"Morris Eagle strikes us once again. Relentlessly, and brilliantly, he examines across these two books every aspect of the major psychoanalytic concepts. And differently from most authors, he does not remain at the theoretical level, but always relates theory to clinical evidence and empirical research, in the best academic tradition. These works will be a classic, an unavoidable reference for our field, and will be used by training programs worldwide."

– **Paolo Migone, MD**, *editor of the journal* Psicoterapia e Scienze Umane *(www.psicoterapiaescienzeumane.it)*

"These two works, both 'Classical' and 'Contemporary', should be in the library of every serious student of psychoanalysis and the psychoanalytic therapies. Applying his wide-ranging critical intelligence to decades of empirical research and cross-disciplinary scholarship, Morris Eagle evaluates seminal psychoanalytic ideas with verve and incisiveness. His comprehensive integration is easy to read, persuasive, and – rare in the professional literature – fascinating."

– **Nancy McWilliams, PhD, ABPP**, *Visiting Full Professor, Rutgers Graduate School of Applied & Professional Psychology*

"In order to prosper it is important for any complex theory in psychology to undergo evaluation of its core constructs to ascertain which aspects have received support, clarify areas in need of modification and also, if we are to be honest and fair, identify those elements that need to be jettisoned. In both 'Classical' and 'Contemporary', Eagle undertakes such an examination of psychoanalytic theory in a thoughtful, clear and incisive review of research evidence, clinical material and conceptual issues. Be forewarned, this is no rubber-stamp of or love letter to psychoanalytic theory. To the contrary, it is a balanced and often critical review of psychoanalytic constructs discussed in an experience-near descriptive manner, eschewing meta-psychological jargon, delivered with a good deal of wit and skillfulness that is typical of Eagle's previous work. Agree or disagree with his conclusions, any serious psychoanalytic scholar or student will benefit a great deal from the discussion contained in these volumes and be much better situated to help psychoanalytic theory evolve and thrive in the contemporary mental health landscape."

– **Mark J. Hilsenroth, PhD**, *Professor, Derner School of Psychology, Adelphi University*

"Morris Eagle's thoughtful, probing, and insightful writings have long stood out as examples of the finest thinking the psychoanalytic tradition has to offer. Bringing a remarkable clarity and rigor of thought to reexamining some of our most fundamental concepts and assumptions, Eagle offers fresh insights that both affirm and challenge analysts of all stripes. These two books, 'Classical' and 'Contemporary', the capstone of a long and brilliant career, are virtually a blueprint for how psychoanalysis can survive in the coming decades."

– **Paul L. Wachtel, PhD**, *CUNY Distinguished Professor, Doctoral Program in Clinical Psychology, City College of CUNY*

"The clarity and richness, the thoughtful analysis and overall assessment of where psychoanalysis stands in these two books by Morris Eagle makes them indispensable for all psychoanalysts and psychoanalytic therapists who are concerned for the future of our field."

– **Otto F. Kernberg**, *Professor of Psychiatry, Weill Medical College of Cornell University; Director of the Personality Disorders Institute of the New York Presbyterian Hospital (Westchester Division), Training Analyst at Columbia University Center for Psychoanalytic Training and Research of New York and Past-President of the International Psychoanalytic Association (IPA)*

"Eagle's integrative work just goes on improving! This is the best, most comprehensive and visionary work so far. He is the best commentator on theoretical and clinical psychoanalysis bar none. A highly recommended book."

– **Peter Fonagy**, *Professor of Contemporary Psychoanalysis and Developmental Science, University College London*

# CORE CONCEPTS IN CLASSICAL PSYCHOANALYSIS

In *Core Concepts in Classical Psychoanalysis*, alongside its companion piece *Core Concepts in Contemporary Psychoanalysis*, Morris N. Eagle asks: of the core concepts and formulations of psychoanalytic theory, which ones should be retained, which should be modified and in what ways, and which should be discarded?

The key concepts and issues explored in this book include:

- Unconscious processes and research on them – what evidence is there for a dynamic unconscious?
- Is there a universal Oedipus complex?
- The importance of inner conflict.
- The concept of defense.

Unlike other previous discussions of these concepts, this book systematically evaluates them in the light of conceptual critique as well as recent research-based evidence and empirical data.

Written with Eagle's piercing clarity of voice, *Core Concepts in Classical Psychoanalysis* challenges previously unquestioned psychoanalytic assumptions and will appeal to psychoanalysts, psychoanalytic psychotherapists, and anyone interested in integrating core psychoanalytic concepts, research, and theory with other disciplines including psychiatry, psychology, and social work.

**Morris N. Eagle, PhD**, is Distinguished Educator-in-Residence at California Lutheran University, Professor Emeritus at the Derner Institute for Advanced Psychological Studies, Adelphi University, and is in part-time private practice. He is the author of *From Classical to Contemporary Psychoanalysis: A Critique and Integration* and many journal articles. He is former President of the Division of Psychoanalysis of the American Psychological Association and recipient of the Sigourney Award, 2009.

## PSYCHOLOGICAL ISSUES BOOK SERIES

DAVID WOLITZKY
Series Editor

The basic mission of *Psychological Issues* is to contribute to the further development of psychoanalysis as a science, as a respected scholarly enterprise, as a theory of human behavior, and as a therapeutic method.

Over the past 50 years, the series has focused on fundamental aspects and foundations of psychoanalytic theory and clinical practice, as well as on work in related disciplines relevant to psychoanalysis. *Psychological Issues* does not aim to represent or promote a particular point of view. The contributions cover broad and integrative topics of vital interest to all psychoanalysts as well as to colleagues in related disciplines. They cut across particular schools of thought and tackle key issues, such as the philosophical underpinnings of psychoanalysis, psychoanalytic theories of motivation, conceptions of therapeutic action, the nature of unconscious mental functioning, psychoanalysis and social issues, and reports of original empirical research relevant to psychoanalysis. The authors often take a critical stance toward theories and offer a careful theoretical analysis and conceptual clarification of the complexities of theories and their clinical implications, drawing upon relevant empirical findings from psychoanalytic research as well as from research in related fields.

The Editorial Board continues to invite contributions from social/behavioral sciences such as anthropology and sociology, from biological sciences such as physiology and the various brain sciences, and from scholarly humanistic disciplines such as philosophy, law, and ethics. Volumes 1–64 in this series were published by International Universities Press. Volumes 65–69 were published by Jason Aronson.

Routledge titles in this series:

**Vol. 75 Psychoanalytic Perspectives on Conflict**
*Edited by Christopher Christian, Morris N. Eagle, & David L. Wolitzky*

**Vol. 76 Death and Fallibility in the Psychoanalytic Encounter**
Mortal Gifts
*Ellen Pinsky*

**Vol. 77 Core Concepts in Classical Psychoanalysis**
Clinical, Research Evidence and Conceptual Critiques
*Morris N. Eagle*

**Vol. 78 Core Concepts in Contemporary Psychoanalysis**
Clinical, Research Evidence and Conceptual Critiques
*Morris N. Eagle*

# CORE CONCEPTS IN CLASSICAL PSYCHOANALYSIS

## Clinical, Research Evidence and Conceptual Critiques

*Morris N. Eagle*

Routledge
Taylor & Francis Group
LONDON AND NEW YORK

First published 2018
by Routledge
4 Park Square, Milton Park, Abingdon, Oxon OX14 4RN

and by Routledge
605 Third Avenue, New York, NY 10017

*Routledge is an imprint of the Taylor & Francis Group, an informa business*



*British Library Cataloguing in Publication Data*
A catalogue record for this book is available from the British Library

*Library of Congress Cataloging in Publication Data*
A catalog record for this book has been requested

ISBN: 978-1-138-84249-6 (hbk)
ISBN: 978-1-138-84250-2 (pbk)
ISBN: 978-1-315-73146-9 (ebk)

Typeset in Bembo and Stone Sans
by Florence Production Ltd, Stoodleigh, Devon, UK

# CONTENTS

*Acknowledgements* *viii*

**Introduction** **1**

**1 Unconscious processes** **5**

**2 Research on unconscious processes** **57**

**3 The Oedipus complex** **94**

**4 Inner conflict** **148**

**5 The concept of defense** **216**

**6 Some concluding comments** **264**

*References* *279*
*Index* *309*

# ACKNOWLEDGEMENTS

I want to express my appreciation to my wife Rita who provided her usual invaluable help with the substance and organization of each chapter; to Robert Holt who commented on selected chapters with his usual care and precision; and to Lauren Jensen for her impressive ability to track down references and most remarkable, her ability to read my handwriting. My appreciation to Kate Hawes for her confidence and flexibility in the simultaneous publication of this book and the companion book. I also want to express my appreciation to Victoria Kelly for her care, competence, and patience in the copy-editing.

# INTRODUCTION

In an important sense, this book is concerned with the future of psychoanalysis. More specifically, it is concerned with the question of what is worth preserving about psychoanalytic theory, what needs to be discarded, and which psychoanalytic hypotheses, concepts, and formulations need to be modified, and in what ways. These issues are considered, not in the light of ever-appearing new "schools," but in the light of research evidence, clinical evidence, and findings from related disciplines, as well as conceptual analysis. I strongly believe that if psychoanalysis is to survive as a viable body of thought, these fundamental issues need to be confronted, boldly and systematically.

As the reader will see, I am quite critical of certain aspects of various psychoanalytic theories and of the kind of thinking that all too frequently is reflected in the psychoanalytic literature. However, my assessments are not those of an outside hostile critic, but of someone who has devoted much of his professional life to the study of psychoanalysis and who strongly believes that psychoanalytic values, insights, and perspectives are very much worth preserving.

Thus, this book is a very personal one in that I have a deep conviction about the views I present. Of course, I have had personal convictions about other papers and books I have written. However, I have a sense of something being different in regard to this book. I think it has partly to do with my advancing age, by virtue of which I feel a need to be as direct, as frank and forthright as it is possible to be. The task I have set myself is to express as clearly as I can the views that I have developed over a period of thinking and writing about psychoanalysis for more than 60 years.

When I described my plans for this book to colleagues who were not in a field connected to psychoanalysis, a not uncommon reaction was essentially "why bother writing about the future of psychoanalysis? We know that psychoanalysis is in a period of decline and does not have much of a future." They are right that psychoanalysis is in a period of decline as far as its standing in the mental health world and larger culture is concerned. However, the fact is that many psychoanalytic insights and formulations have been assimilated by other newer theories, and in that sense, psychoanalysis is still very much alive. But more importantly, I know of no other psychological theory that attempts to grapple with profound human issues in as comprehensive a way as has psychoanalytic theory, particularly Freudian theory. For this reason alone, psychoanalysis needs to have a future.

With respect to the issue of assimilation by non-psychoanalytic theories, several major figures – for example, Beck, the father of cognitive therapy, Perls, the father of Gestalt therapy, and Bowlby, the father of attachment theory – had begun their theoretical work with training in psychoanalysis. And although their later work diverged from that theory, they retained many of its core concepts, albeit in a new guise. For example, while there are certainly differences between them, there is clearly a 'family resemblance' between making the unconscious conscious of psychoanalytic theory and making automatic implicit thoughts explicit of cognitive behavioral therapy. And Bowlby not only had early training as a psychoanalyst, but viewed himself as one throughout his life. One of his main motivations in developing attachment theory was to reform psychoanalysis and align it with the findings of related disciplines such as ethology and cognitive psychology. Attachment theory and cognitive behavioral theory are but two examples of the heuristic and generative value of psychoanalytic theory.

There was a period during the heyday of psychoanalytic influence, when core psychoanalytic concepts and formulations captured the imagination of researchers and theorists from such related disciplines as psychology and anthropology and inspired them to carry out empirical research programs and theoretical reformulations linked to these core psychoanalytic concepts and formulations. Some examples include Sears'(1943; 1944) research program with children and animals at Stanford; Whiting and Child's (1953) anthropological studies at Yale, which followed the tradition of Roheim (1950) and Malinowski (1927) (see also Kardiner, 1939; Kluckhohn, Murray, & Schneider, 1953); Dollard and Miller's (1950) reformulation of Freudian concepts in learning theory terms; and the body of work on conflict and experimental neurosis, which represented a convergence of Pavlovian and psychoanalytic ideas (e.g., French, 1933; Masserman, 1944; 1950; 1953). Writers such as Crews (1995; 1996) who dismiss Freudian theory altogether do not seem to recognize this legacy. It is not that such critics have not identified some legitimate criticisms and concerns. Rather, it is their wholesale and coarse-grained rejection of the entire body of psychoanalysis that is the problem.

Contrastingly, several notable scientists value psychoanalytic theory for its unique attempt to develop a coherent, comprehensive theory of human nature. Recently, I had the pleasure of interviewing the neuroscientist Vittorio Gallese, one of the discoverers of mirror neurons. One of the questions I asked Dr. Gallese was why he, a distinguished neuroscientist, was interested in psychoanalysis. He informed me that before becoming absorbed in neurophysiology, he had flirted with the idea of becoming a psychoanalyst. Dr. Gallese commented that psychoanalytic theory always seemed to him to constitute the most comprehensive and significant theory of human nature and of the nature of mind. A similar sentiment has been expressed by the Nobel Laureate Eric Kandel. Kandel had an abiding interest in psychoanalysis and, as described in his autobiography (Kandel 2007), like Gallese, had also intended early on to become a psychoanalyst. It is clear from his writing that the basis for his interest in psychoanalysis is similar to Gallese's. Kandel is not the only Nobel Laureate with an interest in psychoanalysis. As early as 1947, Lord Adrian, also a neuroscientist and a Nobel Laureate, gave the Ernest Jones Lecture which was published in the *International Journal of Psychoanalysis*.

In short, psychoanalysis has generated concepts that have contributed to an understanding of the nature of mind, infant–mother attachment theory, anthropology, neuroscience and cognitive psychology, among other fields. In addition to this cross-fertilization between psychoanalysis and other areas of study, there is also a considerable amount of psychoanalytic research these days, dealing with the bread and butter issues of therapeutic outcome. However, it is important to remember that Freud believed that the major claim of psychoanalysis on posterity lay in its theoretical propositions about human nature rather than its role as a treatment modality. Similarly, it is clear that figures such as Adrian, Gallese, Kandel, and others became interested in psychoanalysis not primarily as a therapeutic modality, but as a comprehensive theory of mind, human nature, and personality functioning. There is the risk that an increasingly exclusive focus on psychoanalysis as a treatment modality will lead to a neglect of this major contribution of psychoanalysis, confirming Freud's (1926) fear that "the therapy would destroy the science" (p. 254).

My book focuses on psychoanalysis as a theory of human nature and personality functioning rather than as a form of treatment – although some discussion is devoted to the implications of the former for the latter. As such, one of the challenges confronting a book of this kind was to identify and select what in fact are the core concepts in psychoanalytic theory. As we know, over the years, there have been many modifications of the core concepts of classical psychoanalytic theory – many associated with the emergence of new "schools." For example, we have seen papers and books on the "waning" and reconceptualization of the Oedipus complex (e.g., Loewald, 1979); the irrelevance of the "cornerstone" concept of repression for 'today's' patients (e.g., Gitelson, 1963); reformulations of defense and unconscious processes (e.g., Stern, 2003); and the limited therapeutic usefulness of awareness and insight (e.g., Kohut, 1984). Thus, the question must be asked: how does one identify the core ideas of psychoanalytic theory given the fact that different psychoanalytic schools extant today differ regarding the concepts, ideas, and formulations they view as fundamental and/or have reformulated them. One does not want to focus on marginal or peripheral aspects of psychoanalytic theory, which, even if revised or discarded, would have little or no impact on the tenability of core ideas of the theory.

I tried to deal with this issue in the following way: In addition to my own judgment, I examined the chapter on "core concepts" in the revised edition of the *Textbook of Psychoanalysis* (Gabbard, Litowitz, & Williams, 2012) and also asked fifteen colleagues with different theoretical orientations to identify 5–7 core concepts and formulations of psychoanalytic theory. The most frequently cited were: (1) unconscious processes; (2) inner conflict; (3) defense; (4) transference; (5) countertransference; and (6) projective identification. Although not 'nominated' with great frequency, I have also included a chapter on the Oedipus complex because of its central role in classical theory and because it continues to be discussed in the psychoanalytic and interdisciplinary literature.

This book consists of the following chapters:

Chapter 1 – Unconscious processes
Chapter 2 – Research on unconscious processes
Chapter 3 – The Oedipus complex
Chapter 4 – Inner conflict
Chapter 5 – The concept of defense
Chapter 6 – Some concluding comments

The companion book, which deals with core concepts of contemporary psychoanalytic theory includes chapters on transference; countertransference; projection and projective identification; psychoanalytic styles of writing and thinking; and a concluding chapter.

One could perhaps argue that my list of core concepts and formulations is weighted toward classical theory. This may be true to some extent and if it is, it is attributable to the fact that classical theory represents the most systematic and comprehensive version of psychoanalytic theory. However, I do not think that it is a serious problem. For in evaluating these core concepts, one inevitably discusses post-classical critiques and modifications of them. For example, in evaluating the classical concept of repression, one inevitably has to discuss the limitations of that concept as well as newer formulations regarding the nature of defense (e.g., Stern's (2003) discussion of unformulated experiences; Fingarette's (1963) notion of not "spelling out").

For each of the core concepts and formulations, I will address the following questions: (1) What is the evidence?; (2) In the light of conceptual critique and available evidence, does the concept or formulation need to be retained or discarded?; (3) If retained, in what ways does the concept or formulation need to be modified in light of conceptual critique and evidence? An evaluation of core psychoanalytic concepts and formulations, as well as the alterations and reformulations they have undergone, should enable one to make relatively sound judgments regarding their status – and, indeed, the future of psychoanalysis.

# 1

# UNCONSCIOUS PROCESSES

## Introduction

The concept that appeared with the greatest frequency as a response to my query regarding core psychoanalytic concepts and formulations was unconscious processes. More than any other formulation, the central role of unconscious processes in psychological life has been associated with psychoanalytic theory since its inception. Indeed, until recently, it would have been difficult to imagine psychoanalytic theory without the concept of unconscious processes at its center. (I say "until recently" because the concept of unconscious processes does not appear to be central to the contemporary theories of self psychology and relational psychoanalysis.) Many other core concepts associated with psychoanalytic theory, such as defense, drives, wishes and desires, inner conflict, the distinction between manifest and latent content, and the formation of neurotic symptoms presuppose unconscious processes. Understanding of many aspects of psychological experience and behavior seems to require the assumption of unconscious processes. And from a therapeutic perspective, a central classical psychoanalytic goal of making the unconscious conscious would have no meaning without the assumption of unconscious processes.

Two chapters will be devoted to unconscious processes. Chapter 1 deals with conceptual issues, including the question of in what sense unconscious processes can be understood as *mental* processes; the 'debate' between Freud and William James pitting unconscious mental processes against momentary states of consciousness as alternative explanations of certain phenomena; the explanatory role of appeal to unconscious mental motives; the validation of attributions of unconscious mental states; the problem of homunculi; the limitations of explanation in terms of unconscious motives; different theoretical conceptions of unconscious mental processes and states; the relationship between unconscious mental states and psychopathology; the interpersonalizing of the unconscious; the metaphors of surface and depth in psychoanalytic theorizing; and the question of integration of unconscious material in treatment.

Chapter 2 deals with selective research on unconscious processes, including discrimination and encoding of stimuli without awareness (subliminal stimulus studies); neural correlates of discrimination without awareness; unconscious acquisition of 'rules' and algorithms (learning without awareness); encoding and organization of stimuli as a function of degree of awareness and attention; and research on the influence of supraliminal stimuli on behavior without awareness of the influence. The implications of these findings for conceptions of unconscious processes and states are then discussed.

## Unconscious processes: theoretical and conceptual issues

### *Are there unconscious mental processes?*

#### *Freud's answer*

Unconscious processes were recognized and discussed before Freud (see Burston, 1986; Ellenberger, 1970; Rand, 2004; Sand, 2014; Whyte, 1960). Indeed, recognition of unconscious processes goes back to antiquity. Plotinus writes: "The absence of a conscious perception is no proof of the absence of mental activity" (as cited in Whyte, 1967, p. 185). And Aquinas' theory of mind includes "processes in the soul of which we are not immediately aware" (as cited in Whyte, 1967, p. 185). However, at least since Descartes, the concepts of mental and consciousness were generally seen as equivalent. That is, for a phenomenon to be understood as mental meant that it was consciously experienced. Hence, to speak, as Freud did, of unconscious *mental* processes was viewed as a contradiction in terms. And, indeed, at one time, that was a common philosophical reaction (e.g., Field, Averling, & Laird, 1922).

Freud did not merely propose that unconscious mental processes exist, but one, that the major part of mental life goes on outside awareness; two, that "the unconscious is the true psychical reality" (Freud, 1900, p. 613); and three, that the unconscious is the psychic equivalent of Kant's *Ding-an-sich*. He writes that the unconscious "in its innermost nature, is as much unknown to us as the reality of the external world, and it is as incompletely presented by the data of consciousness as is the external world by the communications of our sense organs" (Freud, 1900, p. 613). He also proposes that unconscious thought is organized along different dimensions (primary process) than ordinary conscious thought (secondary process).

It has been commonly observed that, based largely on empirical work associated with the cognitive revolution in psychology, the reality of unconscious mental processes is now widely accepted. Indeed, in accord with Freud's claim, it is also widely accepted that unconscious mental processes are ubiquitous rather than exceptional. For example, Lakoff and Johnson (1999) write that one of three "major findings of cognitive science [is that] thought is mostly unconscious" (p. 3). And Fodor (1983) has asserted that "all psychologically interesting cognitive states are unconscious" (p. 86). This has led some to conclude that Freud's ideas about unconscious mental processes have been fully vindicated. However, matters are more complicated. Most important, the distinctively psychoanalytic claim is not simply the argument for the existence of what Freud (1915c) referred to as the "descriptive unconscious" and what today is often referred to as the "cognitive unconscious" (e.g., Burston, 1986; Eagle, 1987; Kihlstrom, 1987; Weinberger, 2000). It is, rather, the argument for the "dynamic unconscious"; that is, an unconscious of conflicting forces of impulses pressing for discharge and access to consciousness and ego defenses preventing such access. This claim is far from being universally accepted.

## *Searle on unconscious mental processes*

The idea of unconscious mental processes of any kind, cognitive or dynamic, is fraught with philosophical and terminological complexities, including the question of how one understands the term "mental." It is not just Descartes, but also some contemporary philosophers who find the concept of unconscious mental processes problematic in certain respects. For example, Searle (1992) asks: "How could we subtract the consciousness from a mental state and still have the mental state left over?" (p. 52). According to Searle, there are only conscious mental states and neurophysiological brain states with a capacity to cause conscious mental states; there is no ontological realm between the two (Searle's critique is also directed to the positing of unconscious mental processes in cognitive psychology).

Searle acknowledges the explanatory power of positing unconscious mental processes and accepts the need for a psychological 'vocabulary' that employs such terms. However, he rejects the idea that these terms refer to ontological entities or processes that refer neither to conscious experience nor neurophysiological events, but something in between. As McLoughlin (2002) argues, this position is essentially similar to Freud's belief that although the vocabulary of unconscious mental states is necessary for explanation at a psychological level (e.g., to fill in the 'gaps' in conscious mental life), it is not intended to point to an ontological realm that is neither conscious phenomenal experience nor a neurophysiological state. As Freud (1940[1938]) writes:

> Whereas the psychology of consciousness never went beyond the broken sequences which were obviously dependent on something else, the other view, which held that the psychical is unconscious in itself, enabled psychology to take its place like a natural science like any other. The processes with which it is concerned are in themselves just as unknowable as those dealt with by other sciences, by chemistry and physics, for example; but it is possible to establish the laws which they obey and to follow their mutual relations and independences unbroken over long stretches, in short, to arrive at what is described as an "understanding" of the field of natural phenomena in question.
>
> (p. 158)

Following the *Project for a Scientific Psychology*, Freud (1950[1895]) turned to a purely psychological language. However, it is clear from Freud's writings that he was always committed to the neurophysiological as the bedrock for psychological processes. As Freud writes to Fleiss following his relinquishment of the Project:

> I am not at all in disagreement with you, not at all inclined to leave the psychology hanging in the air without an organic basis. But apart from this conviction I do not know how to go on, neither theoretically nor therapeutically, and therefore must behave as if the psychological alone were under consideration.
>
> (Masson, 1985, p. 326)

More than 40 years later, Freud (1940a) writes that because "physical or somatic processes" are more complete than conscious experience, it "seems natural to lay stress in psychology upon these somatic processes, to see in them the true essence of what is mental" (p. 34).

There seems to be relatively widespread agreement that at present we cannot adequately explain certain behaviors by appealing to neurophysiological processes and conscious experience alone (see Dennett, 1969, 1978; Fodor, 1983). We need to employ a vocabulary of unconscious mental processes in order to generate reasonably adequate explanations. More specifically, we need to refer to the language and categories of desires, motives, wishes, intentions, and so on that we normally think of as conscious, while recognizing that the mental states referred to are not consciously experienced. We have little choice in the matter. We will certainly not be able to provide an adequate and rich explanation by referring only to neurophysiological processes, even if, from an ontological perspective, what we refer to as unconscious mental processes are neurophysiological processes.

## *Rubinstein on unconscious mental processes*

Rubinstein, a psychoanalyst and a highly sophisticated philosophical thinker, presents a complex and nuanced discussion of the concept of unconscious mental events. The gist of Rubinstein's (1997) formulation is that "unconscious mental events are neurophysiological events that are classified as mental" on the assumption "that observed phenomena resembling the effects of such phenomenal events as wishing, intending, fantasying, etc. are in fact the effects of these neurophysiological events" (p. 52).

It is important to note that although Rubinstein maintains that unconscious mental events are protoneurophysiological phenomena that point to neurophysiological events, he does not suggest that we rush to translate psychological terms into neurophysiological terms. Different language and different meaning systems underlie these different terms. In our everyday world, including the world of clinical practice, "we are concerned with individuals and with their modes of being-in-the world, not with brains or mental apparatuses" (pp. 64–65). However, we cannot escape the conclusion that "unconscious mental events are neural events by another name" (p. 524), a point of view, as Rubinstein points out, that was held by Freud (See, for example, Freud, 1940[1938], p. 158).

## *Wakefield on unconscious mental processes*

In a sustained and brilliant exposition that is congruent with and further develops Rubinstein's position, Wakefield (1992) maintains that implicit in Freud's conception of unconscious processes are the claims (1) that *representationality* (rather than consciousness) is the essence of the mental; (2) that brains possess the property of representationality; and (3) therefore that nonconscious brain states can be mental. According to Wakefield (2001) Freud's claim "representationality can be realized in nonconscious brain structures and that, therefore, there can be mental states that are not conscious . . . might be the foundation stone on which cognitive psychology rests" (p. 81).

Wakefield (1992; 2001) points to the kinds of empirical phenomena Freud adduced to defend what was and is the jarring argument that certain brain states are mental, that is, possess representationality. These phenomena include behavior following post-hypnotic suggestion and most important, unconscious creative problem-solving. If he were writing today, Freud could have added studies demonstrating unconscious encoding at the semantic level that I will discuss in Chapter 2.

As Wakefield (1992; 2001) shows, Freud's implicit reasoning is that if, like conscious states, nonconscious representational brain states can generate intentionality and intelligent behavior, then one must conclude that it is representational structure, not consciousness, that is the essence of the mental. By this account, consciousness is a contingent, not an essential property of the mental, a startling conclusion arrived at by Freud who writes that "the psychical is unconscious in itself" (Freud, 1940[1938], p. 158).

However jarring this conclusion may be, ultimately, we will likely have little difficulty with the idea that at a particular level of organization, unconscious wishes, motives, etc. are essentially neurophysiological processes. As Chomsky (1965) writes in a different but relevant context:

> [T]he very concept of "physical explanation" will no doubt be extended to incorporate whatever is discovered in this [mental] domain, exactly as it was extended to accommodate gravitational and electromagnetic force, massless particles and numerous other entities and processes that would have offended the common sense of earlier generations.
>
> (pp. 83–84)

Apart from the empirical phenomena that Freud cited in defense of the concept of unconscious mental processes, as Wakefield demonstrates, a programmatic and overarching motive for proposing the inessentiality of consciousness and the corresponding primacy of unconscious processes in psychic life was his ambitious goal to make it possible for psychoanalysis and, indeed, psychology, eventually to take its place as a natural science. Freud (1940[1938]) writes that whereas the psychology of consciousness was woefully incomplete and full of unexplained gaps, "the other view, which held that the psychical is unconscious in itself, enabled psychology to take its place as a natural science like any other" (p. 158). In other words, conscious phenomenal experience alone cannot serve as a basis for psychology as a science, a conclusion radically at odds with the reliance on introspection to provide the fundamental data of psychology, a position espoused by Titchener's (1898, 1909) structuralism.

Implicit in this view is the expectation that, ultimately, we would come to know most of what we need to know about the human mind, not through focusing solely or primarily on phenomenal conscious awareness, but through investigating what Wakefield refers to as "syntactic brain-state causal interactions alone" (1992, p. 92). I would add that this overarching goal began with the Project, which, of course, could not be completed. However, in abandoning the Project, Freud did not abandon his vision. Rather, he developed a psychological and metapsychological language and concepts that were not only heuristic in themselves, but also served as *placeholders* – what Rubinstein refers to as protoneurophysiological terms – for later filling in through discoveries in neurophysiology.

## *Freud versus James on unconscious mental processes*

As noted, Freud's arguments for the existence of unconscious mental processes and states were far from universally accepted. Preceding William James' (1890) ten arguments against admitting the concept of unconscious mental processes into psychology, he expressed the fear that such an admission would open the floodgates to arbitrariness of both explanation and attributions of mental states, unchecked by the individual's ability to either validate or invalidate those attributions on the basis of his or her conscious experience. In response to the question "can states of mind be unconscious?", James (1890) writes in relation to those who posit such states of mind: "they will devote themselves to sapping and mining the region roundabout until it is a bag of logical liquefaction, into the midst of which all definite conclusions of any sort may be trusted ere long to sink and disappear" (p. 107). He also writes that the positing of unconscious mental states "is the sovereign means for believing what one likes in psychology, and of turning what might become a science into a tumbling-ground for whimsies" (p. 163).

James' arguments against admitting the concept of unconscious mental states into psychology are sophisticated and nuanced. The gist of these arguments is to propose momentary and split-off consciousness or brain states as alternatives to unconscious mental states. However, if one pushes the momentary consciousness argument to the extreme, it becomes virtually equivalent to unconscious mental states. That is, if consciousness is so momentary that it cannot be reported, it becomes essentially equivalent to being unconscious. However, this criticism does not apply to James' proposal that brain states serve as an alternative to unconscious mental states.

The debate between Freudian unconscious mental states and James' (as well as Janet's, Binet's, and Prince's) momentary consciousness and split-off consciousness needs to be understood in the context of the history of psychology. James' insistence that mental states need to be linked to consciousness of some sort, even if it is a momentary consciousness or split-off consciousness, was based on his strong belief that the subject matter of psychology must include conscious experience, the "feel" of mental states. This, indeed, was the view of the time. For example, trained introspection of one's experiences was the primary method of collecting psychological data by Titchener (1898; 1909) and his structuralist followers, at one time a dominant school of American psychology. The goal of psychology was to map out the structure of conscious experience. In contemporary terms, one can say that structuralism attempted to identify the fundamental *qualia* of conscious experience.

In part, it was the very meager achievements of structualism that paved the way for the behaviorist school of psychology that, of course, essentially replaced consciousness with overt behavior as the subject matter of psychology. And it was this de-emphasis on conscious experience as well as an emphasis on the role of biological drives that led to the seemingly odd bedfellowship of behaviorism and Freudian psychology. In 1950, Dollard and Miller published an influential book *Personality and Psychotherapy* that translated Freudian formulations into neo-Hullian behaviorist language. One of the factors that made this possible was the convergence of the two perspectives on the downgrading of conscious experience as part of the project of achieving a scientific account of human behavior.

Despite the problems inherent in James' views, his concern that appeal to unconscious mental states might serve as "the sovereign means of believing what one likes in psychology" was not entirely unfounded as evidenced by the misuses of and arbitrary attributions of unconscious mental states found in some of the psychoanalytic literature. That literature is replete with examples of undisciplined attributions of unconscious motives and meanings that are too often dictated by pre-set theoretical formulae that are imposed on the patient material rather than being based on clear and specified clinical evidence.

Consider as an example of such practices the history of psychoanalytic explanations of agoraphobia. Abraham (1913) attributed agoraphobia to the patient's unconscious libidinization of movement; Freud (1926) to unconscious prostitution or 'street-walking fantasies'; and Deutsch (1929) to unconscious murderous wishes toward the patient's trusted companion. Each of the accounts follows a particular formula: if the patient is anxious about moving from the house, then this must be due to the sexualization of movement; if the patient's fear is walking in the street, this must reflect her unconscious wish to be a street-walker or prostitute; and if the patient's anxiety is allayed by the presence of a trusted companion, this must be attributable to the patient's being reassured that the trusted companion is still alive and has not been destroyed by the patient's murderous wishes.

In none of these accounts does the author link his or her presumed explanation to the patient's productions, what he or she thinks or feels. Rather, as noted, the accounts follow a formula dictated by pre-set theoretical views, made possible by the free and undisciplined attribution of unconscious mental states. I am, of course, not suggesting that the concept of unconscious mental events and states be eliminated from psychological explanation or psychological accounts. Rather, I want to point to the special problems and dangers that arise in the attribution of unconscious mental states and, therefore, the special need to discipline such accounts by tying them closely to evidence. This raises the question of how one assesses and validates such attributions.

## Validation of attribution of unconscious mental states

When one attributes a conscious mental state (e.g., a desire or an intention) to another, his or her response to that attribution generally counts in an important way. It has at least some kind of special status and plays a critical role in disciplining the attribution, that is, in validating or invalidating it. However, virtually by definition, this is not the case in attribution of *unconscious* mental states. Acceptance or rejection of such an attribution on the part of the individual to whom the attribution is made plays much less of a part in assessing its validity. Indeed, given the role of defense, one would expect frequent denial of the attribution. How, then, do we assess the validity or accuracy of any interpretation that entails attribution of unconscious mental states.

Thus, although the positing of unconscious mental states may have, as Searle (1992) puts it, indispensable explanatory power, their undisciplined use increases the risk of arbitrary attributions determined by pre-set theoretical views rather than by specified evidence. Examples also include the florid unconscious fantasies attributed to infants in Kleinian theory as well as in the attribution of universal unconscious incestuous and hostile wishes in Freudian oedipal theory (see Chapter 3). One can cite many other examples in which attribution of unconscious mental states is determined more by theoretical loyalties than by disciplined assessment of the evidence (Peterfreund, 1983). Given this risk, if we are to make constructive use of the explanatory power of positing unconscious mental states and processes, it behooves us to develop the discipline of tightly linking attributions of unconscious mental states and processes to clearly specified evidence on the basis of which inferences are made. Unfortunately, this is not a regular habit in psychoanalytic writing and thinking.

I am aware that theory is always under-determined by data or evidence and that the same data can yield an indefinite number of theoretical accounts (Duhem, [1914]1954). Hence, I am not suggesting that a particular set of data always and unqualifiedly points to explanation or theory X and only explanation or theory X. However, what I am arguing for is the need to specify the set of data on the basis of which one has developed one's theoretical account. What I am also arguing is that, in the final analysis, the validity of attributions of unconscious mental states and processes as well as other psychoanalytic accounts is a function of the degree to which, in Freud's (1917[1916–1917]) words, they "tally with what is real (in the patient)" (p. 452) and, one can add, the degree to which they do not contradict the extant evidence on how the mind works rather than on the degree to which they are persuasive (Spence's, 1982, "narrative truth"), coherent (Schafer, 1992; Sherwood, 1969), or aesthetic (Geha, 1984).

The latter qualities may (or may not) be especially relevant in the therapeutic context where one's concern is with helping the patient rather than enlightening or bringing the truth to him or her – two aims that in the history of psychoanalysis have been assumed to converge, but in fact, may not (see Eagle, 2011a). However, as far as theory is concerned, the positing of unconscious mental states and processes can only be said to have explanatory power if it corresponds in some way to something real that needs to be explained in the individual to whom the unconscious mental states and processes are attributed.

How does one assess the degree to which one's attributions of unconscious mental states tally with what is real in the individual to whom the attributions are made? That is, how do we assess the validity of the attributions? Freud's (1917 [1916–1917]) suggestion that only interpretations that tally with what is real in the patient will be therapeutically effective simply does not work. In any case, I want to consider the question more generally rather than limit it to the therapeutic context. One plausible answer provided by Mischel (1966) is that at some point, the individual to whom the attribution is made must acknowledge the attribution if it is to be viewed as valid. I have argued against this position on the ground that the individual may show compelling behavioral evidence of the validity of the attribution, for example, in the content of his or her free associations, dreams, physiological reactions, and predisposition to certain actions, without ever, say due to the persistence of defense, acknowledging the mental contents attributed to him or her (Eagle, 1973). I have argued that the assessment of the validity of the attribution of particular unconscious mental states is somewhat independent of the individual's acknowledgment in the form of conscious experience of the mental state attributed to him or her – either immediately or in the long run. This is especially the case when, along with Rubinstein (1997), one thinks of unconscious mental states as a theoretical term that is answerable primarily to its explanatory power.

Even Descartes (1640/1996) recognized, at least with regard to belief, that an individual's phenomenal conscious experience may not be an adequate guide to his or her mental states. He writes:

> And in order to know what [people's] opinions really were, I needed to pay more attention to what they did, than to what they said, not only because . . . there are few people who are willing to say everything which they believe, but also because *many do not know themselves* (that is, do not know what they believe).
>
> (Discourse, Part III, as cited in Eagle, 1982, p. 361, my italics. Also see Sand, 2014, for a fascinating discussion of what she refers to as "the Cartesian unconscious," p. 67)

I think that Mischel's position is useful in a number of ways, particularly in the therapeutic context. However, much rests on how one understands what it means to acknowledge an unconscious desire or wish. An individual's intellectual acquisition of knowledge of his or her unconscious mental states, so to speak, from the outside (Wachtel, 2009) or in the form of third-person knowledge (Moran, 2001) is likely to be of limited therapeutic value. This is in contrast to the individual's immediate phenomenal experience of and emotional conviction regarding the mental states attributed to him or her, which is experienced from the inside, that is, has the form of first-person knowledge, and is often accompanied by strong emotions. Hence, meaningful acknowledgment of the attribution, often accompanied by emotional conviction, is likely to be an important marker of therapeutic change.

Another reason that Mischel's position is useful is that it serves to discipline our attributions of unconscious mental states and to remind us that the concept of unconscious mental states is parasitic upon the concept of conscious mental states. That is, whether acknowledged or not, it must be *potentially possible* for an unconscious mental state attributed to an individual to be consciously experienced, even if that mental state, for a variety of reasons, including the operation of defense, is never consciously experienced by the individual. In other words, one needs to distinguish between thinking of unconscious mental states as potentially able to be consciously experienced and the employment of actual conscious experience of attributed unconscious mental states as a privileged criterion for the validity of the attribution.

The former consideration also serves to discipline and temper attributions of unconscious mental states, particularly in the therapeutic situation. That is, if it is not possible to conceive of the potential conscious experience of an unconscious mental state attributed to an individual, then one has good reason to doubt that the attributions refer to a mental state in the ordinary sense of the term. This consideration is especially important when one encounters in the psychoanalytic literature attributions of exotic states (e.g. "black holes") with little or no description of how such states would be experienced in consciousness.

There is another problem that needs to be considered, one that dogged logical behaviorism. This is the problem of the under-determination of meaning by behavior – a parallel to the under-determination of theory by data (Duhem, 1954). Another way to put this is to stay that behavior is not always transparent as to its underlying motives and meanings. One can carry out a given behavior for a variety of different reasons and motives (referred to in the psychoanalytic context as the "principle of multiple function" by Waelder, 1936). Furthermore, some of these motives and meanings may be opaque not only to the agent carrying out the action, but also to the observer. In short, sheer behavior alone cannot serve a *criterial* function for inferring unconscious motives and meanings, a consideration I essentially overlooked in my earlier paper (Eagle, 1973).

In ordinary social interaction, although not always the case, most behaviors are generally sufficiently transparent and readable as to the agent's motives and meanings. And despite instances in which this is not the case, we are generally sufficiently able to 'read' motives and meanings from observed behavior to make social interaction and normal communication possible. However, 'reading' or attributing unconscious meaning and motives from behavior is another matter. Virtually by definition, such behavior may be opaque as to unconscious meanings and motives, not only in relation to the agent himself or herself, but also in relation to an observer and/or to someone with whom the agent is interacting. That the latter is the case is made evident by the central role of interpretation in psychoanalytic theoretical and clinical accounts. Were behavior always transparent, the role of interpretation would be much reduced.

Given the above considerations, one can better understand Rubinstein's (1997) proposal that, say, an unconscious desire or wish is a theoretical term. That is, it functions much like a theoretical explanation designed to account for a set of data (e.g., free associations, dreams, slips of the tongue, neurotic symptoms, etc.). And like all theoretical explanation, it is under-determined by the data. I would add that like all theoretical explanation, its validity is determined by a number of factors, including the 'nomological network' in which it is embedded, its predictive capacity, and its congruence with other relevant data.

I think that the above discussion also points to the havoc that florid and arbitrary attributions of unconscious mental states with few or no links to identifiable evidence wreaks on any theoretical account; and to the wisdom of conservatism and constraint in the attribution of unconscious mental states to others. Perhaps in the therapeutic context, unconstrained just-so stories or persuasive and coherent narratives or "interpretive constructions" or "aesthetic fictions," unconcerned with issues of veridicality, may be therapeutically effective, although there is little or no evidence that this is the case. In a theoretical context however, unconstrained attributions of unconscious mental states based on further theoretical speculations and unconnected to identifiable data do not serve psychoanalytic theory well.

A consideration that serves to discipline attributions of unconscious mental states is Mischel's (as well as Searle's and others') insistence that an individual cannot legitimately be said to have an unconscious desire or wish (or any other mental content) unless the desire or wish could potentially become conscious; as we have seen, in a given case, because of other factors such as defense, the unconscious wish or desire attributed to the individual may not in fact become conscious. However, one may be able to predict that under certain specified and independently assessed conditions (e.g., relaxation of defense), the wish or desire would become conscious. In such a case, what one might refer to as conditional first-person acknowledgment, could warrant the inferences or attribution of an unconscious wish or desire despite the individual's failure to acknowledge or even despite explicit denial of the wish or desire attributed to him or her (Eagle, 1973).

There is somewhat of at least a seeming paradox here. The evidence strongly supports the 'expansive' theoretical hypothesis that unconscious mental processes are ubiquitous. However, learning just what those ubiquitous processes are is best served not by an expansive theoretical attitude that freely posits all sorts of unconscious mental processes and states, but by a careful identification of these processes and states, constrained by specific sets of data, both clinical and non-clinical.

Although many unconscious processes may possess features we think of as mental – for example, they appear to be intelligent, – they are nevertheless not capable of being consciously experienced, that is, they are 'impenetrable.' For example, size constancy and phi phenomenon or apparent movement appear to involve intelligent inferential-like processes, a fact that led Helmholtz (1867[1968]) to refer to "unconscious inference."[1]

The inferential-like processes referred to by Helmholtz are automatic computational processes that are 'impenetrable' to conscious experience. That is, one will never consciously experience making Helmholtzian inferences. It is perhaps harmless to refer to these computational processes in psychological terms such as "unconscious inference." The term certainly captures something of the structure of the process. However, perhaps it is not harmless and indeed, may be misleading to think of the computational processes underlying size constancy and phi phenomenon in terms of an *agent* making unconscious inferences that, under certain circumstances, could be made conscious.

For the fact is that these inferential-like processes are inaccessible to conscious experience. Although we certainly consciously experience the *products* of computational processes that underlie the conscious experience of size constancy and phi phenomenon, the *processes* themselves are subpersonal, impenetrable, and not available to conscious experience. Consider as another example the Muller-Lyer illusion in which a horizontal line with arrows pointing out at each end appears longer than a horizontal line with arrows pointing inward at both ends even though both lines are of equal length. Further, knowing that both lines are of equal length does not affect the illusion. That this is so is taken by Fodor (1983) as a piece of evidence for his modular theory of mind. That is, the modular visual system carries out its process independently of what we, as central processes, know. Another way to put this is to point to the distinction between the processing of subpersonal modules and the knowledge as well as beliefs and desires that we, as persons, have.

On the basis of a series of extensive and creative experiments, Rock (1983) proposed that "perception is intelligent in that it is based on operations similar to those that characterize thought" (p. 1). According to Rock, these operations entail "inferential processing" (p. 1) that is similar to logical reasoning. As he puts it:

> By unconscious inference I mean that the process of arriving at the percept is one much like reasoning in which conclusions are drawn from premises, except that in perception the process is not conscious and the outcome is a percept rather than a conclusion.
>
> (p. 272)

However, Rock goes on to note, although "perception is thought-like, it is nevertheless autonomous". That is, by and large, it is not directly affected by consciously represented knowledge" (p. 315). This is made apparent by the evidence that the experience of perceptual illusions is left untouched by knowledge of the true state of affairs. Further, the inferential-like processes that account for the experience and persostence of perceptual illusions are precisely those that serve us so well in veridical perception of the external object.

Another difference between thought and perception, according to Rock, is that perception "is rooted in and constrained by the necessity of accounting for the proximal stimulus" (pp. 339–340). That is, as Rock reasons, since stimuli that impinge on sense organs generate "at best an ambiguous and distortion prone representation of the external object . . ., some mechanism had to evolve to yield reliable, veridical apprehension of such an object" (p. 1). For example, some mechanism had to evolve to assure object constancy despite variation in retinal image as a function of distance, orientation, etc. The mechanism proposed by Rock is a "reasoning-like" one that entails inferential processing. However, the inferential processes proposed by Rock are impenetrable, that is, inaccessible to conscious awareness. They are an example of what has been referred to as the computational unconscious, a kind of unconscious processing that has virtually nothing to do with Freud's dynamic unconscious. It is not clear whether Freud had such 'impenetrable' processes in mind when he stated that the major part of mental life occurs without awareness or whether he included such processes in his conception of the descriptive unconscious.

## *Unconscious processes and the problem of homunculi*

As noted earlier, Freud's (1915) primary justification for invoking unconscious processes and content was his belief that it was indispensable for explaining and understanding much of human behavior. And, as we have also seen, even critics of the concept of unconscious mental contents, such as Searle (1992) and Rubinstein (1997), have acknowledged the explanatory usefulness, even indispensability, of positing unconscious mental processes and contents. However, as I have tried to show, much rests on how that concept is understood and employed. There is little doubt that a wide range of stimuli in the external environment and in one's inner world, of which we are unaware, influence our behavior. There is also little doubt that unconscious processing, some of which is potentially accessible to consciousness and some of which is impenetrable, is ubiquitous. Hence, taking these unconscious factors into account seems indispensable for adequate explanation of a wide range of behavior. And finally, as we will see in the discussion of research on unconscious processes in Chapter 2, there is little doubt that unconscious self, other, and interactional representations, beliefs, expectations, ingrained patterns, meanings, and defenses of which we are unaware strongly influence our behavior, feelings, and thoughts.

One of the problems that arises in appealing to unconscious processes and contents as explanatory accounts, as we have seen identified by James (1890), is the failure to distinguish between the unconscious and the fleetingly conscious.

Another problem is the use of the concept of unconscious processes in the service of reifying unconscious sub-structures of the personality and treating them as quasi-personal agents or homunculi that do things such as pull contents into their orbit, press for discharge, make choices and decisions, and demand punishment.

This last problem is one that Schafer (1976) was acutely aware of and addressed in his *A New Language of Psychoanalysis*. Although he does not state this explicitly, implicit in Schafer's critique is the idea that a theory in which reified subpersonal ids, egos, and superegos seek, do, and decide things parallels and reinforces the patient's tendency to disown aspects of himself or herself and experience them as impersonal and ego-alien "its." Schafer attempts to discourage this kind of theorizing and this sort of language by proposing an "action language," which he believes is the native language of psychoanalysis insofar as the central aim of psychoanalysis is to transform the sense of impersonal and passively endured happenings into personally acknowledged and owned motivations and actions that flow from who one is. Thus, for Schafer, both from a theoretical and clinical perspective, the language of agency is the appropriate language for psychoanalysis.

So, where is the unconscious in Schafer's program? It is certainly not in sub-personal structures of the personality pursuing their own aims. It is in the description of a fully human person or agent carrying out actions that are disclaimed or constitute doing two things at once or showing "an incorrect or faulty way of observing one's own actions" (p. 238). According to this perspective, essential to psychoanalysis is the attempt to "identify a network of intelligible actions where none was thought to exist, thereby expanding the range of acknowledged activity in the analysand's experience of his or her life" (p. 127). Or, as he also puts it, in the course of treatment, "what one presented before as an alien it . . . one now presents as defining aspects of oneself" (p. 257).

There is a recognizable congruence between the central motivation that informs Schafer's action language and both Sartre's and Fingarette's resistance to explanatory accounts that appeal to unconscious subpersonal homunculi. All three privilege choice – such as decisions, aims, desires, and wishes belonging to a person or agent, even if certain aims and desires are pursued unknowingly or ambivalently or self-deceptively. From this perspective, intrapsychic conflict is not a matter of opposing subpersonal structures of the personality (e.g., id versus ego), but rather entails a person or agent pursuing different and conflicting aims, some acknowledged and some disowned, some articulated and some not spelled out. In short, for Schafer, Fingarette, and Sartre, intrapsychic conflict refers to a person or agent at war with himself or herself. In his rejection of psychic structures and replacing those concepts with the central idea of individuals making compromises among different aims, Brenner (2002) seems to take a similar position.

It can be argued that metapsychological formulations that conceptualize sub-personal structures of the personality as homunculi striving for expression, relinquishing resistances, and meting out punishment are merely markers of certain important phenomena that await more adequate explanation, and understood in that light, do no harm. This may well be the case so long as one recognizes:

(1) that ids, egos, and superegos are not mini-persons; and (2) that appealing to an unconscious wish in an explanatory account requires independent evidence of the existence of the wish as well as of the nature of the process through which it exerts its influence. It will not do to say that behavior X occurs because of the influence of wish Y and then also say that we know that wish Y is causally operative because behavior X occurred.

## *Unconscious as hidden meanings*

Many psychoanalytic theorists avoid any talk of causal attributions to unconscious wishes and instead employ the idea of unconscious mental processes in the context of understanding the meanings of behaviors and experiences – of which we are unaware. For example, Lear (1995) locates Freud in a tradition "which goes back to Sophocles and which extends through Plato, Saint Augustine and Shakespeare to Proust and Nietzsche" and is characterized by:

> its insistence that there are significant meanings for human well-being which are obscured from immediate awareness . . . Humans make meaning, for themselves and for others of which they have no direct or immediate awareness . . . this is what Freud meant by the unconscious. And whatever valid criticisms can be aimed at him or at the psychoanalytic profession, it is nevertheless true that psychoanalysis is the most sustained and successful attempt to make these obscure meanings intelligible.
>
> (p. 20)

Of course, Freud has been claimed by many traditions. In locating Freud in the particular tradition that he does, Lear overlooks the Freud of the Project, of the energic model, of the inventor of the structural model, of the constancy principle, and of the theorist who believed that scientific thinking represented the highest level of cognitive development. Be that as it may, it is important to consider the proposition that the essence of the unconscious is not so much repressed wishes and impulses, but rather hidden meanings of which the individual is unaware and the deciphering of which is the main task of psychoanalysis. However, it is equally important to account for the need for hidden meanings and the processes through which meanings are hidden (see Grunbaum, 1990, for a discussion of the focus on meanings in psychoanalysis).

## *Explanation in terms of unconscious wishes and desires as both necessary and incomplete*

As has been noted by many, in appealing to the agent's motives, wishes, intention, desires, and so on in one's explanatory accounts, psychoanalysis mirrors folk psychology. However, it extends and makes more effective that explanatory mode by virtue of including unconscious motives, wishes, etc. in one's explanations.

By doing so, behaviors that seem inexplicable, bizarre and senseless, even random, become intelligible as motivated actions or quasi-actions, but whose motives are hidden from the agent of the behavior. For example, in a recent brief account of a schizophrenic patient's 'senseless' murder of his pregnant fiancée, Stone (2012) renders the murder intelligible as an action the motive for which was to avoid deep humiliation and shame – even though the motive was hidden from the patient. Including this unconscious motive in one's account brings method to the madness.

Knowing the reasons and motives for an action suffices as an explanation in the context of ordinary social interaction. In that context, if you ask someone why they are doing or did X and they give you an answer in the form of a particular reason or motive that bears a rational relationship to action X, that response suffices as an explanation. For example, ordinarily, if someone asks you why you are going to the library and your answer is to get a particular book, your answer suffices as an explanation. And such an account is likely to be indispensable in social interaction and to the idea of being a person.

A psychoanalytic account may broaden the above explanation by introducing the possibility of hidden or unconscious motives. For example, an additional hidden motive for going to the library may be the hope that you will run into one of the librarians to whom you are sexually attracted or you may have unconscious fantasies about what reading the book will accomplish. Although including unconscious motives makes the account of going to the library more comprehensive, it remains in the ordinary explanatory mode of accounting for behavior in terms of the individual's aims and motives. That is, it follows the form of the practical syllogism consisting of an *aim* (i.e., wanting to see the librarian), a *belief* that a particular *action* (i.e., going to the library) will satisfy that aim, and then carrying out the action.

However, as Black (1967) has observed, "As soon as reasons for action have been provided, an inquiring mind will want to press on to questions about the provenance and etiology of such reasons" (p. 656). Implicit in Black's comment is the idea that although explanation in terms of reasons and motives may suffice for ordinary social purposes, it does not suffice for a more complete scientific account of human nature and human behavior (see Sellars, 1963, discussion of the scientific and manifest image of man). And here is where Freud's metapsychology enters the picture. In developing his metapsychology, he is suggesting that accounting for human behavior in terms of reasons and motives, including unconscious reasons and motives, did not suffice for a scientific explanation. For the latter, one needed to know what underlay our reasons and motives. Although Freud's specific metapsychological formulations, including his drive theory, energic model, constancy principle, conception of the mind as a discharge apparatus, and so on may not be adequate, he was, I believe, correct in his belief that a scientific theory required an account not only of the individual's reasons and motives, but also, in Black's (1967) words, of the "provenance and etiology" of those reasons and motives. For Freud, the "provenance and etiology" of motives is largely to be found in our biologically based drives and instincts. From Black's and Freud's perspective, motives and reasons constitute both explanatory accounts (which may suffice for ordinary social interaction) as well as phenomena that themselves need to be explained further.

## *Skepticism toward motivational explanation*

Noting the limitations and incompleteness of appeal to motives as a form of explanation insofar as they constitute both explanations and phenomena that themselves need to be explained nevertheless preserves their usefulness and, so to speak, legitimacy. However, other more extreme forms of skepticism toward motivational accounts have been expressed. Such skepticism has taken various forms. One form, expressed in the context of a dissimulating conception of consciousness (Ricoeur, 1970) is to systematically doubt the validity of the conscious reasons and motives the individual gives for his or her actions. On this view, the motives one gives for one's actions are frequently false and self-deceptive in the sense that they rationalize and 'hide' the 'real' reasons and motives, which are likely to be unconscious wishes. This form of skepticism continues to preserve the legitimacy of the motivational mode of explanation. To be noted here is that this form of skepticism denies the individual's privileged epistemological status regarding his or her own motives and indeed, potentially places greater epistemological weight on the assessment of a knowledgable and sophisticated outside observer (e.g., a psychoanalyst) than on the report of the individual himself or herself (see Eagle, 1973).

A more radical form of skepticism with regard to the explanatory value of motivational accounts is seen in the argument proposed by philosophers influenced by Wittgenstein (e.g., Melden, 1961) that it is a mistake to think of motives and reasons as necessarily specifying the process that precedes and leads to action. Rather, their argument goes, the reasons given may constitute *justifications* for the action after it has already been taken. This form of skepticism is also clearly expressed by Nietzsche (1974) who writes:

> Is the goal, the purpose not often enough a beautifying pretext, a self-deception of vanity after the event that does not want to acknowledge that the ship is *following* the current into which it has entered accidentally? That it 'wills' to go that way *because it must*? That is, has a direction, to be sure, but – no helmsman at all?
>
> (p. 360)

A similar sentiment is expressed by Freud (1923) in his horse and rider metaphor representing the relationship between the id and the ego. He writes:

> Often a rider, if he is not to be parted from his horse, is obliged to guide it where it wants to go in the same way the ego is in the habit of transforming the id's will into an action as if it were its own.
>
> (p. 25)

I refer to this latter form of skepticism as more radical because it appears to virtually do away with the explanatory value of motivational accounts altogether. According to this view, it is not simply that the specific motives and reasons the individual provides for his or her behavior may be self-deceptive. It is also not simply that non-motivational factors influence the desires and motives we have. On both these views, motivational accounts retain some explanatory value. That is, the idea that behavior can be accounted for by referring to reasons and motives is retained even if the reasons and motives we provide are not the only or truly operatives ones, or even if the provenance and etiology of these motives themselves need to be accounted for. On the more extreme view, however, we are *propelled* by impersonal forces of which we are unaware and rationalize or justify our behavior by providing reasons and motives.

The model implicit in this latter view is not that of a rational agent or an agent of any kind, but of a robot-like being who has been programmed by say, evolutionary forces (one product of which is drives) and who has the additional capacity of falsely believing, not only that it has reasons and motives, but also that these reasons and motives influence its behavior. Whatever rationality this robot-like creature has is the rationality that emerges from the 'logic' of the selective advantages inherent in its program. On this view, there is no agent acting on the basis of motives and reasons, conscious or unconscious, but a machine-like entity 'behaving' according to a particular pre-set program.

Although Freud sometimes wrote as if this image represented his model for human behavior (as in the horse and rider metaphor noted above), this is not and could not be his general conception. For one of its implications would be the futility of any psychoanalytic work, particularly work based on the assumptions that motives, reasons, and desires do have an impact on behavior and that awareness and understanding of them may influence and modify their impact.

In any case, both within and outside the psychoanalytic context, we now have a more nuanced view of the various factors that influence behavior. Indeed, given the general acceptance of the psychoanalytic community of the concepts of multiple determination and the "principle of multiple functioning" (Waelder, 1936), I do not think that many analysts would have accepted the horse and rider metaphor as an accurate model of the determinants of human behavior.

I turn now from general conceptual issues regarding unconscious processes to specific psychoanalytic conceptions of unconscious processes.

## Psychoanalytic conceptions of unconscious mental processes and states: Freud's dynamic unconscious

As noted, Freud's distinctively psychoanalytic claim is not the positing of a descriptive unconscious, but the argument for the existence of the "dynamic unconscious." As the term "dynamic" suggests, Freud (1915a) thought of the dynamic unconscious as the product of an interplay of forces: instinctual wishes – or more accurately, the ideas and feelings linked to these wishes – striving to reach consciousness and access to motility versus opposing repressive forces working to keep these mental contents from conscious experience and access to action. As Kris (1947) observes, "psychoanalysis became the psychology of human experience and behavior from the perspective of unconscious conflict" (p. 53).

Unlike the descriptive unconscious, the dynamic unconscious was viewed by Freud (1933) as a "cauldron, full of seething excitations" (p. 84). It is clear that Freud viewed the dynamic unconscious as a sort of place or reservoir of seething repressed wishes pressing for gratification and discharge – much like the witches' brew of Macbeth: "fire, burn, and cauldron bubble." It is also clear that its evocative power notwithstanding, the idea of dynamic unconscious as a reservoir or container of repressed wishes – or for that matter, the idea of the mind as a theatre or stage – is untenable. Further, the idea of unconscious instinctual wishes pressing for gratification and discharge seems equally untenable. Wishes and desires do not press for gratification; they are not subpersonal homunculi that do things. Rather, persons have wishes and desires and are motivated to gratify them. Of course, unconscious wishes and desires may influence what people think and feel and do, and make demands on the mind. But wishes and desires do not think and feel and do things themselves.

## *Freud on unconscious fantasy*

The dynamic unconscious is 'populated' not only by wishes and desires, but also by fantasy. Freud had many things to say about fantasies, including unconscious fantasies. Above all, he viewed fantasies, similar to dreams, slips of the tongue, and neurotic symptoms, as disguised fulfillments of instinctual wishes. He writes: "Like dreams, they are wish-fulfillments" (Freud, 1900, p. 492; see also Arlow, 1969). He also writes in his characteristically confident assertive style: "There can be no doubt that [the phantasies'] sources lie in the instincts" (Freud 1916–1917, p. 368). He also maintained that somatic "hysterical symptoms are the realization of an unconscious phantasy which serves the fulfillment of a wish" (Freud, 1908, p. 163). For example, he interpreted Dora's cough and throat irritation as a somatic expression of an unconscious fellatio fantasy (Freud, 1905[1901], pp. 50–53).

More generally, Freud viewed unconscious fantasy as pathogenic. He writes that "as soon as [day-dreams] have become unconscious they may also become pathogenic" (Freud, 1908, p. 160). And somewhat later, in contrasting fantasy with the healthy models of sublimation and of transforming psychical tension into action in the real world, Freud (1912d) observes that the pathological route is to turn away from reality and "toward the life of phantasy" (p. 232). Further, according to Freud, for people who have pursued satisfaction via fantasies (e.g., masturbation fantasies; incestuous wishes; prostitution fantasies) and now try to pursue satisfaction with the real object, "all of these fall ill from the most laudable efforts, if the earlier fixations of their libido are powerful enough to resist a displacement" (Freud, 1912d, p. 234).

As noted earlier, the main lesson that Lear (1995) takes from Freud's writings on unconscious fantasy has to do with the meanings individuals create of which they are unaware. He writes: "whatever valid criticisms can be aimed at [Freud] or at the psychoanalytic profession, it is nevertheless true that psychoanalysis is the most sustained and successful attempt to make these obscure meanings intelligible" (p. 20). In the context of discussing Freud's stance on actual child seduction versus seduction fantasies, Lear (1995) writes:

> Freud effectively discovered that the mind is active and imaginative in the organization of its own experience . . . Freud called this imaginative activity fantasy, and he argued both that it functions unconsciously and that it plays a powerful role in the organization of a person's experience . . . it is the central insight of psychoanalysis.
>
> (p. 20)

Lear is not alone in believing that recognizing the role of unconscious fantasy in organizing and influencing an individual's life is a central insight of psychoanalysis. Indeed, for some psychoanalytic theorists, identifying the patient's central unconscious fantasies and the role they play in influencing his or her life pattern is *the* primary psychoanalytic task and constitutes the essence of what making the unconscious conscious means (e.g., Litowitz, 2007).

The clearest historical example of an unconscious fantasy, one that Lear refers to, is Freud's reinterpretation of patients' purported reports of childhood seduction as fantasies that in turn were viewed as an expression of incestuous wishes associated with a presumably universal Oedipus complex.[2] Note here the basic elements of Freud's conception of unconscious fantasy, namely, the direct or indirect gratification of unconscious wishes derived from instinctual drives and arising in childhood in the course of psychosexual development.

## *Surface and depth: The unconscious as depth*

For many years, psychoanalysis was referred to as a "depth psychology" (*Tiefenpsychologie*), based on the idea that whereas other psychological theories dealt mainly with the surface of psychological life (i.e., overt observable behavior or conscious experience), psychoanalytic theory focused on the *depths* of psychological life, that is, on unconscious meanings, strivings, desires, wishes, fantasies, anxieties, etc. residing deep in the recesses of the mind. As Wachtel (2003) has pointed out in a cogent paper, given the connotations of "surface" and "depth" one implication of this distinction is that most psychological theories are superficial, whereas psychoanalytic theories are profound. Indeed, Lear (1995) has argued that a central motive for some critiques of Freud (which he refers to as "Freud-bashing") is the unacceptability and even anxiety-provoking effect of a concept of mind as possessing depth.

Lear's comment is consistent with the general psychoanalytic view that most people feel threatened by the thought of powerful impulses and forces – Freud's (1933) "seething cauldron" (p. 84) – residing in their unconscious mind. Indeed, according to psychoanalytic theory, defenses are erected to keep derivatives of these impulses and forces from reaching conscious experience. In short, from the perspective of Freudian theory, the powerful unconscious impulses and urges hidden in the recesses of one's mind constitute the greatest psychological threat to the individual and the most fertile source of psychopathology. (Interestingly, they are also believed to be a rich source of creativity.)

The above perspective can be and has been challenged in a number of ways. Wittgenstein's (1938/1966) reaction to reading Freud was twofold: one, he believed that he was a genius; and two, that his theory was misleading and dangerous. Misleading in what way? According to Wittgenstein, most people are often flattered rather than threatened by the thought of powerful and mysterious unconscious forces residing deep within them. According to Wittgenstein, what is truly threatening to the individual is the idea that there is nothing beneath the surface. The idea that we harbor dark, mysterious, and powerful impulses and desires can be reassuring and even flattering, particularly if one's typical conscious experience is one of emptiness and if one's greatest fear is that one is shallow.

Bertrand Russell (1921) makes a similar point. He writes that the Freudian unconscious:

> becomes a sort of underground prisoner, living in a dungeon, breaking in at long intervals on our daylight respectability with dark groans and maledictions and strange atavistic lusts. The ordinary reader, almost inevitability, thinks of this underground person as another consciousness, prevented by what Freud calls the 'censor' from making his voice heard in company, except on rare and dreadful occasions when he shouts so loud that everyone hears him and there is a scandal. Most of us like the idea that we could be desperately wicked if only we let ourselves go. For this reason, the Freudian 'unconscious' has been a consolation to many quiet and well-behaved persons.
>
> (pp. 37–38)

This is captured by a rather cruel *New Yorker* cartoon some years ago in which a psychiatrist is saying to a patient: "Deep down you're shallow."

One is also reminded of Ibsen's Peer Gynt who wants to convince the Button-Molder that he does not deserve the mundane fate shared by ordinary mortals of being molded down into a formless mass by arguing that he is special, that the terrible deeds he has committed in his lifetime mark him for a different and special fate. The Button-Molder disdainfully dismisses Peer Gynt's claim with the observation that what Peer Gynt thinks of as terrible deeds are petty and mundane and do not mark him off from the mass of humankind. The point here is that Peer Gynt's narcissism is deeply wounded by his shallowness and ordinariness and is salved by the thought that a dark evil lurks somewhere deep within him.

Classical psychoanalysis, both as a theory and as a form of treatment, has traded on the idea that its theorists as well as its practitioners are privy to dark and terrible secrets of human nature buried deep in the unconscious, secrets that most people are not privy to and cannot confront. For example, who among us could tolerate with equanimity the presumed terrible truth of incestuous wishes? Witness Oedipus' blood-curdling response to his recognition that he had committed incest. The psychoanalytic practitioner, as an expert on the unconscious, it is claimed, can help the patient, under relatively safe conditions, to become aware of and confront these terrible secrets. And the psychoanalytic theorist, also an expert on the unconscious, can help all of us to become at least intellectually aware of and confront the dark secrets of the unconscious mind. And as for those who balk at and reject the insights and truths the theory offers, given their unanalyzed state, it is understandable that they are not ready to confront the dark and deep forces and secrets that reside in the unconscious mind.[3,4]

In contrast to Freud's (1933) "seething cauldron" (p. 84) of repressed impulses, the unconscious of contemporary psychoanalytic theories is one of representations – of self, other, and self–other interactions based on repeated experiences with caregivers. The latter may not be easily accessible to conscious experience, but not because they are 'deeply' repressed, but rather largely because they have been acquired (i.e., learned) early in life and have become in Lyons-Ruth's (1999) words, part of our "implicit relational knowing" or procedural knowledge. Further, individuals are generally better able to understand and have at least intellectual access to their representational patterns than to presumably repressed wishes and fantasies (e.g., of incestuous wishes and fantasies). Thus, in a certain literal sense, the former are more on the surface (i.e., more readily accessible to conscious awareness) and the latter are deeper (i.e., less accessible to conscious awareness). However, for some, this translates into superficial versus profound in the sense of degree of importance and degree of impact on the individual's life. As we will see, even contemporary Freudians such as Gray and his followers emphasize in their clinical work material that is just below the surface rather than deeply repressed in their clinical work. Further, as will also see, for some, analytic work focuses not so much on bringing repressed wishes and desires to conscious awareness but on helping the patient understand how his or her mind works and learning to reflect on one's own and others' mental states.

As Wachtel (2003) also observes, deeper is often equated with developmentally earlier which, in turn, implies archaic, primitive, and more serious psychopathology. Thus, "preoedipal" pathology is not only presumably deeper, but also more serious and intractable. Further, normal early developmental stages are described in pathological terms such as "the paranoid–schizoid position" and "the depressive position"; and adult psychopathology is understood as a developmental arrest at or regression to these early normal developmental stages. Some authors refer to a "psychotic core" (e.g., Eigen, 1993; Loewald, 1979) that is presumably universally present in early stages of development, is covered over and unconscious in most individuals, and becomes manifest when someone becomes psychotic. In other words, the "psychotic core" is deeply buried in the unconscious and comes to the surface when psychosis erupts. One implication of this formulation is that the 'deepest' level of analysis is reached when one taps that "psychotic core." Despite cogent critiques of the tendency in the psychoanalytic literature to equate adult pathology with early stages of normal functioning (e.g., Klein & Tribich, 1982; Peterfreund, 1978; Zeanah, Anders, Seifer, & Stern, 1989), this kind of theorizing persists.

Thus, those who take this perspective, a presumably excessive focus on such 'surface' matters as representational patterns would call for a 'deepening' of the treatment characterized by a turn to an emphasis on the 'deeply repressed' – often based on the implicit assumption, for which there is no good evidence, that only the latter focus accomplishes thorough and deep personality change. In short, there is an equation, for which there is little evidence, among the deeply buried, the early stages of development, the 'primitive,' and the more seriously pathological.

The factors that may strongly influence the trajectory of an individual's life may often be, so to speak, right on the surface, even if not in conscious awareness. As an example, consider the well known study by Rutter, Quinton, and Hill (1990) who investigated the adult outcomes of institution-reared children. One of their important findings was that a critical factor in influencing the developmental trajectory of the women in the study was something as seemingly mundane and 'superficial' as having good experiences at school. This factor, in turn, reinforced the girls' confidence in planning and made more probable such outcomes as staying in school longer, getting better jobs, having contact with a more wholesome peer group, marrying later, becoming pregnant later, and having a more supportive spouse. The point here is that the relatively 'surface' factor of school performance had a profound influence on the various 'choice-points' in the girl's life. The profundity of influence of a given factor on an individuals' life may be relatively unrelated to issues of surface and depth as they are understood in a psychoanalytic context. The results of the Rutter et al. (1990) study are important and can be understood quite apart from any considerations of the role of unconscious factors in the girls' life – although perhaps consideration of such factors as unconscious guilt, unconscious fantasies, and unconscious self-representations could enrich understanding in a given individual case. (The idea that seemingly surface factors, for example, quirks of character interacting with chance events, can have a profound impact on an individual's life is captured by great novelists such as Eliot, Trollope, and Austen.)

During the time I was working on this chapter, I viewed the excellent PBS documentary on the Roosevelts, the first installment of which dealt with Theodore Roosevelt. He was a puny, sickly, and fearful child who would not leave his home unless he was accompanied by his younger brother. As a way of coping with his frail constitution, and with the encouragement of his deeply admired and beloved father, Theodore took on an assortment of physical challenges later in life and became a sturdy young man. When he became President of the United States, he openly and forcefully advocated military power and an aggressive imperialism.

As one of the documentary commentators remarked, "he loved war." In thinking about his development, one can see virtually a direct line from Theodore's attempts to deal with his childhood frailty and weakness to his worship of physical strength and power to his imperialistic policy and worship of war.

On the domestic political front, before he became President, Theodore Roosevelt devoted himself to rooting out corruption and, when he became President, to limiting the monopolistic power of corporations and implementing very progressive policies. Here, too, one can draw virtually a direct line from Theodore Roosevelt's admiration of his morally upright father and his determination to uphold the values he had internalized. There is, of course, a great deal that can be said regarding Theodore Roosevelt's policies and psychological dynamics. However, in the present context, the point I want to make is the degree to which a relatively adequate psychological account of both his domestic and foreign policies is provided by reference to relatively surface factors (i.e., readily accessible), albeit powerful and profound in their influence. Further, appeal to more esoteric and presumably 'deeper' factors, such as, for example, a death instinct, would likely add little or nothing; indeed, would likely serve to obfuscate a relatively clear and relatively adequate account.

We often make the assumption that the depths of horror of actions requires an explanatory account that is commensurate with the actions, that is, that appeals to primeval depths within the actor's personality. This issue is addressed by Arendt (1963) in *Eichmann in Jerusalem*, in her discussion of the "banality of evil." Given the horror and evil of Eichmann's actions, we expect to confront a monster of extraordinary proportions, harboring 'primitive' motives. Instead, we see an ordinary man, a good father and husband and an ambitious bureaucrat whose job happens to be shipping humans to their death rather than, say, cars to car dealers.

There has been much debate regarding Arendt's description of Eichmann and her concept of the "banality of evil," particularly as applied to Eichmann. New information has been uncovered indicating that Eichmann was a dedicated Nazi ideologue and a passionate anti-Semite and not simply the petty bureaucrat who could not think and could not grasp what he was doing. However, despite all the academic excitement this new information generated, Eichmann's personality and personal motives are of limited relevance to the concept of the "banality of evil." As Smith (2007) observes, the data from the Nuremberg trials showed that "high-ranking Nazi war criminals . . . participated in atrocities without diagnosable impairments that would account for their actions" (General Sir John Hackett, as cited by Smith, 2007). "They were as diverse a group as one might find in our government today, or in the leadership of the PTA" (as cited in Smith, 2007, p. 4). Further, as for the rank and file that carried out the killings in concentration camps, "there is not a shred of evidence to suggest that they were anything other than ordinary German citizens" (Smith, 2007, p. 4). Many of them were ordinary middle-aged family men without either military training or ideological indoctrination. Waller writes the "truth seems to be that the most outstanding characteristic of perpetrators of extraordinary evil lies in their normality, not abnormality" (as cited in Smith, 2007, p. 4). This fits the profile painted by Primo Levi of the Nazi jailers at Auschwitz as "average human beings, averagely intelligent, averagely wicked" (as cited in Smith, 2007, p. 4).

Thus, although contrary to Arendt's claim that Eichmann was incapable of thinking and evidence demonstrating that he was a passionate anti-Semite and Nazi ideologue, the fact is that his actions do not appear to entail the eruption of dark and deeply buried unconscious forces, but rather reflect well organized plans motivated by Nazi ideology and ambition. Eichmann was not a psychotic individual whose ego was overwhelmed by the sheer intensity of the aggressive instinctual drive. Indeed, he would not have been able to efficiently supervise the mass murders as efficiently as he did were his own ego functions not relatively intact.

One can make a similar point with regard to the mass killing of war. Although war may require a selected capacity for aggression, it is made possible largely by the 'surface' social factors of conformity, patriotism, not wanting to be seen as a coward, love of country, identification with presumed national interest, and so on. Whereas a psychotic individual's killing spree may perhaps be understood in terms of eruption of unconscious forces – although I have my doubts that this constitutes an adequate explanation – war requires social organization and relatively intact ego functioning of its participants, including its leaders.

Finally, I want to address the issue of surface and depth by referring to two recent papers. As noted earlier, Stone (2012) describes the case of a paranoid schizophrenic man who became psychotic (for the second time – the first time was in graduate school) when his fiancée told him she was pregnant and who ended up killing her after "powerful forces" commanded him to do so. Stone writes that the "mysterious forces" and persecutory delusions "were nothing more exotic than the prospect of husbandhood and fatherhood, along with the necessity to function well professionally so as to provide adequate monetary and emotional support for his family" (p. 19). For this young man, given that the options of abortion (adamantly opposed by his fiancée) and abandonment (too shameful) were not possible, a persecutory delusion commanding murder "allowed him to save face" (p. 19).

Contrast Stone's rather straightforward account with Kogan's (2012) description of the offspring of Holocaust survivors in terms of "psychic hole" and "black hole," as "a body that encapsulates all of the unconscious fantasies connected to the parents' traumatic past" (p. 8). In contrast, to Stone's description which, despite the horror of the patient's act, deals with ordinary 'surface' motives (such as avoiding shame and protecting one's self-image), Kogan's account is 'deeper' in that it deals with presumably primitive, inaccessible, and even ineffable phenomena. However, the costs of such presumed depth include hyperbole (e.g., traumatizations result in "a sort of shocking infantile catastrophe associated with stark terror and may lead to primitive mental disturbances" (pp. 7–8), lack of evidence, and above all, lack of applicability, and enormous distance between the account and the lives of real individuals (there is no evidence that Kogan's description generally applies to children of Holocaust survivors). It is important to note that whereas Stone's description was intended to demonstrate that psychoanalytic insights could contribute to understanding a psychotic act, Kogan's paper was stimulated by understandable deeply personal reactions to a visit to the Jewish Museum in Berlin.

I make much of Kogan's account because I think it is illustrative of similar problematic accounts in the psychoanalytic literature, problematic mainly because they are true neither to the individual's experience (i.e., the children of Holocaust survivors; they fail as accounts from the inside) nor to the requirements of a clear and testable theoretical explanation (they fail as accounts from the outside). That is, although personally meaningful to the author, they lack *ecological validity* in both realms.

## Contemporary psychoanalytic conceptions of unconscious mental processes and states

Despite its centrality in Freudian theory, the concept of the dynamic unconscious, at least the way Freud understood it, does not play a dominant role in some contemporary psychoanalytic theories. There is little reference to unconscious dynamic processes and the references that are present are mainly to a cognitively oriented unconscious. For example, one finds few references to unconscious processes in the index of Kohut's (1984) last book and the few references one does find are comments on Freudian theory. Most important, self psychology theory does not require a prominent role for unconscious processes and states. There is little in the structure and logic of self psychology theory that has to do with conflicting unconscious motives or with unconscious wishes and desires striving for gratification. Rather, much like Rogerian theory, there is one general and over-arching motive, namely, striving for self-cohesiveness and for realization of one's ambitions and ideals in the light of one's talents and aptitudes., what Kohut (1984) refers to as one's "nuclear program" (p. 132). Also, in contrast to what Kohut (1984) refers to as "structural conflicts" (p. 45), the concept of self-defects does not require a concept of the dynamic unconscious.

Other contemporary psychoanalytic theories do provide a more prominent place for unconscious processes, but primarily for a more cognitively oriented (although accompanied by affect) rather than a dynamic unconscious in the Freudian sense. The unconscious of contemporary psychoanalytic theories is mainly an unconscious of "relational configurations" (Mitchell, 1998), internal objects and internalized object relations (Fairbairn, 1952); "interactional structures" (Beebe & Lachmann, 2002), "internal working models" (Bowlby, 1980), "representations of interactions generalized" or RIGs (Stern, 1985), "pathogenic beliefs" (Weiss & Sampson, 1986), and "implicit relational knowing" (Lyons-Ruth, 1999). There is room for conflict in these representations, but not between impulses and defense. That is to say, it is mainly a cognitive unconscious of representations, expectations, and beliefs rather than a "cauldron, full of seething excitations" (Freud, 1933, p. 73) (see Eagle, 2011a). This is not to say that contemporary psychoanalytic conceptions of unconscious processes ignore the role of affect. This will become apparent in the elaboration below of these contemporary conceptualizations.

Common to the concepts of "relational configurations," "interactional structures," "internal working models"; "RIGs," "unconscious pathogenic beliefs," and "implicit relational knowing" is not only their representational structure, but also the assumption that they have been acquired early in life in the course of repeated interactions with parental figures. That is to say, they are based on early learning. Other elements common to these concepts are the ideas, (1) that these representations are not necessarily consciously experienced, that is, are often unconscious, but not unconscious due to repression; and (2) that these early representations strongly influence one's later relationships with significant figures.

Let me provide some specific examples. According to Bowlby (1980), based on early interactions with one's attachment figure(s), one develops an internal working model consisting of representations of the attachment figure, of what to expect from the attachment figure, and corresponding representations of oneself. For example, based on repeated experiences of rejection, one may develop a representation of the attachment figure as rejecting, expect rejection in response to seeking to meet one's attachment needs, and acquire a representation of oneself as unworthy of love. Furthermore, this internal working model is likely to influence one's representations and expectations later in life in relation to actual and potential attachment figures.

It is important to note that according to attachment theory, the internal working models acquired early in life are likely to include contradictory unconscious and consciously accessible models existing side by side, the latter defensively motivated and the former reflective of actual but defensively excluded experiences. For example, an individual may describe his or her parent on the Adult Attachment Interview (AAI) (Main & Goldwyn, 1998) as ideal and wonderful, and yet, either may not be able to provide concrete instantiations of the image he or she portrays or may provide concrete examples that contradict the idealized picture, suggesting that the latter is a defensively motivated idealized conscious representation that exists alongside the individual's unconscious internal working model.

Another example: According to Weiss and Sampson's (1986) Control–Mastery theory, based on certain implicit parental communications early in life, the child may develop unconscious beliefs, some of them pathogenic. For example, based on implicit parental communications to the effect that if you become independent and separate from me, you will be harming or destroying me, the child may come to experience guilt in relation to normal strivings for independence and separation. Or, as another example, based on implicit parental communications to the effect that if you are successful and outdo me, you will incur my wrath or will humiliate me, the child may come to experience anxiety and/or guilt in relation to his or her ambitions and strivings for success (I will return to this topic in Chapter 4).

Thus, in contrast to the unconscious as a "cauldron, full of seething excitations," the unconscious of contemporary psychoanalytic theories is comprised of representations, beliefs, and expectations, and their accompanying affects. However, these cognitive representations, beliefs, and expectations – which are more accurately characterized as cognitive–affective representations – are saturated with such affective issues as the need to avoid the pain of rejection or the warding off of anxiety and guilt or rage at not having one's needs met or conflicted efforts to meet one's attachment needs or guilt-ridden strivings for separation and success.

One virtue of contemporary psychoanalytic conceptions of unconscious processes and states is the enhanced possibility of carrying out empirical research on these matters; another related virtue is the greater points of contact between psychoanalytic and other theories dealing with similar phenomena. Consider the large body of attachment research on attachment patterns and their underlying internal working models. Such research provides data that enable one to make plausible inferences regarding an individual's representations of attachment figures and expectations regarding his or her attachment needs. I have already noted, as an example of such research, the finding on the AAI suggesting a conscious idealized representation of a parental figure and a contradictory unconscious representation. As another example, consider the research of Waters and Waters (2006) on attachment "scripts." Their findings suggest that individuals vary in the degree to which they have available in their cognitive repertory – without necessarily being aware of it – representations of the attachment figure as a safe haven and the expectation that the figure will be available as a secure base when one is distressed.

## *The unconscious as unarticulated*

A number of general critiques of the Freudian conception of unconscious processes as well as alternatives to that conception that have been presented are not linked to a particular psychoanalytic theory. An important example is Fingarette's (1963) proposal, based on Sartre's (1956) critique of the Freudian unconscious, that the repressed unconscious is better understood as unarticulated, as not spelled out. And as we will also see, in the psychoanalytic context, Stern (2003) further elaborates Fingarette's view through his conceptualization of unconscious mental contents as unformulated.

As Olafson (1967) writes in elucidating Sartre's position:

> our choices or "projects" are not necessarily the objects of a reflective self-awareness. A properly conceived psychoanalytic method would therefore address itself to the task of interpreting the system of choices that our actions express and would reject all reductions of these choices to occult non-choicelike states of the unconscious.
>
> (p. 292)

In accord with a Sartrean perspective, Fingarette's alternative to Freud's dynamic unconscious is captured by the description of an individual engaging in a project – for example, a woman who is complicit in an ongoing seduction – without spelling out both the project in which she is engaged as well as her 'policy' to fail to spell it out. In more ordinary discourse, one can say that the woman does not spell out either the motives for her behavior or her inclination – in Sartre's language, her 'choice' and in Fingarette's language, her 'policy' – to either not articulate her motives or to find motives that she finds comfortable and that allow her to continue in her behaviors – that is, to cooperate in the seduction.

Sartre's objection to the Freudian unconscious is based on his insistence on preserving the primacy and sufficiency of the role of the agent and his or her choices in accounting for human action; and his rejection of any 'reductive' explanation that weakens the hegemony of agentic choice in human action by appealing to subpersonal mechanisms. However, one does not have to accept Sartre's existentialist rejection of the influence of any non-choicelike or subpersonal factors in human action in order to recognize that he has pointed to certain problems with the Freudian unconscious.

Recall the language Freud (1914) employs in his discussion of resistance, compulsion to repeat, and working-through. He writes about promising "the ego rewards and advantages," about "the ego decid[ing] to relinquish its resistances" and its "difficulty in rendering the repressions," and so on. It is a language in which a part or structure of the personality – the ego – does all the sorts of things that persons do – responding to rewards and advantages, deciding, undoing repressions, and so on. One finds similar language in regard to other structures of the personality. For example, id impulses press for discharge and gratification and there is an "attraction exerted by the unconscious prototype upon the repressed instinctual process" (Freud, 1926, p. 159). And by virtue of its need to punish, the superego "opposes every move towards success, including, therefore, the patient's own recovery through analysis" (p. 159).

In these accounts, subpersonal structures of the personality are described as homunculi, indistinguishable from persons. From the perspective of Sartre's critique, what leads to this way of thinking is the positing of "occult non-choicelike states of the unconscious" (Olafson, 1967, p. 292). It seems to me that one needs to distinguish between the very tenable and empirically supported idea that unconscious factors influence our behavior and conscious mental states – our choices, desires, fantasies, etc. – and the positing of unconscious homunculi as mini-agents of behavior and mental states.

The above distinction can be made clearer by noting a critical contrast between robots and human agents. One gets robots to carry out certain tasks by programming specific behaviors. Human agents, however, are influenced not simply by programming specific behaviors, but by factors, including unconscious factors, that influence what they think, feel, desire, and want to do. So, it is not unconscious egos that are deciding or relinquishing, or unconscious superegos that punish and oppose success. Rather, it is both conscious factors and unconscious factors of which we are unaware that influence what we, as human agents, strive for, decide (or cannot decide), and feel guilty about (see Dennett, 1969; 1978, for a different view).

Consider an important paper by Money and Erhardt (1972) on the behavior and preferences of females who had been fetally androgenized due to their pregnant mothers being given an androgen-related hormone as a means of preventing miscarriage. These girls tended to show a variety of common characteristics including tomboyism, lack of interest in playing with dolls, little interest in feminine clothes, and greater interest in career than marriage and family. It is clear that fetal androgenization influenced the girls' behavior, in ways of which they were unaware. However, fetal androgenization did not exert its influence through directly programming specific behaviors – as would be the case in programming a robot – but rather in exerting an influence on what the girls wanted and did not want, what they preferred and did not prefer, what captured their interest and what did not. Further, each of the girls studied offered specific reasons and motives for her behavior rather than report a blind compulsion in robot-like fashion to carry out certain behaviors and avoid other behaviors.

Consider as another example an individual who has experienced early oral deprivation and as an adult engages, more than most individuals, in a variety of 'oral' activities such as smoking, chewing, talking, and overeating. How does one understand these activities and their relationship to early oral deprivation? It is not likely that early oral deprivation directly influences later oral activities the way a program directs a robot. Rather, early oral deprivation may influence the individual's wants, desires, and pleasures.

I think the above examples illustrate the way that unconscious factors normally influence our behavior. This is different from a formulation in which unconscious impulses and wishes, kept in check only by ego controls, are ever ready to erupt into consciousness and overtake motility in the manner of a dybbuk or demon. It is true that under certain circumstances, such as addiction, individuals will report feeling compelled by peremptory desires and impulses to engage in certain behaviors (e.g., using the drug to which one is addicted). However, although physiologically based, the peremptory desire is a conscious one motivated by the anticipation of pleasure and/or relief from distressful states. If the peremptory desire or impulse is experienced as beyond the individual's control (i.e., the irresistible impulse), this is not because the dybbuk or demon or unconscious wish has taken control of the individual's mind, but because the anticipated pleasure is too intense to resist and/or because the need for relief from unbearable states overrides all other considerations.

There are circumstances, such as psychosis, in which something like a dybbuk or demon seems to take over the personality in the form of voices telling the individual what to do, for example, kill himself or herself or someone else. From a psychoanalytic perspective, such voices are often interpreted as unacceptable and unacknowledged unconscious wishes that have been rendered into foreign 'not me' voices and can, therefore be acted on. (See Stone's, 2012, description of a schizophrenic patient who killed his pregnant fiancée because voices told him to do so.) However, do such psychotic phenomena indicate that deeply buried within all of us are unconscious murderous impulses and wishes (as well as other unconscious instinctual impulses and wishes) that press for discharge and are normally kept in check by ego controls? Formulations of the unconscious as a "cauldron, full of seething excitations" (Freud, 1933, p. 84) as well as the claim that deeply buried within all of us is a "psychotic core" (Eigen, 1993) seems to constitute a "yes" to the above question.

A response of "yes" to the above question is also implied by the formulation that in mental states such as sleep, fatigue, intoxication, and free associating on the couch, characterized by loosening or disinhibition of ego controls, derivatives of instinctual drives and wishes that are always pressing for discharge will be more likely to erupt into consciousness. We have known since Plato (and likely before) that in certain states such as sleep and dreaming certain thoughts and feelings that are ordinarily censored are now more likely to be expressed and communicated both to oneself and to others. However, does this mean that these thoughts and feelings have existed in an unconscious state, are constantly pressing for expression and discharge, and await the 'opportunity' of loosened ego controls to escape censorship and achieve expression in consciousness? The answer in both classical Freudian theory and contemporary psychoanalytic ego psychology to this question seems to be "yes." For example, Gray (1990) writes:

> The theoretical and clinical framework within which I examine therapeutic action is the analysis of those problems that arise when instinctual derivatives, searching for more adequate discharge, encounter conflicts that force the ego to turn primarily to unconscious rather than conscious solutions.
>
> (p. 1084)

There is, in my view, a more tenable alternative to the above formulation. For one thing, it is not just "instinctual derivatives" but also other thoughts and feelings that are censored and kept from oneself and others. Second, instinctual derivatives are not homunculi "searching for more adequate discharge." And most germane in the present context, it is very likely that the thoughts and feelings that are experienced and expressed under conditions of loosened ego controls have already been consciously experienced, even if fleetingly, and then pushed out of awareness and/or inhibited from expression under normal conditions.

Recall Freud's (Breuer & Freud, 1893–1895) description of Lucy R. as an example of this phenomenon. Freud tells Lucy R.: "I believe that really you are in love with your employer, the Director, though perhaps without being aware of it yourself" (p. 117). Lucy R. responds: "Yes, I think that's true." Freud replies: "But if you knew you loved your employer, why didn't you tell me?" Lucy R. answers: "I didn't know – or rather I didn't want to know. I wanted to drive it out of my head and not think of it again; and I believe latterly I have succeeded." And she adds later on: "People would laugh at me if they had any idea of it" (p. 117).

Consider also the actor Mel Gibson's expression of blatantly anti-Semitic sentiments when he was inebriated. Would we say these anti-Semitic thoughts and feelings were unconsciously searching for more adequate discharge, and then found such an opportunity when ego controls were loosened? This is simply implausible. It is far more likely that Gibson harbored conscious anti-Semitic thoughts and feelings and, under normal conditions, knew well enough not to express and communicate them to others and perhaps, at times, to himself. The expression *in vino veritas* does not refer to repressed unconscious mental contents that are unavailable to consciousness and emerge only when the individual is under the influence. It refers, rather, to one's true attitudes, thoughts, and feelings that are and have been available to consciousness, even if perhaps fleetingly, but that, due to propriety, socialization, and similar factors, have been withheld from full articulation, expression, and communication.

It is, of course, true that we are often unaware not only of the factors that influence what we strive for, decide, and feel guilt about, but also, in varying degrees, of the nature of our strivings, decisions, and feelings themselves. However, this does not mean that it is unconscious subpersonal homunculi that are the mini-agents of these strivings, decisions, and feelings or that these strivings, decisions, and feelings somehow reside in the unconscious. Rather, as Fingarette (1963) and Stern (2003) have argued (and as I believe is implicit in Gray's (2005) "close process monitoring"), it means that we are motivated to not spell out, to not formulate, and to not put into words certain thoughts and feelings that are associated with dysphoric affects and are inimical to one's self-image. Even in Freud's (Breuer & Freud, 1893–1895) account of Lucy R. – a presumed example of repression – we learn that she was, indeed, aware, even if fleetingly, of her fantasies about her employer, but then pushed them out of her mind. That is, she did not attend to them or spell them out.

## *Are unconscious mental contents indeterminate?*

At least some contemporary psychoanalytic theorists have essentially proposed that the meaning of unconscious mental contents is indeterminate. Thus, Stern (1983; 2003) not only defines unconscious mental contents as unformulated contents, but also proposes that these unformulated contents can be formulated in a variety of different ways and, so to speak, await formulation as a function of the social interactional context.

It should be clear that Stern is not saying that unconscious (i.e., unformulated) mental states have a determinate context that may be difficult to identify – that would be an epistemological observation. Rather, he is saying that unconscious mental contents have no determinate meaning and are given determinate meaning via social interaction – that is an ontological proposition.

My colleagues and I have argued against Stern's position (Eagle, Wolitzky, & Wakefield, 2001) and I do not want to repeat the full argument here. However, a central element of our argument is perhaps worth repeating. According to Stern (2003), "lack of formulation as defense means never allowing ourselves to interpret our experience in the first place. The refusal to formulate is quite simple; one just restricts one's freedom of thought and the 'offending' experience is never created" (p. 63). The problem here is that, however vague and fleeting it may be, there must be some "offending" determinate content that triggers the defensive step of not formulating any further. However, if it is conceptualized otherwise, if there are no determinate unconscious mental contents, why is defense against such contents ever necessary? To do away with the idea of some determinate meaning for unconscious mental contents is to do away with the concept altogether. Indeed, it is difficult to understand what could possibly be meant by unconscious mental contents that have no determinate meaning.

One can argue that bodily sensations (e.g., experiencing a rapid heartbeat) may have an indeterminate meaning and are then given determinate meaning through cognitive structuring influenced by the situational context. Thus, as Schachter and Singer (1962) have shown in their classic study, the same physiological sensations are given different meanings by individuals (e.g., fear versus excitement) depending upon the situation to which they are exposed. However, the experience of a rapid heartbeat is neither indeterminate nor unconscious, including in the sense of being unformulated; it is the formulated experience of a rapid heartbeat. What may be indeterminate is the further meaning given to the experience in the sense of labeling and attributing it to fear or excitement.

There is a complex and technical philosophical debate around the question of indeterminacy of reference and meaning associated, for example, with the work of Quine (e.g., 1969). As I understand Quine (1969), his claim, a form of logical behaviorism, as Wakefield (2001) puts it, is that "only behavioral facts are relevant to reference" (p. 38). According to this view, the reference of any statement is indeterminate. For example, when an individual utters the word "rabbit," he may be referring to a whole rabbit or part of a rabbit or X. Further, the correlation between external events and the individual's utterances will be the same for any of these references. Hence, the meaning of the utterance "rabbit" is indeterminate. Furthermore, on this view, one cannot bypass the indeterminacy by asking the individual what he or she means because any response will be subject to the same indeterminacy. This, however, is not the kind of indeterminacy of meaning implicit in Stern's formulation.

## *The unconscious as implicit*

The term "implicit" rather than "unconscious" is frequently employed in the non-psychoanalytic literature to refer to the processes that are out of awareness, but not repressed. Such processes include knowledge we have, operations we carry out, 'rules' we follow, or discriminations we make, all without explicit awareness, that we have the knowledge, are carrying out these processes, following these 'rules' or making these discriminations. Recently a group of psychoanalytic theorists have focused on implicit processes in their understanding of phenomena of central interest to psychoanalysis (Lyons-Ruth and her colleagues – e.g., Lyons-Ruth, 1999; Process of Change Boston Study Group, 1998).

Lyons-Ruth (1999) refers to "implicit procedural" knowledge that is manifested in an "enactive form" that "does not require reflective thought or verbalization to be, in some sense, known" (p. 578). It will be recognized that the representations of internal working models (IWMs), representations of internalizations generalized (RIGs), role relationships, unconscious pathogenic beliefs, and so on discussed earlier, can be thought of as instances of implicit procedural knowledge. That is, they take the form of implicit 'rules' that are expressed through relational enactments and/or inferred on the basis of narrative structure (e.g., as in the AAI or Waters and Waters' (2006) attachment script narratives). As noted earlier and also noted by Lyons-Ruth (1999), although these representations are out of awareness, they are implicit rather than repressed. Lyons-Ruth (1999) employs the term "implicit procedural unconscious" (p. 586) – a knowing how knowledge – to refer to "implicit relational procedures [that] are often neither conscious and verbalizable nor repressed in a dynamic sense" (p. 589).

Further, these implicit relational procedures are saturated with strong affects, the poor regulation of which is a central feature of psychopathology. According to Lyons-Ruth and her colleagues, therapeutic change consists in "creating new representational structures" and new forms of "being with others" (p. 608). Such change is not likely to occur, Lyons-Ruth maintains, primarily through insight or verbal symbolic knowledge. Rather, "the work of elaborating new implicit procedures for being with others must occur at enactive as well as symbolic levels" (p. 608). This perspective places a great deal of emphasis on the therapeutic relationship, that is, on the interactions between patient and therapist, as the primary agent of therapeutic change. In this regard, it constitutes a variation on the theme of corrective emotional experience as a central factor in therapeutic change. More specifically, on this view, it is such experiences that play a central role in altering old representational structures and old ways of being with others an in "elaborating new implicit procedures for being with others" (p. 608).

Note that there is little talk in the above of making the unconscious conscious or making the implicit explicit. Indeed, as the above quote indicates, the new and presumably more adaptive procedures for being with others that are acquired remain at the implicit level. This assumption is consistent with the general observation that implicit or what Polanyi refers to as "tacit" knowledge is relatively unsusceptible to influence or refutation by explicit verbalized knowledge (See Polanyi & Prosch, 1975). Thus, Lyons-Ruth (1999) argues that not only is implicit procedural knowledge acquired nonverbally (i.e., through early implicit relational interactions) and expressed through nonverbal enactments, but also that old implicit procedural knowledge is changed and new implicit procedural knowledge is acquired largely through nonverbal interactions.

As can be seen, Lyons-Ruth's virtually exclusive emphasis is on implicit relational representations, that is, ways of being with others. There is little or no attention given to representations, such as self representations, that, although largely the product of early relational interactions, once formed, are essentially trait-like non-relational structures. For example, once formed, a representation of self as unlovable or unworthy or 'bad,' has much to do with ways of being with oneself as with ways of being with others. Although ways of being with oneself may be largely the product of early relational interactions, insofar as they are internalized, they become stable *intrapsychic* structures. Freud's concept of superego and Fairbairn's concepts of internalized objects and internalized object relations are exemplars of such intrapsychic structures. Although they strongly influence ways of being with others, they primarily represent ways of being with oneself. It is this latter consideration that identifies them as internalized object relations rather than relations with an external and actual other.

One would expect that therapeutic work would be as much directed toward problematic and maladaptive ways of being with oneself as with problematic ways of being with others. As Strachey (1934) observed, a harsh and punitive superego is often a central factor in psychopathology and an important goal of treatment is softening this harshness and punitive attitude toward oneself. Similarly, in discussing the relationship between the libidinal and anti-libidinal ego, Fairbairn (1952) points to the individual's contemptuous and condemning attitude toward his or her own needs as a central feature of psychopathology that needs to be addressed in treatment.

At the risk of belaboring the point, I want to note again that although these implicit attitudes toward oneself may be the product of early relational interactions, once formed, they function as intrapsychic structures relatively independent of and resistant to change by relational interactions. Indeed, they strongly influence relational interactions. Further, were these intrapsychic structures easily influenced by relational interactions, bringing about therapeutic change would be a far less arduous task. It is the very rigidity and adhesiveness of these attitudes and structures, their relative refractoriness to later experiences that makes treatment so difficult and challenging.

Before leaving the topic of implicit processes, I want to note briefly the distinction between the conception of the unconscious as unarticulated or not spelled out and the unconscious as implicit. One way of clarifying this distinction is to note that whereas the unarticulated or not spelled out refers to the declarative knowledge one has, but defensively does not make explicit, the implicit knowledge of interest to Lyons-Ruth and her colleagues is procedural knowledge that is manifested through enactments, and that is implicit, not only by virtue of defense, but as a consequence of having been acquired early in life, sometimes at a preverbal level.

## Unconscious mental processes, inner conflict, and psychopathology

With perhaps the notable exception of self psychology theory, classical and some contemporary psychoanalytic theories share the assumptions that unconscious mental processes play a special and distinctive role in psychopathology; and that bringing unconscious material to consciousness (making the unconscious conscious) plays a special and distinctive role in therapeutic success. Indeed, these assumptions mark the birth of psychoanalysis, as expressed in the ideas that the incompatibility between the ego and a wish rendered unconscious by repression is at the root of hysteria; and that bringing repressed material to consciousness is curative. Given its longevity and centrality, there is remarkably little direct systematic evidence for the assumed link between psychopathology and unconscious or implicit mental processes and content (with the exception of the relationship between certain internal working models and maladaptive behavior).

Even prior to the introduction of the concepts of inner conflict and repression, Breuer and Freud, as well as Charcot and Janet, accepted as fundamental the idea that mental contents isolated from normal consciousness are pathogenic. Charcot refers to them as a "parasite" (as cited in Macmillan, 1991, p. 65); Janet refers to them as a "virus" that is inaccessible to the subject, works subconsciously, and "brings about all disorders of hysteria and of mental disease" (as cited in Ellenberger, 1970, p. 149); and Freud (Breuer & Freud, 1893–1895) also refers to them as "a sort of parasite" (p. 49). Thus, it is not simply the incompatibility between the ego and particular mental contents (i.e., inner conflict per se) that is pathogenic, but the isolated and *unintegrated* status of the mental content. Thus, according to this view, a conscious conflict between the ego and a wish would not necessarily possess the same pathogenic potential were the wish not isolated from the rest of the personality. And the primary means of isolating a mental content from the rest of the personality that Freud came to focus on was rendering it unconscious.

Why should the unconscious status of mental contents and processes per se have pathogenic potential? After all, unconscious processes operate in much of normal psychological functioning. This is not an unimportant question insofar as, among other things, this fundamental assumption of the pathogenic potential of unconscious mental contents provides the rationale for central psychoanalytic treatment goals such as making the unconscious conscious and achieving insight.

A number of answers to the above question have been offered in both classical and some contemporary psychoanalytic theories. One answer provided by Freud (Breuer & Freud, 1893–1895, p. 9) early on is that when an idea is repressed, the "quota of affect" associated with it remains in a strangulated state and is 'converted' into somatic hysterical symptoms. Another answer Freud provides in the context of trauma is that when a mental content is rendered unconscious and thereby isolated from the rest of the personality, it is not subject to the associative rectification provided by other ideas. As Freud (Breuer & Freud, 1893–1895, p. 9) puts it, when an idea enters "the greatest complex of associations, it comes alongside other experiences, which may contradict it, and . . . subject [it] to rectification by other ideas." This cannot happen when the idea is isolated from the rest of the personality. In ordinary language, one would say that because the mental contents are unconscious and isolated from the rest of the personality, they are not put into perspective and are relatively inaccessible to evaluation and correction by "higher mental processes" (Dollard & Miller, 1950).

Still another reason provided by classical psychoanalytic theory is that when a wish or desire is conscious, one can take steps in reality to gratify it or when that is impossible or unwise, one can attempt either to sublimate the wish or 'renounce' or 'repudiate' it. Both steps free the individual from having to engage in the "constant expenditure of energy" needed to defend against the emergence of the wish in conscious experience, thus liberating the ego from this enervating and depleting task. Here, the pathogenic potential of unconscious mental contents lies not primarily in their unconscious status, but in the energy expended in keeping the mental contents unconscious. In effect, this points to the pathogenic consequences of efforts of defense rather than of unconscious status per se.

What answers are provided to the above question by contemporary psychoanalytic theories? As noted, the mental contents emphasized by contemporary psychoanalytic theories are not instinctual wishes pressing for discharge, but representations such as "relational configurations" (Mitchell, 1988), "internal working models" (IWMs) (Bowlby, 1980), "representations of interactions generalized" (RIGs) (Stern, 1985), "interactional structures" (Beebe & Lachmann, 2002), and "pathogenic beliefs" (Weiss & Sampson, 1986). However, in common with classical theory, an assumption made in these theories is that the unconscious or implicit status of these representations is a major factor in their pathogenic potential.

According to contemporary theories, although these representations may have constituted an adaptive response early in life, they have become largely maladaptive in one's current life circumstances. For example, an avoidant attachment pattern may have been adaptive early in life, while later in life it has the maladaptive potential to interfere with the capacity for emotional intimacy. Further, the unconscious or implicit status of these representations renders them relatively inaccessible to evaluation in the light of self-reflection and current reality. They are likely to remain rigid, unquestioned, and not responsive to new experiences. Hence, the rationale for bringing these implicit and unquestioned representations to consciousness is to facilitate reflection and evaluation in the light of the reality of one's current life.

## Unconscious fantasy revisited: its links to psychopathology

In Freud's view, fantasy is opposed to reality and accordingly, a turning toward fantasy necessarily entails turning away from reality – hence, the association between fantasy and pathology. As we have seen, according to Freud, a characteristic of fantasy, one that renders it pathogenic, is that it turns the individual away from pursing satisfaction through interaction with a real object in external reality. Thus, according to this formulation, fantasy is largely an intrapsychic phenomenon that distorts interactions with real objects in reality. Fairbairn (1952) echoes Freud's view in identifying as a significant marker of psychopathology the individual's tendency to turn inward toward fantasy and away from objects in the external world. Indeed according to Fairbairn, this schizoid tendency is at the core of a wide range of psychopathology.

The concept of unconscious fantasy has been broadened beyond Freud's formulations in a number of ways. Indeed, Lear's conception of fantasy noted earlier as the imaginative elaboration of the meanings of experience already goes beyond positing a necessary link between unconscious fantasy and gratification of instinctual wishes. The notion of fantasy as the imaginative elaboration of experience is consistent with the general idea, much supported by empirical research, that along with a focal meaning, virtually every experience at the, so to speak, center of consciousness, also triggers a network of other meanings that are unconscious (not in the sense of repressed) or on the periphery of consciousness. Let me cite a simple example: when reading or hearing a word, we usually respond to its denotative meaning. However, it can be shown in a variety of ways that not only is the denotative meaning of the word encoded, but also that a network of connotations and associations is activated (e.g., Grossman & Eagle, 1970). G. S. Klein (1976) referred to a "connotative hierarchy" that is elicited in everyday experience. Poetry would not be possible without this process.

According to classical theory, in the analytic situation of relatively loosened ego controls, it is instinctual drives that exert the strongest influence on the associative meanings and the accompanying affect that emerge in free association. That is, the analytic situation facilitates, in Rapaport's (1967) words, the drive organization of cognition. However, there is another way to look at the entire situation. The analytic situation, including the use of the couch, the anonymity and location of the analyst, and free association instructions, may facilitate the emergence of 'peripheral' associative meanings or meanings lower in the "connotative hierarchy" that, under normal circumstances, would not emerge in consciousness. Whether these associative meanings are likely to be drive-related is an empirical question, as is the question of whether they are likely to be linked to repressed mental contents.

I would suggest that the penumbra of unconscious or perhaps preconscious meanings that are part of every experience are the raw material not only of poetry, but also of fantasy. That is, these meanings constitute an important source for the imaginative elaboration and organization of experience to which Lear refers. According to this view, fantasy is not necessarily opposed to reality, but may entail imaginative elaboration of experiences of aspects of reality. Hence, contrary to Freud, unconscious fantasies are not always necessarily pathogenic. They may or may not be. Further, Freud's (1916–1917) confident assertions notwithstanding, given the lack of evidence, it is unlikely either that the sources of our imaginative elaborations of experience always "lie in the instincts" (p. 368) or that they are invariably wish-fulfillments. Imaginative elaborations of experience may be saturated with fear, anxiety, and rejection rather than disguised or undisguised wish fulfillment. And in childhood, the sources of these imaginative elaborations may have as much to do with such factors as immature cognition and parental cues as with instincts.

The conception of fantasy as the imaginative elaboration of experiences and the idea that every experience is idiosyncratically encoded along different meaning dimensions should go some way toward demonstrating the untenability of a dichotomy between 'actual events' and fantasy. Sandler (1976) has substantially broadened what was mainly an intrapsychic concept of fantasy through his observation that individuals may act to create role relationships in external reality as a means of actualizing an unconscious fantasy. And, one might add, the creation of these role relationships often also entails object choice in the real world. For example, a rescue fantasy entails not only the creation of a role relationship of victim and rescuer, but also predisposes the individual to the choice of an object who, he or she senses, will acquiesce, permit, or actively cooperate in the creation of a particular role relationship.

What links unconscious fantasy to psychopathology is not the imaginative elaboration of experience – that, indeed, enriches experience – but rather the substitution of fantasy for reality. Thus, the actualization of an unconscious fantasy may include experiencing the object less in terms of who he or she actually is and more as a stand-in for an early object, the interactions with whom constitute the source of the early fantasies repeated in the current relationship.

Implicit in Fairbairn's (1952) theorizing is the idea that the core of pathology lies not in attempting to create a particular role relationship whatever difficulties it leads to. That, at least, entails attempting to actualize a fantasy in external reality. For Fairbairn, the core of psychopathology lies primarily in relating to the other as a stand-in for an internalized object. In doing so, the individual is relating, not to a real object in the world, but to an aspect of himself or herself, that is, to his or her own creation. Thus, for Fairbairn, at the core of psychopathology is a schizoid imprisonment in one's own solipsism. One cannot break out of that imprisonment to reach an object in the real world. Indeed, for Fairbairn one important criterion for mental health is the individual's ability to relate to a real external other in terms of who that other actually is rather than as a stand-in for an internalized object.

## *The interpersonalizing of the unconscious*

Sandler transformed the language of unconscious instinctual impulses and wishes blindly pressing for discharge to a language in which a person harbors unconscious wishes and fantasies that are always characterized by self and other in particular roles and interactions. To take a concrete example, for Sandler, exhibitionism is not expressed simply as an impulse pressing for discharge or as a wish to exhibit oneself, but as a wish or fantasy in which one exhibits oneself to another who observes what one is exhibiting. This is one of those important truths that has been there all along and becomes seen as obvious once it is made explicit.

Sandler's insistence that there is no such thing as a wish that does not have an object relational context reflects the influence of Klein (1946/1975), in particular, her claim that, contrary to Freud's (1915) formulation that drive and object are initially separate, they are inherently linked. Indeed, Klein's emendation of Freud's view constitutes an early foundation for the later development of an object relations theory. Paralleling Winnicott's (1965) statement that there is no such thing as a baby, but only a baby–mother unit, one can say that for Klein and Sandler, there is no such thing as a wish, but only a wish in which one is in a particular relationship with another.

Sandler's 'interpersonalizing' of the concepts of unconscious wishes and fantasies brings traditional psychoanalytic theory closer to contemporary psychoanalytic theories, including the relational theory of Mitchell and his colleagues, Weiss and Sampson's Control–Mastery theory, Kernberg's formulations, and Bowlby's attachment theory. As noted earlier, contemporary psychoanalytic conceptions of the unconscious essentially replace Freud's (1933) "cauldron, full of seething excitations" (p. 84) with an unconscious of representations of self, other, and prototypic interactions between self and other (e.g., representations of interactions generalized or RIGs (Stern, 1985); internal working models (IWMs) (Bowlby,

1980); representations of self and other linked by positive or unconscious or negative affects (Kernberg, 1984); unconscious pathogenic beliefs (Weiss & Sampson, 1986); and internalized objects and object relations (Fairbairn, 1952)). One can place Sandler's concept of role relationship created in the service of actualizing an unconscious fantasy or wish alongside these other concepts – while recognizing that Sandler's (as well as Kernberg's) formulation is distinguished from the others by his retention of the centrality of unconscious instinctual drives and wishes.

Indeed, it is Sandler's continued emphasis on instinctual wishes that, I believe, creates problems for his clinical–theoretical formulations. In his 1976 classic paper where he articulates his formulations of unconscious fantasy and the role relationship concept, Sandler presents a clinical vignette intended to illustrate his formulation in which he hands a tissue to a patient when she cries, something she does quite frequently. On one occasion, when he does not hand her the tissue, she explodes and accuses him of being uncaring. Sandler then goes on to discuss the links between the created role relationship of patient crying and analyst providing tissue and the patient's early fantasy of soiling herself with no one there to clean her up. He suggests that this abiding unconscious fantasy plays a central role in the patient's pathology.

It seems to me that Sandler's emphasis on the concrete act of soiling (perhaps due to an adherence to the classical theory of psychosexual development) as central to the patient's pathology is misplaced. It seems doubtful that early experiences specifically of soiling oneself and not being cleaned up per se are, in themselves, pathogenic. There is certainly no evidence for that proposition. However, it is far more likely that early experiences of being neglected and not being adequately cared for – whether that takes the concrete form of not being cleaned up after soiling oneself, or not being fed when hungry, or not being soothed when distressed, or not being engaged with wanting interaction, and so on – are pathogenic. There is much evidence for that proposition.

Furthermore, a caregiver who does not clean up after her infant soils herself is likely to be neglectful in other areas of child caregiving. Thus it is very likely that it is the cumulative effects of a general neglectful pattern that is pathogenic rather than the discrete experience of not being cleaned up after soiling. To make the point more sharply, one can pose the following hypothetical question: If mother had been an ideal caregiver in all other respects, but had been relatively neglectful in the one area of not cleaning her infant after she had soiled herself, would we expect pathological consequences? In short, it seems very likely that the patient's fearful fantasy of soiling herself with no one there to clean her up is best understood as both a discrete episodic memory as well as a metaphor, a concrete instantiation of the procedural knowledge of being neglected and not having her needs met.

The interaction between patient and analyst described by Sandler of patient crying and analyst handing her a tissue can be understood in the same light. That is, the patient is distressed and the analyst responds in a caring way, opposite to that of the patient's caregiver.[5] From the perspective of Weiss and Sampson's (1986) Control–Mastery theory, one can describe this interaction in terms of the patient unconsciously presenting a test to the analyst (i.e. "Will you be the same as or different from my neglectful mother?") and the analyst passing the test (i.e., by handing her the tissue, thus not repeating mother's presumed neglectful behaviors). Central to Weiss and Sampson's view is the idea that the patient's test-passing behavior – which, in Sandler's terms, entails creating a particular role relationship – is an adaptive attempt on the part of the patient to avoid being retraumatized at the hands of the analyst.

In contrast to Weiss and Sampson's perspective, Sandler views the patient's attempt to create a particular role relationship as a means of actualizing his or her unconscious wishes and fantasies in a disguised way; and "in doing so, he resists becoming aware of any infantile relationship which he might be attempting to impose" (p. 43). In other words, despite his departure from classical theory in other respects, Sandler continues to view transference primarily in terms of the patient attempting to gratify unconscious infantile wishes and fantasies and, accordingly, to induce the analyst to take on a role that serves to accomplish such gratification.

For Sandler, identifying his patient's unconscious wish to have someone around to clean her up should she soil herself gets to the infantile roots of her pathology and somehow is seen as constituting a 'deeper' insight than the formulation that she wishes to be taken care of when distressed; and as noted, that the memory of soiling herself and not being cleaned up serves as a metaphor for that wish. (Note the assumption that the soiling fantasy is assumed to be "deeper" and more fundamental in some way than the wish to be cared for.)

For Freud and for many classical analysts, as an *infantile* wish, the patient needs not only to become aware of and understand the role it plays in her life, but also to *relinquish* it if she is to overcome her pathology. However, if one understands the fantasy as a metaphor for a wish to be taken care of when distressed, one would not likely conclude that it needs to be relinquished. For *that* wish, in different age appropriate forms, one would argue, is a lifelong rather than an infantile one.

There are other more subtle and nuanced issues at play here. In contrast to wanting to be taken care of when distressed, there is, indeed, an infantile quality to the fear that one will soil oneself and that there will be no one around to clean up. If however, one understands the latter as a metaphor for the former, one could say that the patient experiences and expresses the wish to be taken care of in an *infantile form*, in the language and categories appropriate to infancy and childhood of soiling and being cleaned up. When understood this way, what follows is not the necessity and desirability of relinquishment as a therapeutic goal, but an exploration of why the wish to be taken care of when distressed is expressed in the infantile imagery of soiling and not being cleaned up.

Thus, even if the patient's soiling and not being cleaned up fantasy is a metaphor for the general wish to be taken care of when distressed, why does it take the infantile form of soiling and being cleaned? One answer brings to mind Freud's (1915b) account of one of the consequences of repression. He writes:

> the repressed instinct-presentation . . . develops in a more unchecked and luxuriant fashion. It ramifies, like a fungus, so to speak, in the dark and takes on extreme forms of expression . . . [which] reflect an extraordinary strength of instinct. This illusory strength of instinct is the result of an uninhibited development of it in phantasy and of the damming-up consequent on lack of real satisfaction.
>
> (p. 149)[6]

Keeping Freud's observation in mind, one can speculate that because the patient's wish to be taken care of is unacceptable to her and therefore repressed, it "takes on extreme forms of expression" and "uninhibited development in phantasy" and is experienced as symbolically equivalent to the shameful act of soiling herself and wanting to be cleaned up. That is, the patient's shame at wanting to be taken care of is expressed in the shameful fantasy of soiling herself and not being cleaned up.

I have been struck in clinical work by how frequently patients who report not being adequately cared for in childhood find ways of expressing that need in adulthood in ways that are unrealistic and doomed not to be met. From a classical perspective, this would be understood largely in terms of the repetition compulsion and the persistence of infantile wishes (e.g., oral wishes). It could also be understood, however, in terms of the patient's inner conflict about the wish to be cared for, which, in turn, could be understood in terms of the wish eliciting shame and anxiety related to the early "danger situations" (Freud, 1926, p. 125). The point here is that patients often express their needs and wishes in ways that cannot be met in reality, not only or not necessarily because they are, in fact, infantile, *but because they themselves view them as infantile and shameful* and therefore, have condemnatory and contemptuous attitudes toward those aspects of themselves that have such wishes and needs.

Further, such attitudes are often attributed to the other, including the therapist, with the result that the conflictual wishes and needs are expressed either in a disguised way or in a manner (e.g., accusatorily, angrily) that virtually guarantees their non-fulfillment. The condemnatory and contemptuous attitudes can also be expressed through object choice. That is, the individual may choose a partner who is likely to share his or her self-critical attitudes and then bitterly and chronically complain that his or her needs are not being met.

## Implications for treatment: agreements and disagreements

### *Freud and Fairbairn: repressed infantile impulses versus repressed internal objects*

Let me turn now to the implications of different views of the unconscious for approaches to treatment. For Freud, the unconscious is 'populated' by infantile instinctual wishes and impulses that are inherent threats to the ego, are inherently anti-social, and are inherently unrealistic. Therefore, central goals of treatment include ownership of one's wishes followed by either sublimation or renunciation rather than continued futile and maladaptive attempts at their gratification. (Ironically, according to this perspective, the patient's fears that his or her wishes and fantasies are 'bad' and worthy of condemnation are, in a certain sense, reinforced by the idea that they need to be renounced or transformed through sublimation.)

The unconscious of Fairbairn is 'populated' by relationships among internal objects that develop as a consequence of rejection and deprivation. There is no counterpart in Fairbairn's formulations to Freud's positing of inherently infantile and anti-social impulses and wishes that the patient tries to gratify and hence, there is little or no talk of renunciation or sublimation of unconscious wishes. Rather, the patient is conflicted and self-critical in relation to largely legitimate needs. On this view, it is not the patient's wishes that are problematic (i.e., infantile and anti-social), but rather his or her critical and condemnatory attitudes toward them.

These contrasting conceptions of the unconscious generate somewhat different therapeutic attitudes, approaches, and process goals. For Freud (1933, p. 80), as expressed in where id was, there shall ego be, an overriding psychoanalytic goal is to own and acknowledge as part of oneself (as part of the "I" or *Ich*) what was defensively disowned and experienced as an impersonal "it" (*Es*). For Fairbairn, an overriding psychoanalytic goal is, in an important sense, *to disown* – in Fairbairn's (1952) words, to "exorcise" – the internal objects that were defensively made part of the self. *In short, whereas for Freud the goal is to own and acknowledge what one defensively tried to rid oneself of, for Fairbairn, the goal is to rid oneself of what one defensively made part of oneself.*

One can see that, for Freud, the main source of pathology lies in the individual's attempt to rid himself or herself through repression or disavowal of wishes and impulses that are an inherent part of our psychobiological nature. Although repressed and unconscious, insofar as they are part of our psychobiological nature, they continue to make demands on the mind that must be addressed; they cannot simply be done away with and made to disappear. Hence, the harmfulness and relative futility of the attempts to deny them a place in one's personality and one's sense of who one is.

For Fairbairn, the main source of pathology lies not in excluding what is, whether one likes it or not, inescapably part of oneself, but in *taking in and making part of oneself what should have remained external.* More specifically, the internalization of the 'bad object' leaves one at the mercy of an "internal saboteur" (Fairbairn, 1952, p. 101), the consequence of which is not only "splitting of the ego" (p. 8), but also a chronic sense of shame and self-contempt in response to one's own needs. Thus, whereas for Freud, the inevitability of some degree of pathology is a product of our very nature and the human condition (i.e., the primary antagonism between id and ego and between id and society), for Fairbairn, pathology is the consequence of those negative environmental experiences (i.e., rejection and deprivation) that lead to the child's defensive internalization of the 'bad' object.[7]

## Warded-off mental contents

There appears to be wide agreement among various psychoanalytic theories, that keeping certain mental contents from conscious awareness is pathogenic; and that bringing warded-off material to consciousness is a therapeutic process goal. Although they may have different theoretical rationales, the central assumption that bringing warded-off material into conscious experience is therapeutic is not limited to psychoanalytic theory, but also includes most, if not all, of the "talking therapies": cognitive behavioral theory, Rogerian theory, Winnicott's formulations, Sullivanian theory, intersubjective theory, and Gestalt therapy. Thus, an important process goal of cognitive behavioral therapy is making implicit automatic thoughts presumably implicated in psychopathology explicit. Rogers (1959) writes that people do not adequately attend and heed to their visceral sensations, their gut feelings, because they are associated with "conditions of worth," that is, they have been invalidated; and has as a therapeutic goal a greater in-touchness with these gut feelings. Rogers' account is quite similar to Winnicott's (1965) conception of a "true self," a main characteristic of which is experiential access to organic sensations and impulses. Sullivan's (1953) contribution to this general framework is represented in his concept of "selective inattention." According to Atwood and Stolorow (1984), one manifestation of psychopathology is restriction in the individual's "regions of experience" and "horizons of awareness" and a central goal of treatment is removal of these restrictions and consequent expansion of the range of experience and awareness. Similar to Atwood and Stolorow, in the context of Gestalt therapy, a primary marker for psychopathology is restriction of experience and a primary goal of treatment is increasing the range and depth of experience, particularly emotional experience. And finally, in Control–Mastery theory, the emphasis is on helping the patient become aware of his or her unconscious or implicit representations, including construals, expectations, and pathogenic beliefs.

## Surface and depth in psychoanalytic treatment

Here we return to the issue of surface and depth in the context of psychoanalytic treatment. When Freud (1894) first introduced the concept of repression, he viewed it as a conscious strategy, consisting of pushing certain thoughts and ideas out of one's mind – thus, indistinguishable from suppression (see Erdelyi, 2006). We have seen the operation of suppression in Lucy R.'s response to Freud: "I didn't know – or rather I didn't want to know. I wanted to drive it out of my head and not think of it again; and I believe that latterly I have succeeded" (Breuer & Freud, 1893–1895, p. 117).

Note that Lucy R.'s wishes and fantasies are not deeply buried in her unconscious requiring special and determined efforts to bring them to consciousness. Rather, they are just below the surface and become fully conscious when attention is focused on them. In Fingarette's (1963) words, Lucy R.'s wishes and fantasies are not "spelled out," but are acknowledged when attended to and articulated.

It should be noted that inner conflict is as present and focal in this early account as it is in Freud's later writings. In that sense, the dynamic unconscious, that is, the struggle between the conscious experiences of certain wishes and fantasies and the forces in the personality opposing such experiences, is as present in Freud's early formulations as it is in his later ones. The concept of the dynamic unconscious does not require the assumption that conflictual wishes and fantasies are always deeply buried and inaccessible to conscious experience without the intervention of special procedures.

The above notion of the nature of unconscious wishes and fantasies becomes radically altered in Freud's later writings, particularly with the advent of drive theory and the structural model. The 'deep' unconscious is now described as "a cauldron full of seething excitations" (Freud, 1933, p. 84), the source of which are instinctual drives pushing for discharge. These instinctual drives can never themselves be consciously experienced; only instinctual derivatives in the form of thoughts and feelings (and somatic symptoms) can be consciously experienced. And a central process goal of psychoanalytic treatment is to bring these instinctual derivates to consciousness, a therapeutic stance that has been referred to as id analysis.

With the advent of ego psychology, the focus on id analysis has given way to an emphasis on the ego function of defense, that is, defense analysis – reaching its apotheosis in the work of Gray (2005) and his followers (e.g., Busch, 2009; Davison, Pray, & Bristol, 1990; Portuges & Hollander, 2011; Sugarman, 2006). In this latter perspective, making the unconscious conscious primarily refers not to uncovering deeply repressed wishes, but helping the patient understand how his or her mind works through attention to defensive processes. Further, the pursuit of this goal entails "close process monitoring" of patient behaviors that are right at or just below the surface of conscious awareness.

Consider the following exchange between Anna Freud and Joseph Sandler with regard to the unconscious status of defended against mental contents:

> *Anna Freud:* "Heinz Hartmann would say that it can become automatic."
> *Joseph Sandler:* ". . . I still think that there must be awareness of the impulse to evoke the response."
> *Anna Freud:* "Hartmann and I discussed it at the time, in 1936 and 1937. There must be a momentary awareness."
> *Joseph Sandler:* "An unconscious awareness?"
> *Anna Freud:* "It could even be a momentary conscious awareness."
> (as cited in Erdelyi, 1990, pp. 13–14)

Apparently, James' hypothesis of fleeting and momentary awareness remains alive and well.

It is important to note that although Gray writes from the perspective of classical theory in focusing exclusively on "drive derivatives," his formulation is relevant to defense against any set of conflictual thoughts, feelings, and fantasies that carry the potential of generating dysphoric affects and threats to one's self-esteem and self-image. Gray's claim notwithstanding, it is unlikely that such thoughts, feelings, and fantasies are limited to derivatives of libidinal and aggressive drives.

In important respects, Gray's formulation of unconscious processes and content is similar to that of Weiss and Sampson (1986) and oddly enough, to Stern's relational and Atwood and Stolorow's (1984) intersubjective formulations. Central to Weiss and Sampson's "Control–Mastery theory" is the idea that patients need to determine that it is safe, that is, that they will not be retraumatized, before presenting warded-off material to the therapist.[8] This is quite similar to Gray's observation that for the patient "to put into words what comes to mind in the presence of the analyst is to create some kind of risk" (p. 1086). Atwood and Stolorow (1984) make a similar point when they state that the patient's "regions of experience" and "horizons of awareness" were in the past and are in the present strongly influenced by his or her, respectively, dangers entailed in relation to parental figures and the analyst's reactions to the presentation of certain 'forbidden' thoughts and feelings. Further, there appears to be general agreement that the patient will ward off mental contents (i.e., desires, wishes, aims, feelings, and thoughts) that are associated with negative affects (i.e., anxiety, guilt, shame, and so on) generated by parental disapproval and invalidation.

To sum up, the conceptualization of unconscious processes and contents implicit in the formulations of Gray, as well as to some extent, in those of Weiss and Sampson and Atwood and Stolorow (1984) appears to be not that of deeply buried mental contents or of a "cauldron, full of seething excitations" (Freud, 1933, p. 84). Rather, it is an unconscious of mental contents that are fleetingly experienced and then pushed out of conscious awareness – much like the kind of unconscious suggested by Lucy R.'s description of pushing her fantasy about her employer out of her mind (Breuer & Freud, 1893–1895) or by Fingarette's (1963) formulation of not "spelling out" as well as Stern's (2003) not formulating the unformulated. It is also an unconscious that is as much influenced by what one feels is safe to communicate to another as by what one feels it is safe to tell oneself (See Chapter 5 for a discussion of interpersonalizing of defense).

Let me provide an example taken from Davison et al.'s (1990) account of "close process monitoring":

> *Patient:* "I am so angry with Betty. I could strangle her . . . [he elaborated for a while, then he became hesitant] . . .on the other hand, she has many fine qualities, etc."
>
> *Analyst:* "Now you are focused on her fine qualities, a moment before you were experiencing very different feelings, then your feelings shifted. Can you see what happened here?"
>
> *Patient:* "I was afraid you would think I was a brute for feeling so angry at her."
>
> (p. 620)

In this example and in others provided by Davison et al. (as well as by Gray and his colleagues), the analyst does not make 'deep' interpretations of repressed material, but rather calls the patient's attention to certain behaviors such as a shift in content. The analyst's intervention, in effect, says: "look what you do when you are uncomfortable about having and expressing angry feelings and thoughts." Further, although the patient appears to be aware at some level of the shift and the motive for it, it is the analyst's calling attention to the shift in thoughts and feelings that brings it into the focus of awareness and keeps it from being immediately pushed out of the patient's mind. In short, as Gray (2005) observes, interventions from the perspective of a "close process monitoring" stance enable the patient "to put into words what comes to mind."

At the risk of belaboring the point, I want to note again that the unconscious implied in Gray's (2005) "close process monitoring," as well as in the other theorists I have cited, is a far cry from Freud's unconscious of deeply repressed instinctual impulses. It is an unconscious of what was fleetingly conscious and then pushed out of awareness, of not putting it into words what comes to mind, and not making connections and understanding the significance of what one has experienced. In these respects, it is an unconscious that, in certain respects, is closer to James' (1890) fringe of consciousness and to Freud's (1915) preconscious than to his "dynamic unconscious." It is also worth noting once again that the fleetingly conscious unconscious I am describing is, in certain respects, as much a *dynamic* unconscious as Freud's conception of the dynamic unconscious insofar as anxiety, conflict, and other motives and forces influence whether what is fleetingly experienced will be fully experienced or pushed out of awareness.

## *What is warded off?*

Beyond convergence on the idea that what is warded off is linked to parental disapproval, disagreements arise with regard to the particular mental contents that each theory assumes are associated with parental disapproval and consequent negative affects. Employing Freudian language, one can say that each theory has a somewhat different conception of the particular mental contents that are associated with the "danger situations" and that, therefore, are likely to be warded off. For Gray, it is drive derivatives. For Control–Mastery theory, it is pathogenic beliefs based on early parental communications. For Rogers, it is gut feelings. And so on.

Consider the brief exchange between patient and analyst cited above by Davison et al. (1990). The analyst calls attention to the patient's shift from expressing anger toward someone to noting that the object of his anger has many fine qualities. The patient responds by saying "I was afraid you would think I was a brute for feeling so angry at her." In this interaction, the analyst tries to help the patient become more fully aware of his attempt to ward off aggressive feelings by not staying with those feelings and 'compensating' for them by saying nice things about the object of his aggressive feelings. Further, the analyst's intervention appears to facilitate the patient's acknowledgment that his shift from aggressive feelings to looking for nice things to say was motivated by his concern that the analyst would think poorly of him due to his expression of anger.

### *Bringing warded-off contents to conscious awareness or understanding how one's mind works*

As Sugarman (2006) has noted, contemporary ego psychologists focus less on bringing specific repressed mental contents to consciousness and more on helping the patient understand how his or her mind works. A decreasing emphasis on making the deeply buried unconscious conscious is also seen in the current emphasis on enhancing mentalization, particularly in treatment of individuals with borderline personality disorder. As Bateman and Fonagy (2006) have noted, the concepts of mentalization and reflective capacity, although somewhat different in certain respects, bear a strong family resemblance to the classic psychoanalytic concept of the observing function of the ego. One thing to be noted is that the goal of strengthening the observing function of the ego refers to enhancing a capacity or function or, perhaps one should say, a skill. In the context of Freudian theory, a primary purpose of strengthening the observing function of the ego was understood as better equipping the patient to do what the analyst did, namely, bring conflicted and defended-against wishes, desires, and impulses to consciousness and then deal with them by pursuing gratification in reality, sublimating them, or repudiating them. (One sees in the posited necessity of gratification or sublimation of certain mental contents traces of the early idea that "strangulated affect" must be dealt with in a way that permits adequate discharge if one is to avoid symptomatic compromise formation).

In contrast to the above aims of strengthening the observing function of the ego, the primary purpose of enhancing mentalization and reflective capacity is not rendering unconscious wishes, desires, and impulses conscious, but rather strengthening one's capacity to *reflect* both on one's own and others' mental states. Both the classical and contemporary views entail expansion of consciousness, but in somewhat different ways. According to the traditional view, consciousness is expanded through increased conscious access to defended-against mental contents. According to the current conception of mentalization, consciousness is expanded through one's increased capacity not only to reflect on one's own and others' mental states, but also through an increased capacity to reflect on one's rigid and unquestioned perspectives, construals, and expectations. Expansion of consciousness is primarily characterized not by increased access to a greater number of hitherto unconscious specific mental contents (e.g., incestuous wishes), but by an increased capacity to take different perspectives and to understand how one's mind works (Sugarman, 2006).

## The issue of integration: "Where id was, there shall ego be"

From its earliest days, a fundamental assumption made in psychoanalytic theory is that making the unconscious conscious is therapeutic, indeed, is the overarching goal of psychoanalysis. In his later writings, Freud (1933) replaced or, at least supplemented, that aim with "where id is, there shall ego be" (p. 80) as a primary goal of psychoanalytic treatment. There are various ways of understanding "where id was, there shall ego be." One interpretation is: where peremptory instinctual impulses were, there shall greater ego controls be (see Apfelbaum, 1966, for a cogent critique of this view). Another, in my view, more meaningful interpretation, rests on the original German *das Es* and *das Ich* which is accurately translated as the (impersonal) it and the (personal) I. On this interpretation, Freud's adage becomes: where impersonal 'it' was, there shall personal 'I' be. This is equivalent to saying: those aspects of oneself improperly and defensively rendered impersonal and experienced as ego-alien shall be acknowledged as and integrated into a personal part of oneself. In this shift from making the unconscious conscious to where id was, there shall ego be as the overriding goal of psychoanalysis, Freud was essentially giving pride of place to integration rather than awareness per se as a psychoanalytic ideal. This becomes clear when based on the original German of *Es* and *Ich*, Freud's adage becomes where impersonal 'it' was, there shall personal 'I' be.

In the present context of discussing the role of unconscious contents and processes in psychopathology and treatment, it is important to recognize the distinction between conscious–unconscious and integrated–unintegrated. The two dimensions are not identical. One can consciously experience thoughts and feelings as ego-alien (as in the case of obsessive thoughts and compulsions); and unconscious mental contents can be smoothly integrated into the personality. Indeed, Freud (1926) wrote that in health, it is difficult to distinguish between id and ego.

As noted earlier, an assumption shared by Charcot, Binet, Janet, and Freud is that mental contents isolated from the rest of the personality function as pathogens (analogous to parasites and viruses). On this view, it is not the unconscious state of these contents per se, but the isolated, that is, the *unintegrated* status of the mental contents that renders them pathogenic. Indeed, the primary reason that hypnosis failed as an effective treatment is that although it may have succeeded in bringing mental contents to consciousness, they remained *unintegrated*. Hence, any change brought about by hypnosis was evanescent. In reaction to this, Freud replaced bringing material into conscious awareness through hypnosis with an emphasis on the importance of associative rectification of the traumatic mental contents, that is, on the integration of these mental contents into the rest of the personality, the "dominant mass of ideas" that constitute the ego (Breuer & Freud, 1893–1895, p. 116). In short, although there has been an overwhelmingly predominant emphasis on unconscious processes in accounts of psychoanalytic theory, inherent in the logic of the theory is at least an equal, if not greater, emphasis on the integration of unintegrated aspects of the personality. Even if one maintains that making the unconscious conscious may be a necessary ingredient in successful treatment – and even that may not always be the case – it is certainly not sufficient. It is difficult to see what would be therapeutic about making unconscious conscious were it the case that what was made conscious remained unintegrated and even ego-alien. The importance Freud gives to integration is seen in his comments at various points, that the overarching goal of psychoanalysis is to achieve unity of the personality.

He also writes that in an ideal state of health, there is a unity between the id and the ego and that it is difficult to detect a sharp difference between the two structures of the personality.

The psychoanalytic emphasis on integration and unity of the personality is one expression of an age-old philosophical and spiritual quest. Confucius wrote that at seventy he could follow the dictates of his heart for what he desired no longer overstepped the boundaries of right (Lau, 1979). And Kierkegaard (1886/1948) contrasts "double-mindedness" with "purity of heart" and writes that "purity of heart is willing one thing." Although Kierkegaard was struggling with issues of faith rather than commenting on psychopathology, there is a thematic continuity between his "double-mindedness" and Freud's (1894) early identification of "splits in consciousness" as the hallmark of hysteria. Prominent in the classical psychoanalytic literature the idea that a hallmark of psychopathology is a riven personality, the individual at war with himself or herself. For Sartre too, the issues that psychoanalysis or any other discipline that is concerned with the human condition needs to deal with have to do with double-mindedness or, in his words "bad faith" (*mauvaise foi*), which he locates in the conflict between re-reflective consciousness and the self of "impure reflection."

When it became clear that making the unconscious conscious was most frequently not sufficient for therapeutic change insofar as it often did not entail integration of what had been unconscious (the same problem that Freud encountered in the use of hypnosis), the concepts of emotional insight (versus intellectual insight) and *working–through* were introduced, the latter almost as an afterthought. The concept of working through is intended to address the question of how the patient makes disowned and unacknowledged aspects of his or her personality into integrated parts of himself or herself. However, no more than three or four pages are devoted to this vital topic in the entire corpus of Freud's work. (Freud, 1914a, also devotes two pages to the concept of "working-over"; working-over, although bearing some similarity to working-through, focuses on assimilating traumatic experiences and is virtually identical to his early concept of associative rectification of isolated mental contents.) Furthermore, Freud's brief discussion of working-through links it entirely to the vicissitudes of resistance and the compulsion to repeat and is inadequate as an explanatory account of degree of success or failure of integration.

A careful consideration of these concepts, particularly that of working-through makes it clear that they essentially refer to the process of integration, that is, rendering an insight or perspective or a way of viewing oneself an integral part of oneself. But given its importance, the goal of integration cannot rest on the thin conceptual reeds of emotional insight and working-through, concepts that are secondary, both in terms of theoretical and clinical primacy, to lifting repression and making the unconscious conscious. For one thing, there are ways of facilitating integration other than through the lifting of repression and the expansion of conscious awareness. (See, for example, Kohut's, 1984, concept of "transmuting internalization" (p. 71) and Lyons-Ruth's, 1999, concept of "implicit relational knowing".)

The role of failure of integration in psychopathology and the corresponding therapeutic importance of integration are more apparent in a number of theoretical and clinical contexts. These include discussions of splitting in borderline personality disorder, lack of self-cohesiveness in narcissistic personality disorder, and dissociative disorders. Even a brief consideration of the concept of splitting in borderline personality disorder makes it clear that, on that view, the failure of integration of ego states (what has been referred to as a vertical split) rather than the unconscious status of mental contents through repression (referred to as a horizontal split) is the primary pathological condition; and correspondingly, that the primary therapeutic aim is integration of unintegrated cognitive–affective ego states rather than lifting repression and thereby making repressed mental contents conscious.

## Notes

1 Size constancy refers to our perception of an object at different distances as approximately the same size despite variations in retinal images. However, when all cues to distance are removed, a 4-foot square 4 feet from the observer will be perceived as the same size as an 8-foot square 8 feet from the observer. Such phenomena have led to the conclusion that in normal perception an unconscious inferential-like computational process that takes size and distance into account underlies size constancy. As for phi phenomenon or apparent movement: If a triangle (or any other form) is flashed on at point A in a visual field and then, at an appropriate interval, at point B, one will experience the triangle moving from A to B, even though no actual movement has occurred. It is as if the viewer is making the "unconscious inference" (Helmholtz, 1868/1871], p. 217) that if an object is here at A in the field at time one, is there at B a short time later, then it must have moved. Of course, no conscious inference is experienced. But the apparent movement is just what would be experienced for the kind of inference I described. As Rock (1970) puts it, "movement will be perceived whenever the total information available adds up to the inference that an object has changed its location" (p. 9). The inferential nature of induced movement is also demonstrated by the fact that the experience of movement can be eliminated by, so to speak, "forcing" a different inference. Thus, if simultaneously with the flashing on of B, A also reappears in its original location, one will experience no movement. Since A is in its original location, one need not "deduce" that it moved. Similarly, if a card with a window is moved back and forth revealing now A and then B, giving the impression of two objects being successively uncovered and covered, again no movement is experienced. As Rock (1970) notes, "it follows that if the first object is covered over, it has not moved to location B but remained where it is" (p. 9). "Once again, the spontaneous perceptual experience will follow the inference that best fits the available data or will be identical to what would occur if one engaged in a conscious, problem solving inference that represented the most elegant solution to the problem" (Eagle, 1987, pp. 156–157).

2 I add "purported" because there is little evidence that Freud's patients *actually* reported seductions to him. Rather, as Israëls and Schatzman (1993) have shown, it is Freud's interpretation of his patients' reports that introduces the topic of childhood seduction.

3 Along with others, Tuch (2016) argues that many criticisms of psychoanalytic theory are motivated by fear and the need to avoid what psychoanalysis reveals.

4 The dark secrets of the unconscious mind in contemporary perspectives appear to have as much do with presumably repressed memories of external trauma as with inner 'terrible' wishes, desires, and fantasies.

5 It is important to note that we do not know how the patient's caregiver actually dealt with her soiling herself as an infant. We only know the patient's report. Indeed, it is

possible that the patient's soiling memory is a fantasy that serves as a metaphor for among other things, a general sense of having been neglected.

6 This is one of the few times – perhaps the only time – that Freud suggests that the "strength of instinct" may be illusory, the consequence of a fantasy that is unchecked because it has not been exposed to the light of reality.

7 There is a family resemblance between Fairbairn's goal of 'excorcising' the bad object or the "internal saboteur" and Strachey's (1934) emphasis on softening the harshness of the superego as a central aim of treatment. This becomes particularly evident when one recalls that the model for Fairbairn's internal object is Freud's concept of the superego.

8 Weiss and Sampson and also Gray, on occasion, employ the term "warded off" rather than repressed. I do not want to make too much of choice of words, but I cannot help but observe the differences in connotations between the two terms. In contrast to "repressed" or "unconscious," which suggests unavailable to conscious experience, the connotation of "warded off" is more ambiguous and could include at least fleeting conscious experience from which one turns away and does not fully confront.

# 2

# RESEARCH ON UNCONSCIOUS PROCESSES

## The descriptive unconscious

The advent of the cognitive revolution in psychology and the flourishing of cognitive neuroscience have seen the emergence of a huge research literature on unconscious processes. As noted in the previous chapter, cognitive psychologists devote a great deal of attention to unconscious processes. For example, Fodor (1983) has written that "all psychologically interesting cognitive states are unconscious" (p. 86). And Lakoff and Johnson (1999) have stated that one of the three "major findings of cognitive science [is that] thought is mostly unconscious" (p. 3).

The research literature on unconscious processes is too large to cover in a single chapter. Hence, I will focus on selected research on unconscious processes that is of some relevance to psychoanalysis. With few exceptions, the psychological research on unconscious processes has to do with the "descriptive unconscious" rather than the "dynamic unconscious" or "the unconscious" as a topographical realm or place.

Freud (1900) distinguished between a "descriptive" and a "dynamic" unconscious (pp. 614–615); and his strategy in his essay *The Unconscious* was first to make the case for the existence of a descriptive unconscious, which would then strengthen the case for positing a "dynamic unconscious." (Freud, 1915a). However, although the existence of a descriptive unconscious may be a necessary, it is not a sufficient, condition for vouchsafing the "dynamic unconscious," which is, after all, the concept most directly relevant to at least classical psychoanalytic theory. This should be kept in mind in reading the discussion of empirical research on unconscious processes.

## Discrimination and encoding of external stimuli without awareness (subliminal studies)

A large body of studies appear to demonstrate that external stimuli of which subjects are unaware (i.e., subliminal stimuli) are nevertheless registered, discriminated, and encoded as indicated by their effects on subsequent behavior. The means by which the stimuli are rendered subliminal as well as the behaviors that reveal their effects vary. With regard to the former, the largest set of studies employ a backward masking method. However, other methods such as binocular suppression have also been employed. Backward masking refers to the fact that when a stimulus (A) is presented at a particular duration and followed at an appropriate interval by a supraliminal stimulus (B), the A stimulus is masked and not consciously perceived. However, although not consciously perceived, the A stimulus influences or "primes" subsequent behavior that can include speed of lexical decisions, learning, attitudes, judgments, impression formation, affects, physiological responses, and various brain processes.

A good deal of the work in this area is carried out with little or no reference to psychoanalytic theory. Indeed, not infrequently, when psychoanalytic theory is referred to at all, it is in the context of a disclaimer that the unconscious or nonconscious processes with which the investigator is concerned are different from the Freudian concept of the dynamic unconscious. However, much of the early work on subliminal phenomena was carried out by psychoanalytically oriented researchers and theorists largely through the work of Charles Fisher (e.g., 1954) and researchers at the psychoanalytically oriented New York University Research Center for Mental Health during the 1950s and 1960s. As Fisher observed, one of the few empirical studies referred to by Freud was an investigation by Pötzl (1917) on the role of unattended (preconscious) stimuli in the formation of dream content. Pursuing this work further, Fisher and his colleagues (e.g., Fisher, 1954; Fisher & Paul, 1959; Paul & Fisher, 1959) investigated the effects of briefly exposed pictorial and verbal stimuli on dream content. He reported that elements of the stimuli appeared in the subjects' dreams, but were subjected to various primary process distortions, including fragmentation, condensation, and symbolic transformation.

Fisher's pioneering efforts were followed by a series of studies at New York University Research Center for Mental Health that focused on the effects of subliminal and incidental stimuli on cognition. These studies were largely motivated by an interest in the question of how stimuli not in focal awareness, but nevertheless unconsciously or preconsciously discriminated, are encoded and organized. Such information, it was expected, would shed light on the nature of unconscious processes and influences, including the role of awareness in influencing primary and secondary process organization.

In one early study at the NYU Research Center for Mental Health by Smith, Spence, and Klein (1959), the words HAPPY or ANGRY (A-stimuli) were presented subliminally and immediately followed by a supraliminal neutral face (the B-stimulus). The results showed that the A-stimuli differentially influenced the perception of the B-stimulus in accord with the meanings of "happy" and "angry," indicating that, although not consciously perceived, the A-stimuli were encoded at the level of semantic meaning.

Many later studies reported similar effects using a variety of masked stimuli and different dependent variables. For example, Robles, Smith, Carver, and Wellens (1987) reported that subliminal stimuli of positive (smiling cartoon faces), negative (threatening and violent), and neutral (gray featureless images) stimuli inserted into a computer graphics sequence, differentially influenced participants' reports of state anxiety (but not trait anxiety). State anxiety scores in the positive condition were significantly lower than state anxiety in the neutral condition, which, in turn, were significantly lower than state anxiety in the negative condition.

In a study somewhat related to the Robles et al. (1987) study, and employing a backward masking method, Ohman and Soares (1994) reported that skin conductance response (SCR) was of greater magnitude to phobic stimuli (snakes and spiders) then to neutral (flowers) stimuli. Most important, spider-fearful and snake-fearful subjects showed a larger SCR response to the phobic stimuli than non-phobic subjects. In general accord with these findings, Shevrin et al (1992) reported that the event-related potentials of phobic subjects classified unconscious conflict words (as assessed by clinicians who interviewed the participants) better subliminally than supraliminally, with the reverse being the case for conscious symptom words.

In a priming study employing backward masking, Lee, Kang, Lee, Namkoong, and An (2011) found that compared to a neutral subliminal prime, subliminal fear and disgust facial expressions influenced reactions to a supraliminal slightly happy target face. The subliminal fear prime influenced both the subjects' affective (pleasant–unpleasant) and genuineness ratings of the target face, whereas the subliminal disgust prime influenced only genuineness ratings. The authors speculate that compared to disgust, the threatening nature of fear leads to a broader priming affect.

It is known that when subjects are asked to make a decision as to whether a target stimulus is a real word or a non-word, their decision times are faster when the prime and target are semantically related (e.g. bread–butter) rather than unrelated. Employing a binocular pattern masking procedure, Kemp-Wheeler and Hill (1992) investigated the effects of subliminal words on a lexical decision time task in which subjects had to decide whether a supraliminal target was a real word or a non-word. One-third of the subliminal words were emotionally related to the target words (unpleasant); one-third were semantically related; and one-third were neither emotionally nor semantically related to the target word.

In one experiment, the mean lexical decision time was significantly slower when the subliminal primes were unrelated to the target word than when emotionally or semantically related. In the second experiment, compared to unrelated subliminal primes, only the semantically related subliminal primes influenced lexical decision times in the predicted directions. Especially noteworthy is Kemp-Wheeler and Hill's claim that the subliminal stimuli were presented below the objective detection threshold.

In a study by Krosnick, Betz, Jussim, and Lynn (1992), subjects were asked to rate a supraliminal target person on their attitudes toward the person (good–bad), their beliefs about the person's personality characteristics, and the person's physical attractiveness. The target person stimulus was preceded by subliminal positive-affect-arousing or negative-affect-arousing photos. The results showed that subjects in the positive-affect condition reported a more favorable attitude toward the target and rated the person's personality characteristics and physical attractiveness more favorably. However, the latter differences were not statistically significant. These results partly replicate the findings of an early study by Eagle (1959), who found differential ratings of a target supraliminal B-figure (a drawing of a boy with a neutral expression) as a function of whether the target stimulus was preceded and masked by a subliminal A-stimulus of a benevolent (the boy handing a birthday cake to someone) versus an aggressive (the boy about to stab someone) action.

In an intriguing study by Ric and Muller (2012), participants were asked to respond to whether a target symbol presented to them supraliminally (which was either a number or a letter) was a number. Two digits presented at each side of the fixation point (flankers) preceded the target. A subliminal prime of "add" or "*relativize*" also preceded the target. Compared to the prime "*relativize*," participants primed with "add" were faster at identifying a digit when the target was the sum of the flankers than when it was not. Adding to the repertoire of unconscious capacities, the authors conclude that "the unconscious can do (at least simple) arithmetic such as addition" (p. 1).

Tsuchiya and Koch (2005) and Tsuchiya, Koch, Gilroy, and Blake (2006) have reported that subliminal stimuli can influence direction of attention as a function of differences in gender and sexual orientation. They reported that such differences predicted attention responses to interocularly suppressed (and therefore presumably not in conscious awareness) images of naked men and women. Heterosexual men's attention was deployed to female nudes and repelled in relation to male nudes, whereas homosexual men's attention was directed to male nudes.

As a final example, subliminal stimuli have also been reported to influence behaviors such as levels of eating. In one study, subliminal presentation of abandonment cues led to greater levels of eating, whereas unification cues reduced levels of eating (Waller & Barter, 2005).

## Neural and physiological correlates of subliminal stimuli

Subliminal stimuli have also been reported to influence physiological and neural responses. Given the availability of new techniques, there have been a spate of neuroimaging studies in recent years demonstrating that subliminal stimuli can activate various brain responses. I have already briefly noted the Shevrin et al. (1992) study showing event related potential (ERP) responses to subliminal stimuli. Other studies have shown autonomic, skin conductance, and increased amygdala activity associated with emotion in response to subliminal stimuli (Anderson, Christoff, Panitz, DeRosa, & Gabrieli, 2003; Andino, Menendez, Landis, & Pegna, 2009; Esteves, Dimberg, & Öhman, 1994; Morris, de Gelder, Weiskrantz, & Dolan, 2001). It is also interesting to observe that personality variables such as individual differences in trait anxiety are lawfully related to basolateral amygdala response to subliminal fearful faces (Etkin et al., 2004).

Bernat, Shevrin, and Snodgrass (2001) reported brain ERP evidence for differential processing of pleasant and unpleasant words at both subliminal and supraliminal levels of exposure. Strikingly, the subliminal words were presented unmasked for one millisecond duration. Differential ERP responses were also found for subliminal exposure of fear and neutral faces (Liddell, Williams, Rathjen, Shevrin, & Gordon, 2004). Liddell et al. (2005) reported that a subliminal fearful face (masked) elicited activity in the amygdala as well as other brain regions. They conclude that "this network may represent an evolutionary adaptive 'alarm' system for rapid alerting to sources of threat, without the need for conscious appraisal" (p. 235).

This conclusion seems somewhat strained insofar as in the natural environment, the threats that require a rapid response prior to full conscious appraisal are generally not subliminal but supraliminal. Liddell et al. (2005) could argue that this rapid alerting system is also implicated in response to threatening subliminal stimuli. This interpretation is supported by Nasrallah, Carmel, and Lavie's (2009) finding of enhanced sensitivity to subliminal negative words compared to positive words, as reflected in the accuracy of subject's categorization of words as emotional. One can conclude "that negative stimuli [and presumably, therefore, more threatening] enjoy preferential access to perceptual processing" (p. 616).

The inhibition of behavior in an experimental situation is associated with a larger amplitude of the P3 component of an ERP across frontal-central-parietal brain sites (Smith, Johnstone, & Barry, 2007). Employing this measure, Hepler and Albarracin (2013) carried out two experiments in which participants were subliminally primed with action words (go, run, move, hit, start), inaction words (still, sit, rest, calm, stop), and controls that were scrambled action and inaction words. The participants were instructed to press a button when they saw X on a screen (go condition) and not to respond when they saw Y (no-go condition). The focus was on the P3 ERP response taken from EEG recordings during no-go Y trials (where participants are instructed to inhibit a response). There was a main effect for prime that indicated that inaction primes resulted in significantly greater P3 amplitude than action primes. However, the nature of the prime did not influence the proportion of correct no-go trials.

Experiment 2 was identical to Experiment 1 save for the larger number of trials and prime detection and recognition tasks following the completion of the experiment. The results were similar to those found in Experiment 1. Inaction word primes resulted in significantly larger P3 amplitude than action and control primes; and action primes resulted in significantly smaller P3 amplitude than control primes. As in Experiment 1, despite inaction primes resulting in larger P3 amplitude, the nature of the prime did not influence the proportion of correct no-go trials.

Although Hepler and Albarracin downplay this result, it is, I believe, as important as the main findings they emphasize. Thus, the triggering of an inhibitory brain process did not appear to influence the behavioral response; that is, it did not override the participants' conscious intention to respond in accord with the instructions they were given. Of course, it is possible that the triggering of increased P3 amplitude could have influenced behavior in subtle ways not measured in the experiments. However, it would still remain the case that the increased P3 amplitude did not influence the consciously driven task-oriented behavior.

Perhaps the most interesting finding of these experiments is that P3 amplitudes vary with the semantic meaning of the subliminal words presented. This is still another finding demonstrating that despite lack of conscious awareness of a stimulus, it can nevertheless be encoded at the semantic level. I find these demonstrations quite challenging to our ordinary notion that *persons*, not component brain processes, respond to semantic meanings of words. Because the participant perceives nothing beyond perhaps a flash of light, in our ordinary way of thinking, we would not say that he or she, *as person or agent*, has encoded the meaning of words such as "calm" or "go" (let alone more lengthy and complex phrases). But we find that despite the person having no awareness that even any word has been presented, brain processes vary as a function of the semantic meaning of these words. Although I can readily understand the role of subpersonal modules processing 'low level' information (Fodor, 1983), it is more difficult to understand subpersonal modules engaged in semantic processing.

In an fMRI study that is especially relevant to psychoanalytic theory, Lieberman et al. (2007) reported that compared to other responses (e.g., matching) verbal labelling of affective stimuli diminished amygdala and other limbic responses to negative emotional images. Affect labeling also resulted in increased activity in the right ventrolateral prefrontal cortex (RVLPFC). "Finally, RVLPFC and amygdala activity during affect labeling were inversely correlated, a relationship that was mediated by activity in medial prefrontal cortex (MPFC)" (p. 421).

These findings suggest that labeling can reduce negative affect. However, one cannot label one's affective responses unless one is consciously aware of them. From a clinical perspective, linking negative affects to the triggers that activate them is also important. The latter is obviously not possible when the stimuli that trigger affective responses are not in conscious awareness. Hence, the results on the effects of labeling provide indirect support for the value of making the unconscious conscious through putting into words affects that are triggered.

## Critique of subliminal studies

Even a brief survey of subliminal research cannot be complete without at least noting criticisms directed to this work. That we are influenced by a wide array of stimuli of which we are unaware is not in dispute. And that some filtering out of sensory input prior to conscious perception occurs is also not especially controversial (e.g., Broadbent & Broadbent, 1987; Deutsch & Deutsch, 1963; Treisman, 1969). What is at issue is the stronger claim that the "semantic meaning of a visual stimulus can be processed without awareness and that this information can influence higher cognitive functions" (Hannula, Simons, & Cohen, 2005, p. 247). Although, given the repeated reports of subliminal effects at the semantic level, we have become accustomed to this claim, it is nevertheless a striking one. As noted above, I must confess that I find the conclusion that external stimuli presented below the detection threshold can be processed at the level of semantic meaning jarring and one that automatically triggers my skepticism. It always raises for me the specter of a very clever unconscious homunculus that is able to detect and decipher the semantic meaning of external stimuli without the individual having any conscious awareness of the stimulus or of the fact that its semantic meaning has been encoded. It jars my assumption that only persons, not subpersonal mechanisms, can decipher semantic meaning.

My skepticism is shared by others who have based it on more substantial grounds than feeling jarred. For example, Hannula et al. (2005) have articulated a number of criticisms of the subliminal effects studies. They include: (1) the distinction between a perceptual experience and the report of it, the latter being influenced by the perceiver's decision criterion; (2) the variation of conscious sensitivity over time, thus perhaps raising some doubt as to whether stimuli at an exposure level that in earlier tests yielded chance discrimination are truly subliminal during the experiment proper; and (3) different displays used to establish thresholds and in the experiment proper. However, Hannula et al. (2005) go on to state that one could have greater confidence of claims of implicit perception if combined with "rigorous measures of conscious perception," neuroimaging and physiological evidence "reveal brain circuits or pathways that are distinct from those typically responsible for conscious processing" (p. 252). As we have seen, such evidence appears to have been provided.

Some of the reported findings on neural correlates of subliminal stimuli have been interpreted as demonstrating subcortical processing of fearful faces. However, as Straube, Mothes-Lasch, and Miltner (2011) have observed, a number of authors (e.g., Lipka, Miltner, & Straube, 2011; Pessoa & Adolphs, 2010) have pointed to some methodological problems with masking procedures: (1) not ruling out interactions with the mask; (2) the possibility of awareness of some cues; and (3) contributions of pathways other than subcortical ones to the amygdala. Based on these problems, Straube et al. (2011) conclude that "taken together, there is no clear-cut evidence that the amygdala can be activated differentially to emotional versus neutral faces by a subcortical route" (p. 7 of online publication). Thus, they view LeDoux's (e.g., 2000) proposal of a 'fast' subcortical thalamus–amygdala route of processing that coexists with a 'slower' cortex–amygdala route as an interesting hypothesis rather than one supported by clear-cut evidence.

The debate on whether fleeting and momentary conscious cues are available in subliminal studies not only harks back to the Freud–James 'debate' discussed in Chapter 2, but also implicitly raises the issue of the distinction between an experience and the verbal report of that experience. That issue is particularly important in the case of the experience of rapid exposure of external stimuli. As Sperling (1960) and Averbach and Sperling (1961) have shown in their classic papers on storage of briefly exposed visual information, we consciously process more information than we can report, not only to others, but also to ourselves. Employing a method of partial report, they were able to estimate the total information the subjects had processed when briefly exposed to a stimulus array of 9 to 12 letters. They showed that a visual image of the stimulus array was "momentarily available" (p. 357) to the subjects for a brief period before fading, with the result that only a portion of the 'iconic image' found expression in verbal report.

These studies raise the general and rather core issue of the distinction and 'gap' between immediate phenomenal experience and the *report* of that experience. In both studies, although exposed for a brief duration, the stimulus array was presented at a supraliminal level. Hence, the results do not have to do directly with subliminal effects and unconscious processing. Rather, reminiscent of James' (1890) alternative to positing unconscious processes, they have to do with fleeting and momentary conscious experience that remains unrepresented in verbal report. Sperling (1960) and Averbach and Sperling (1961) were able to infer momentary and fleeting conscious experience and to estimate the total information processed by employing a highly sensitive and ingenious method. As has been noted by Holender (1986), Panksepp (2005), and others, this is not always the case in studies of subliminal effects, with the result that we do not always have accurate data on how much information has been momentarily consciously experienced and processed.

The 'gap' between immediate phenomenal experience and the report of that experience is influenced by how we deploy attention. In a series of recent experiments by Chen and Wylie (2015), the participants' task was to report on the location of a target letter. When given a surprise memory test to report the identity or color of the letter, they performed no better than chance. The authors refer to this phenomenon as "attribute amnesia." That is, when asked to identify one aspect of a fully supraliminal stimulus (e.g., color), one has 'amnesia' for other aspects of the stimulus (e.g., its identitiy). It is an instance of what Mack and Rock (1998) refer to as "inattentional blindness." It would have been interesting in the Chen and Wylie study to see whether the non-remembered attribute could influence some aspect of the participants' response, for example, association to the stimulus or reaction time, when the non-remembered attribute is relevant to the task and could, therefore, prime a response, similar to a subliminal prime.

## *Unconscious influence of supraliminal stimuli on behavior*

There are a number of studies that deal with unconscious processing in the context of supraliminal stimuli. In these studies, what is claimed to be unconscious is not the stimuli that are presented to subjects, but rather the fact that they have influenced their behavior. Again, because these studies are too numerous to cover adequately, I will provide some representative examples in different categories. Although varying in a number of respects, the studies share in common the facts that (1) the stimuli employed are supraliminal; (2) what the participants are unaware of is not the stimuli presented to them, but the *influence* of these stimuli on various aspects of their behavior.

Over the last number of years, a series of studies have been published that purport to demonstrate that exposure to ordinary objects and words prime our behavior in ways of which we are unaware. In one of the most well known of these studies, Bargh, Chen, and Burrows (1996) reported that compared to a control group, participants who were exposed to words suggestive of old age (through unscrambling scrambled sentences) walked significantly more slowly to an elevator upon leaving the laboratory.

In studies with a similar design, Williams and Bargh (2008) found that participants who briefly held a cup of hot versus iced coffee evaluated a target person as having a "warmer" personality (e.g., generous, caring); and participants holding a hot versus cold therapeutic pad were likely to choose a gift for a friend rather than for themselves. There are many other studies along the same line reporting similar effects, for example, the effects of an elderly stereotype prime on grasping actions (Banfield, Pendry, Mewse, & Edwards, 2003); the effects of exposure to backpacks and briefcases on, respectively, cooperative and competitive behaviors; and the priming effect of exposure to briefcases on the cognitive accessibility of a competition construct (Kay, Wheeler, Bargh, & Ross, 2004).

Background smells have also been shown to influence behavior without the individual's awareness, as reported by Holland, Hendriks, and Aarts (2005). They found that participants who were unobtrusively exposed to citrus-scented all purpose cleaner identified cleaning-related words faster in a lexical decision task, reported cleaning-related activities more frequently when describing behavior they expected to engage in during the day, and were more likely to keep their direct environment clean during an eating task. The authors account for these results as due to the greater "mental accessibility of the behavior concept of cleaning" (p. 689).

Other sensory modalities have also been shown to influence behavior. Ackerman, Nocera, and Bargh (2010) reported that "heavy objects made job candidates appear more important; rough objects made social interactions more difficult; and hard objects increased rigidity in negotiations" (p. 1713). Some other examples: Dijksterhuis and van Knippenberg (1998) primed participants with the trait "intelligence" or "stupidity," who were then asked to complete an ostensibly unrelated general knowledge test. The participants primed with "intelligence" did significantly better than non-primed participants; and participants primed with "stupidity" did significantly poorer than non-primed participants.

In a fascinating and well thought out series of studies, Maier, Elliot, and Lichtenfeld (2008) reported that relative to the color gray, incidental exposure to the color red negatively affected performance on an IQ test (the 20-item numeric subtest of the Intelligence Structure Test (Amthauer, Brocke, Liepmann, & Beauducel, 1999)). Furthermore, they demonstrated the mediating effects of the color red on evoking "an avoidance-based constricting of attentional focus, which in turn undermines performance attainment" (p. 1537).

Why should exposure to the color red evoke an attentional avoidance response in an achievement context? There are a number of possible explanations. As Maier et al. (2008) note, in many cultures, red is associated with the danger of failure in academics (teachers use red to mark mistakes and errors) and with inhibitory signals in general contexts (traffic lights). These associations, the authors note, may be reinforced by or derived from an evolutionarily selected-for predisposition to respond to red as a signal of danger (in some species of ape, red signals the dominance or attack-readiness of an opponent (Pryke, Andresson, & Lawes, 2001; Setchell & Wickings, 2005)). I would add that in humans, red is often associated with blood and with anger (e.g., the face can become red with anger).

In a very useful discussion, Maier et al. (2008) raise the issue of context and observe that red is also associated with love, romance (e.g., Valentines), sexual attractiveness (e.g., lipstick), and lust (e.g., red-light district). Hence, in these contexts, as opposed to an academic achievement context, red may be more likely to elicit approach rather than avoidance responses. In short, "the influence of red on motivation and behavior is not invariant but is sensitive to context" (p. 1538).

I have spent all this time on the Maier et al. (2008) study not because I believe that color psychology is of special interest to psychoanalysis, but because the issues the authors raise are relevant to psychoanalysis as well as to properly understanding the findings of the above studies I have briefly described. One such issue is the role of context in influencing the *associative meaning* of stimuli to which one is exposed, which, in turn, may influence the effects of these stimuli on the individual's behavior. Thus, as we have seen, whereas in an academic performance context, red is more likely to activate failure- and threat-associated meanings, which, in turn, is more likely to evoke avoidance responses, in an interpersonal context, red is more likely to activate romantic and sexual associative meanings, which, in turn, is more likely to evoke approach responses (Barelli, Heistermann, Boesch, & Reichard, 2007; Dixson, 1983; Elliot & Niesta, 2008).

The findings of the above studies are intriguing and have made quite a splash. For example, that one would walk more slowly because one has been exposed to words suggesting old age is certainly not something one would normally expect. Similarly, one would also not normally expect that holding a cup of hot coffee would influence one's judgment of another or that holding a hot therapeutic pad would make one more generous. These sorts of findings, if replicated, suggest not only that we are constantly being influenced by external stimuli without our awareness, but also that we are frequently, perhaps characteristically, not aware of the *nature* of these influences, for example, on our motor behavior (e.g., pace of walking), interpersonal judgment, generosity, and cooperative versus competitive attitudes.

The surprising, even startling, nature of some of the findings is precisely the quality that has elicited a good deal of skepticism, expressions of which have been publicized is such sources as the *Chronicle of Higher Education* and the *New York Times*. At least some degree of skepticism is buttressed and justified, not only by the startling nature of some findings, but by failure to replicate them.

Employing an objective and automatic method of timing (infrared beams) rather than a manually operated stopwatch, Doyen, Klein, Pichon, and Cleeremans (2012) reported a failure to replicate Bargh et al.'s (1996) results. In a second experiment, in which they manipulated the experiment's expectations, using a stopwatch, those experimenters who expected primed subjects to walk slower reported significant differences in that direction between prime and no-prime conditions; and those experimenters who expected primed subjects to walk faster reported significant differences between prime and no-prime conditions in that direction.

Other fascinating results were reported. With regard to the objective measure of timing in the second experiment, primed subjects walked significantly slower than non-primed condition (thus replicating the Bargh et al. (1996) effect), but only in the slow experimenter condition. Thus, experimenter expectation in the fast condition did not lead to faster walking when objectively measured. Further, independent of prime versus no-prime, subjects in the slow experimenter condition walked significantly slower than in the fast experiment condition, suggesting the effect of experimenter cues.

During the debriefing in both experiments, an attempt was made to assess the subjects' awareness of the prime, of their primed behavior, and of the link between the prime and the primed behavior. Only four subjects reported awareness that the scrambled sentences they were asked to unscramble were related to the stereotype of old people. There was little direct evidence that subjects were aware of any link between the prime and their behavior. However, some indirect evidence was forthcoming. Doyen et al. (2012) presented subjects with four pictures (i.e., athletic person, Arabic person, handicapped person, and elderly person) and asked them which category could have been used as primes. In both Experiments 1 and 2 the primed subjects chose the picture of the old person above chance, whereas subjects in the no-prime condition were equally likely to choose any of the four pictures.

How does one understand the above findings? For one thing, they raise the strong possibility that the Bargh effect may have been due to a combination of (1) the experimenter timing error; (2) unwitting subtle cues communicated by the experimenter to subjects; and (3) some subjects' awareness of the nature of the prime. With regard to the latter factor, the fact that subjects in the prime condition chose above chance the old person picture as the category that could have been used as a prime above chance suggests that they were not unaware of the prime category (i.e., elderly). Because Bargh et al. (1996) did not test for awareness of the prime, this cannot be ruled out as a factor in their results.

What is especially interesting in the Doyen et al. (2012) study is the finding that priming alone did not produce the effect, but priming combined with experimenter expectation. As noted, this suggests that the experimenter was communicating subtle behavioral cues to subjects. As Doyen et al. (2012) put it, "it is likely that experimenters who expect their participants to walk slower behave differently than those who expect their participants to walk faster and that such behavioral cues are picked up by participants" (p. 5).

There is a good deal of (unintended) irony in this account. On the one hand, Doyen et al. (2012) did not replicate the Bargh effect. That is, they demonstrated that primes of which the subjects are (presumably) unaware do not influence walking speed. On the other hand, their findings suggest that the experimenter's behavioral cues of which the subjects are presumably unaware influence their walking speed. If this is true, one must then conclude that the experimenter's behavioral cues prime the subjects' walking speed without their awareness of either the prime or the link between the prime and their behavior. In effect, they have replicated the Bargh effect through the unintended use of a different prime, namely, the experiment's behavioral cues. This raises the questions – assuming that Doyen et al.'s (2012) own results are replicable – of (1) the nature of the experimenter's behavioral cues; and (2) the nature of the process through which these cues influenced the subject's walking speed.

Answers to these questions would seem to have a good deal of relevance not only to understanding interpersonal influence in general, but also to understanding the influence of therapist cues on the patient's behavior in the therapeutic situation. In this context, the interest is not, of course on such behaviors as walking speed, but rather in such matters as topics the patient brings up or fails to bring up, the nature of his or her associations, feelings of safety, and so on.[1] Masling and Cohen (1987) have reviewed illustrative cases in which the therapist's unwitting cues influenced the kind of material the patient produced in the therapeutic session. In one case, the therapist was Carl Rogers (Murray, 1956); and in another case, the therapist was Rogerian (Truax, 1966). This is especially important because despite the fact that Rogerian therapists view themselves as *non-directive*, these cases indicate that they can nevertheless influence the themes brought forth by patients through emitting subtle cues. This is also undoubtedly the case with classical analysts who (mistakenly) assume that their 'blank screen' stance (the psychoanalytic version of being non-directive) guarantees that they are not influencing their patients' free associations. Greenson (1967), a classical analyst, provides a description of his subtle differential response to the patient saying negative things about Roosevelt.

Indeed, one of the great and long-lasting illusions that lay behind the classical emphasis on the analyst as a 'blank screen' was the unwarranted assumption that taking this stance could eliminate the analyst's communication of unwitting cues to the patient. This assumption was based on the failure to recognize that any human interaction entails bi-directional communication of cues, including unwitting and subtle cues. Furthermore, although unwitting and subtle, these cues can exert a strong influence on behavior, particularly in such emotionally loaded interactional contexts as the therapeutic situation.

A recognition of the inevitability of emitting unwitting cues led to a radical change in contemporary psychoanalytic conceptions of the analytic stance and of transference and countertransference. It was recognized that no one, including an analyst, can really be a blank screen if that means emitting no cues. As Gill (1994) pointed out, even silence – the orthodox analyst's usual way of presumably being utterly opaque – can be a powerful cue. Furthermore, as Gill and others reasoned, if emitting of cues is inevitable it follows that, for the most part, the patient's transference reactions are not best thought of simply in terms of the patient's projections onto a blank screen analyst. Rather, transference entails the patient's interpretation, selection, and response to actual cues emitted by the analyst. Similar considerations apply to how one understands countertransference.

## *Unconscious thought paradigm*

A series of studies have been carried out, largely by Dijksterhuis and his colleagues, that reported the positive effect of superiority of purported unconscious thought on various behaviors. The standard design employed was to compare various responses in three conditions: (1) immediate response; (2) response after a period of conscious thought and deliberation; and (3) response after a period of distraction during which unconscious thought is hypothesized to take place.

In a series of experiments, Dijksterhuis and his colleagues have reported the superiority of various responses in the "unconscious thought" condition. For example, Dijksterhuis and Meurs (2006) reported that when asked to generate items according to a specific instruction (e.g., generate place names starting with the letter "A"), participants in the "unconscious thought" condition generated more original responses. In another study, Dijksterhuis and van Olden (2006) found that when asked to choose one of five art posters, compared to the immediate choice and choice after deliberate thinking condition, participants in the distraction (and presumed unconscious thought) condition expressed greater satisfaction with their choice when phoned 3 to 5 weeks later. As a final example, Dijksterhuis (2004) reported that in making a complex decision in which multiple attributes were involved (e.g., choosing a possible roommate), the distraction condition generated better choices than the immediate and conscious deliberation conditions. Other studies have reported similar results with regard to impression formation, prediction of athletic events, stereotyping, and problem solving.[2]

Dijksterhuis and Nordgren (2006) have proposed that the presumed 'superior' performance of unconscious thought for complex decisions is due, among other reasons, to (1) the greater cognitive capacity of unconscious thought; (2) its better weighting of multiple attributes; and (3) its characteristic divergent rather than the focused and convergent thinking characteristic of conscious thought.

As we have seen with the studies on the unconscious influence of supraliminal cues on various behaviors, all is not entirely well with the unconscious thought paradigm. As is the case with the former studies, there have been a number of failures to replicate the findings of Dijksterhuis and his colleagues on the superiority of the unconscious thought condition in complex choices and judgments (e.g., Acker, 2008; Newell, Wong, Cheung, & Rakow, 2009; Payne, Samper, Bettman, & Luce, 2008; Rey, Goldstein, & Perruchet, 2009; Runnion, 2009; Thorsteinson & Withrow, 2009). Indeed, in a series of experiments (Calvillo & Penaloza, 2009) on complex decisions (i.e., choosing a car), contrary to the findings of Dijksterhuis and his colleagues, whereas participants in the "unconscious thought" condition were unable to distinguish between the best and worst alternatives in a complex set, participants in the immediate condition were able to do so. In a series of papers,

Newell and his colleagues have identified serious problems with the studies by Dijksterhuis and his colleagues, including failure by other investigators to replicate findings and serious methodological errors (e.g., Newell, 2015).

Also, both Gonzales-Vallejo and Phillips (2010) and Waroquier et al. (2009) have identified methodological and statistical problems in some of the unconscious thought studies. Further, Waroquier, Marchiori, Klein, and Cleeremans (2009) failed to replicate the finding that a complex decision task (i.e., selecting among applicants for an engineer position) was facilitated in the distraction condition. They also note a theoretical puzzle with regard to the unconscious thought paradigm. Normally, submitting participants to a concurrent task (distraction) while, at the same time, requiring a response on another task (i.e., making a complex choice or decision) has been viewed as a constraint on cognitive capacity (e.g., Fiske & Newberg, 1990; Gilbert & Hixon, 1991) rather than as a means of facilitating unconscious thought.

There is also a serious conceptual and methodical problem with the unconscious thought studies. Let us assume that the findings reported by Dijksterhuis and his colleagues are indeed reliable and replicable. What we could warrantedly say in that case is that the distraction condition leads to different results ('better' performance) than the immediate and conscious thought conditions. We would have no direct evidence that these differences were attributable to unconscious thought in the distraction condition or even that unconscious thought linked to the task occurred. The differences could be due to the detrimental effects of conscious deliberation rather than the facilitating effects of the distraction condition. Indeed, in one study, Nordgren and Dijksterhuis (2009) themselves found that the difference in preference consistency "was due to the impediment of deliberation and not to the benefit of nondeliberation" (p. 39). Thus, even if one assumes that unconscious thought occurs in the distraction condition, we do not know whether it is task-relevant unconscious thought. It may be that not thinking about the task at hand at all (either consciously or unconsciously) but about other matters for a period of time is conducive to choice satisfaction, better prediction, less stereotyping, 'better' choices, and so on.

Hence, the following breezily offered advice given by Dijksterhuis and Nordgren (2006) on the basis of their research is not warranted:

> When a decision strategy warrants the careful and strict application of one specific rule . . ., use conscious thought. When matter becomes more complicated and weighting is called for . . . use unconscious thought. In addition, when the amount of relevant information increases and strictly following a single rule ceases to be feasible (such as when buying a house), use unconscious thought.
>
> (p. 105)

> In short, consciousness should be used to gather information, and the unconscious should be used to work on it.
>
> (p. 107)

> [P]eople tend to engage in a great deal of conscious thought when they deal with complex problems, whereas they should engage more in unconscious thought.
>
> (p. 108)

Once again, individual differences are ignored. These homilies are offered without any consideration given to individual differences in decision strategies and with insufficient consideration given to differences in the nature of the decision task confronted by the individual. With regard to the latter, Dijksterhuis and Nordgren (2006) offer their advice based on (1) the distinction between simple versus complex tasks; and (2) a limited number of tasks within the complex rubric (e.g., buying a car, choosing a roommate, selecting an art poster). Beyond simple versus complex, no attention is given to developing a taxonomy of tasks or to possible interactions between decision strategies and type of task. It defies plausibility to believe that the rule 'conscious thought for simple task (or for information gathering) and unconscious thought for complex tasks' holds for all tasks and for all individuals.

## *Acquisition of 'rules' without awareness*

In a series of experiments employing hidden covariations among stimuli, Lewicki and his colleagues (e.g., Lewicki, Hill, & Czyzewska, 1992) have reported that participants can process information and acquire information-processing algorithms and heuristics without conscious awareness that they have acquired these heuristics or of their influence on forming and making judgments. These algorithms are presumably based on unconscious detection of covariation among features in the world. For example, nonconscious processing of a covariation between a nonsalient facial feature X and a personality characteristic Y often results in a tendency to attribute to a subsequent person with the facial feature X the personality characteristic Y – without the awareness that he or she has formed an inferential 'rule' or algorithm that guides his or her judgments. One can see the family resemblance between this form of procedural knowledge and various phenomena of interest to psychoanalysis, including transference, the formation of early representations and pathogenic beliefs, and their influence on later behavior.

It needs to be noted however, that Hendrickx, De Houwer, Baeyens, Eelen, and Van Avermaet (1997) have been only partly successful in their attempt to replicate findings reported by Lewicki, Hill, and Czyzewska, (1997) who, in turn, have argued that deviations from the original methodology are responsible for Hendrickx et al.'s failure to replicate the findings. (However, see Shanks & St. John (1994) for a cogent critique of studies, including those of Lewicki and his colleagues, reporting learning without awareness.)

As another example of the unconscious acquisition of 'rules,' in a study by Bowers (1984; 1987), subjects were presented with word triads and were asked to think of a word that the triad of words all have in common. Some of these triads can be solved and others cannot. Subjects were asked to indicate which triads can and cannot be solved. Bowers reported that although they could solve the solvable triad, subjects could nevertheless discriminate with considerable accuracy between the solvable and unsolvable triads. These results suggest that in distinguishing between the two sets of word triads the subjects were employing cues or 'rules' they could not articulate.

As has been noted by many, although we normally utter and write grammatically correct sentences and are able to distinguish between correct and incorrect sentences, we frequently cannot articulate the syntactical rules we employ (Chomsky, 1965). A number of investigators have demonstrated this phenomenon in the laboratory through construction and use of artificial grammars (e.g., Reber, 1976, 1989; Broadbent, FitzGerald, & Broadbent, 1986). Subjects learn how to use the artificial grammar correctly, but cannot articulate the rules they are employing.

The above studies do not deal with the kinds of 'rules' implicit in the concepts of internal working models, RIGs, and unconscious pathogenic beliefs. However, in addition to the findings of these studies being of interest in their own right and contributing to our understanding of how the mind works, by demonstrating that our behavior can be influenced by 'rules' of which we are unaware and cannot articulate, they lend additional credence to psychoanalytic propositions that require the assumption that such phenomena are within our mental capacities. Were that not the case, we would be entitled to be more skeptical about these propositions.

As is the case with studies on subliminal effects, a frequent criticism of learning without awareness (implicit learning) studies centers on the question of degree to which some cues and information have been consciously – even if fleetingly – processed. Common to these critiques is the argument that the possibility of conscious cues has not been excluded.

There is, however, at least one study on the unconscious acquisition of 'rules' where the criticism of possible conscious cues does not seem to hold because even focal attention does not result in the subjects' awareness of the 'rules' that influence their behavior. Turvey and Fertig (1970) presented lists of words to subjects:

| List one | List two |
|---|---|
| farm | wife |
| prevent | burn |
| uncle | silence |
| sea | debt |
| car | sing |
| play | young |
| religious | disease |
| action | box |
| develop | window |

Before proceeding further, let me describe the Osgood Semantic Differential (Osgood, Suci, & Tannenbaum, 1957). It allows one to rate a given stimulus (e.g., a word) on the negative–positive poles of three dimensions: Evaluative (good–bad); Potency (strong–weak); and Activity (active–passive). In list 1, the words are normatively rated high on the positive poles of one of the dimensions of the Osgood Semantic Differential, which include evaluative (good–bad), potency (strong–weak), and activity (active–passive), and neutral on the other two dimensions. In list 2, the words are drawn from the negative pole of the Semantic Differential. Before presenting the study and its results, let me briefly describe the phenomenon of proactive interference (PI). The interference of learning list A with the learning and recall of a subsequent list B is referred to as PI. In other words, learning list A proactively interferes with the recall of list B. There are many studies identifying the dimensions of list A and the relationship between lists A and B that influence PI. Further, and most important for this study, one can manipulate the factors that will produce release from PI. For example, one gets release from PI when there is a shift in the category of items from list A to list B.

Now to the results of the study. When there was a shift in Osgood Semantic Differential polarity (from positive to negative or negative to positive), a release from PI occurred, that is, there was significant improvement in recall. This did not occur when there was a shift across dimensions within the same polarity (e.g., shift from all words high [or low] in polarity from evaluative to potency). In other words, a distinction between negative and positive polarity was made tacitly. What is striking about this finding is that even when informed about the properties of the two lists, the distinction cannot be made explicitly. As Turvey (1977) writes:

> Imagine if the words in the two columns were simply mixed together and you were ignorant of the Semantic Differential (as were the subjects in the experiments). I doubt if you could even begin to sort them into the two categories I have described.
>
> (p. 177)

And yet, this sorting is implicitly made. One should note that the release from PI does not work when there is a shift between nouns and verbs, a distinction that is readily available to explicit knowledge.

The findings of the above studies suggest that stimuli are organized differently as a function of tacit versus explicit knowledge. The release from PI data reported by Turvey and Fertig (1970) indicate that participants implicitly organized stimuli along polarities of positive versus negative on the dimensions of evaluation (good–bad), potency (strong–weak), and activity (active–passive), although they did not know they were doing so and could not explicitly make these distinctions. Furthermore, these forms of organization are different from those we use for explicit knowledge and in certain contexts may not even be available to explicit knowledge. Although these forms of organization are not directly equivalent to primary versus secondary process organization, they bear a distant family resemblance to that dimension. It would be interesting to carry out a study similar to the Turvey and

Fertig (1970) study where the dimensions of the stimuli presented lend themselves to drive organization. Would one find evidence of implicit drive organization as indicated by proactive interference and release from proactive interference?

## *Not knowing the reasons for our behavior*

An important set of studies has been summarized in a classic paper by Nisbett and Wilson (1977). In all these studies participants were unaware of the factors that influenced their behavior, but nevertheless gave reasons for their behavior that, it was shown experimentally, were not the actual reasons. For example, in one study, women selected hosiery on the basis of its position (the last bin explored), but gave as the reason for their choice the sheerness, knit, and weave of the hosiery although all of the hosiery samples were identical on these dimensions. As another example, although the probability of helping intervention behavior by a bystander is a function of the number of people present, this factor is virtually never mentioned as the individual's reason for his or her behavior. Rather, people tend to refer to such factors as the victim's need and the likelihood that their behavior will be helpful. As a final example, individuals who viewed a film under conditions of noise and distraction tended to report that their evaluation of the film was negatively influenced by these factors. However, their evaluations were virtually identical to those of a control group who viewed the film under normal conditions.

Nisbett and Wilson conclude that frequently when people are asked to give reasons for their behavior, they arrive at their reasons not through introspection of their experience or by "consulting a memory of a mediating process, but by applying or generating causal theories" (p. 248) derived from general models learned in a culture or subculture. In some respects, Nisbett and Wilson's conclusion is similar to Wittgenstein's (1938/1966) earlier noted argument that frequently the reasons one gives for one's behavior constitute justifications rather than simply explanations.

One cannot help but recognize the link between Nisbett and Wilson and Wittgenstein's accounts and the psychoanalytic concept of rationalization. However, the former go beyond the context of defensive function and are intended to be applicable to much of normative behavior. That is, we are often unaware of the factors that actually influence our behavior and instead generate reasons and motives either when we are asked by others or ask ourselves to do so. (However, see critiques of Nisbett and Wilson – e.g., Smith & Miller, 1978; Howe, 1991.)

## *Influence of degree of awareness and attention on stimulus organization*

A question that is of special interest to psychoanalytic theory is the relationship between degree of awareness and attention and stimulus organization. The Turvey and Fertig (1970) study discussed above can be understood as demonstrating that implicit 'rules' of organization, that is, 'rules' of which we are unaware, are different from explicit 'rules' and may not be accessible to conscious awareness. Studies on this issue are relevant to a psychoanalytic theory of thinking, particularly to the psychoanalytic idea that stimuli are differentially encoded and organized as a function of degree of awareness; with relative lack of awareness facilitating primary process organization and focal awareness facilitating secondary process organization (see Rapaport, 1967). As Klein (1959) observed, the Pötzl experiments "were among the very few that intrigued Freud" (p. 10). The so-called "Pötzl phenomenon" was investigated many years later in a series of studies by Fischer and his colleagues (e.g., Fisher & Paul, 1959; Paul & Fisher, 1959) who reported that unattended stimuli were more prone to primary process organization.

In many instances, it might be more profitable to think in terms of degree of awareness rather than in terms of a sharp dichotomy between conscious and unconscious. From this perspective, what would be interesting and important would be the question of whether the forms and levels of encoding and the kind of influence they have on behavior vary with the degree of awareness (defined in terms of phenomenal experience) with which stimuli have been experienced. For example, does the level of awareness with which a stimulus is experienced influence primary process versus secondary modes of encoding? Focusing on this sort of issue may be more heuristically profitable than protracted methodological debates on whether subliminal stimuli yield an absolutely zero level of consciously available information.

The effect of level of attention on type of cognitive processing also interested Jung (1920) who hypothesized that a low level of attention would be associated with a more 'primitive' kind of cognitive processing. In support of this hypothesis, Eagle and Ortof (1967) found evidence that compared to a high level of attention, when subjects were presented a list of words under conditions of low attention (manipulated through a distraction task), their processing of the stimulus words were more likely to be based on acoustic features (e.g., rhymes) rather than the semantic meaning of the words (see Craik & Lockhart, 1972, for an important paper on levels of processing).

During the 1950s a number of studies on the question of degree of awareness and attention and stimulus organization were carried out at the New York University Research Center for Mental Health (e.g., Eagle, 1959; Eagle, Wolitzky, & Klein, 1966; Klein, Spence, Holt, & Gourevitch, 1958; Paul & Fisher, 1959; Pine, 1960, 1961; Smith, Spence, & Klein, 1959; Spence & Holland, 1962). A few of these studies, which I will describe below, dealt with the differential effects of subliminal and incidental versus supraliminal stimuli on mode of processing.

In accord with the psychoanalytic theory of primary versus secondary process organization of cognition, a number of early studies attempted to demonstrate that in contrast to stimuli that are attended to and reportable in phenomenal awareness, subliminal and incidental stimuli – that is, stimuli associated with a low degree of attention and awareness – will be more likely to show primary process organization. This hypothesis was the basis for much of the early work on subliminal and incidental stimuli at the New York University Research Center for Mental Health.

In one study, Pine (1960) reported that compared to focal stimuli, incidental stimuli influenced subjects' subsequent imaginative stories in accord with the latter's symbolic meanings. More specifically, when the incidental stimulus was a description of "cow" which included 'oral-passive' descriptors such as "warm," "soft," "contented," and so on, subjects' subsequent imaginative stories included more interpersonal themes of receiving and the presence of children relative to adults in the stories.

When the incidental stimulus was a description of a "hook," which included "phallic-aggressive" descriptors such as "metallic hardness," "stark", "prong," and "power," the subsequent imaginative stories included more themes of intruding and greater presence of adults in the stories. The differences did not appear when the "cow" and "hook" stimuli were in focal awareness. The influence of the focal stimuli on the imaginative stories were more direct rather than transformed. For example, in the focal "cow" condition, the stories were more likely to include words such as "nice," "countryside," foodstuffs, and presence of animals; in the focal "hook" condition, the stories were more likely to include words such as "effective work," "working hard," and themes of repairing things and going to engineering school. Pine interpreted these findings partly as a function of the relationship between decreased awareness and greater susceptibility of stimuli to transformations of drive organization.

Similar to Pine (1960), Spence and Holland (1962) investigated the relationship between degree of awareness and stimulus organization. However, unlike Pine, they employed subliminal rather than incidental stimuli. After exposing the word "cheese" either subliminally or supraliminally, subjects heard a list of 26 words that included both "cheese" associates and control words, and were then asked to recall the words. There was also a 'blank' condition in which subjects heard the 26 words without prior exposure to the word "cheese." The subjects in the subliminal condition recalled significantly more "cheese" associates than subjects in the supraliminal and 'blank' conditions. In addition, the number of cheese-related "intrusions" (i.e., "recalled" words that were not in the target list) were significantly higher in the supraliminal than subliminal condition and consisted mainly of food associates (e.g., sweet, taste, meat). Other findings reported were that the subliminal stimulus had a stronger effect on the recall of more distant associates of "cheese," and that subjects who reported partial cues in the subliminal condition tended to recall words that were structurally similar to "cheese" (i.e., contained a common letter, for example, "chair," "arch"). Spence and Holland concluded that these results supported the Freudian hypothesis that "thinking below awareness tends to fan out over a large network of traces" (p. 164) and "that a supraliminal stimulus had a more restricting effect on recall than a subliminal stimulus" (p. 170) and that "apparently the subliminal stimulus follows laws that are independent of those which determine conscious associations" (p. 169).

Unfortunately, a number of attempts to replicate Spence and Holland's (1962) findings were unsuccessful. Also, some of the findings reported seem to contradict theoretically based expectations. For example, Spence and Holland reported that the greater the discrimination in the threshold task (i.e., discriminating "something" from "nothing") the greater the recall of words structurally similar to "cheese" (e.g., "chair") and the fewer the recall of words similar in meaning to "cheese" (e.g., "mouse"). They account for this finding by speculating that subjects who showed higher discrimination in the threshold task were more likely to pick up partial cues (e.g., single letters) during the experiment and thus recall more words that were structurally similar to "cheese." Contrastingly, their reasoning continues, subjects who discriminated no or minimal information were not likely to be influenced by partial structural cues and therefore responded solely in terms of the semantic meaning of subliminal stimulus.

According to this reasoning, at least within a certain range, the lower the amount of cues or information of a stimulus that is consciously perceived, the more likely the stimulus will be processed at the semantic rather than the graphic level. Spence and Holland's reasoning is that when a stimulus is truly subliminal, that is, when no cues are consciously perceived or reported, it will be more likely to be processed at the semantic level because of the absence of partial cues that, if present, prime structurally related rather than semantically related words. This hypothesis posits a highly sensitive unconscious discriminating apparatus that if not 'misled' by consciously available partial cues can precisely encode semantic meaning.

Not only does this proposition seem implausible, but it appears generally incongruent with the earlier noted findings reported by Eagle and Ortof (1967) that reduced attention to a stimulus tends to limit its processing to a graphic level and impedes processing at a semantic level. More generally, the evidence that reduced attention interferes with or prevents encoding of words at the semantic level needs to be reconciled with reports of semantic encoding of subliminal stimuli, where the conditions (e.g., masking) preclude the deployment of any attention to these stimuli. If reduced attention leads to phonetic rather than semantic encoding, should not subliminal verbal stimuli influence subsequent responses in terms of the former's phonetic structure rather than semantic meaning?

It needs to be noted that although Spence and Holland's specific findings were not replicated, Marcel (1980) reported results that tend to support their general hypothesis regarding the restricting effects of supraliminal stimuli. He found that when the word PALM was presented subliminally, it facilitated the lexical classification of WRIST, whether preceded by HAND or TREE, whereas when it was presented supraliminally, it had an inhibitory effect on the classification of WRIST when preceded by TREE.

In a series of experiments, Farooqui and Manly (2015) reported that whereas supraliminal cues significantly improved performance in a situation in which the cue predicted which of two tasks the participants should perform, supraliminal cues did not influence performance. This was likely so because when the cues were supraliminal they were deemed irrelevant by the participants, whereas when they were subliminal, participants "could not, by definition, apply the same gating" (p. 8). These findings are especially interesting because they suggest that under certain circumstances not having to make judgments about the relevance of cues can enhance performance.

Similar findings were reported by Lin and Murray (2015). Comparing the effects of subliminal and supraliminal cues, they found that whereas subliminal cues facilitated performance in a cue location task (is the cue on the right or the left?), supraliminal cues did not. The authors attribute these results to the need to suppress task-irrelevant information (an inhibition effect) that is associated with conscious awareness, but not with subliminal stimuli outside awareness.

## *Subliminal and supraliminal stimuli are associated with different neural responses*

A number of studies have shown differences in the effects of stimuli on neural responses as a function of whether or not they are reportable in phenomenal awareness. For example, as noted earlier, Shevrin et al. (1992) reported that subjects' ERP responses classified unconscious conflict words related to their phobia when presented subliminally, whereas ERP responses to supraliminal words classified conscious symptom words. As another example of differences between subliminal and supraliminal encoding, Stenberg, Lindgren, Johansson, Olson, and Rosen (2000) reported that consciously reported stimuli were associated with neural activity in different brain areas than unreported (subliminal) stimuli, which suggests that explicit (i.e., reportable, in phenomenal awareness) and implicit perception (i.e., not reported) "are separable neural processes" (Hannula et al., 2005, p. 252).

Williams et al. (2006) also reported that compared to a neutral expression, subliminal facial expression of fear elicited greater amygdala activity and also skin conductance responses. There was a trend for greater right amygdala response for subliminal stimuli and greater left amygdala response for supraliminal stimuli. There were also differential cortical responses to the subliminal and supraliminal faces. Quite interesting, subcortical amygdala activity was relatively persistent in response to the subliminal faces, whereas the supraliminal faces were associated with more sustained cortical activity. One can speculate that different neural responses may be associated with different kinds of stimulus organization. Recall also Lieberman et al.'s (2007) report that compared to neutral stimuli, labeling of affective stimuli diminishes amygdala and other limbic responses to negative emotional images and resulted in increased activity in the right ventrolateral prefrontal cortex.

## *Individual differences*

Implicit in Maier et al.'s (2008) discussion of the importance of context is the idea that *the individual meanings associated with the stimulus to which one is exposed* will influence its effects on behavior. The reason that context matters, Maier et al. (2008) tell us, is that it influences the associative meanings given to the stimulus. But differences in associative meanings given to a stimulus can be generated not only by different conditions (e.g., two different contexts) but also by idiosyncratic factors such as the individual's unique history and his or her particular associative network within a given condition (something assumed in the use of free association in the psychoanalytic situation). This would suggest the importance of studying not only differences between conditions, but also interactional effects (i.e., condition X individual difference variables).

A frequent comment made by psychoanalytic as well as other clinicians is that general findings such as mean differences between experimental and control groups typically reported in research papers are not of much use to them when they are dealing with individual patients and their particular psychic reality. I think the comment is justified. Individual differences are often treated as error variance rather than meaningful phenomena to be studied in their own right. In the studies I have discussed, no account is taken of individual differences. Rather, only differences between conditions are reported: for example, participants exposed to 'elderly' words walk more slowly than those exposed to non-elderly words. Or, participants who held a cup of hot coffee rate someone more 'warmly' than those who held a cup of iced coffee. These results are certainly interesting, even startling, and are certainly worth reporting (assuming they are reliable and replicable phenomena). However, not all subjects show these effects, and it may be possible to obtain statistically significant differences as the result of the responses of a minority of subjects. However, the impression given is that the results reported (e.g., walking slower as a result of exposure to 'elderly' words; 'warmer' evaluations of others as a result of holding a cup of hot coffee) are general phenomena characteristic of most, if not all, people.

In developing a fully adequate explanatory account, it would be important to have some understanding of why some subjects showed the effect and others did not. It is likely that one factor that accounts for these differences is the different associative meanings given to the stimuli to which the participants were exposed. It is difficult to believe that identical associative networks were evoked in *all* subjects. For example, is it not possible, even likely, that some subjects had 'warm' associations to iced coffee (e.g., hot summer days) and negative associations to hot coffee (isolated from adults)? As another example, it is difficult to believe that all subjects had 'cooperative' associations to backpacks and 'competitive' associations to briefcases.

There are a small number of early studies that have dealt with individual differences in sensitivity to subliminal stimuli. In one study on subliminal effects (Eagle, 1962), participants were also administered a battery of psychological tests, asked to write a brief autobiography, and administered two quasi-clinical interviews. They also participated in a sensory deprivation study. Based on this material, staff members of the New York University Research Center for Mental Health rated 180 descriptive statements covering motives, defenses, thought processes, interpersonal patterns, affects and inner states. Of interest in the present context, participants who showed the greatest effects of subliminal stimuli were rated high on the "Receptivity to Inner Cues" scale, which consisted of items such as "Is highly given to inference – tries to figure out hidden meanings"; "Is intuitive, reaching conclusions without knowing why"; "Has vivid imagery." Subliminal sensitivity was negatively correlated with the following items: "Avoids and resists fantasy, clinging rigidly to reality"; "Use of repression"; "Fantasy life minimal and stereotyped."

Degree of subliminal sensitivity was also lawfully related to participants' reports of experiences in the sensory deprivation situation. Participants high in subliminal sensitivity tended to report pleasant affect, were more relaxed, and had fewer thoughts of quitting. Contrastingly, participants low in subliminal sensitivity tended to express more negative affect and reported significantly more thoughts about quitting.

## Research on the dynamic unconscious

In contrast to the descriptive unconscious, the dynamic unconscious implies opposing forces in the personality. More specifically, mental contents enmeshed in inner conflict are banned from consciousness by defense. Further, the situation is a dynamic rather than a static one in the sense that wishes and desires are constantly striving for discharge and for access to conscious awareness and motility; and defenses against these wishes and desires require "an uninterrupted expenditure of force" (Freud, 1915b, p. 151). Given this conception of the dynamic unconscious, it is apparent that most of the research described thus far deals mainly with the descriptive rather than the dynamic unconscious. There are, however, a number of studies that are relevant to the dynamic unconscious, and I want to at least briefly note here some examples of research in this area. As one might imagine, it is very difficult to devise and carry out experimental research on dynamic unconscious processes. This is at least partly so because the complex interaction between urges and defenses against them is an ongoing 'natural' process that is difficult to capture in the experimental laboratory. It is also difficult to capture and measure unconscious urges and fantasies. Often, the best one can do is investigate 'something like' the dynamic unconscious and infer certain phenomena and processes as well as the interaction between them. It is important to keep these limitations in mind in reviewing a few studies that bear some relevance to the dynamic unconscious.

Luborsky (1973) demonstrated that "momentary forgetting" in psychotherapy sessions was reliably preceded by conflictual and anxiety-provoking material; Luborsky, Blinder, and Schimek (1965) found that sexual visual material is associated with fewer eye fixations and poorer recall by participants identified as repressors; and Szalai and Eagle (1992) showed that participants who employ repressive defenses have more difficulty acquiring an aggressive concept in a concept formation task, which appears to be mediated by their tendency to avoid attending to the aggressive content in the stimuli. Thus, in all three studies, conflictual material was kept from awareness through the use of avoidant/repressive defenses.

In a study of more direct relevance to the dynamic unconscious, Adams, Wright, and Lohr (1996), demonstrated that in a sample of explicitly heterosexual men, compared to non-homophobic men, homophobic men showed a significantly greater increase in penile erection in response to male erotic homosexual stimuli. Further, whereas reports of subjective arousal were consistent with penile responses for non-homophobic men, for homophobic men this was not the case with regard to a homosexual video. The discrepancy appeared to be due to underestimates of arousal by the homophobic men.

An issue raised by the Adams et al. (1996) study is the status of the homophobic men's presumed repressed homosexual thoughts and feelings. Referring to them as repressed implies that they are 'deeply' unconscious and inaccessible to conscious awareness. However, it is entirely possible, even perhaps likely, that in viewing the homosexual video, the homophobic men more readily experienced anxiety-provoking homosexual thoughts and feelings that, like Lucy R., they pushed out of consciousness. Note that once again we confront issues of fleeting conscious awareness and reluctance to report versus unconscious and inaccessible.

In a study by Wolitzky, Klein, and Dworkin (1975), an attempt was made through hypnosis to create a conflict between the wish to be comforted and the sense that the wish was inappropriate. The results showed that compared to the control condition, participants in the conflict condition recalled fewer conflict words from a story read to them that contained the conflict theme. Also, in a word association task, galvanic skin responses (GSR) to the forgotten conflict words were of greater magnitude than non-conflict words. The authors conclude the participants in the conflict condition repressed the conflict words, and further, that the repressed conflict words continued to exert an influence on behavior as indicated by the GSR responses.

In two studies, Schmeing et al. (2013) reported that word associations accompanied by greater SCR magnitudes, longer reaction times, and activation of the anterior cingulated cortex were more likely to be subsequently forgotten. They interpret these results as indicating that words that elicit internal conflicts evoke a repressive "mechanism for avoiding conscious access to conflict-related material" (p. 9).

It is notable that with the exception of the Adams et al. (1996) study, in all the above studies, forgetting is the operational index for the unconscious status of a mental content. Further, the forgetting is assumed to be a *motivated* one, in particular, the motive to avoid conscious experience of conflictual material that would elicit negative affect. In the Adams et al. (1996) study, the discrepancy between self-report of low arousal and increases in penile erection is the basis for the inference that thoughts and feelings elicited by the erotic stimuli and that led to increases in penile erection were rendered unconscious. Whether or not this inference is justified, the study fits a later conception of the dynamic unconscious in which unacceptable contents such as erotic thoughts and feelings rather than memories are barred from conscious experience through the operation of defense.

One may refer to a dynamic unconscious not only in regard to wishes and desires, but also in regard to conflicting representations. There is inferential evidence that individuals who are classified as avoidant–dismissive on the Adult Attachment Interview (AAI) have conflicting internal working models (IWMs) of their parental figures. One model is conscious and idealized and the other, which is more realistic, is unconscious and defended against (e.g., Hesse, 2008, p. 565; Mikulincer & Shaver,

2008, p. 519). This conflict, however, is not one of impulses striving for expression and held down by counterforces, but one of certain information being kept from awareness, what Bowlby (1988) refers to as "defensive exclusion" (p. 35).

## Implications of research findings for psychoanalytic conceptions of unconscious processes

In important respects, the picture of unconscious processes and influences that emerges from the studies discussed in this chapter is quite different from psychoanalytic conceptions of these processes and influences. From a classical psychoanalytic perspective, the predominant image is that of the individual strongly influenced, at times buffeted about, by the inner forces of instinctually based motives, wishes, impulses, and fantasies of which he or she is unaware – lived by his id, as Groddeck (1923/1976) put it. Although in some contemporary psychoanalytic theories, these inner forces are representations and symbolic equivalences linked to early external events rather than instinctual wishes, both Freudian and contemporary psychoanalytic theories share the emphasis on the determining influences of inner forces acquired early in life on the subsequent trajectory of the individual's life.

The contrasting image that emerges from much current research on unconscious processes is that of individuals strongly influenced by external stimuli of which they are either unaware or, if aware of the stimuli, are unaware of their influence. Thus, if primed with words redolent of the elderly, he or she walks slower. If exposed to hot objects, he or she is warmer and more generous, and so on. As noted, there is no attention given in these studies to the question of individual meanings and associations given to elderly related words or to hot versus iced coffee. That is, there appears to be little concern with individual differences in psychic reality. From the psychoanalytic perspective, the assumption is made that inner processes, such as conflict, defenses, desires, fantasies, and one's idiosyncratic history will influence the meanings of and associations to external stimuli.These possibilities are not investigated in much of the research discussed. Instead, the implicit assumption made is that the external stimulus has the same meaning for all subjects and will influence their behavior in the same way.

The research findings on unconscious processes, some of which I have described, have been cited by some (e.g., Berlin, 2011; Luborsky & Barrett, 2006) as providing strong support for various aspects of Freudian theory of unconscious processes. However, let us take a careful and close look at the different components of this claim. The subliminal studies lend some weight to the claim that we are capable of unconsciously registering and processing a wider range of information than we may have thought possible. Also, with the very important caveat that reliability and replicability have yet to be clearly established, the findings reported by Bargh and his colleagues as well as those of other similar studies suggest that our behavior is constantly being influenced by stimuli without our awareness of the nature of the influence or even of the fact that we are being influenced. Both of these sets of findings tend to support the broad psychoanalytic claim that unconscious processes as well as their influences on our behavior are ubiquitous.

However, beyond that general claim, many of the empirical findings have only limited relevance to psychoanalytic theory. As noted, most of the studies carried out in this area deal with the processing and effects of *external* stimuli. The fact is, however, that psychoanalytic theory has relatively little to say about unconscious processes in relation to *external stimuli*. Freud (1900) assumed that insofar as perception of external stimuli served the main ego function of reality-testing in relation to the external world, the role of unconscious mental processes was minimal. In the language of ego psychology, perception is normally relatively autonomous, relatively uninfluenced by unconscious motives. The function of perception is to accurately represent external reality and it does so best when it operates relatively freely of unconscious motives. Somewhat paradoxically, perception serves drive gratification most effectively when it functions independently of unconscious drive influences; in short, as an ego function, the task of perception in reality-testing of the external world, which can only function properly when it is relatively impervious to unconscious factors.

I know of no post-Freudian or post-ego psychology 'schools' of psychoanalysis that pay much attention to the role of unconscious processing of external stimuli that are out of awareness. In short, the priming effects of external stimuli per se may not have direct relevance for psychoanalytic theory. However, the findings of these studies may have *indirect relevance* to psychoanalytic theory insofar as they speak to the capacities of unconscious processes. The reports of processing of subliminal stimuli to the level of semantic meaning as well as the findings that we can acquire 'rules' and algorithms without conscious awareness and along dimensions that are not accessible to conscious awareness support the claim that unconscious processing is not limited to 'dumb' and simple lower levels, as has been argued by some (e.g., Greenwald, 1992; Abrams & Greenwald, 2000), but can be 'smart' and complex. Thus, one can say that research findings on unconscious processes largely provide evidence for a descriptive rather than a "dynamic unconscious."

Of course, as Freud (1926) has noted, "an undesirable instinctual impulse [can be] aroused by some external perception" (p. 94). In accord with this idea, an assumption sometimes made by psychoanalytically oriented researchers on subliminal effects that would make their work more relevant to psychoanalytic theory is that subliminal stimuli trigger and even gratify unconscious wishes and fantasies and that the effects observed are mediated by the activation of unconscious fantasies and wishes (e.g., Silverman, 1979). But no evidence is presented in support of this assumption. Indeed, the reasoning is somewhat circular: how do you know that unconscious wishes and fantasies have been activated and gratified? Because of the effects of subliminal stimuli on behaviors such as symptom reduction or enhanced performance (Silverman & Weinberger, 1985). And what accounts for symptom reduction and enhanced performance? The activation and gratification of unconscious wishes and fantasies. Hence, we are left with data – interesting and important in themselves – suggesting that external stimuli that are exposed too quickly to be consciously perceived or reported can nevertheless be processed, it appears, at a semantic level and can influence subsequent behavior.

The finding that a negative subliminal stimulus (e.g., a fearful face) can acti vate the amygdala (e.g., Liddell et al., 2005) or trigger enhanced skin conductance response has been interpreted as providing support for Freud's concept of the dynamic unconscious (e.g., Berlin, 2011). However, although some findings can perhaps be interpreted as providing some indirect support for the psychoanalytic claim that an unconscious mental content can trigger something such as signal anxiety, what such findings do not show is that the signal anxiety, if it does occur, triggers a defense that prevents the mental content from reaching conscious awareness. It is, however, this latter component that is at the core of the concept of the dynamic unconscious. Hence, all that one concludes is that unconscious mental contents corresponding to an external subliminal stimulus (in contrast to an endogenous wish) elicit physiological, neural, and psychological responses.

The external versus the internal source of the mental content is of critical importance. Liddell et al. (2005) write that the response of the amygdala and other brain regions to the subliminal fearful face "may represent an evolutionary adaptive 'alarm' system for rapid alerting to sources of threat, without the need for conscious appraisal" (p. 235). They are obviously referring to external threat requiring action, not threat generated by an unacceptable wish or desire, which can be dealt with by repression or suppression. Under normal circumstances, it would hardly be adaptive to respond to an external threat requiring action by repressing or suppressing one's reaction to the threat.

We need to make a distinction between the unconscious processing of external stimuli that have been rendered unavailable to conscious experience through such external manipulations as brief exposure and masking, and unconscious processing of internal mental contents that have been rendered unavailable to conscious experience through the operation of defensive motives and processes. It is important to keep in mind that from a psychoanalytic perspective, unlike subliminal stimuli, unconscious desires and wishes are not inherently unavailable to conscious experience; they are *made* unavailable by motivated defense and would presumably be available to conscious experience were it not for active defensive processes. It is these phenomena that are of central interest to psychoanalysis. In the studies on unconscious processing of subliminal stimuli, the stimuli are made unavailable through manipulation of external conditions. Thus, once again, one has to conclude that these studies are primarily relevant to the 'descriptive unconscious,' rather than to the 'dynamic unconscious.'

There are two sets of studies that are, however, more pertinent to psychoanalytic theory: (1) those having to do with the implicit acquisition of 'rules' and algorithms; and (2) those having to do with the relationship between degree of awareness and attention and the organization of stimuli. The former is relevant to the contemporary psychoanalytic emphasis on the acquisition of 'rules' and representations in the course of development, as well as their influence on behavior, both without conscious awareness.

I refer here to the emphasis in contemporary psychoanalytic theory on the acquisition and effects of unconscious representations of parental figures, of self, and of prototypic interactions with parents. As we have seen earlier, examples include "internal working models" (IWMs) (Bowlby, 1980); "representations of interactions generalized" (RIGs) (Stern, 1985); "interactional structures" (Beebe & Lachmann, 2002); and "unconscious pathogenic beliefs" (Weiss & Sampson, 1986). For each of these concepts, the assumption is made that the representations that are formed are unconscious, or perhaps one should say, implicit. Without necessarily knowing that one has done so, one forms representations – or perhaps one should say algorithms – that reflect an abstracting out of prototypic interactions and experiences.

These representations can include such 'cold' scripts as going to a restaurant or 'hot' scripts such as what happens when I try to have my attachment needs met. What distinguishes the 'cold' and 'hot' scripts from each other is the facts that, one, the latter entail vital interactions with parental and other significant figures; and two, are likely to entail strong affects. One important implication of these facts is that the unconscious or implicit status of 'hot' representations or scripts that are formed is not likely to be simply a product of straightforward implicit learning, but is likely to include various motives, including defensive motives.

Ironically it appears that, in general, studies that deal with the unconscious effects of fully supraliminal stimuli seem to be of greater relevance to psychoanalytic theory and practice and have greater ecological validity than studies of unconscious processing of external subliminal stimuli. The former studies include evidence, illustrated for example by the work of Lewicki and his colleagues, that one forges connections among stimuli without conscious awareness that one has done so. They also include evidence of different principles of organization as a function of implicit versus explicit processing. And finally, the work of Nisbett and his colleagues (e.g., Nisbett & Wilson, 1977) demonstrates that, unaware of the factors that have influenced his or her behavior, the individual supplies plausible reasons, based on mini-causal theories that can be shown not to be the actual reasons. From a psychoanalytic perspective, the findings of these studies not only suggest the ubiquitousness of unconscious processes, but are far more relevant to psychoanalytic theory than the findings of subliminal studies that require contrived circumstances that one is not very likely to encounter in one's daily life.

## *Personal versus subpersonal processes*

The following considerations point to further complexities inherent in relating empirical research findings on unconscious processes to psychoanalytic theory. As the use of the language of desires, fantasies, wishes, etc. indicates, unconscious mental states were viewed by Freud (1923, pp. 13–14), as "personal-level" phenomena (Dennett, 1969, ch. 4). That is, in O'Brien and Jureidini's (2002) words, "they apply to the whole person rather than the cognitive and perceptual parts from which they are made" (p. 143). This conception of unconscious processes is radically different from a computational unconscious that is at the center of contemporary cognitive psychology.

Underlying many forms of intelligent behavior and experience (e.g., perception; understanding sentences) are unconscious processes that entail complex interactions among representations. These computational processes consist in modular operations distributed across the brain. That is, they are "sub-personal" (Dennett, 1969, ch. 4) rather than personal-level phenomena such as desires, beliefs, etc. Further, these representations are unconscious, not as a function of countervailing forces and motives, but as a result of the "computational architecture of the brain" (O'Brien & Jureidini, 2002, p. 146; see also Fodor, 1983).

Because these processes appear so intelligent and thought-like, we tend to attribute to them person-like capacities and describe them as a homunculus doing things such as making unconscious inferences. However, these computational processes are nevertheless subpersonal rather than "personal-level" phenomena. In contrast, the unconscious desires, beliefs, fantasies, etc. of interest to psychoanalytic theory refer to personal–level phenomena in the sense that only persons – not parts of persons – have desires, beliefs, fantasies, etc. As O'Brien and Jureidini (2002) put it, desires, etc. apply to "the whole person rather than the cognitive and perceptual parts from which they are made" (p. 143). We recognize that only persons rather than parts of persons can have conscious desires, beliefs, and fantasies. Further, if as Freud (1915, p. 168) tells us, unconscious desires are not essentially different from conscious desires save for the fact that they are not in conscious awareness, one would have to conclude that at least from a Freudian perspective, only persons, not parts of persons, can have unconscious desires, etc.

Although we may have little choice but to employ personal-level terms in referring to unconscious wishes, desires, and fantasies, as Rubinstein (1997) has observed, these terms are proto-neurological ones in the sense that they refer to brain states. However, unlike the brain states associated with cognitive computational processes, which are inaccessible to consciousness, the assumption is made that the experiences linked to brain states referred to by a term such as unconscious desire are potentially recoverable in consciousness.

Perhaps we should make a distinction between an unconscious computational *process* and an unconscious mental *state*. As has been noted by many, the way our brains work is that we are generally aware of the *product* 'produced' by *processes* of which we are unaware. For example, we consciously experience *percepts*, not the unconscious computational processes that generate the percepts. Furthermore, as noted, however intelligent and thought-like they may be, these computational processes consist in subpersonal processes and modular operations that are 'impenetrable' to consciousness.

The situation is not essentially different in the case of consciously experiencing a desire or fantasy, save that it involves inner rather than external stimuli. That is, just as is the case with a perception of an external object, so it is also the case that when we experience a conscious desire, we are consciously aware only of the *product*, the desire, not of the *processes* that generated the desire. Analogously to the unconscious and 'impenetrable' computational processes that 'produce' a conscious percept corresponding to an external object, there are undoubtedly unconscious and 'impenetrable' processes that generate a consciously experienced desire. Whereas the 'raw materials' for the computational processes that generate the percept are physical stimuli from the external world, the 'raw materials' for the processes that generate a conscious desire are bodily states. And their associated meanings.

From the above perspective, an unconscious mental state is a brain state that can influence behavior in various ways and, particularly important, has the capacity to generate conscious mental states such as desire. From this perspective, when we attribute an unconscious mental state to another, we are essentially employing a marker for a brain state that can influence the individual's behavior without his or her awareness and that can generate a particular conscious mental state. In an important sense, to attribute an unconscious mental state, such as an unconscious desire, to another or to oneself is to point to an unconscious *process* that has the capacity to generate the *product* of a consciously experienced desire.

Hence, in making the unconscious conscious, we are not making an unconscious desire conscious – one that has been there all along waiting to be uncovered (see Mitchell, 1998). That is because there is no such entity as an unconscious desire that is identical to a conscious desire. Rather, in accord with Rubinstein's (and Searle's) formulations, what are referred to as unconscious desires are neural processes that influence our behavior in various ways and that have the capacity to generate conscious desires. And even that description is too simple to be adequate. For the experience of any mental content is not an all-or-none matter, but one of degree of awareness as well as degree along other properties and dimensions such as clarity, articulation, verbal labeling, avowal in consciousness, personal import, duration, spelled out, and so on. Of course, underlying everything we do and feel and think are neural processes. But it is not the neural processes that do and think and feel. To formulate neural processes as thinking, etc. is to confuse levels of discourse and to be guilty of a category error.

Freud's struggle with the issue of subpersonal versus personal-level phenomena is reflected in the ongoing tension in the corpus of his work between what has come to be known as his clinical versus his metapsychological theories and perspectives (see Holt, 1976). As Rubinstein (1997) has shown, the two perspectives are far more interrelated than the critics of Freud's metapsychology have recognized. However, my intention is not to revisit that debate, but to point to the ongoing tension in Freud's theorizing as well as his struggle to understand the relationship between formulations in terms of persons feeling, thinking, and doing things and formulations in terms of the complex interplay of impersonal and subpersonal forces and energies. One can gain an important insight into Freud's work by recognizing that he was constantly struggling to understand the relationship between, in Ricoeur's (1970) words, meaning and mechanism. Further, of all of Freud's central formulations, the concept of unconscious processes is located somewhere between meaning and mechanism.

## Summary and conclusions

### *Concluding comments*

All the material discussed in this and the previous chapter – research findings, clinical evidence, conceptual critiques, and new theoretical developments – warrant the following conclusions regarding the psychoanalytic concept of unconscious mental processes:

1) Despite some cogent critiques of subliminal studies, there is a good deal of evidence that unconscious processing, including processing at the semantic level, can occur. These findings provide support for Freud's claim that mental processing of a relatively sophisticated nature can occur without conscious awareness. However, although such evidence provides support for the positing of a 'descriptive unconscious,' it does not speak directly to the positing of a 'dynamic unconscious.'

That a subliminal stimulus that is consciously experienced, at best, as a flash of light can prime behavior indicating that what was consciously experienced as a flash of light has nevertheless been processed to the semantic level is, at least to me, quite remarkable, and raises questions regarding how such processing occurs. Insofar as the person who is presented the subliminal stimulus is not aware of processing any content (beyond a flash of light), the findings of subliminal studies appear to support a modular theory of mind. That is, the processing of the subliminal stimulus appears to be carried out by a module of the mind unlinked to agency and subjectivity. Although the positing of a module that is capable of as sophisticated a task as semantic encoding raises the specter of the homunculus problem (and a clever homunculus at that), I do not see any clear alternative that would adequately account for the findings of subliminal studies.

2) Most contemporary cognitive psychologists would agree with Freud that the major part of mental life goes on outside awareness. However, here too, the focus is on the 'descriptive unconscious' rather than the 'dynamic unconscious.' A further distinction needs to be made between 'penetrable' and 'impenetrable' unconscious processes. Many of the unconscious computational processes that underlie our conscious experiences, for example, the inference-like unconscious processes underlying the experience of size constancy, are 'impenetrable,' that is, inherently inaccessible to conscious awareness. Although 'intelligent,' there would be no uniform agreement that these processes can be rightfully viewed as *mental* processes.

3) Supraliminal incidental or background external stimuli can also influence our behavior without our awareness of the nature of the influence or even of the fact that they are exerting an influence. What makes these findings of some interest to psychoanalysis is the fact that it is the *associative meanings* of these incidental stimuli rather than their literal denotative meanings that appear to exert the influence. This is clear in the Pine studies discussed earlier but, although perhaps less obvious, is

also the case in later studies. For example, that handling and drinking a cup of hot coffee leads to a judgment of a target individual as more positive (assuming such results can be replicated) is obviously due to the connotative associative meanings (e.g., warm, generous) elicited by the cup of hot coffee. Although the associative meanings may be outside awareness, they are likely to be readily accessible to conscious awareness when attention is directed to them. Hence, from a psychoanalytic perspective, they can be viewed as preconscious rather than unconscious. Thus, once again, the findings in this area are relevant to a discussion of the descriptive rather than the dynamic unconscious.

4) There is a good deal of evidence that we acquire 'rules' and algorithms that influence our behavior without awareness that we are employing them. We also categorize stimuli along dimensions of which we are unaware. Further, quite often we are unable to identify the nature of the 'rules' and algorithms we are following or the dimensions along which we categorize stimuli.

These findings are especially relevant to such contemporary psychoanalytic concepts as unconscious pathogenic beliefs, internal working models (IWMs), and representations of interactions generalized (RIGs). That is, based on repeated interactions with parental figures, the child (and the adult) abstracts out 'rules' and expectations, often not in awareness, regarding the behavior of significant others. Although dynamic factors may be present (e.g., the need to have an idealized image of parents), the unconscious status of these representations is largely due to implicit learning and, to lesser extent, to defensive exclusion. Hence, once again, these findings have more to do with the descriptive than the dynamic unconscious.

5) There is evidence that level of awareness and attention influences the dimensions along which we organize stimuli. Although the research in this area deals mainly with non-affective stimuli, the findings are relevant to psychoanalytic hypotheses regarding different organization (i.e., primary versus secondary process organization) as a function of level of awareness and level of attention.

6) The picture that emerges from many of the above studies discussed is that of the individual somewhat at the mercy of influence from *external* stimuli of which s/he is unaware. This is the reverse of the Freudian image of the individual who is subject to the pervasive influence of *inner* stimuli such as wishes, desires, and fantasies, of which s/he is unaware. Quite fittingly perhaps for twenty-first century America, the individual of Freudian theory – the one who, in Groddeck's (1923/1976) words, is lived by his id – is replaced by the individual of social psychology, the individual whose behavior is constantly being influenced by the array of external stimuli s/he confronts. Thus, the analyst who could understand the dark recesses of the other's mind has been partly replaced by the experimental psychologist who is an expert on how external stimuli influence one's feelings, thoughts, and behavior without one's awareness.

7) There is relatively little research relevant to the dynamic unconscious. The few studies that have been carried out demonstrate poorer recall of stimuli associated with conflict or threat, which is largely a function of deployment of attention; and dissociation between self-report (e.g., of sexual arousal) and non-verbal indices (e.g., penile erection). All this research deals with external stimuli rather than inner wishes and desires. The assumption is made in some studies that the external stimuli (e.g., the picture of a nude woman in the Luborsky et al. (1965) study and the erotic stimuli in the Adam et al. (1996) study) elicit inner mental contents and affective reactions (e.g., anxiety) that, in turn, result in either forgetting of the stimuli (as in the Luborsky (1973) and the Wolitzky et al. (1975) studies) or in defensive denial of threatening affective reactions evoked by the stimuli (as in the denial of sexual arousal in the Adams et al. (1996) study).

However, in order to link these studies more directly relevantly to the dynamic unconscious, one needs to demonstrate not only that the external stimuli presented are conflictual and elicit implicit negative affective responses (as reflected, for example, in increased SCR), but also that unconscious defensive measures have been taken by the individual to keep mental contents and their associated negative affects from being consciously experienced. This is not uniformly demonstrated in the studies discussed. Thus, in the Wolitzky et al. (1975) study, it may simply be the case that anxiety tends to disrupt recall. This parsimonious explanation does not require the assumption that the poorer recall of the anxiety-laden words is due to a *motivated defensive forgetting*. As for the Adams et al. (1996) study, the dissociation between self-report of sexual arousal and penile erection may not be due to repression of sexual feelings, but failure to acknowledge sexual arousal to the experimenter and/or oneself. Indeed, this could be a conscious, even if perhaps fleetingly conscious, defensive strategy having more to do with the *report* of one's mental contents than with unconsciously banning these mental contents from conscious awareness.

In short, the most one can say is that the studies I have described are relevant to 'something like' or an altered version of the dynamic unconscious. The findings of these studies certainly do not support the classical formulation that infantile sexual and aggressive wishes are banned from conscious awareness by a mechanism (i.e., repression) that is, itself, inaccessible to conscious awareness. Indeed, there is no good evidence for this formulation in regard to *any* unacceptable mental contents. A more plausible account of how we keep from experiencing and acknowledging conflictual and threatening mental contents is provided by concepts such as not spelling out (Fingarette, 1963) and failing to formulate (Stern, 2003).

8) There is a radical de-emphasis of the "cornerstone" concept of repression and correspondingly, of deeply buried instinctually derived unconscious impulses, wishes, desires, and fantasies. To a large extent, this is the product of a corresponding de-emphasis in contemporary psychoanalytic formulations on Freud's drive theory.

9) There has been an increased emphasis on unconscious representations that are unconscious, not primarily by virtue of repression, but largely because they have been acquired early in life, often pre-verbally. Indeed, it would be more accurate to refer to these representations as implicit and as a kind of learning without awareness – as in Lyons-Ruth's (1999) concept of "implicit relational knowing" – rather than unconscious as in repressed.

10) The emphasis on the implicit rather than the repressed unconscious is also reflected in accounts of the motivated failure to articulate one's thoughts, feelings, and intentions and one's motives for doing certain things. One implication of this view is that one's unarticulated motives and other mental contents may be fleetingly experienced in consciousness rather than deeply repressed – much like Lucy R.'s description of her experience and much like the description of unconscious processes in the exchange between Anna Freud and Sandler noted earlier. It turns out that William James' (1890) emphasis on fleeting and momentary consciousness is alive and well in contemporary developments.

11) The issue of fleeting consciousness versus the deeply repressed arises in another context. A topic remarkably absent, even in the literature of relational psychoanalysis, is what I refer to as the *interpersonalizing* of the unconscious. That is, although closely linked, there is a distinction to be made between what one will tell oneself and what one will tell others.

12) For a long time, psychoanalysis was referred to and referred to itself as a *depth* psychology. As Wachtel (2003) has observed, we use the metaphors of surface and depth to equate surface with superficial and depth with profound. During the heyday of psychoanalysis, analysts traded on these metaphors by presenting themselves as *mensch kenners* who could read the depths of the individual's mind, regions where the individual himself or herself could not go. Hence, the idea that what was referred to as repressed may, in fact, be fleetingly available to consciousness had to be a threat to the image of the analyst as someone with a special mind-reading capacity, as someone who does not deal with surface phenomena (read superficial) but with deep and dark phenomena.

One contemporary development in psychoanalysis is an increasing emphasis on more surface phenomena. This is especially evident in the "close process monitoring" approach of Paul Gray and his colleagues (e.g., Gray, 2005). It is also implicit, I believe, in the contemporary emphasis on the transference–countertransference choreography between patient and analyst. Interpretations and attention are directed toward material just below the surface rather than to presumably deeply buried repressed contents. In this approach, much of the material addressed may be fleetingly experienced and pushed out of awareness or, indeed, may be consciously available but not communicated.There is an interesting disconnect between, on the one hand, descriptions of clinical work that focus on relatively surface, that is, at least fleetingly feelings and thoughts available to the patient and, on the other hand, theoretical accounts that refer to deeply buried mental contents and processes inaccessible to conscious experience.

13) An early emphasis on uncovering repressed mental contents as an overarching process goal has essentially been replaced by the goals of understanding how one's mind works and by enhancing the patient's capacity to reflect on his or her mental states and those of others with whom he or she interacts.

14) There is relatively little research on the axiomatic psychoanalytic claim that unconscious dynamic processes and psychopathology are inextricably linked, specifically, that unconscious processes play a causal role in psychopathology. The only studies I can think of that are somewhat relevant to this claim are those that show that labeling as well as cortical processing can inhibit amygdala activation in response to negative stimuli, which suggests that putting feelings into words can serve to inhibit negative affect.

Although there is evidence that a "repressive style" exacts costs, there is also evidence demonstrating its benefits. As I have suggested elsewhere (Eagle, 2011a) the positive link between unconscious processes and psychopathology and the corollary identification of making the unconscious conscious as an overriding therapeutic goal may be as much a reflection of the Enlightenment roots of psychoanalysis as conclusions warranted by clinical research evidence.

Finally, it may be the case that to the extent that the unconscious status of mental states is linked to psychopathology, it is largely due to the fact that these mental states are not integrated into the personality rather than to their unconscious status per se.

## Overall conclusions

The pervasive role of unconscious process and contents in mental life is almost always seen as the hallmark of psychoanalytic theory. And indeed, research on unconscious processes tends to support this general idea. However, most of the research on unconscious processes is not especially relevant to distinctive psychoanalytic claims that are inherent in the concept of the dynamic unconscious, including the "cornerstone" concept of repression or in the inextricable link between unconscious processes and psychopathology. Ironically, Freud's formulations of the descriptive unconscious are far more relevant to contemporary cognitive theory and research. These formulations include the ubiquitousness of unconscious processes, the claim that the unconscious is the true psychic reality, the radical idea that the essence of the mental is somatic, and the corresponding implications that representationality and intentionality, not consciousness, are the essence of the mental and that brain states have representational capacities. Indeed, as noted in Chapter 1, Wakefield (1992; 2001) has argued that in articulating these foundational ideas, Freud can rightfully be seen as the father of contemporary cognitive theory.

## Notes

1 Of course, one also wants to understand the influence of patient cues on the therapist's thoughts, feelings, and behavior. The bi-directional nature of cues communicated between patient and therapist is discussed in the psychoanalytic literature under the rubric of transference–countertransference interactions as well as so-called projective identification. These topics are discussed in later chapters.

2 It will be recalled that the sudden emergence of a solution to a problem after a period of not thinking about it was taken by Freud as evidence of unconscious thought (see Wakefield, 1992; 2001).

# 3

# THE OEDIPUS COMPLEX

## Does the Oedipus complex exist?

### Introduction

The main issue I address in this chapter is the question of the evidence for the existence of a universal Oedipus complex, defined by Freud (1900, p. 262) as incestuous wishes toward the opposite sex parent and rivalrous and hostile wishes toward the same sex parent. Although the existence of a universal Oedipus complex may no longer be uniformly posited as a core assumption of all psychoanalytic "schools," there is little doubt that it occupied a central place in Freudian theory and continues to occupy a central place for many analysts. Freud (1905) writes: "With the progress of psychoanalytic studies the importance of the Oedipus complex has become more and more clearly evident; its recognition has become the shibboleth that distinguishes the adherents of psychoanalysis from its opponents" (p. 226, fn. 1, added in 1920). He also writes: "I venture to say that if psychoanalysis could boast of no other achievement than the discovery of the repressed Oedipus complex, that alone would give it a claim to be included among the precious new acquisitions of mankind" (Freud, 1940[1938], pp. 292–293). For many years, acceptance of the assumption of the universality of the Oedipus complex, along with the positing of its central role in the development of neurosis, gender identity, the formation of the superego, and the degree of integration between love and sexual desire was viewed by many in the psychoanalytic establishment as an essential bona fide for being seen as a true analyst (Simon, 1991).

As for contemporary psychoanalytic theorists, in a recent issue of an Italian psychoanalytic journal, *Psicoterapia e scienze umane*, leading psychoanalysts were asked to respond to 13 questions regarding the current status and future of psychoanalysis. One of those questions concerned the respondents' views regarding the centrality of the Oedipus complex for current psychoanalytic theory. The majority of respondents, who represented a variety of theoretical approaches, stated that they continued to view the Oedipus complex as a core aspect of psychoanalytic theory.

Debates about the Oedipus complex, particularly the question of its universality, also have a long history in anthropological studies highlighted by the work of Malinowski (1927) in the Trobriand Islands, who questioned the universality of the Oedipus complex and the critiques of his conclusions by Jones (1952) and Roheim (1950) (see also Kardiner, 1939). The debate has continued long past the early work of Malinowski and others. In 1982, Spiro, a psychoanalytically oriented anthropologist, published a book in which he reanalyzed Malinowski's data and concluded that the Oedipus complex is even stronger in the Trobriand Islands than in the West.

A voluminous literature, primarily in anthropological, but also in psychoanalytic, journals, on various issues related to the Oedipus complex continues to the present day. It is impossible to cover all this material, past and present, in a single chapter. Instead, this chapter will provide a general assessment of the concept of the Oedipus complex in the light of the available evidence and the critical discussions that have taken place.

The chapter is organized as follows: I begin with a description of the Oedipus complex in classical theory followed by eight arguments presented for its presumed universality. I then discuss the Westermarck hypothesis, the clearest alternative to the theory of a universal Oedipus complex. This is followed by a consideration of the proposition of classical psychoanalytic theory that how the individual resolves oedipal conflicts is a powerful determinant of important aspects of psychological development. The topic of oedipal betrayal, a less frequently commented on aspect of the Oedipus complex is then discussed. This section is followed by a discussion of the presumed evolved function of the Oedipus complex and the presumed relationship between oedipal betrayal and the Oedipus complex. I conclude that, whereas there is much evidence for a universal incest *taboo*, there is little or no evidence for the claim of the existence of universal incestuous and death wishes. I also conclude that alternative theoretical formulations of phenomena, such as the split between love and desire and so-called castration anxiety, that have been attributed to the Oedipus complex, are more parsimonious and more in accord with the evidence. One of these formulations accords a central role to the separability and partial antagonism between the attachment and sexual systems in accounting for the split between love and desire and in contributing to mate selection. Another formulation, Control–Mastery theory, accounts for certain phenomena (for example, as guilt and fear of punishment in relation to ambitious strivings) described as castration anxiety as at least partly attributable to parental communications rather than to oedipal incestuous and hostile wishes. Finally, I discuss reconceptualizations of the Oedipus complex that essentially redefine it in terms of strivings for separation and autonomy rather than incestuous and hostile wishes.

## The nature of the Oedipus complex

The Oedipus complex includes the following components: universal incestuous wishes toward the opposite sex parent and rivalrous and hostile wishes toward the same sex parent; the incest taboo; castration anxiety; choice of mate based on a template of a parental figure; and the claim that how the individual resolves oedipal conflicts plays a determinative role in psychological development, including sexual identity, superego formation, and the capacity to integrate love and desire.

The broader theoretical context for the Oedipus complex includes Freud's conception of the sexual instinct, his theory of infantile sexuality and psychosexual development, and his account of the basis for infant–mother attachment. Freud assumed that infantile sexuality is a universal feature of psychosexual development. More specifically, he maintained that the pleasures linked to the erogenous zones are essentially sexual in nature. According to Freud, in the course of psychosexual development, the child finds the caregiver as an object of sexual desire (Freud, 1905, p. 272) who, in the course of her ministrations has provided "an unending source of sexual excitation" (Freud, 1905, p. 223). He also assumed that psychosexual development follows a regular progression, marked by the salience of different erotogenic zones (i.e., oral, anal, phallic). According to this scheme, the culmination of psychosexual development in childhood is the phallic stage and the emergence of the Oedipus complex.

Freud (1915a) maintained that initially the sexual instinct does not have an object. He writes: "[The object] is what is most variable about an instinct and is not originally connected with it, but becomes assigned to it only in consequence of being peculiarly fitted to make satisfaction possible" (p. 122). Indeed, Freud (1915a) defined the object as "the thing in regard to which or through which the instinct achieves its aim" (p. 122). Insofar as mother is the object who is most intimately linked to the pleasures of infantile sexuality, she becomes the first love object for the infant. This happens early in the infant's life prior to the oedipal stage. However, during the preoedipal period, the infant's libidinal tie to the love object is based on oral and anal pleasures. It is only during the phallic stage that incestuous wishes emerge. Hence, on this view, given the unfolding of psychosexual development to include the phallic stage and given the fact that caregiving entails prolonged ministrations of a sensual nature, incestuous desires are inevitable.

Although there is evidence for the existence of infantile sexuality in primates and the human infant, it does not tend to support the specifically Freudian account of psychosexual development. For example, infant chimpanzees mount mother when her estrus cycle returns and male infants can have erections and even appear to reach orgasm while feeding (Ingham & Spain, 2005). According to the Freudian account of psychosexual development, however, early on infantile sexuality is oral and anal, not phallic or genital, the latter not emerging until the oedipal stage at 4 to 6 years of age. Thus, it is difficult to say what the implications are of the findings that male infants may have erections while feeding for Freud's theory of the Oedipus complex, in particular, for the hypothesis of universal incestuous wishes.

In an important sense, in the Freudian account of the Oedipus complex, incestuous wishes are primary and hostile wishes are secondary. For, according to this view, in the mind of the Oedipal child, the source of hostile wishes toward the same sex parent is that that parent, as a rival, stands in the way of gratifying incestuous wishes. Were that not the case, there would be less reason for the child's hostile wishes toward the same sex parent.[1] (As we will see, this is much clearer in the case of the boy and murkier in the case of the girl.) The point here is that in debates on the Oedipus complex, there is a good reason to focus on claims of universal incestuous wishes and the incest taboo as the critical components of the Oedipus complex. Given the forbidden nature of both incestuous and hostile wishes, the Oedipus complex entails intense conflicts. More specifically, given punitive and disapproving parental responses expressions of these forbidden wishes evoke, they trigger castration anxiety as well as anxieties linked to the other "danger situations," including loss of the object and loss of the object's love (Freud, 1926a).

According to classical theory, how one resolves Oedipal conflicts plays a key role not only in the individual's capacity to libidinally cathect an "extraneous object" outside the family, but also in the formation of gender identity, superego structure, development of neurosis, and object choice. According to this theory, in normal development, the oedipal boy not only relinquishes incestuous wishes in the face of castration anxiety, but also "identifies with the aggressor," thus contributing to male identity. Another presumed outcome of such identification is the creation of the superego. In that sense, the superego is "the heir to the Oedipus complex" (Freud, 1923, p. 48). As for the relationship between the Oedipus complex and psychopathology, Freud (1926b) writes that "It became ever clearer that the [Oedipus complex] was the nucleus of every case of neurosis" (p. 198), one feature of which is a relative failure to integrate love and desire. As for the Freudian view of the choice of mate, although an adequate resolution of the Oedipus complex entails relinquishment of incestuous wishes and libidinally cathecting an "extraneous object" outside the family, the enduring influence and reach of the Oedipus complex are seen in the fact that for all men, mother remains the template for all future love objects. I will return to this topic later in the chapter.

## Arguments for the universality of incestuous wishes

There are at least 11 different arguments presented in support of the claim that incestuous wishes are a universal aspect of development:

1. There would be no need for a powerful incest taboo were it not for the existence of equally powerful universal incestuous wishes.
2. Mother's sensual gratification of erogenous zones makes her a 'natural' incestuous object during the oedipal stage of psychosexual development.
3. Freud's interpretation of patients' presumed reports of actual seduction by family members as seduction fantasies.
4. Freud's 'discovery' of components of the Oedipus complex in his self-analysis.
5. Widespread legends and myths with presumed oedipal content.
6. The argument that erotic desire is characterized by a "sense of transgression" that is derived from overcoming of oedipal prohibitions (Kernberg, 1995).
7. The claim that choice of mate is based on a template of the opposite sex parent.

8. The claim that the commonly observed split between love and desire is attributable to the persistence of incestuous wishes.
9. Castration anxiety as a reaction to death wishes toward the same sex parent.
10. Anecdotal reports of little boys wanting to marry Mommy and little girls wanting to marry Daddy.
11. One could also add Freud's (1909) universalization of the case of Little Hans (who he refers to as "a little Oedipus who wanted to have his father 'out of the way', to get rid of him, so that he might be alone with his beautiful mother and sleep with her" (p. 111)) as a source of evidence appealed to by him to support his argument for the universality of incestuous wishes and the Oedipus complex. However, see Wakefield (2007a,b,c) who obtained new material on Little Hans from the Freud Archives and who presents a highly convincing case that Little Hans' phobia is better explained by appeal to attachment theory rather than to oedipal theory.

Let us examine each of these arguments:

## *1. There would be no need for an incest taboo were there not universal incestuous wishes*

Instead of presenting direct evidence, the standard psychoanalytic argument has been that the very presence of a powerful and universal cultural incest taboo is sufficient ground for inferring the existence of equally universal and powerful incestuous wishes that the taboo is intended to keep in check. His reasoning is that "it would not be clear why such severe prohibitions [i.e., the incest taboo] were called for, which would point rather to the presence of a strong desire for it" (Freud, 1916–1917, p. 210).

> Such an inexorable prohibition of it in law and custom would not be needed if there were any reliable natural barriers against the temptation of incest. The truth is just the opposite. A human being's first choice of an object is regularly an incestuous one, aimed in the case of the male, at his mother and sister.
>
> (Freud, 1917/1916–17, pp. 334–335)

The same argument is spelled out later by Lindzey (1967) who writes:

> One may argue persuasively that the mere universal existence of the incest taboo, together with the powerful effects of emotions that are associated with its violation, constitute convincing evidence for the existence of a set of general tendencies that are being denied. It seems unlikely that there would have been universal selection in favor of such a taboo if there were not rather widespread impulses toward expression of the prohibition.
>
> (p. 1055)

The argument that there would be no universal and powerful incest taboo were there not universal and powerful incestuous wishes against which the taboo operates is, I believe, a faulty one. One effective rejoinder to this argument is that the role of the incest taboo is not to guard against powerful incestuous wishes, but to bolster innately backed incest avoidance mechanisms (Bixler, 1981; Van den Berghe, 1990). It seems highly unlikely that evolution would have selected for desires against which we need to defend and that seem to offer no selective advantage. Also, that we have universal taboos against, say, suicide or murder or eating feces does not constitute adequate evidence for positing universal suicidal or murderous impulses or universal urges to eat feces (Eagle, 2007a). As Fox (1980) points out, "we need not assume that we have laws against murder because we all have murderous natures, but only because some murder occurs and we don't like that" (p. 8).

"Similarly, one would say that we have an incest taboo not because we all have incestuous natures, but because the cost of even *some* incest is to be avoided." Fox observes that "there are many tribes and nations . . . that do not effectively punish either, but that are not overwhelmed with incest or murder" (p. 7). He suggests that the proper question is not, "Why do human beings not commit incest?" but "Why do human beings not *want* [italics added] to commit incest all that much?" (p. 7). Fox goes on to observe with regard to incest that "*unease* and *avoidance* seem to be the common denominators – not fierce sanctions or lust reined in by the power of taboo" (p. 9). And, as Pinker (2009) comments in regard to the claim that the experience of very strong discomfort when one imagines incest suggests a repressed desire: "By that reasoning we may conclude that people have an unconscious desire to eat dog feces and stick needles in their eyes" (p. 456).

Of course, Freud would counter that one finds unease and avoidance and not fierce *conscious* incestuous desire because such desire has been defended against and thus has become unconscious. Indeed, just as Lindzey (1967) does, Freud would take the general unease and avoidance in response to incest as *betraying* unconscious incestuous desire. But this does not take one very far in responding to the challenge of presenting more direct evidence for the claim that powerful incestuous wishes and impulses – even if unconscious ones – are universal.

Freud assumed that whereas incestuous wishes are universal across cultures and species, the incest taboo was a uniquely human cultural product. He was not aware and could not be aware at the time he wrote that incest avoidance is also characteristic of animal species.[2] Freud's view of things fit very well with his general conception of human nature as made up of primitive drive-related impulses kept in check by an overlay of internalized social prohibitions. Thus, like other animals, we too harbor incestuous impulses. But unlike other animals, these impulses are kept in check by the forces of civilization. This view was held not only by Freud, but by many others. Indeed, the great anthropologist Lévi-Strauss (1949/1969) viewed the incest taboo as a prime example of the entry of human culture into biology. He writes: "Before it [i.e., the incest taboo], culture is still non-existent; with it, nature's sovereignty over man is ended. The prohibition of incest is where nature transcends itself" (Levi-Strauss, 1949/1969, pp. 30–31). However, that is not the way things are. If anything, one needs to turn Freud's and Lévi-Strauss' argument on its head and reverse their proposal that incestuous wishes are biologically given and that the incest taboo is a culturally imposed restraint. There is much evidence that it is incest avoidance that is biologically based (i.e., the product of natural selection), whereas incestuous desires and actions, when they do occur, appear to be the product of environmental factors such as dysfunctional families and maladaptive child-rearing. For example, Erikson (1993) reported that incestuous wishes are present mainly in children who have experienced disruptive bonding.

## *2. Mother's gratification of erogenous zones*

From the perspective of Freudian psychosexual theory, because mother's ministrations entail gratification of the infant's erogenous zones, it is natural that during the course of psychosexual development, when the child reaches the phallic stage, his phallic impulses will be directed toward mother in the form of incestuous wishes. If one accepts the Freudian theory of psychosexual development, this is perhaps a plausible implication, one that constitutes a basis for positing the inevitable emergence of the Oedipus complex.

There is little doubt that the caregiver's ministrations, including feeding, changing diapers, bathing, and so on, entail sensual pleasures for the infant. In that sense, mother's ministrations introduce the infant into the world of bodily sensuality. It is, therefore, perhaps plausible to hypothesize that mother constitutes a template for an object who provides sensual pleasures.

However, there is a great and problematic distance from the recognition that mother is the first object who provides sensual pleasures to the assumption of an Oedipus complex at the center of which are incestuous wishes (see G. S. Klein's (1976) suggestion that one replace "infantile sexuality" with "infantile sensuality"). One needs some kind of reliable evidence to support that claim.

Another serious problem with Freud's formulation is that according to its logic, insofar as mother provides early sensual pleasures for females as well as males, one would expect that for both genders mother should be the object of incestuous desires. We know, as Freud did, that that is not the case. According to Freudian theory, it is father who is the incestuous object desire for heterosexual girls. And to account for that presumed fact, Freud (1924, pp. 177–179) weaves a complex and arbitrary narrative involving the girl's anger at mother for bringing her into the world without a penis and developing the fantasy of having a baby with father as a substitute for the absent penis. The just-so and arbitrary nature of this story, in effect renders the Oedipus complex inapplicable to half of humankind. Thus, oedipal theory is essentially a theory of male psychosexual development – and a problematic one at that.

Finally, as the child develops beyond infancy, the sensual pleasures associated with early ministrations become less central. The primary developmental challenges and tasks confronting the child now include exploration, separation–individuation, relatedness, and autonomy. And the corresponding role that mother (as well as father) now need to play includes the provision of a safe haven and a secure base for exploration. It is just as plausible – indeed, more plausible given the evidence of attachment research – to hypothesize that the figures who carry out these functions contribute to the child's template for an object who serves similar functions.

## 3. Reports of seduction

Freud's understanding of presumed reports by patients of seduction by family members as seduction fantasies rather than actual seduction hardly constitutes an adequate ground for positing universal incestuous wishes. Even if these seduction reports did actually occur – which is highly questionable – one could hardly legitimately universalize on the basis of a handful of patients – a disturbing tendency of Freud's. There are, however, additional problems with these presumed reports of seduction. For one thing, as Israëls and Schatzman (1993) have shown (see also Schimek, 1987), the patients who purportedly reported seduction did not in fact, actually do so. Rather, the presumed occurrence of seduction was based on Freud's *interpretations* of the material they produced, interpretations that were often resisted by the patient. Further, in Freud's shift from actual seduction to the positing of seduction fantasies, it is not as if new evidence was introduced. Rather, the shift was 'required' by his theory of infantile sexuality and the Oedipus complex. Also, it is important to note that when the incest taboo is violated and incest occurs, it is initiated by the adult, not the oedipal child. That is, the direction of incest is generally from adult to child, not as Freud's theory proposes, from child to adult or from child to sibling.

Notwithstanding this fact, Jones (1953) writes:

> Freud has discovered the truth of the matter; that irrespective of incest wishes of parents toward their children, and even occasional acts of these kinds, what he had to concern himself with was the general occurrence of incest wishes of children towards their parents.
>
> (p. 322)

## 4. Freud's self-analysis

With regard to Freud's self-analysis as an evidential basis for this oedipal theory, Sachs (1944) writes that "Freud had made his own mind his chief laboratory, his untiring self-analysis became the basis for all his analytic discoveries" (as cited in Gedo, 1968, p. 99). Gedo (1968) cites Freud's "discovery of the universal Oedipus complex by achieving insight into his infantile libidinal wishes toward his mother and aggression against his father [as a] prominent example" (p. 99) of the role of Freud's self-analysis in his theorizing (see also Kris, 1950). However much Freud's self-analysis inspired his theorizing, it can hardly be said to constitute an adequate evidential basis for the positing of universal incestuous wishes.

## *5. Legends and myths*

We are left with the more substantial and challenging evidence based on common themes found in the legends, myths, and folklore of different cultures. Whatever one may think of this approach, its strength lies in its appeal to evidence generated not by analysis of a limited number of patients, or by the self-analysis of a single individual, or by reference to a single myth, but by appeal to a large data set. This evidence possesses an additional advantage. From a Freudian perspective, one could argue that because of the incest taboo, incestuous wishes will be unconscious and not in consciousness and will not be reported in undisguised form by patients. Rather, the expression and outlet for such material will be more likely to be socially acceptable and therefore 'safer' imaginative products.

There is a huge literature in this area, one certainly too large to cover in a single chapter. And I am certainly not a knowledgeable expert on folklore, legends, and myths. However, it is clear that one of the main issues in appealing to myths and legends as evidence for the universality of the Oedipus complex is how the meanings of these myths and legends are interpreted. Despite having a positive attitude toward the Freudian interpretation of world literature on legends and myths, Johnson and Price-Williams (1996) note that the "gap between strict and loose interpretations leaves plenty of room for argument over exactly what an oedipal story is" (p. 3).

As Miller (1984) has noted, Freud's selective interpretation of *Oedipus Rex* is revealed in his failure to take adequate note of the fact that King Laius wanted to kill Oedipus. As Ross (1982) observes, based on the story of *Oedipus Rex*, one can just as readily refer to a "Laius Complex" – the father's hostile wishes and generational envy toward the son – as to an Oedipus complex (See Kohut, 1984 for a discussion of the role of father to son generational envy in the vicissitudes of the Oedipus complex; (Sheleff, 1981 refers to the "Rustum complex" after an old Persian legend in which the father kills the son). Although I cannot cover much of the myths and legends literature with regard to the universality of incestuous wishes and the Oedipus complex there are useful selective summaries available (e.g., Johnson & Price-Williams, 1996).

Some of the legends and myths contain one presumed component of the Oedipus complex, whereas others contain another component. It is rare to find legends and myths that contain all elements of the Oedipus complex. Finally, and perhaps most important, even if one could demonstrate that different cultural legends and myths unambiguously contain all the components of the Oedipus complex, that would not, in itself, constitute evidence for the hypotheses that: (1) the 4–6 year old boy harbors incestuous wishes toward his mother; and (2) that incestuous wishes constitute a predictable stage of psychosexual development that is a component of a natural progression of erotogenic zones; and (3) that these incestuous wishes emerge out of the sensual gratifications that are part of the mother's ministrations. After all, it is these hypotheses taken together that constitute Freud's theory of the Oedipus complex.

It is interesting to observe that despite providing the namesake for the complex, the story of Oedipus is a rather poor instantiation of the Freudian theory of the Oedipus complex. For one thing, insofar as he was not raised by his biological mother Jocasta, did not know she was his mother, and most important, did not experience the sensual psychosexual pleasures at her hands. Thus, according to the logic of Freudian theory, there is no good reason for Oedipus to have incestuous wishes toward Jocasta – unless one wants to hypothesize that genetic similarity alone is a sufficient basis for the emergence of incestuous wishes. After all, Jocasta was not the object through which the instinct achieved its aim.

There are many themes in myths and legends, for example, about cannibalism, murder, narcissism, magical powers, human embodiments of God who can rise from the dead, and so on. The question is what do they tell us about who we are. They certainly may reveal much about the nature of our imaginations and about the kinds of thoughts, fantasies, and even desires we are capable of having. Whether, however, every theme that appears in legends and myths can be assumed to reveal universal desires and impulses in childhood, many of which have been repressed, is another matter. Also, there are subtle distinctions among such processes as imagination, fantasy, and desire. For example, one can commonly observe young boys and teenagers avidly killing off characters playing their video games. Thus, killing is certainly part of their imagination and fantasy world. However, is this behavior evidence that each of these boys harbors murderous desires and impulses that he would carry out were it not for internal and cultural restraints? I think not. Similarly, although incest, murder, and other themes may be common in myths and legends, one cannot directly translate from the presence of these themes in myths and legends to universal desires and impulses that are kept in check by restraints but nevertheless appear in imagination and fantasy. The links between imagination and fantasy, on the one hand, and desires and impulses on the other, are likely to be more complex than that. For example, common themes in imagination and fantasy are as likely to be as concerned with dreads and fears (and attempts to master them) as with desires and impulses.

## *6. Erotic desire and a sense of transgression*

Kernberg (1995) has argued that the source of the "sense of transgression" (p. 16) that characterizes erotic desire has to do with "the overcoming of the prohibition implied in all sexual encounters, a prohibition derived from the oedipal structuring of sexual life" (p. 16). Thus, he is suggesting that this presumable "sense of transgression" in relation to sexual impulses and behaviors constitutes evidence for the Oedipus complex. Or, to put it another way, a sense of transgression in relation to sex would not be experienced if it were not for the (presumed) fact that sexual desire and sexual behavior always include oedipal (i.e., incestuous) elements and therefore always encounter oedipal prohibitions. In short, Kernberg is suggesting that all erotic desire includes incestuous elements – hence, the "sense of transgression" and forbiddenness that enhance sexual excitement. As he puts it, "erotic desire is characterized by sexual excitement linked to the oedipal object" (p. 16).

I think Kernberg's hypothesis is interesting. However, it rests on the questionable assumption that a sense of transgression is a universal feature of erotic desire and sexual excitement. That is, if one is to hypothesize that the Oedipus complex is universal and if a sense of transgression in relation to sex constitutes evidence for that hypothesis, then one must assume that the latter is universal, that is, cross-cultural. However, there is little evidence that that is the case and much evidence that a sense of transgression in relation to sex is culture specific and, within a culture, varies with one's early upbringing. Also, there may be reasons other than oedipal-related ones for a sense of transgression in relation to sex when it does exist. For example, prohibitions instilling guilt and shame in relation to sex can serve as a means of institutional control (e. g., religious and governmental) over individual desire and behavior (See Orwell's *Nineteen Eighty-Four*).

## *7. Choice of mate*

Freud argued that one important expression of the Oedipal complex, as well as of the influence of infantile sexuality, is the presumed fact the choice of a mate is based on a prototype of one's parental figure. He asserts that "there can be no doubt that every object-choice whatever is based . . . on these prototypes. A man, especially looks for someone who can represent his picture of his mother" (Freud, 1905, p. 228). He also writes that the object will "still be chosen on the model (image) of the infantile ones" (Freud, 1912c, p. 181). For Freud, the man's choice of a mate based on a prototype of mother is taken as evidence of the persistence of infantile incestuous wishes. Indeed, according to Freud (1912c), so powerful and persistent are these incestuous wishes that "the realization of complete satisfaction" will be barred because "the final object of the sexual instinct is never any longer the original object but only a surrogate for it" (p. 189). For "civilized man" (p. 184) the path "to be really true and happy in love" (p. 186) is barred. One can only settle for substitutes.

According to Freud (1905), the child's incestuous wishes toward another are based on the "sexual excitation and satisfaction" (p. 223) her ministrations provide. Hence, on this logic, to the extent that mother is the main caregiver, both the male and female child should experience incestuous wishes toward her. Why should the little girl form a template of father early in development "as a guide to the selection of a similar mate" (Morehead, 1999, p. 367). If the infant's early experiences of infantile sexuality determine the prototype of one's object choice, it is mother who should represent that prototype for both men and women. As we have seen, Freud (1924; 1925, p. 254) attempts to deal with this challenge by weaving a complex, highly speculative and arbitrary narrative in which the little girl observes that she does not have a penis, experiences resentment against her mother "who sent her into the world so insufficiently equipped," and leads to "a loosening of the girl's relation with her mother as a love object" (p. 254).

The little girl "gives up her wish for a penis and puts in place of it a wish for a child: and with that purpose in view she takes her father as a love-object" (p. 256). There is no empirical evidence for this highly speculative narrative, with the result that most theorists who write about the Oedipus complex, including Morehead, limit their discussion to males.

### *The Westermarck hypothesis*

The theory that most directly contrasts with Freud's oedipal theory, particularly with regard to the issue of choice of mate, is the Westermarck (1894) hypothesis. In a quite sophisticated early formulation, Westermarck proposed that the proximal mechanism for incest avoidance is evolutionarily selected-for lack of sexual interest and even sexual aversion in relation to those with whom we are reared. The Westermarck hypothesis was anticipated by Jeremy Bentham (1789/1907), who observed:

> It is very rare that the passion of love is developed within the circle of individuals to whom marriage is forbidden. There needs to give birth to that sentiment a certain degree of surprise, a sudden effect of novelty. . . . Individuals accustomed to see each other and to know each other, from an age in which neither is capable of conceiving the desire nor of inspiring it, will see each other with the same eyes to the end of life.
>
> (p. 220)

Since we are likely to have a close genetic link to those with whom we grew up, this proximal mechanism serves the distal evolutionary function of preventing incest and its biological costs and facilitating exogamy. Westermarck wrote:

> Generally speaking, there is a remarkable absence of erotic feelings between persons living very closely together from childhood. Nay, more, in this, as in many other cases, sexual indifference is combined with the positive feeling of aversion when the act is thought of.
>
> (Westermarck, 1984, p. 80)

The absence of erotic feeling, even sexual aversion, in these circumstances, Westermarck proposes, serves to effect the avoidance of incest and the facilitation of exogamy. Freud was aware of the "Westermarck effect," but summarily dismissed it at various points. At one point, he writes (Freud, 1917/1915–1916):

> If living together dampens sexual desire toward those with whom one grows up, an avoidance of incest would be secure automatically, and it would not be clear why such severe prohibitions were called for, which would point rather to the presence of a strong desire for it.
>
> (p. 210)

According to Morehead (1999), who wants to demonstrate that at least a revised and modernized version of oedipal theory can be preserved, there is evidence that "a template of internal image of early associates, primarily the opposite-sex parent is formed early in development and is later used as a guide for the selection of a similar mate" (p. 367). And further, according to Morehead, the evidence supports that component of oedipal theory that suggests "that early familial experience forms a model for adult sexual mate choice and establishes patterns of adult sexual relationships" (p. 347). What is the evidence regarding choice of mate? Do we in fact, select mates and are we attracted to mates who represent a 'prototype' of our parents? And if that is the case, does it provide support for the Oedipus complex and the universality?

Although the Westermarck hypothesis continues to be controversial, particularly in its original form, there is a good deal of evidence supporting it. Across a wide range of species, prolonged propinquity and familiarity dampen sexual interest and arousal, whereas unfamiliarity, novelty, and diversity intensify them. For example, as Fox (1980) notes, "Evidence exists from animals, moths, and birds that opposite-sex creatures reared together during immaturity copulate less readily than strangers when mature" (p. 24).

There is also evidence in humans that prolonged propinquity early in life discourages marriage among people reared together. In one study, Talmon (1964) looked at 125 marriages in three well-established kibbutzim and found not a single case where two people reared in the same peer group had married. In a much larger study, Shepher (1971) obtained the records of 2,769 marriages of children raised on kibbutzim. He found only 16 cases where people reared together in the same group married. Furthermore, in all 16 of these apparent exceptions, the children had not been reared together between birth and six years of age. In other words, of 2,769 marriages, not a single one occurred between people who had been reared together when they were younger than six years of age. In accord with the Westermarck hypothesis, Shepher concludes that a "negative imprinting" with regard to sexual interest in those with whom one was reared is established during the first six years of life.

Shor and Simchai (2009) recently presented a critique of the Westermarck hypothesis and, in particular, of the Shepher study. They conducted 60 in-depth interviews with individuals who grew up on kibbutzim and reported that "almost none of the interviewees reported sexual aversion toward their peers" (p. 1822). Rather, 53% reported strong or moderate sexual attraction toward at least some of their peers and 43% reported feelings of indifference. However, many interviewees, including those who felt strong sexual attraction, "saw the relationship as something 'different' and often they could not envision full intercourse and a romantic relationship as a full option" (p. 1824). Shor and Simchai also cite the atmosphere of prohibition in relation to sex among peers at the kibbutz as a factor in Shepher's results and also report the prediction of degree of sexual attraction by group cohesion: the higher the group cohesion, the lower the sexual attraction.

The Shor and Simchai findings suggest that one may need to modify the Westermarck hypothesis to state that prolonged propinquity may *reduce* sexual attraction rather than necessarily generate sexual aversion. The fact is that almost half of the interviewees reported sexual indifference toward their kibbutzim peers – a rather large percentage for young people who are interacting with each other. And even those who reported sexual attraction for a peer felt something "different" and often could not envision sexual intercourse and a romantic relationship with that peer. As Shor and Simchai note, however, reports of aversion and disgust were reserved for thoughts about sex with siblings. That factors other than prolonged propinquity, such as group cohesion, were shown to influence degree of sexual attraction does not contradict a modified version of the Westermarck hypothesis. Rather, it demonstrates the role of additional factors. Further, if anything, according to Kernberg's (1995) reasoning, the atmosphere of prohibition and transgression in relation to sex among peers at the kibbutz should have intensified rather than attenuated sexual attraction.

Although Westermarck proposed that the relationship between sexual inhibition and prolonged propinquity was selected for in the course of evolution, he did not specify the proximal mechanisms that mediate this relationship. Over the years, a number of neo-Westermarckian hypotheses have been proposed that identify a or *the* mechanism that may account for the Westermarck effect. Some examples follow.

## *Olfactory mediation*

Schneider and Hendrix (2000) have suggested that the Westermarck effect is mediated olfactorily. They hypothesize that both in animals and humans "familiarization with scent [is] a likely cause of aversions" (p. 66) in mate selection. They summarize evidence that kin recognition is mediated by the major histocompatibility complex (MHC) gene segment, which is linked to individual and familial scent, and that "some avoid cosocialized associates on this basis" (p. 65). For example, both male and female mice appear to recognize differences in MCH genotype and mate preferentially on this basis (Egid & Brown, 1989; Potts, Manning, & Wakeland, 1991, 1992; Yamazaki et al., 1976, 1979; Yamaguchi et al., 1981). In humans, female students found the odor of shirts worn by men who were less similar to them in MHC significantly more positive than the odor of shirts worn by men more similar to them in MHC.

## *Habituation as a mediator*

Fraley and Marks (2010) have proposed that the primary factor that accounts for reduced sexual interest (rather than aversion) with prolonged propinquity is simple habituation. As they note, "there is evidence that sexual passions often wane as people become increasingly habituated to one another (Call, Sprecher, & Schwartz, 1995; James, 1981)" (p. 1210) (see also Bateson, 1983; 2004). Hence, reduced sexual interest in someone who is too familiar may be partly due to a habituation effect.

However, the habituation hypothesis does not account for expressions of aversion and even disgust in relation to imagining sex with close kin.

## Genetic kinship estimator as a mediator

Still another account of the Westermarck effect has been proposed by Lieberman, Tooby, and Cosmides (2003), who posit an implicit and selected-for "genetic kinship estimator" (p. 821). According to this model, when an estimate of genetic relatedness between self and other is sufficiently high, sexual aversion toward the other is triggered. Further, the "genetic kinship estimator" is influenced by such factors as prolonged propinquity. Hence, the model purports to explain such findings as the relative absence of marriages among children reared together. It is as if the "genetic kinship estimator" is 'fooled' by prolonged propinquity and other factors to estimate greater genetic relatedness than in fact there is.

It is likely that there is no single factor that accounts for the phenomena addressed by the Westermarck hypothesis. Further, in considering the evidence for the Westermarck effect, one needs to be clear whether one is referring to relative lack of sexual interest – which can be accounted for by such factors as habituation and the observation that sexual excitement is enhanced by novelty, an "obstacle" (Freud, 1912b), and illicitness (Kernberg, 1995) – and sexual aversion which is not easily accounted for by these factors. One should note that Westermarck (1894) himself referred to both "sexual indifference" and "the positive feeling of aversion" (p. 80). However, indifference and aversion are quite different phenomena and are not likely to be explicable in the same way. For example, one could argue that aversion rather than indifference is more compatible with Freud's hypothesis that the incest taboo is erected against powerful incestuous impulses.[3]

In a recent study, Fraley and Marks (2010) report findings that, they claim, contradict the neo-Westermarck hypothesis and support Freud's account of mate attraction. In one of a series of experiments by Fraley and Marks (2010) subjects were asked to rate the sexual attractiveness of 100 faces. For both the experimental and control subjects, the faces were preceded by the subliminal exposure of a photograph of the experimental subjects' opposite sex parent. The subjects who were primed by the subliminal image of their own parent found the faces significantly more sexually attractive. However, although the differences were statistically significant, they were not especially large. On a rating scale from 1 (low) to 7 (high), the mean for the experimental group was 3.82 and for the control group was 3.56 – hardly a robust difference to support a claim of universality.

In the second experiment, when the experimental subjects' own face was morphed into the faces of opposite sex strangers in varying degrees, they rated the morphed faces as significantly more sexually attractive than control subjects who rated non-morphed faces. The authors interpret these results as contradicting the neo-Westermarckian hypothesis that genetic relatedness dampens sexual appeal insofar as the "self is a prototype for someone who shares 100% of the participant's genetic variance" (p. 1206). In Experiment 3, when the subjects were falsely told that the faces they were rating for sexual attractiveness were faces that included their own morphed face, they rated these faces as significantly *less* attractive to them than the control group who were not given the false information. One should note that only the experimental subjects were given the description: "We are interested in studying incest. We want to know how attractive people find faces that are designed to resemble genetic relatives such as parents, brothers, and sisters" (pp. 1207–1208). The authors interpret these findings to indicate that whereas non-awareness of genetic relatedness (the conditions of Experiments 1 and 2) leads to diminished ratings of sexual attraction, "conscious awareness of the purported genetic relatedness between self and other leads to diminished feelings of desire, even when the actual degree of resemblance is zero" (p. 1208). The authors are over-interpreting the data here. The participants were asked to rate the attractiveness of faces, not report on feelings of desire.

Fraley and Marks (2010) conclude that the "data suggest that there may be some truth in Freud's claim" to the effect that were it not for the fact of "nonconscious processes that lead people to be sexually attracted to family members . . . there would be no need for such powerful taboos concerning incest" (p. 1208). They go on to say, however, that in the "evolutionary psychodynamic framework" they are proposing, "attraction for kin arises not because people harbor natural incestuous urges . . . but because the mechanisms that promote familiarity, bonding, and attraction are more likely to operate on inputs experienced in the early family environment" (p. 1209).

There is a good deal one can comment on about the Fraley and Marks' (2010) findings and how they are interpreted. Let me limit myself to a few comments:

1. There is a leap between ratings of faces for sexual attractiveness and overall feelings of sexual attraction and a huge leap between such ratings and choice of mate. One should not draw any conclusions about the latter based on these findings.
2. As noted, whereas the differences between a mean rating of 3.82 (the experimental group in Experiment 1) and 3.56 may be statistically significant, given how small the differences are, it is not clear what ecological validity or significance they have.
3. The fact that (in Experiment 2) participants rated faces that had elements of their own face as more sexually attractive suggests that a sense of familiarity and trust may have been the primary factor in the participants' ratings in both Experiments 1 and 2. Indeed, DeBruine (2002) has shown that facial resemblance to oneself enhances trust. Fraley and Marks interpret these findings in terms of a positive relationship between degree of genetic relatedness and ratings of sexual attractiveness. They argue that "because self is a prototype for someone who shares 100% of the participant's genetic variance" (p. 1207), rating faces that have elements of one's face as more sexually attractive demonstrates this relationship. More generally, they argue that according to what they refer to as a neo-Westermarckian hypothesis of Lieberman et al. (2003), a detection

of high genetic relatedness by a "genetic kinship estimator" (p. 821) should lead to lower not higher ratings of sexual attractiveness. Hence, they conclude, their findings contradict the neo-Westermarckian hypothesis that predicts an inverse relationship between degree of genetic relatedness and ratings of sexual attractiveness.

Fraley and Marks (2010) interpret the findings of both Experiments 1 and 2 in terms of the relationship between genetic relatedness and ratings of sexual attractiveness. However, they are very different experiments. In Experiment 1, the faces rated by the participants bear no genetic relationship at all to them. The issue of genetic relatedness is introduced because the faces rated were subliminally preceded (primed) by the face of participant's opposite sex parent. It is not clear why genetic relatedness is at all relevant. What we do know is that preceding a face with a subliminal exposure of an image of the participant's opposite sex parent leads to a small increase in ratings of sexual attractiveness compared to a control group. How that comes about is an interesting question. But we cannot assume that the process through which this occurs is that the priming subliminal face (of the opposite sex parent) somehow leads to the face that is rated to be unconsciously perceived by the participant as more genetically related (or more similar) to himself or herself. That assumption begs the question regarding the relationship between genetic relatedness and sexual attractiveness. There is no independent evidence that the faces subliminally primed by exposure of the image of one's opposite sex parent are 'detected' as genetically related by a "genetic kinship estimator."

Also, it seems to me that there is something odd in assuming that the primary factor operating in rating faces similar to oneself as more sexually attractive is unconscious detection of degree of genetic relatedness. The issue of what Freud (1914*b*) refers to as narcissistic object choice needs to be considered.

4. As for the findings of Experiment 3, it is hardly surprising that subjects would rate as less sexually attractive faces that they are told were constructed by morphing their own face into those of a stranger's as a way of "simulating the appearance of kin" (p. 1207), and when they are also told: "we are also interested in studying incest. We want to know how attractive people find faces that are designed to resemble genetic relatives such as parents, brothers, and sisters" (pp. 1207–1208). One cannot make too much of these results.
5. Fraley and Marks (2010) assume that their results demonstrate that subjects were more attracted to faces that resemble kin and take this as partial support for Freud's hypothesis that people are "sexually attracted to family members" (p. 1208). However, one needs to note again that the faces that were rated as more sexually attractive were not faces that more closely resembled kin, but rather faces that were preceded by subliminal exposure of an image of the participants' opposite sex parent. There was no evidence that the subjects perceived these faces as more closely resembling kin.

Most important, Fraley and Marks (2010) write that:

> [A]ccording to an evolutionary psychodynamic framework, attraction for kin arises not because people harbor relational incestuous urges . . . but because the mechanisms that promote familiarity, bonding, and attraction are most likely to operate on inputs experienced in the early family environment.
> (p. 1209)

Thus, in effect, they do not interpret their results as supporting a core assumption of Freud's theory of the Oedipus complex. They go on to write: "For example, if sexual imprinting really takes place in humans, then one's early interactions with primary attachment figures can play an influential role in shaping the 'ideal' for what kinds of people one will find attractive" (p. 1209).

There is evidence that both animals and humans prefer mates who are similar but not identical to those with whom they were reared. For example, in one study, quail preferred members of the opposite sex who were first cousins to those who were third cousins, siblings, and unrelated (Bateson, 1983). And mice, too, show greatest sexual interest in mates of intermediate relatedness, often second cousins (Barnard & Aldhous, 1991; Barnard & Fitzimmons, 1988). There is also evidence from bird and rodent species that these animals avoid mating with close kin but tend to choose mates who are similar in appearance.

A similar pattern referred to as positive assortative mating is found in humans (e.g., Bereczki, Gyuris, &Weisfeld, 2002; Buss, 1984; Zajonc, Adelmann, Murphy, & Niedenthal, 1987). That is, people tend to select mates who are similar to themselves (and therefore, presumably similar to family members) in physical, social, and psychological characteristics. Indeed, in many non-industrialized cultures, marriages to first and second cousins were quite common. In short, there appears to be evidence that both animals and humans tend to select mates who are similar to themselves and to family members.

Do the above findings on mate choice provide compelling evidence for even a diluted claim of a universal biologically based Oedipus complex, at the center of which are incestuous wishes? The research cited by Morehead indicates that animals and humans tend to select mates who are similar, but not too similar, to family members and oneself. However, there is little or nothing on specific similarity to the opposite sex parent. Thus, Morehead's account does not accurately reflect the findings that he presents in his paper. Most important, even if it could be shown that we tend to select mates who are similar to the opposite sex parent would this finding support oedipal theory?

One problem with the hypothesis of an Oedipus complex is that it does not take into account the near universality of offspring–parent incest avoidance among animals. As noted earlier, Freud assumed that whereas incest was rampant among animals, incest avoidance was unique to humans and required uniquely human explanations such as the role of repression and castration anxiety. However, given the universality of incest avoidance among different species, the uniquely human account is not as cogent. It is far more parsimonious to assume that, insofar as we are part of the animal kingdom and the evolutionary process, there will be some continuity and commonality between animals and humans in the factors that account for incest avoidance.

Another problem with the Oedipus complex hypothesis is one I have noted earlier: It does not adequately account for incest avoidance in females. If mother becomes the child's first libidinal object through her provision of sensual pleasures, this will be true for both males and females. We are then at a loss to understand female heterosexuality. And Freud's convoluted account does not supply that understanding. Again, it is far more parsimonious to assume that, although there are likely to be differences, at least some of the factors that account for incest avoidance are common not only to animals and humans, but also to males and females.

However, oedipal theory does not account very well for the data on choice of mate for either males or females. As noted, the general pattern that emerges is that both animals and humans tend to select mates of intermediate degree of relatedness rather than mates based on a prototype or template of the opposite sex parent. Further, the most adequate explanatory account of that pattern lies not in the assumption of universal incestuous wishes, but in a number of other considerations and theoretical formulations. At the distal level of explanation, the most parsimonious and plausible hypothesis seems to be represented by Bateson's (1982; 1983; 2004) hypothesis that mate choice based on an intermediate degree of relatedness best balances the costs (and benefits) of inbreeding and outbreeding.

At the level of proximal explanation, there are a number of factors that contribute to mate choice based on an intermediate degree of relatedness as well as an intermediate degree of similarity between oneself (and one's family) and potential mates. We know, for example, that in humans, the single best predictor of who one marries is propinquity. And further, people who live in the same neighborhood or occupy the same physical and social environments are more likely to be more similar to each other on a number of dimensions than people who live in very different environments.

Lorenz (1970) has shed some additional light on this question of parent as a template for choice of mate. As he has shown, many birds and mammals use either parents or siblings as a template for potential mates. For example, a mallard drake raised by graylag goose foster parents and living with mallard siblings will flock with mallards, but court greylags. As other examples, a jackdaw reared by a human will court humans; and, unlike the mallard drake and the jackdaw, a Muscovy drake raised by a human and with surrogate siblings will court mallards. Quite importantly, in none of these cases does the animal court either the surrogate parent or the siblings with whom it has been raised. Rather, the early figure (surrogate parent or sibling) serves as the schema for the *type of object* the animal will court.[4]

## *Mate choice and compromise between the attachment and sexual systems*

The proximal factors that are of greatest interest, however, in the present context are those that have to do with the individual's personal feelings and attitudes.

As I have proposed elsewhere (Eagle, 2007b), mate choice based on an intermediate degree of similarity balances the 'demands' of two major motivational systems: attachment and sexuality. Whereas sexual arousal is heightened by novelty, unfamiliarity, and the exotic, security of attachment is associated with the familiar. Hence, the choice of a mate who is very dissimilar to family members might maximize sexual interest, but render the formation of an attachment bond more difficult. Conversely, the choice of a mate who is too similar to family members might maximize the formation of an attachment bond, but due to the incest taboo, make sexual interest and excitement more difficult. So, a choice made on the basis of an intermediate degree of similarity seems to represent the optimal compromise between the somewhat conflicting 'demands' of the sexual and attachment systems. It represents a 'best fit' compromise between the pulls and demands of the two systems, insofar as it is responsive to incest avoidance as well as feelings of relative comfort because the mate is experienced as familiar, safe, and redolent of family members, including one's attachment figure. Hence, it permits *both* sexual feelings *and* attachment feelings. Thus, contrary to Morehead (1999), even when there is evidence that choice of mate is based on a prototype or template of parent or sibling, it does not necessarily support oedipal theory.

Morehead (1999) attempts to preserve some semblance of oedipal theory by stating:

> But analytic theorists do not need to prove that the Oedipal boy would have sex with his mother if only he could, nor do they need to show that sexuality is the prime motivation of all the Oedipal boy's wishes. They need only to demonstrate the presence of sexual elements in early attachments.
>
> (p. 368)

But even if the boy's mate selection could be shown to be influenced by a template or representation of mother, this could be mainly based not on "sexual elements," but on experiences of mother as a safe haven and secure base. To say that that influence demonstrates "the presence of sexual elements" begs the very question that is being debated, namely the extent of these "sexual elements" in early attachments and their influences on later choice of mate.

Morehead's diluted re-formulation of the oedipal complex radically alters its meaning. If, as he claims, it is not the case that the theory of the oedipal complex indeed posits that the "Oedipal boy would have sex with his mother if only he could"; and if, as he also claims, it is not the case that it also posits that "sexuality is the prime motivator of all the Oedipal boy's wishes" (p. 368), then the meaning of the Oedipus complex has been changed beyond all recognition. Thus, although Morehead makes clear that his intention is to preserve some semblance of oedipal theory, his reformulation of it is essentially equivalent to a relinquishment of it, without acknowledging that that is what his supposed reformulation entails.

The primary question here is whether the infant's and child's 'imprinting' in relation to his or her attachment figure is primarily sexual in nature. If the 'imprinting' mechanisms also entails the factors of "familiarity and bonding," then one cannot attribute choice of mate based on similarity to kin specifically to "sexual imprinting." A far more adequate explanation is provided by a variation of Bateson's (1982; 1983) model of optimal outbreeding. I say "variation" of Bateson's model because, according to that model, choice of mate tends to be a composite product of early sexual imprinting – which leads one to find individuals similar to kin as sexually attractive – and habituation – which weakens sexual desire. Hence, one 'searches' for a mate who resembles one's kin, but not too much.

I have proposed that the mate choice of "optimal similarity" is the compromise product of the 'pulls' of the attachment and sexual systems (Eagle, 2007b; 2013). That is, one is attracted to a potential mate who is sufficiently novel to trigger sexual interest and excitement and sufficiently familiar to one's attachment figure to generate feelings of safety and trust. This compromise product permits sexual interest without triggering incest avoidance responses. To be noted here is that according to this formulation, choice of mate based on 'optimal similarity' does not require the assumption of early sexual imprinting. Indeed, according to this formulation, it would be more accurate to refer to early 'imprinting' of attachment patterns.

As Fraley and Marks (2010) (and others – e.g,, see Morehead, 1999) have observed, people tend to marry individuals who are similar to them and therefore to kin – a phenomenon referred to variously as homogamy and positive assortative mating. Indeed, this phenomenon has led some to argue that a sexual imprinting process takes place, which is characterized by finding desirable and 'searching' for mates who are similar to people with whom they were reared (e.g., Bereczkei, Gyuris, Koves, & Bernath, 2002; Bereczkei et al., 2004). That is, this finding appears to contradict the claim that sexual desire and attraction are inhibited toward those with whom one was reared. How does one account for this seeming contradiction? It seems to me that the solution to this puzzle is quite clear and is provided by the "optimal similarity" hypothesis discussed earlier as well as some additional considerations. As I have noted elsewhere (Eagle, 2007):

> The choice of a mate who is very dissimilar to family members might maximize sexual interest, but render the formation of an attachment bond more difficult. Conversely, the choice of a mate who is too similar to family members might maximize the formation of an attachment bond but, in accord with the Westermarck hypothesis, make sexual interest and excitement more difficult. So, a choice made on the basis of optimal similarity seems to represent the optimal compromise between the somewhat conflicting "demands" of the sexual and attachment systems.
>
> (p. 43)

Previous theorists, I believe, have made the error of assuming that mate selection is based solely or primarily on sexual attraction and not also on other factors such as early attachment experiences and the internal working model of the attachment figure. As Fox (1980) observes, there is a distinction between sexual attraction and mate selection. In a *New York Times* article on Iraqi marriages, the reporter John Tierney (2003) notes "cousin marriages were once the norm throughout the world" (p. 12) and reports an interview with an Iraqi woman who responded to her uncle's proposal that she marry his son by stating, "I was a little surprised, but I knew right away it was a wise choice. It is *safer* (my italics) to marry a cousin than a stranger" (p. 1). Tierney cites the anthropologist Fox's point that in much of the world the world is divided into two groups: kin and strangers; and as the Iraqi woman's comment suggests, kin are safer. I was struck by the Iraqi woman's comment that marriage to her cousin was "safer." That is, her judgment that marriage to her cousin was a "wise choice" was very likely not based on sexual attraction to him, but feelings of safety that are associated with the familiarity of kin. In the present context, one can say that such feelings represent a solid basis for an enduring attachment bond.

It needs to be noted that although someone similar to oneself is also more likely to be more similar to kin, one cannot rule out the possibility that it is the former not the latter that is primarily operative in homogamy or positive assortative mating. That is, in those instances, mate choice may be more a matter of narcissistic object choice than similarity to kin.

It seems to me that the tendency for sexual interest to become intensified with novelty and diversity, and dampen with prolonged propinquity provide a plausible mechanism and a parsimonious account for the tendency of animals and humans to select an "extraneous object" (Freud, 1912b, p. 181) rather than an incestuous object. It seems highly unlikely that nature would first select for universal and powerful incestuous desires and then add a universal incest taboo to prevent the satisfaction of these desires.

## 8. The split between love and desire

The split between love and desire, or between the "affectionate and sensual currents" is taken by Freud (1912b) to be a quintessential expression of the Oedipus complex. Freud (1912c) described a group of men suffering from "psychical impotence" as: "where they love they do not desire and where they desire they cannot love" (p. 183). He also noted that this split between love and desire was quite common in both men and women and was expressed in the lack of sexual interest and enjoyment in relation to one's spouse. Freud (1912b) attributed this split in men to "an incestuous fixation on mother or sister which has never been surmounted" (p. 180). To the extent that the woman triggers incestuous wishes and fantasies, the man becomes impotent or cannot experience sexual interest and enjoyment. The man cannot feel sexual toward women who trigger the "affectionate current" or who are held in "high psychical estimation" (p. 183) – hence, the so-called whore–madonna complex. In short, for Freud, the split between love and desire is due to unresolved oedipal conflicts, in particular the persistence of incestuous wishes.

## *Attachment and sexuality as separable and partly antagonistic behavioral–motivational systems*

In what follows, I present a formulation that recognizes the universality of the incest taboo, but does not require the questionable assumption of universal incestuous wishes. I begin by observing that what Freud refers to as love and desire, or the affectionate and sensual currents, is essentially equivalent to attachment and sexuality. This is an important point because it enables us to recognize two core components of long-term adult relationships. Although they interact with each other, attachment and sexuality are distinctive and separable behavioral systems. Further, as I will try to demonstrate, in certain respects, they operate in mutually antagonistic ways – a fact that goes some way toward explaining the split between love and desire (Eagle, 2007).

### *Physiological evidence*

There is a good deal of evidence that both on a physiological and psychological level, attachment and sexuality are separable behavioral systems. They are mediated by different biological processes. As Liebowitz (1983) observes:

> Biologically, it appears that we have evolved two distinct chemical systems for romance; one basically serves to bring people together and the other to keep them together. The first is [sexual] attraction . . . the second, which helps keep people together, is attachment. Attachment has more to do with feelings of security than of excitement.
>
> (p. 90)

There is a good deal of animal and human research indicating that oxytocin and vasopressin play an important role not only in maternal behavior and mother–infant bonding, but also in adult attachment bonding. For example, monogamous prairie voles, mice, and primates have different distributions of oxytocin and vasopressin receptors than non-monogamous prairie voles, rodents, and primates (Insel & Young, 2001). Further, injection of either oxytocin or vasopressin facilitates monogamy in non-monogamous prairie voles; and when an oxytocin receptor antagonist is injected into a monogamous prairie vole, the usual monogamous preference for a partner is blocked.

Wingfield (1984) reported that subcutaneous implantation of testosterone in monogamous birds renders them polygamous. Physiological evidence for the separability of attachment and sexuality in humans includes the finding that single men and women have higher levels of testosterone than partnered men and women. However, partnered men who reported greater desire for uncommitted sex had the same level of testosterone as single men. And partnered women who reported more frequent uncommitted sexual behavior had the same level of testosterone as single women (Edelstein, Chopik, & Kean, 2011).

In a study of 890 men, Kuzawa, Gettler, Muller, McDade, & Feranil (2009) found that young fathers had a lower level of testosterone than single men. In another study, Kuzawa, Gettler, Huang, & McDade (2010) reported that young mothers and partnered women had lower waking testosterone than single women. This was particularly true of mothers of young infants. Furthermore, these findings were independent of breastfeeding, contraceptive pill use, sleep quality, menstrual cycle, employment, and socio-economic status.

In a rather striking finding, Gettler et al. (2011) reported that although there was no change in testosterone level, levels of cortisol and prolactin declined minutes after men played with their children. And finally, in a study of more than 700 elderly men and women, Pollet, van der Meij, Cobey, and Buunk (2011) found testosterone level was associated with number of lifetime sex partners reported by men even after controlling for possible confounding variables such as age, level of education, and ethnicity. A similar but weaker relationship was found for women.

## *Psychological evidence*

As for the psychological evidence regarding the separability of the attachment and sexual systems, as Holmes (2001) and Fonagy (2001) have commented, it is not uncommon to observe intense attachment without much sexual interest and sexual interest without attachment. This is not surprising in view of the fact that the factors that are involved in the development of an attachment bond are different from those that influence sexual interest and excitement. For one thing, the development of an attachment bond requires prolonged propinquity, whereas sexual interest and arousal can be virtually instantaneous. Most important, familiarity is necessary for someone to serve as an attachment figure, whereas novelty and unfamiliarity, – which the poet Byron refers to as "fresh features" – which are incompatible with the development of an attachment bond, intensify sexual arousal and excitement. Indeed, there is a good deal of evidence from animal and human research that intensity of sexual excitement is reduced by familiarity and prolonged propinquity and enhanced by novelty.

Consider a phenomenon found in the animal kingdom that is referred to as the "Coolidge effect," based on the following story:

> One day the president and Mrs. Coolidge were visiting a government farm. Soon after their arrival they were taken off on separate tours. When Mrs. Coolidge passed the chicken pens she paused to ask the man in charge if the rooster copulates more than once each day. 'Dozens of times' was the reply. 'Please tell the President,' Mrs. Coolidge requested. When the president passed the pens and was told about the rooster, he asked 'same hen every time?' 'Oh no, Mr. President, a different one each time.' The president nodded slowly, then said 'Tell that to Mrs. Coolidge.'
>
> (Bermant, 1976, pp. 76–77)

In many mammalian species, after copulating with a female and ejaculating several times, sexual activity wanes and then eventually ceases. However, if a new estrous female is introduced, the male immediately begins to copulate again. Symons (1979) writes that "while males of many species are indiscriminate in that they will copulate with any estrous females of their species, they are extremely discriminating in that they recognize females individually, and they are partial to variety and prejudiced against familiarity" (p. 210). From an evolutionary perspective, this pattern has the adaptive consequence of increasing the likelihood that the male's genes will be propagated.

It is important to note that although widespread, the, so to speak, degree or intensity of the Coolidge effect may vary with different species. The Coolidge effect does not appear to be prominently present in two species. Pierce, O'Brien, and Dewsbury (1992) investigated the Coolidge effect in old-field mice and prairie voles, both of which are generally monogamous. In an attempt to tease out the factors involved in resuming copulation after satiety, Pierce et al. (1992) studied the resumption of sexual behavior of male prairie voles with original females, a new but familiar female, and a novel female. When a rigorous criterion for satiety was employed, three of the ten males achieved ejaculation following reintroduction of the original female compared with seven of ten males achieving ejaculation with the familiar and novel females, a difference that did not reach statistical significance. Also, males showed significantly more mounts, thrusts, and intromissions and achieved ejaculation more quickly with novel and familiar females (combined) than with the original females. The authors conclude that male prairie voles fail to show a Coolidge effect, although there was a trend in that direction. In my reading of the results, however, including the significant difference between novel and familiar females versus original females, in mounts, thrusts, and intromissions as well as latency of ejaculations, there is, indeed, some evidence of a Coolidge effect. More research needs to be done, however. For, as the authors note, factors other than sexual interest – for example, mate guarding – may influence resumption of copulation in both polygamous and monogamous species.

Furthermore, the phenomena I have been discussing, in particular, the relation between novelty and variety versus familiarity and sexual interest, have been widely and independently observed in humans (See Kinsey, Pomeroy, & Martin, 1948). The most obvious expression of this relationship is the widespread prevalence of extramarital sex. As Diamond (2003) notes, both the institution of marriage and the occurrence of extramarital sex have been reported from all human societies. The partial antagonism between attachment and sexuality is also seen in Freud's (1912c) observation that "the psychical value of erotic needs is reduced as soon as their satisfaction becomes easy. An obstacle is required in order to heighten libido" (p. 187). It is also noted by Mitchell (2002) who observes that security, predictability, and safety are inimical to the experience of desire and passion. He writes: "We become attached and we want objects of our own attachment to stay fixed, unchanging – so ironically enough, attachment is the great enemy of eroticism" (p. 87). Paralleling Freud's (1912b) observation and Lacan's (1966/2002) discussion of the insatiability of desire, he also writes that "the precondition of romantic passion is lack, desire for what one does not have" (p. 56).

That sexual interest and attraction are heightened by newness and unfamiliarity and dampened by familiarity is, in certain respects, highly adaptive in the original family situation insofar as it encourages the mating choice of "extraneous objects" (Freud, 1912c, p. 181) and discourages the "choice" of a family member. However, to the extent that these characteristics of sexuality, that is, intensification by newness and dampening by familiarity, continue to operate, they constitute potential threats to the stability and longevity of established long-term relationships. For, in such relationships, the originally "extraneous object" becomes a familiar one and others outside the relationship are now "extraneous objects" towards whom sexual interest may be directed. Insofar as one's spouse is generally both ones attachment figure and one's sexual partner, this presents challenges to a long-term relationship that need to be met if it is to be satisfactorily maintained.

There is a good deal of evidence that in long-term relationships, the longer the couple have been together, the fewer the passionate and the more the companionate features characterize the relationship (Sprecher & Regan, 1998). In a study conducted by the National Opinion Research Center, Michael, Gagnon, Laumann, and Kolata (1994) found that the frequency of sexual intercourse of married couples declined markedly as a function of years of marriage. The data support Briffault's (1928) assertion that it is companionship, not sex, that is the central factor in long-term relationships. This phenomenon suggests that habituation dampens sexual desire in ongoing relationships that were initially characterized by strong sexual attraction.

To be noted here is that quite apart from any question of incestuous wishes or even incest taboo, the separability and partial antagonism of the attachment and sexual systems goes some way toward accounting for the split between love and desire. Another way to put it is to say that, given how these two systems operate, the integration between love and desire is not a given, but a developmental psychological challenge and achievement. As Hazan and Zeifman (1994) observe, sexual attraction, which they refer to as the "psychological tether," often brings and holds two adults together for a long enough time to provide an opportunity for a strong emotional bond to form. However, the longevity of the relationship, will, in large part, be determined by the couple's ability to maintain that emotional bond in the face of the relatively decreased role of sexual intensity. And, indeed, a good deal of evidence suggests that sensitive and responsive care, not sexual attraction, is the most accurate predictor of relationship longevity (e.g., Kotler, 1985).

In a study on factors that contribute to the experience of intimacy in romantic relationships, Farrugia and Hogans (1998) found that attachment to partner made the greatest contribution followed by sensitivity to caregiving. The authors note that "a surprising finding was that measures of sexual behavior . . . did not make a unique contribution to intimacy in romantic relationships" (Farrugia & Hogans, 1998, p. 11). This finding is especially noteworthy given the young age of the sample. It should be noted, however, that the sample was predominately female and that the authors did not report results for males and females separately. Nevertheless, the results tend to support the conclusion of Waring, Tillman, Frelick, Russell, and Weisz (1990) "that sexuality is considered part of intimacy by most people, although it is not considered to be the primary component" (p. 4).

The above findings support Diamond's (2003) argument that although "the evolved processes underlying sexual desire and affectional bonding are often experienced in concert, they are governed by different social-behavioral systems that have evolved to serve different goals" (p. 174). According to Diamond (see also Fisher, 1998), "desire is governed by the sexual mating system" (p. 174), the goal of which is reproduction, "whereas romantic love is governed by the attachment or pair-bonding system . . . the goal of which is the maintenance of an enduring association" (p. 174) for the purpose of survival of dependent offspring.[5]

### *Individual differences in integrating attachment and sexuality*

Although the separability and partial antagonism between the attachment and sexual systems presents a general developmental challenge, the fact is that there are individual differences in the degree to which integration between attachment and sexuality or love and desire is successfully achieved. As Freud (1912a) observed, some men suffer from "psychical impotence" in relation to their spouse, but not in relation to other women, particularly women who are not held in "high psychical estimation" (p. 183). And many other men, as well as many women, he also observed, even if they do not suffer from symptoms, such as "psychical impotence," nevertheless show a significant split between love and desire evidenced by not being able to experience much sexual interest and enjoyment with their spouse.

I would suggest that a significant factor in the individual's success in integrating attachment and sexuality is the degree to which s/he unconsciously equates current partner with early attachment figure. For the male, to the extent that one's romantic partner becomes one's attachment figure, she takes on a maternal role. For these men who have difficulty relinquishing ties to early objects, the unconscious equation between spouse and mother would be especially intense and unyielding. This in turn, would intensify the incest taboo, which would make it difficult to experience sexual feelings toward spouse. In Freud's (1912) language, the affectionate–attachment current is split off from the sensual–sexual current, the latter being safer and easier to experience with an "extraneous object" outside the home who is not one's attachment figure. It is important to note that in this account while the incest *taboo* plays a central role in the above account, one need not invoke incest *wishes*.

Virtually by definition, insecure attachment in an adult relationship entails unresolved attachment issues (Eagle, 2007b; 2013). In particular, it entails responding to one's current partner as if she were a stand-in for one's early attachment figure. For example, the avoidantly attached individual avoids expressing attachment needs as if s/he continues to expect the rejection s/he experienced at the hands of his early attachment figure; and the preoccupied individual behaves as if s/he continues to expect the inconsistency and abandonment s/he experienced at the hands of his or her early attachment figure. In both cases, the individual's pattern with early attachment figures persists and characterizes later adult relationships. Hence, because the current relationship is 'contaminated' by unresolved early ties and the unconscious equation between current partner and early attachment figure, the former is likely to become a taboo sexual object, making it more difficult to experience sexual interest and feelings toward him or her. Once again, note that one can hypothesize the activation of the incest taboo without the necessity to assume the presence of powerful incestuous wishes.

There is evidence indicating that different attachment patterns are associated with different patterns of sexual behavior. For example, avoidantly attached males tend to separate sexual from attachment feelings; are more likely to endorse the use of sex for fun rather than as an expression of emotional depth (Feeney & Noller, 1990); show greater fear of intimacy (Latchaw, 2010); and report more infidelity (Allan & Baucom, 2004; Cohen, 2005). Anxiously attached individuals report frequent, intense, and short-term love experiences (Feeney & Noller, 1990); show more sexual conflict (Latchaw, 2010); tend to experience sex as reassurance (Davis et al., 2004); and also report more infidelity, but out of a feeling of neglect and desire to be cared for (Allan & Baucom, 2004) (for a fuller description of findings in this area, see Eagle, 2013).[6]

## *9. Castration anxiety: unconscious wishes or symbolic equivalence*

Castration anxiety is viewed as a central component of the Oedipus complex. According to Freudian theory, it is based on parental threats in response to endogenously generated death wishes and fantasies in relation to the same sex parent that is a component of a universally programmed oedipal complex. Given the presumed universality of castration anxiety, one would have to assume that parental castration threats are equally ubiquitous.

However, this is simply implausible. Hence, it makes more sense to think of the Freudian concept of castration anxiety as an endogenously generated fantasy in which, so to speak, the punishment (i.e., castration) is made to fit the crime (i.e., killing of the father in order to safely fulfill one's incestuous wishes). In contrast to this view is the proposition that castration anxiety stems not from indigenous and programmed hostile wishes, but from pathogenic beliefs based on parental communications (see Eagle, 1987). The essence of these communications is that if you outdo me or separate from me, you will harm me or incur my displeasure. These actual experiences can then be elaborated to include a symbolic equivalence between pursuing or succeeding in one's ambitions and destroying the other or inviting the other's wrath. Thus, pursuit of and success in one's ambitions becomes fraught with a degree of danger, anxiety, and guilt that is based on but goes beyond actual experiences.

Consider as another example of a pathogenic belief, Modell's (1983) discussion of "survivor guilt" and "separation guilt" based on the emotional conviction that 'if I separate from my parents and lead a separate and autonomous life, I will be abandoning them.' However, once again, although actual parental messages and cues may form the basis for this pathogenic belief, its further development and elaboration may include a symbolic equivalence between the developmentally normal pursuit of separation–individuation and abandoning and destroying others. One can say that repeated episodic experiences of certain parental cues and messages become transformed into if–then implicit or procedural knowledge. That is, the implicit belief is that if I lead a successful and independent life, it is necessarily at the expense of someone close to me. Furthermore, to the extent that this if–then 'rule' is implicit, it cannot be reflected on and is difficult to disconfirm (Polanyi & Prosch, 1975). It is also important to note that parental denial that they are communicating certain cues and messages contributes importantly to the implicit or unconscious status of pathogenic beliefs (see Eagle, 1987).

Kohut (1984) presents a similar account of oedipal conflicts and anxieties. He maintains that under optimal conditions, the oedipal stage is joyfully entered – presumably because it marks the child's new developmental experiences and strivings. It is, Kohut maintains, only in the context of inappropriate parental seductiveness and generational envy that oedipal conflicts and anxieties, including castration anxiety, arise.

Viewing unconscious fantasies as based on endogenously generated forbidden unconscious wishes versus seeing them as elaborations of parental responses to developmental strivings has important theoretical as well as clinical implications. If one adopts the Freudian perspective, one will be more likely to devote one's clinical efforts to uncovering repressed hostile wishes and fantasies that are assumed to be universally present. If, however, one entertains the possibility that castration anxiety may be based on parental communications and is a fantasy in which ambition, success, and self-assertion are unconsciously experienced *as if* they constituted hostile wishes meriting dire punishment, one's focus will more likely be on the idiosyncratic personal meanings the patient has unconsciously given to normal developmental strivings, for example, on the unconscious equation of ambitious strivings with hostility toward the parental figure. This unconscious equation is understood as the source of expected punishment both from the other and from oneself, that is, the internalized other in the form of the superego. I want especially to note the contrast between a stance of uncovering that, based on one's theory, one 'knows' is unconsciously there, but repressed in every patient, and a stance in which one's efforts are devoted to deciphering the unconscious idiosyncratic meanings given to certain wishes and strivings.

I am not suggesting that children do not ever have hostile wishes toward their parents. Of course, they do. What I am questioning is the claim that such wishes are universal and are based on a biologically based program of psychosexual development. Furthermore, in some cases, it may be that it *is parental* hostility and rivalry toward the child's achievements and competitive strivings, what Kohut (1984) refers to as generational envy, that triggers hostile impulses in the child toward the parent.

Following his replacement of his seduction theory with a theory of unconscious seduction wishes and fantasies, Freud radically de-emphasized the role of actual events in favor of universal endogenous factors. After abandoning his seduction theory, Freud displayed a striking and persistent blindness towards adult aggressive and sexual behavior towards children (Klein, 1981; Sheleff, 1981). As Milton Klein (1981) observes, at the very time that Freud reported in a letter to Fliess his own dream in which he experienced sexual feeling towards his 11 year old daughter, he also wrote in his notes: "Hostile impulses against parents (a wish that they should die) are also an integral part of neurosis" (Freud, 1887–1902, p. 207). Klein writes, "What is striking is that Freud made a theoretical turn-around by theorizing about the child's impulses toward the parent on the same day that he gave a personal account of the parent's impulses toward the child" (p. 197).

And although Freud studied the Oedipus trilogy and borrowed one of his central concepts from it, as noted earlier, he ignores the striking fact that Laius, the father, ordered that the infant Oedipus be put to death. (In this connection, see also Sheleff, 1981, who describes an old Persian myth in which the father kills the son.) Another example of Freud's neglect of the role of actual adult behavior towards children include his failure to note and give weight to the degree to which Dora was being used as a pawn by her father in his affair with Frau K.

Freud's neglect of the effects of adult and parental behavior, and his exclusive emphasis on the libidinal and aggressive impulses and fantasies of the child, were necessitated by a theory that located the origins of pathology almost entirely in intrapsychic unconscious instinctual impulses and the conflicts that surrounded them. Hence, actual events (e.g., parental envy or seductiveness) serve only as "releasers," or perhaps facilitators, of what are, in any case, universal, biologically laid down, vicissitudes. As Freud (1919b) puts it at one point, "It is in the years of childhood between the ages of two and four or five that the congenital libidinal factors are first awakened by actual experiences and become attached to certain complexes" (p. 184). Or, as Jones (1953) states, "Freud had discovered the truth of the matter: that irrespective of incest wishes of parents towards their children, and even of occasional acts of the kinds, what he had to concern himself with was the general occurrence of incest wishes of children towards their parents" (p. 322). In other words, whatever parents did or did not do in reality, incestuous and aggressive wishes of children towards parents are universally present.

## *10. Anecdotal evidence*

Anecdotal accounts, presumably attesting to the ubiquitousness of incestuous wishes should also be at least briefly considered. When I discuss the Oedipus complex with colleagues, there are at least one or more individuals who will say something like: "I didn't believe in the Oedipus complex until I had children and repeatedly heard my 4 or 5 year old son announcing that he wanted to marry me and that he viewed Daddy as a rival" – or "heard my 4 or 5 year old daughter saying she wanted to marry Daddy." Of course, the question is how one interprets these anecdotes. Can one assume that when a 4 or 5 year old little boy says he wants to marry Mommy, he is expressing incestuous wishes? Could he be expressing rather a desire to have Mommy's exclusive attention? We do not know what a 4 or 5 year old means when he says he wants to marry Mommy. One thing, however, we can be sure about – even from a psychoanalytic point of view – is that when a 4 or 5 year old boy says he wants to marry Mommy, his understanding of 'marry' is not the same as the adult's and is likely to be suffused with fantasy and evidence of immature cognitive development appropriate to his age (See Eagle, 2001; Erreich, 2003; 2015). Indeed, the very meaning of "incestuous wishes" is undoubtedly markedly different for an adult and a 4 or 5 year old – let alone for an adult and a young infant who, according to Klein (1975, p. 2), shows evidence of the Oedipus complex.

As another example of anecdotal evidence, I was recently told by a colleague who works with children that it is not uncommon for her to hear boys of age four and older express fears that their penis will recede into their pubic area and disappear, and to hear girls of the same age express castration concerns and penis envy in the form of the fantasy that instead of having a penis like boys have, their penis had been cut off. According to my colleague, rather than being unconscious, these fantasies and fears were often openly expressed.

Let us assume that my colleague's anecdotal account is reasonably accurate. The question is whether these fantasies and fears support the classical Oedipal complex theory. In order to support oedipal theory, the boy's fear that his penis will disappear would have to be experienced at some level as punishment for incestuous and hostile wishes; and the girl's fantasy that her penis had been removed would have to be fitted in the classical account that in compensation for not having a penis, the little girl entertains the fantasy of having a baby with father. Although according to classical theory, incestuous and hostile wishes and impregnation fantasy are presumably unconscious, some evidence, direct or indirect, linking the presumably openly expressed castration fears and penis envy to the oedipal account must be present. Young children may have all sorts of fantasies, some frightening, about their bodies, including the fantasy that their penis will disappear or that they once had a penis. However, such fantasies, by themselves, do not provide support for the propositions that these fantasies are the product of universal incestuous and hostile impulses.

I recall seeing a Mr. Rogers television program in which he, in his usual sensitive manner, reassures young children that they will not disappear down the drain as the bath water does when the plug is removed. Apparently, Mr. Rogers was aware that at least some children have the frightening fantasy that they will disappear. My point here is that young children have many different bodily fantasies, based on immature cognition and a variety of fears. The questions are whether a subclass of such fantasies and fears constitute support for oedipal theory and the kind of evidence that would be needed for that support to be forthcoming.

It would be quite interesting to carry out ecologically valid research to investigate what young children mean – the specific representations and fantasies involved – when they talk about wanting to marry Mommy or Daddy or express other fantasies that are invoked as evidence for the Oedipus complex. This could perhaps bring to bear clinically relevant data to better adjudicate this issue – an alternative to one's position being determined by one's fealty to this or that psychoanalytic 'school.'

In one of the few empirical studies on "oedipal behaviors", Watson and Getz (1990) obtained parents' reports of children's (ages 3 to 6) affectionate and aggressive behavior toward them. They also obtained the children's doll-play narratives as a means of assessing their "role-level understanding," "oedipal preferences," "understanding of age relativity," and "belief in parental omniscience." Oedipal behaviors were defined in terms of affection for opposite sex parent and aggression toward same sex parent, rather diluted criteria. They found that "oedipal behaviors" were found at four years of age and began to decline at five years. They also found that changes in the children's "oedipal behaviors" were lawfully related to their level of understanding of behavioral and social roles. As an example of the latter, the highest level of understanding was scored when a child showed that he or she understands "that a person can be in at least two roles simultaneously, for example, both mother and grandmother or both mother and wife" (p. 35). Children who demonstrated this level of role understanding showed very few "oedipal behaviors" in their doll-play narratives.

An interesting and unexpected finding reported by Watson and Getz "was a shift in children's explanations for choices in the hypothetical stories, namely, from responses demonstrating their strong personal preferences (e.g., "Tommy wants to go with his mother because he loves her") to responses showing a fairness strategy (e.g., "Tommy went with Daddy last time, so that it's only fair that he goes with Mommy this time") (p. 41). This fairness strategy was not present at three years of age, minimally present at four and five years, and characteristic at six years of age. The authors suggest that this more balanced strategy replaces the stronger parental preference pattern that defines oedipal behavior and can be taken as indication of the passing of the oedipal phase.

I think this study is an interesting one in a number of ways. It demonstrates that what are referred to as "oedipal behaviors" (e.g., "I want to marry Mommy" or "I want to marry Daddy") do, indeed, occur in children at a certain age. However, it also helps one understand these behaviors in the context of the child's cognitive development and his or her struggle to understand shifting roles in the family structure. For example, at a certain age children begin to "see male and female roles as complementary and constant" (p. 32), but may not be able to "realize that they can love each parent while their parents continue to love each other. In other words, children may not see how their parents can be both parents to them and spouses to each other and maintain both relationships simultaneously" (p. 32).

The results of the Watson and Getz (1990) study indicate that, as one aspect of oedipal theory predicts, at a certain age children tend to show affection for the opposite sex parent and aggression toward the same sex parent. However, contrary to oedipal theory, the pattern begins to decline at age five. Most important, the emergence of "oedipal behaviors" as well as their decline are related to the child's level of understanding of social roles and family structure. This supports the idea that so-called oedipal behaviors reflect the child's developmental struggle to understand triangularity.

A number of additional points are worth noting. One, the patterns described by Watson and Getz were general trends that admit of many exceptions rather than the universal patterns claimed by oedipal theory. Two, although the term "oedipal behaviors" is employed by Watson and Getz, it refers to expressions of affection for opposite sex parent and aggression toward same sex parent rather than, as oedipal theory dictates, incestuous and death wishes. There is perhaps no harm in using the somewhat question-begging term "oedipal behaviors" loosely and descriptively so long as one understands that the "oedipal behaviors" referred to (i.e., expressions of affection and aggression) are quite different from the behaviors posited by oedipal theory, namely, incestuous wishes toward the opposite sex parent that persist into adulthood and death wishes toward the same sex parent. To assume that the child's affectionate and aggressive behaviors constitute evidence for oedipal theory is to beg the very question at issue and to have a very watered down conception of the Oedipus complex. One must keep in mind that Watson and Getz present no evidence for the direct or indirect (e.g., in fantasy) expressions of incestuous or death wishes. However, their findings can perhaps be taken as support of such a highly diluted version of the Oedipus complex that one has to question whether another term with less misleading connotations should be used.

As Mayes and Cohen (1996) write:

> [B]etween 3 and 5 years of age, a marked reorganization of psychological life occurs, formally demarcated in psychoanalysis as the oedipal period. The process of "oedipalization" involves dramatic shifts in neural activity, cognitive capacities, symbolic thinking, and social-affective life.
>
> (p. 127)

Note that the dramatic shifts referred to have little to do with incesutuous and hostile wishes; also, the term "oedipalization" is employed in a vague sense.

There are findings of other studies that tend to contradict predictions of oedipal theory. For example, Panksepp (1998) reported that 26.8% of mothers endorsed the item "Tries to touch mother's or other women's breasts" in regard to their 2–5 year old boys. However, that item was also endorsed by 43.7% of mothers in regard to their 2–5 year old *girls*. Another finding was that children with behavior problems showed more sexual behaviors and that sexually abused children had the greatest frequency of sexual behaviors.

## *Does resolution of the oedipal conflicts play a key role in various aspects of psychological development?*

As noted earlier, according to classical oedipal theory, how the individual resolves oedipal conflicts has a powerful influence on various aspects of psychological development, including gender identity, superego formation, integration of love and desire, and object choice. What is the evidence for these rather strong claims? In answering this question, much depends on how one understands the resolution of oedipal conflicts. If, as is the case in classical theory, one defines it as relinquishment of incestuous and hostile wishes and identification with the aggressor, then one would have to say that there is no good empirical support for this formulation insofar as there is no compelling evidence for the existence of universal incestuous wishes in the first place that need to be relinquished.

There is an odd inconsistency in Freud's thinking about resolution of the Oedipus complex. On the one hand, adequate resolution is understood in terms of relinquishment of incestuous wishes. On the other hand, Freud (1912c) tells us that "anyone who is to be really free and happy in love must . . . have come to terms with the idea of incest with his mother or sister" (p. 186). And he also tells us that because of the incest taboo, "the final object of the sexual instinct is never any longer the original object, but only a surrogate for it" (p. 189). These statements suggest that were it not for cultural restraints, the ideal 'solution' to the oedipal complex would not be relinquishment of incestuous wishes, but their acceptance and fulfillment – a state of affairs, he (incorrectly) believed, characterized animal life. Because of the restraints of civilization, humans, on the other hand, have to settle for 'second best' surrogates.

## *Evolved function of oedipal conflicts*

In an interesting paper, Josephs (2010) speculates about "the evolved function of the oedipal conflict" (p. 937). His basic claim is that "incestuous and sexual rivalrous feelings in relation to the parents are normative and can serve an adaptive function in enabling children to develop working models of romantic love triangles" (p. 938), which, in turn, "provide intuitive strategies of coping with some of the sexually competitive threats to monogamous romantic relationships in adulthood such as infidelity and mate poaching" (p. 939). In other words, experiencing and acquiring coping skills to deal with oedipal conflicts in childhood provides a practice arena for coping with the vicissitudes and dangers (e.g., being cuckolded or being subject to punishment and mutilation if caught poaching) of romantic love triangles in adulthood.

Josephs' speculations are interesting and imaginative. However, they have little or no bearing on the question of whether there is a universal Oedipus complex. Rather, his speculations essentially take the following form: These are possibly the evolved functions of what oedipal conflicts would be if one took for granted that the Oedipus complex exists and is universal. But this is no argument for the existence of a universal Oedipus complex nor a substitute for direct empirical evidence. What needs to precede hypotheses about the evolved function of X is evidence for the existence of X. One cannot legitimately begin with speculations about the evolved function of X as an argument for the existence of X. Doing so presents the risk that one is largely generating just-so evolutionary function stories, however interesting they may be.

## *Oedipal betrayal as an aspect of the Oedipus complex*

Up to this point, I have dealt with the Oedipus complex as it is usually understood, where the primary emphasis is on incestuous wishes, rivalry, and the incest taboo. However, a number of commentators have called attention to what they view as an important but relatively under-emphasized aspect of the Oedipus complex, namely, the oedipal child's experience of the parental sexual relationship as a betrayal, "as an act of infidelity by the desired but unfaithful parent" (Josephs, 2006, p. 423). According to these commentators, the experience of oedipal betrayal by the desired parent is as regular and integral an aspect of the Oedipus complex as incestuous and rivalrous wishes. Furthermore, according to this view, the sense of oedipal betrayal is especially important in understanding the experiences and dynamics of both the one who is the object of infidelity and the one who carries it out. I will discuss two recent papers that illustrate this perspective.

The first paper is by Elise (2012). There are essentially two major themes in the paper. One theme that remains closer to the clinical material and is described with great sensitivity is how infidelity undermines not only trust in the other, but perhaps most important, "trust in one's own mind in relation to one's objects" (p. 701). She describes the reaction of several female patients who reacted to their partner's or spouse's infidelity with an "anxious preoccupation with a need to 'reconstruct' past reality" (p. 698) – to check phone records, credit slips, etc. as part of an effort to learn when and how long the betrayal was going on. Elise writes: "I could appreciate and interpret the imperative to regain a grasp of the past, in order to restore confidence in the capacity for reality testing" (p. 699). As noted, in this part of the paper, there are close links among the patient's reported experiences, the analyst's formulations, and her clinical interventions.

The second theme of the paper focuses on oedipal betrayal. Elise's basic argument here is that the woman's experience of infidelity is essentially a re-experience of "being cheated on, a repetition of the original oedipal injury in being the passive recipient of betrayal" (p. 80). For both sexes, according to Elise, "recognition of the mother's desire going elsewhere can feel to the child like a betrayal by the mother: I thought you were mine alone, but now I see that you've been involved with him [i.e., father] all along"! "For both sexes, deception takes place first in relation to the maternal object, who is, as Freud (1935) puts it, a 'faithless seducer' " (p. 682). However, according to Elise, the girl has been "dumped" twice, once by the mother – her "first object of desire" (p. 681) – and then by father when the oedipal girl turns to him. Hence, on this view, infidelity is likely to be especially traumatic for women.

I do not know whether or not there is evidence for the above conclusion. As far as I know, there is no evidence that the pattern described by Elise is a frequently observed one. However, what I want to focus on here is Elise's claim that infidelity is regularly (universally?) experienced by women as oedipal betrayal, as "a repetition of the original oedipal injury" (p. 80). In what I refer to as the first theme of the paper, Elise presents poignant clinical material supporting her formulation regarding the effect of infidelity in undermining trust in one's mind. For example, the patient states with much emotion: "I'd been lied to for some time and *my* reality that I'd *lived* was *not* true – it was dissolved in seconds, shaken apart, as if my memory banks were melting down" (p. 686). And Elise's interventions are empathic and directly linked to her patient's experiences.

In contrast to how the first theme is presented, in Elise's discussion of the second theme, namely, infidelity as oedipal betrayal, no clinical material is presented that constitutes direct or inferential evidence that the patient experienced the infidelity of her partner as a repeat of an earlier oedipal betrayal. Rather, Elise notes that the patient's father had cheated on her mother when the patient was seven and then writes "Thus, with his affair her father had symbolically cheated on Eva and cheated her out of a secure home and family, as well as out of a positive identification with a mother loved faithfully by her husband" (p. 685). However, the relevance of the father's cheating is thrown into question when, later in the paper, Elise writes: "The oedipal child must come to grips with the grim realization that the parents, though they do indeed love the child, have indeed 'cheated' on him or her by their 'affair' with one another" (p. 695).

Much of the discussion of infidelity as the re-experience of oedipal betrayal in the paper is in the above vein, that is, theoretical formulations and speculations about what the oedipal child presumably experiences. For example, Elise writes: "Often a new sibling provides incontrovertible evidence of a mother's infidelity (Freud, 1910), intensifying the sense of injury in a most poignant way. The girl realizes that her wish to have a baby with her mother is doomed" (p. 697). No evidence, clinical or otherwise, is presented supporting the idea that the generic girl wishes to have a baby with her mother. Rather, it is stated as a given.

The only place in the paper in which Elise attempts to relate her speculations regarding the link between infidelity and oedipal betrayal to the clinical material is when she writes: "A narrative construction of oedipal injuries in relation to mother and father, *which for the most part could not be directly recalled* [my emphasis], was accessed only when those injuries surfaced in the transference" (p. 701). If oedipal injuries were not directly recalled, what is the clinical basis for inferring that they occurred? Elise seems to assume that the patient felt betrayed by the analyst when she recognized another patient in the waiting room who worked in the same corporation as she did. On what basis does Elise assume the patient's reaction constitutes evidence of her sense of oedipal betrayal in relation to mother and father? The only basis seems to be Elise's theoretical assumptions regarding oedipal conflicts. Why isn't it an expression of sibling rivalry or some other set of feelings? A meaningful way of addressing these questions is to look to the clinical material produced by the patient rather than impose one's theoretical speculations (see Peterfreund, 1983).

I raise the above issue not to comment on Elise's technique or clinical interventions, but to illustrate the relative independence of a theoretical assumption regarding the Oedipus complex from the clinical material presented. As noted, this is in contrast to the close link between Elise's formulation and the clinical data in her discussion of the effects of infidelity on the patient's sense of her capacity to test reality in relation to her objects. Perhaps this is so because the latter formulation is more experience-near, less theoretically 'loaded,' and more theoretically neutral. Perhaps this better enables the analyst to look at the clinical material for what it is rather than through a pre-set theoretical lens. Contrastingly, if one assumes the universality of the Oedipus complex and also assumes that it always includes a sense of betrayal and the "grim realization" that one's parents have "cheated" on oneself by virtue of their "affair" with one another, then one will look for it and find it in one form or another in all patients who have experienced infidelity on the part of their partner.

Elise cites a paper by Josephs (2006) who highlights an aspect of the Oedipus complex noted by Freud (1910b, pp. 170–171), but as he notes, is relatively neglected in the psychoanalytic literature. That aspect is the boy's feeling of betrayal by mother who has "granted the favor of sexual intercourse, not to himself, but to his father" (Freud, 1910b, p. 171). According to Josephs, the unconscious desire for revenge in response to this experience of oedipal betrayal is a key factor in impulses and acts of infidelity. As Josephs (2006) puts it, "The child will avenge him- or herself by growing up to become an adult who will seduce and betray others as he or she has felt seduced and betrayed" (p. 424). In other words, the unfaithful individual turns passive into active. Further, Josephs suggests that in addition to the "danger situations" (Freud, 1926) of loss of the object, loss of the object's love, etc., "the trauma of oedipal seduction and betrayal may be a universal situation of danger" (p. 435), one relatively neglected by Freud and other psychoanalytic theorists.

What is the evidence that the child perceives parental intercourse as an act of infidelity by the desired but unfaithful parent? Instead of addressing this question, Josephs cites Freud. On what basis does Josephs maintain that adult infidelity is motivated by a desire for revenge owing to oedipal betrayal? In neither case does Josephs cite clinical or other sources of evidence. Without addressing the question of the basis of these speculations and formulations, what standing can they have beyond that of imaginative stories? As is the case in the Elise paper, the clinical material that Josephs presents, which is intended to be illustrative of his formulation bears little actual relationship to it. No clinical evidence is presented that points to the patient's experience, conscious or unconscious, of oedipal betrayal as a child or that could reasonably form a basis for an inference of such an experience.

In just about all the clinical material presented there is little or no material supporting the inference that the infidelity of the patient discussed by Joseph toward her husband is motivated by revenge for oedipal betrayal. Josephs (2006) writes that "the issue of oedipal infidelity did not explicitly emerge in the material until relatively late in the treatment after much of the negative transference had been worked through" (p. 434). However, what Josephs refers to as "oedipal infidelity" that emerged had to do not primarily with interactions between the patient and father, but with her father's flirtation with other women in front of her and her mother and the belief on the part of some family members "that her father had extramarital affairs" (p. 434). To refer to this material – which has to do with possible infidelity of father in relation to mother – as reflecting the emergence of "the issue of oedipal infidelity" begs the question rather than constitutes evidence for it or evaluating its tenability.

In general, Josephs has a question-begging and over-inclusive conception of oedipal infidelity. For example, he cites Freud in noting:

> [O]edipal infidelity is a huge narcissistic injury that incites fantasies of revenge. The murderousness felt toward the unfaithful parent [i.e., unfaithful toward the child] certainly equals that felt toward the rival parent.
>
> (p. 424)

Josephs then goes on to observe that "Shakespeare's Othello is the best dramatization of the desire to punish sexual betrayal with a death sentence" (p. 424). But, Othello is responding to his belief that his wife not his mother has betrayed him. To assimilate this account to "*oedipal*" infidelity or betrayal is, once again, to beg the very question that is at issue, namely, can Othello's sense of betrayal and desire for revenge be legitimately seen as psychologically equivalent to *oedipal* betrayal?

Let me cite another example of a somewhat arbitrary assimilation of phenomena to the context of oedipal theory. As noted earlier, Elise (2012) refers to Freud's idea that "often a new sibling provides incontrovertible evidence of a mother's infidelity (Freud, 1910, 1919a), intensifying the sense of injury in a most poignant manner" (p. 697). She goes on to state, "the girl realizes that her wish to have a baby with her mother is doomed" (p. 697) – presumably because she recognizes father's role in the birth of the sibling. What is striking here is that the child's reaction to a new sibling is discussed not in terms of sibling rivalry, and of being displaced by the newborn sibling, but in terms of mother's sexual infidelity. This is especially striking given the ubiquitous observable evidence (as contrasted with speculation) on how children react to the arrival of a new sibling, the broad evidence of sibling rivalry in a wide range of species, and based on such evidence, the status of sibling rivalry as one of Darwin's great principles.

On what basis does Elise maintain that girls generally wish to have a baby with mother? Did her patient express such a wish? Have her patients generally expressed such a wish? Is there evidence available from any source that girls generally have such wishes? Can one think of ways to determine whether or not girls regularly have such a wish? Unless these questions can be adequately addressed, one would have to conclude that Elise's formulation is an imaginative speculation – a just-so story – that bears little relationship to the girl's experiences or psychological life.

There are larger issues at play here having to do with such matters as the nature of evidence and the very nature of psychoanalytic theorizing. Both Elise's and Josephs' papers are replete with speculations about why people cheat on their partner, the motivations underlying this behavior, what children feel about the relationship between mother and father, the relationship between early feelings and fantasies, such as girls wanting to have a baby with mother, and infidelity, splitting between faithful and unfaithful aspects of the self, seduction by the desired parent, hatred toward the desired parent in response to feeling betrayed, and so on and so on. In each of these papers, selected clinical material is presented which, for the most part, has only the most distant relationship to the speculations and formulations presented. That is, their evidential import is highly questionable.

Here we have a major divergence in attitudes and values between this type of psychoanalytic theorizing and an empirically grounded discipline, including grounding in clinical material. From the latter perspective, if one stated that children regularly perceive parental intercourse as betrayal, the very next step would be to think of ways to determine whether or to what degree children do, in fact, perceive, parental intercourse that way. Similarly with Elise's claim that girls want to have a baby with mother. One would want to know whether they, in fact, have such wishes. As difficult as it would undoubtedly be, one would go about trying to determine the best way to address that question.

There is an interesting irony contained in the above discussion. One of the sources of tension between clinicians and researchers is the former's emphasis on idiographic approaches – what Hoffman (2009) refers to as the "consequential uniqueness" of each case – and the complaint that researchers impose nomothetic formulations on the individual case. But if interpretations of clinical material of individual cases are derived from presumed nomothetic laws (e.g., all infidelity is experienced as a repeat of an earlier betrayal), the clinician is engaging in the same practice that is the basis for his or her objection to research practices. More egregious, the nomothetic formulations relied upon by the clinician are not supported by evidence, either clinical or research evidence.

I want to make one final comment regarding the claim that children experience their parents 'intimate' sexual relationship as a betrayal. One implication of this formulation is that the more intimate and clearly sexual the relationship between parents, the greater the likelihood the child will experience oedipal betrayal, the more intense that experience of betrayal will be, and the more difficulty the child will have in resolving oedipal conflicts. And conversely, the more distant and nonsexual the parental relationship, the lower the likelihood that the child will experience oedipal betrayal and if he or she does, the less intense it is likely to be, and therefore, the less burdened the child will be in his or her resolution of oedipal conflicts. However, the evidence suggests that parental discord and distance is associated with more rather than less difficulty in resolving oedipal conflicts. Indeed, the evidence suggests that components of the Oedipus complex (i.e., incestuous and rivalrous wishes) are likely to be manifested in largely troubled families (e.g., Ascherman & Safier, 1990; Flores, Mattos, & Salzano, 1998; see also Hamilton.

1982). The oedipal betrayal hypothesis does not seem to take into account the likely possibility that the child's experience of the parents as close and intimate, including sexually intimate, can be reassuring in the sense of generating feelings of safety, security, and family stability, and can serve as a model of commitment and fidelity.

## *Reconceptualizations of the Oedipus complex*

A number of attempts have been made to preserve some version of the Oedipus complex by reformulating it in various ways. I have already noted Morehead's (1996) efforts to preserve some version of oedipal theory. He writes that "Human and animal evidence supports the Westermarck hypothesis," but suggests that such evidence does not contradict "recent analytic theory on the Oedipus complex [which] does not require the existence of a central, powerful, incestuous sexual drive" (p. 347). As I have argued above, an Oedipus complex without incestuous wishes is no longer an Oedipus complex, but rather a relinquishment of the concept.

There are a number of other ways in which the Oedipus complex has been reconceptualized. One way is to define the Oedipus complex in terms of the transition from dyadic to "triadic object relations" (Fairbairn, 1952, p. 122) in which the sexual is not primary. According to this view, when oedipal sexuality does become prominent, it is due to the unavailability of parental love and is motivated by "a desperate attempt to make emotional contact with the object" (p. 122). A similar position is taken by Kohut (1984) who distinguishes between the Oedipus complex, which is a pathological phenomenon due to inappropriate parental seductiveness and intergenerational envy and a developmental oedipal stage, which when adequate parental mirroring is available, is characterized by age-appropriate affection and non-hostile assertiveness. Why age-appropriate affection and assertiveness are referred to as oedipal is not addressed by Kohut.

The increasing prominence of triadic relationships in the life of the child may be an important aspect of development and therefore worth studying. Indeed, one can perhaps understand the child's conflicts, not in the literal sense of incestuous wishes, etc., but in the metaphoric sense of highlighting triadic conflicts, jealousies, competition for attention and nurturance, etc. within the family structure. Understanding so-called oedipal conflicts in this way may contribute to an understanding of the developing child's experience, the interaction between the child and his or her parents, and certain aspects of the interaction between mother and father. For example, as noted earlier, it is not at all uncommon to observe a family dynamic in which the birth of a child triggers the husband's envy and rivalry in relation to his wife's meting out of attention and nurturance. Thus, one can speak of not only the child entering the triadic relationship, *but also the father.* Should one refer to this dynamic as a reverse oedipal complex? As far as I know, Freud did not comment on this dynamic. (See Simon, 1991, for a discussion of the role of parental behavior in inducing the child's competition and hostility.)

Another way that the Oedipus complex has been redefined is illustrated by Loewald's (1979) statement that "the Oedipal attachments, struggles, and conflicts must also be understood as new versions of the basic union–individuation dilemma" (p. 775). According to this reconceptualization, the Oedipus complex is no longer primarily about incestuous wishes, but rather primarily about fantasies of symbiotic merger. The developmental struggle to achieve differentiation and some degree of independence and separation from parents is undoubtedly a universal issue for a wide range of species, including humans. However, it is not an oedipal issue, at the center of which is the need to deal with incestuous and hostile wishes. In short, once again, this supposed redefinition of the Oedipus complex, too, is not a redefinition, but a relinquishment of the concept.

In effect, the presumed redefinition states something like the following: 'We were mistaken in believing that incestuous wishes are universal. We have come to believe that what we took to be the Oedipus complex is essentially the expression of the individual's struggle to achieve differentiation and separation.' It would be refreshing and clarifying if we were told directly that the theory of the Oedipus complex had been rejected and also the evidential basis for assigning primacy to the role of struggles for separation–individuation.

Tracing the vicissitudes of the reconceptualizations and redefinitions of the Oedipus complex can be instructive in examining how theory change typically comes about in psychoanalysis. Instead of reaching a relatively clear verdict that the evidence does not support the viability of oedipal theory and looking for alternative theoretical explanations (of the important phenomena that oedipal theory addresses), the Oedipus complex has been redefined, which gives the impression not that it has been relinquished in the light of the evidence, but that it is alive and well, but has simply been modestly altered.

One of the problems with retaining the term "Oedipus complex" and, at the same time, understanding it in a metaphoric sense is that the latter may have little to do with the Oedipus complex as a universal stage of psychosexual development, as it is generally understood. Also, it contributes little to an understanding of a number of issues, including gender differences, for example, the question of why the increased prominence of triadic relationships takes the form of the little girl's increased interest in Daddy. Above all, to conceptualize the oedipal stage primarily in terms of the emergence of triadic relationships, without the presence of incestuous and hostile wishes, is to redefine the Oedipus complex out of existence. Retaining concepts such as oedipal stage and Oedipus complex obscures this fact.

As for the relationship between resolution of oedipal conflicts and psychopathology, there is a far more compelling case for the claim that how one resolves so-called oedipal conflicts influences subsequent psychological development when one redefines these conflicts in terms of differentiation and separation–individuation. I think it is fair to say that there is a relative consensus among contemporary psychoanalytic theorists and clinicians that persistence of early modes of relating and clinging to early object ties are pathological and, correspondingly, that developmental growth in modes of relating and object ties is an essential aspect of optimal development and mental health. An early expression of this point of view is seen in Fairbairn's (1952) conception of mental health in terms of the move from infantile dependence to mature dependence, from the "regressive lure of identification to the progressive urge toward separation" (p. 43), and the individual's capacity to relate to the other not as a stand-in for an early internalized object, but in terms of who the other actually is. This conception of mental health is also seen in Mahler's (1968) formulation of symbiosis–separation–individuation, Loewald's (1979) emphasis on differentiation, and the emphasis of attachment theory on flexible versus rigid internal working models (Bowlby, 1980) (see Eagle, 2013).

In short, it would make sense and contribute to conceptual clarity to address issues of differentiation and separation–individuation in their own right rather than conceptualize them as somehow a redefined version of the Oedipus complex. Viewing something as an expression of oedipal conflicts should be reserved for phenomena that have to do with such matters as the relative failure to integrate love and desire due to the activation of an incest taboo triggered by an unconscious equation between parent and current partner.

On this revised view of the Oedipus complex, what needs to be resolved is the unconscious equation between parental figure and romantic partner so that the latter is not experienced as an incestuous object. However, it needs to be noted once again, from the fact that the incest taboo is activated in the equation between parental figures and current romantic partner, it does not follow that incestuous desires are involved. To put it conversely, from the fact that A's response to his wife as if she were his mother activates the incest taboo and leads to interference with sexual desire, it does not follow that this has come about due to early incestuous wishes toward mother that have persisted into adulthood. Rather, the mere symbolic equation between mother and wife is sufficient to activate the incest taboo.

## Implications of relinquishment of the Oedipus complex for the role of sexuality in psychoanalytic theory

There is little of a systematic nature in the psychoanalytic literature that deals with the question of the impact of altering or relinquishing one or more components of a theory upon the rest of the theory. This issue is particularly pertinent in the case of Freudian theory, which has an architectural structure of different interlocking components that have a close logical relationship to each other. The de-emphasis on the Oedipus complex as a central factor in the development of neurosis and the increasing emphasis on the issue of differentiation and separation–individuation raises questions regarding the role of sexuality in a wide range of psychopathology. It also raises questions regarding the proper role of sexuality and its interaction with other motivational systems in psychic life.

What are the implications of relinquishing or modifying the classical conception of the oedipal complex for a psychoanalytic general theory of psychological development as well as a more specific theory of the nature of sexuality, the integration of attachment and sexuality, choice of mate, and other related phenomena?

One implication of this theoretical change is the idea that at the core of a wide range of psychopathology are not the persistence of conflicts around incestuous wishes and fantasies, but rather issues having to do with differentiation and separation–individuation. Of course, patients continue to report sexual difficulties, such as the split between love and desire. However, there is little evidence that these difficulties are mainly due to the persistence of early incestuous wishes.

Consider, for example, conceptualizations of borderline personality disorder (BPD). There is little evidence that oedipal conflicts (defined in the traditional sense) or more generally, sexual conflicts, are at the core of BPD. Rather, borderline pathology is characterized by such features as loss of boundaries, hypersensitivity to rejection, fear of abandonment, and impulsivity – features that have little to do with incestuous wishes and much to do with issues of differentiation and separation–individuation as well as of affect regulation.

Consider as another example, the conceptualization of agoraphobia, a syndrome that was conceptualized in classical theory virtually exclusively in terms of sexual and aggressive impulses (see Eagle, 2009). I think it is fair to say that much of the evidence, including clinical evidence, supports the view that agoraphobia is best understood as entailing a separation–individuation conflict – what Fairbairn (1952) referred to as "the conflict between the regressive lure of identification and the progressive urge toward separation" (p. 43). There is little or no evidence that at the core of agoraphobia are classical oedipal conflicts.

It has been argued, that whereas oedipal conflicts are at the core of neurosis, so-called pre-oedipal issues are at the core of other forms of psychopathology such as BPD or agoraphobia or narcissistic personality disorder. Therefore, the reasoning goes, whereas the theory of the Oedipus complex is appropriate for neurosis, it is not appropriate for pre-oedipal pathology. There are a number of problems with this 'compromise' which preserves some area of psychopathology to be understood in terms of classical oedipal conflicts. As we have seen from the earlier discussion, even quintessentially neurotic and presumably oedipal problems, such as the split between love and desire, are not adequately accounted for by the theory of the Oedipus complex.

Another problem with the 'compromise' lies in the terms "pre-oedipal" and "oedipal." A common assumption found in the psychoanalytic literature is that the roots of more serious psychopathology such as, say, BPD or schizophrenia, are earlier, that is, pre-oedipal issues, whereas the roots of less serious psychopathology, such as neurosis, are later, that is, oedipal issues. Aside from the problem that this formulation begs the question of whether there are, in fact, pre-oedipal and oedipal stages of development, there is little or no evidence that the roots of more severe psychopathology are earlier than those of less severe psychopathology.

It should be noted that the issues being discussed are not only of theoretical import, but also have important implications for treatment. Thus, if, for example, based on one's theoretical convictions, one believes that all male patients harbor unconscious incestuous wishes toward mother and hostile wishes toward father, one will be more likely to 'find' and interpret them in the patient's productions.

Also, based on cues emitted by the therapist, patients may comply and produce material compatible with the therapist's theoretical predilections (see Masling & Cohen, 1987). As Marmor (1962) noted quite a while ago, Freudian patients tend to have Freudian dreams, Adlerian patients Adlerian dreams, and so on.

All the talk about creative pluralism, the theory-saturated nature of data, co-construction, and master narratives notwithstanding, I do not believe that our aim for a psychoanalytic treatment is or should be one in which the therapist's theoretical predilection or bias or conviction is a major determinant of how the patient is understood. I think it is incumbent upon therapists not only to be aware of the danger of foreclosing understanding of the patient through imposition of theoretical biases and convictions, but also to mitigate this danger by educating themselves about evidence contrary to their convictions. This has been a recurrent theme throughout this book. With regard to the Oedipus complex specifically, there is, fortunately, a rich literature that can provide the therapist with an informed background in listening to the patient's productions.

The discussion of the Oedipus complex should lead one to re-assess the overriding role given to sex and aggression not only in the development of psychopathology, but also in psychological functioning and development in general. The presumed centrality of the Oedipus complex in neurosis and in psychological development was predicated on the virtually exclusive emphasis given to infantile sexual and aggressive instinctual forces in psychological life by classical psychoanalytic theory. From early on, acceptance of the primacy of sexual wishes and fantasies in psychic life became the essential credential of being a Freudian or even being a 'real' psychoanalyst. Freud maintained that conflictual sexual wishes and fantasies were at the core of hysterical symptoms – a position that the more cautious and deliberate – and yes, more scientific – Breuer believed was too rash and not adequately supported by evidence. Breuer's objections notwithstanding, Freud never wavered from his insistence on the central role of the sexual instinct in psychopathology and psychological life and elaborated on this idea in the later formulations of psychosexual stages, drive theory, the Oedipus complex and even his conception of the primary function of the "mental apparatus" as discharge of (mainly sexual) excitation. Those, such as Jung or Adler, for example, who did not accept this basic assumption were viewed as heretics (unfortunately, these theorists developed their own orthodoxies).

Indeed, throughout the history of psychoanalysis, this attitude continued and was directed toward later figures such as Sullivan, Fromm, and Horney who were not only viewed as heretics, but were also dubbed "superficial" because they presumably focused on 'surface' phenomena such as cultural and social influences rather than on 'deep' processes such as the sexual instinct and 'primitive' sexual wishes and fantasies. And somewhat later, an egregious example of this attitude was seen in the psychoanalytic establishment's reactions to Bowlby's work. Such reactions included not simply theoretical disagreements, but virtually excommunication of Bowlby on the grounds that attachment theory was not really psychoanalytic.

My strong impression is that, to some extent, a softened version of this attitude continues to the present day in many psychoanalytic institutes, including those institutes that feel that they must keep up with the times and offer at least a few seminars on attachment theory. Their sense of estrangement, condescension, and perhaps threat in regard to attachment theory is not helped by the fact that it is embedded in an empirical research program usually associated with a university setting rather than in clinical training at psychoanalytic institutes.

This attitude of discomfort with and even hostility toward empirical research is not limited to classical 'schools' and institutes. It extends to newer 'schools' and institutes, including those associated with relational psychoanalysis and self (see Hoffman, 2009; and Mitchell's, 1998, comments on the "Grunbaum syndrome" which he satirically describes as a syndrome characterized by feelings of guilt one develops in response to not doing research, and a syndrome one soon gets over). Although psychoanalytic 'schools' may differ in their theoretical approach, they share a guild-like attitude in which loyalty to one's 'school,' institute, and charismatic leaders counts far more than empirical evidence.

The rejection of Freudian oedipal theory does not imply the rejection of infantile sexuality. There is a good deal of evidence for the presence of sexual behaviors among young non-human primates (e.g., Anderson & Bielert, 1990; Clark, 1977; De Waal, 1990; 2007) as well as children, particularly in cultures that have an open and permissive attitude toward sexuality (see Josephs, 2011). There is little doubt that infants are, literally, highly sensual creatures (see G. S. Klein, 1976). However, it should be clear that the existence of infantile sensuality or infantile sexuality does not in itself support the hypothesis of the oedipal complex nor does it in itself inform us regarding the role of sexuality in psychological life.

To argue that the evidence taken as a whole does not support Freud's theory of the Oedipus complex is not equivalent to denying that sexual desires and impulses are a vital motivational aspect of psychological and social life. At a recent study group in which I participate, the reduced importance of sexuality in contemporary psychoanalytic theories was brought up for discussion. One of the participants who decried this trend noted, as evidence of the continuing preoccupation with sexuality in our culture, that pornography was the fastest growing industry in the United States. And, of course, one can also point to the ubiquitousness of sexual themes in advertising and entertainment (i.e., movies) as still another expression of the central role of sexual content in our social and psychological life. We pay attention to and think and fantasize about sex with great frequency. I recall reading a study some years ago in which it was reported that men think about sex with great frequency throughout the day. In short, there is little doubt that sexual content and themes occupy a central place in our thoughts, feelings, and motives. From an evolutionary perspective, this makes a good deal of sense in view of the fact that sexual motives and behavior serve the survival of the species and serve to propagate our genes (see Freud's, 1900, prescient discussion of this issue).

To recognize the frequency, intensity, and importance of sexual motives is not, however, equivalent to the proposition that infantile sexuality plays a central role in personality development, including the development of psychopathology. It is theoretically possible, for example, that despite the importance of sexual motives in influencing a wide range of behaviors and in capturing our attention, interest, and behavior, sexuality and its vicissitudes may not be a central factor in the development of certain forms of psychopathology or in the development of certain areas of personality functioning (e.g., the development of memory or reality-testing). The latter possibility is, after all, implicit in the concepts of primary and secondary ego autonomy.

One also needs to recognize that there are other motives and motivational systems, such as the regulation of self-esteem, the need for status and power, the acquisition of money, aggression, loyalty, and attachment, that are also prominent in psychological life and that interact with sexual motivations. It is not entirely clear why we should assume that the sexual motivational system and sexual motives are necessarily and always primary and higher in the hierarchy of motives than other motives as far as their influence on development and personality functioning is concerned – let alone why we should reductively assume that these other motives can be understood as secondary derivatives of primary sexual motives.

Along with Hullian learning theory (e.g., Hull, 1943, 1951; see also Dollard & Miller, 1950), Freud assumed that virtually all motives were secondary derivatives of so-called primary drives – in Freud's case, the sexual drive. From early on, Freud (Breuer & Freud, 1893–1895) attributed hysterical symptoms to forbidden and conflictual sexual wishes and, as noted, the primacy of sexuality became the sine qua non of loyalty to Freudian theory. The primacy given to sexuality was not based mainly on clinical evidence, but on the need to link psychoanalysis to the organic, to the body. And, as Makari (2008) points out, Freud found this link in the sexology of his day.

To sum up, the issue is not whether there is room for sexuality in psychoanalytic theory. Of course, there is. There are, however, other motivational systems that psychoanalytic theory must also provide room for (see Lichtenberg, 1989) and that cannot be reduced to sexuality – just as sexuality cannot be reduced to other motivational systems. The challenge is to understand the role that sexual desires and motives play in psychic life and to delineate the interactions and relationships among different motivation systems such as aggression, self-regulation, caregiving, and attachment – without reducing one to the other (see Eagle, 2007b; 2011c; 2013, for a discussion of the relationship between sexuality and attachment).

Finally, apart from the question of the universality of the Oedipus complex, it is simply not plausible that more than any set of factors, the vicissitudes of infantile sexual wishes are at the core of psychological development and of a wide range of psychopathology, including severe psychopathology such as schizophrenia, or what Freud (1914a) referred to as "paraphrenia." Indeed, Freud himself understood paraphrenia more in terms of the vicissitudes of narcissism than of sexuality.[7] One does not have to discount of the importance of sexuality in psychological life in order to make this point.

In raising the question of "Is there room for sexuality in theory?" Green (1995) echoes a concern that goes back more than 100 years. As Makari (2008) makes clear, more than any other single issue, the primacy of sexuality and Freud's libido theory were at the center of psychoanalytic divisions and splits. It seems to me that the appropriate question is not "Is there room for sexuality in psychoanalytic theory," but rather "what role does sexuality play in various aspects of psychological functioning and development, including the development of psychopathology." There is no doubt that sexuality is a vital psychological and biological force in animal and human life and that sexual selection is one of the central evolutionary principles. For much of the animal kingdom, including humans, the sexual instinct is necessary for the perpetuation of the species (as is undoubtedly the case in a less obvious and salient way for other instinctual-motivational systems such as aggression, territoriality, attachment, fear, and exploration). However, this distal evolutionary function of the sexual system does not translate easily to the role of sexuality in psychological functioning and ontogenetic development at the level of proximal motives and factors.

There is also no doubt that there is, so to speak, a natural affinity between sexuality and the life of the imagination and fantasy and that both conscious and unconscious sexual motives can energize a wide range of behaviors that are themselves not directly and obviously sexual in nature. These facts about sexuality partly account for the central role that it has played in psychoanalysis and the arts as well as the fruitful relationship between the two. However, a recognition of these facts about sexuality does not constitute a theory of the role of sexuality in development and psychological functioning.

Finally, there is no doubt that sexuality, both on a biological and psychological level, is a distinctive instinctual system with its own distinctive features. For example, as Freud (1915a) observed, the relatively loose connection between the sexual drive and the object accounts for the wide range of fantasied and actual things that can be the object of sexual desire and imagination – for example, from parts of the body, as in part objects, to inanimate objects such as shoes, as in fetishes, to dead bodies, as in necrophilia, to whole persons, as in the integration of love and desire. A distinctive feature of sexuality that may partly account for its great impact on psychological life is, as Freud (1912c) observed, that "an obstacle is required to heighten libido" (p. 187). And as a final example, as both Freud (1912c) and Lacan (1966/2002) commented, the seeming insatiability of sexual desire. As Freud (1912c) puts it, "we must reckon with the possibility that some thing in the nature of the sexual instinct is unfavorable to the realization of complete satisfaction" (pp. 188–189).

These and other distinctive features of sexuality and sexual desire make it apparent that they cannot be reduced to other instinctual–motivational systems. I make this point because of the reductionistic tendency in psychoanalytic theorizing. As we know, in Freud's theorizing, sexual motives are primary and a wide range of explicitly non-sexual behaviors are seen as derivatives and indirect and disguised expressions and gratifications of ubiquitous sexual motives. This is a form of what one could refer to as sexual reductionism. However, in some psychoanalytic theorizing there is a tendency to replace sexual reductionism with object relational reductionism. For example, Fairbairn (1952) writes that "the function of libidinal pleasure is essentially to provide a sign-post to the object" (p. 33), suggesting that seeking the object is primary and that sex is a derivative and mainly a means of expressing and gratifying object relational motives. Of course, Fairbairn's position is welcomed by relational psychoanalysis and is cited approvingly by Mitchell (1988). Thus, sexual reductionism is replaced by object relational reductionism.

To take another example, according to Kohut (1984), certain forms of sexuality are understood as shoring up a non-cohesive self. Although, as noted, Kohut refers to compulsive sexuality, he has very little to say about the nature of non-compulsive sexuality and its role in psychological functioning. Hence, one is tempted to conclude that Kohut's view is that sexual motives are derivative and mainly a means of expressing and gratifying one's needs for self-cohesiveness. That is, it is clear from Kohut's writings that he views self motives as primary and sexual motives are secondary.

It is, of course, the case that one set of behaviors and desires, say sexual behaviors and desires, can, indeed, be a means of expressing and addressing other motives, say object relational or self-cohesiveness motives. For example, as G. S. Klein (1976) noted some years ago, sexual gratification can be linked to "self values." And this is true across a whole range of motivational systems. However, that sex can serve "self-values" and object relational motives – say, the need to feel close to another – does not mean that sex can be reduced to "self values" or object relational needs. After all, there are various ways to enhance the self or feel close to another. We would want to know what is going on when it is sex that serves as the means for expressing and pursuing these motives. Also, that sex can express and gratify other motives does not mean it is only or primarily "a sign-post to the object" or that it does not have distinctive and unique properties that are not shared by other motivational systems.

Consider the finding noted earlier that different attachment patterns are associated with different patterns of sexual behavior. Thus, individuals, particularly women, who are classified as preoccupied not only show distinctive sexual patterns, but also tend to 'employ' sex as a means of dealing with fears of abandonment and experiencing reassurance. Other non-sexual aspects of their behavior will also reveal their preoccupation with fears of abandonment and their attempt to cope with these fears. One is reminded here of Waelder's (1936) principle of multiple functioning which states that any given behavior serves multiple functions and serves multiple motivational aims. Although for the purpose of conceptualization and construction of theory, we divide behavior into separate motivational systems, in 'real life,' behavior entails the continual interaction of different motivational aims and systems.

One way of understanding this continual interaction among different motivational systems is to think in terms of hierarchies of motivational systems and aims for a given behavior or set of behaviors. Thus, in the above example of preoccupied attachment, at the top of the hierarchy motivating the individual's sexual behavior are fears of abandonment and need for reassurance. It may seem odd to say in regard to a behavior that is sexual in content that high in the hierarchy of its motivations are attachment-related fears of abandonment and need for reassurance and lower on the hierarchy are sexual motivations and needs. However, the sense of oddness may be dispelled if one distinguishes between the content of a behavior and the primary motives and aims associated with the behavior. In the above example, the individual's behavior is sexual and will therefore show many of the invariant physiological and psychological features of the sexual system. In that sense, sexuality is not being reduced to other motivational systems. However, the sexual impulses themselves are at least partly motivated by the need for reassurance. So, we have here not a reduction of one motivational system to another, but a case of the interaction and mutual influence of different motivational systems, with the recognition that this interaction will be characterized by a hierarchy of motives.

One of the ways that different motivational systems interact is by influencing the specific characteristics of the behavior through which the individual's motives and aims are expressed. Thus, the preoccupied individual's fear of abandonment and need for reassurance will undoubtedly be expressed in the idiosyncratic characteristics of his or her actual sexual behavior. I am referring here not only to the experiences of sexual impulses that are motivated by the need for reassurance that we have already discussed. I am referring also to the very nature and form of the specific sexual behavior itself. Although there is little or no research in this area, one regularly observes in clinical work the influence of other motivational systems upon such specifics of sexual behavior as achievement of orgasm, sense of satisfaction, nature of sexual fantasies, feelings of intimacy, post-coital mood, and so on.

Implicit in the positing of a hierarchy of motives is the idea of primary and secondary motives and aims in a non-reductive sense. I think there would be general agreement that in the above example of preoccupied attachment, the individual's fear of abandonment and need for reassurance are primary, whereas his or her sexual impulses are secondary, that is, are largely motivated by the need for reassurance. This way of 'ordering' the hierarchy of motives expresses not only how one understands the individual's personality organization, but in congruence with that understanding, would also be reflected in the clinical focus in the treatment situation.

It seems to me intuitively right to talk about both sexual behavior and impulses being motivated mainly by sexual desire in which case, sexual motives are primary, as well as sexual behavior being motivated mainly by something like need for reassurance or need for self-cohesiveness or need for power, in which cases, these motives are primary, with sexual motives being lower on the hierarchy of motives. I think I am describing in the theoretical language of hierarchy of motives what we naturally do in clinical work all the time.

It makes intuitive and clinical sense to understand the idea that, in certain circumstances, sexual impulses can be motivated by other motives However, interestingly enough, it seems more difficult to imagine circumstances in which sexual impulses 'trigger' object relational, attachment, and self motives and behaviors through which the primary sexual motive will be expressed and perhaps satisfied. Thus, whether or not one agrees with it, the statement "sex is a sign-post to the object" makes sense, particularly if one interprets it in the non-reductionist way that I have been discussing. However, would it make sense to say that object-seeking is a sign-post to sex, that is, that we engage in object-seeking primarily as a means of expressing and gratifying sexual motives and needs? Indeed, the Freudian proposition that the basis for the infant's attachment to the caregiver is the latter's role in drive reduction – a version of the idea that object-seeking is a sign-post to sexual satisfaction – receives little empirical support.

And yet, it might be recognized that the statement that object-seeking is primarily a sign-post to sex, however, odd it may sound when stated precisely in this way, is essentially the Freudian theoretical position, as expressed in libido theory, the relationship between the drive and the object, the secondary drive theory of attachment, the theory of infantile sexuality, and the conceptualization of the mind as a discharge 'apparatus.' When embedded in a theoretical framework, the claim that object-seeking is a sign-post to sex appears less odd and jarring and not immediately dismissible largely because the concept of sexuality has now been sufficiently broadened so that it is essentially equivalent to the pleasure principle. One can then at least imagine – whether or not it is empirically supported – that we may engage in object-seeking (as well as a wide range of other activities) as a means of experiencing pleasure and/or avoiding unpleasure. The point here is that built into Freudian theory, virtually by definition, or perhaps one should say as an axiomatic assumption, is the idea that sex (or libido) – now broadly defined – is *always* primary, whereas other motives and aims are *always* secondary in the sense of being derivatives of transformations of libidinal motives.

To be noted here is that the necessary primacy of sexual motives is not the product of empirical or clinical findings, but rather definitionally built into the Freudian conceptualization of human nature. One consequence of all this is that sexual "derivatives" are found (i.e., inferred) in clinical work even when on the surface, the material produced by the patient (e.g., free association, dreams) is not explicitly sexual in content. Further, the distinction between manifest and latent and the central role of interpretation in analytic work are critical factors in 'finding' mainly supportive evidence for the a priori primacy of sexual motives in psychological life. And when such supportive evidence is not reported with sufficient frequency in the psychoanalytic literature, articles appear rhetorically asking, "Is there room for sexuality in psychoanalytic theory?", the implication being that faint-hearted contemporary psychoanalytic theorists are defensively avoiding sexuality.

The fact is that sufficient evidence has accumulated to render entirely untenable the claim that such behaviors as object-seeking, the infant's attachment to caregiver, and our attachment to each other are primarily motivated by or based on sexual motives – however broadly one defines sexual motives – or by the need of the sexual drive to find an object. There are many areas of human behavior characterized by the primacy of object relational and self motives and the secondary status (i.e., lower in the hierarchy of motives) of sexual motives. As noted earlier, there also seem to be areas of psychopathology, for example, attachment pathology or borderline personality disorder, in which the vicissitudes of sexual motives do not appear to be primary either in an etiological sense or in terms of current functioning – although these forms of psychopathology may entail their own distinctive expressions of sexual patterns.

One can, of course, restrict the province of psychoanalysis to sexuality or, even more narrowly, to infantile sexuality. This is essentially the approach taken by Widlöcher (2002) who has proposed that the proper arena for psychoanalytic theory and practice is limited to the influence of auto-erotic fantasies associated with infantile sexuality on the psychological life of adults, in particular, their influence on the individual's ability to love a 'real' other. According to Widlöcher (2002), infantile sexuality is characterized by the quest for auto-erotic pleasures and by auto-erotic fantasies that "express[es] an imaginary relation to the object" (p. 31) and in which "[the object] is only the actor called upon to play a role in an imaginary scenario" (p. 13). Furthermore, psychological life is characterized by a constant and "conflictual interweaving of love for the other and the quest for auto-erotic pleasure" (p. 31). Widlöcher suggests that the conflictual interweaving of love for the other and auto-erotic pleasures based on the fantasies of infantile sexuality is the distinctive and proper arena not only for psychoanalytic theory but also for psychoanalytic clinical intervention. That is to say, the theoretical and practical area of distinctively psychoanalytic knowledge and expertness lies in the exploration of the impediments to love for the other constituted by the auto-erotic fantasies of infantile sexuality.

Widlöcher's (2002) view is shared by other French analysts, including other contributors to the volume, *Infantile Sexuality and Attachment*, edited by Widlöcher. For example, Scarfone (2002) writes: "I place . . . outside the specific domain of psychoanalysis, attachment behaviors, primary love, and infantile sexuality, understood here as what is continuous with adult sexuality" (p. 99). In other words, the exclusive and limited domain of psychoanalysis is infantile sexuality itself (not as a precursor to adult sexuality) and the auto-erotic fantasies with which it is associated. On the view of Widlöcher and Scarfone (as well as others who take a similar position), concern with phenomena other than infantile sexuality is best left to other disciplines such as developmental psychology and attachment theory.

An important implication, then, of Widlöcher's formulation is that psychoanalytic theory and clinical intervention are applicable primarily or perhaps only to those aspects of psychological functioning at the center of which are conflicts between love for the other and impediments to that achievement in the form of auto-erotic fantasies associated with infantile sexuality. There is perhaps something appealing and more realistic about a more modest 'narrowed scope' in contrast to the "widened scope" (Stone, 1954) carved out for psychoanalysis. However, this 'narrowed scope' rests on the assumption that the primary impediments to love for the other are the residues of auto-erotic fantasies associated with infantile sexuality, a questionable assumption that appears to be predicated on a theoretical axiom rather than the complex reality of psychological life and for which little evidence is provided. In any case, whatever its assets and liabilities, this restricted view of psychoanalysis rules out any general claim it may have as an adequate theory of mind, of development, or of psychological functioning.

## Conclusions

The following conclusions seem warranted by the foregoing evidence and discussion:

1. Where there is much evidence for a universal incest taboo or incest avoidance among animals and humans, there is little evidence for the existence of a universal Oedipus complex, when it is defined in terms of universal incestuous wishes and rivalrous (death) wishes appearing at a particular stage of psychosexual development.
2. There is ample evidence attesting to the commonly observed split between love and desire. However, that phenomenon is parsimoniously accounted for, at least in large part, in terms of the factors of the separable and partly antagonistic relationship between the attachment and sexual instinctual systems, triggering of the incest taboo, and parental seductiveness.
3. There is little evidence that choice of mate is based mainly on a template of the opposite sex parent. Rather, there is evidence that both humans and animals prefer mates who are similar, but not too similar to oneself and therefore to kin. This pattern can be interpreted as the product of a 'best fit' compromise between the pulls of the attachment and sexual motivational systems. Further, even if choice of mate were based on a template of parent, it would not necessarily support the theory of the Oedipus complex. It could just as well be attributable to the fact that parent is an attachment figure.
4. There is also little evidence that the nature of one's resolution of oedipal conflicts plays a determinative role in the development of gender identity, superego, or neurosis.
5. There is a good deal of evidence in support of at least of the neo-Westermarck hypothesis, which represents a major alternative account of the nature and origins of the incest taboo. There appears to be evidence for the hypothesis that being reared together is associated with reduced sexual interest and also, in some circumstances, sexual aversion. Various processes that mediate the Westermarck effect have been suggested, including habituation, an olfactory mechanism, and a "genetic kinship estimator."
6. The presumed widespread appearance of oedipal-like themes in myths and legends is an important phenomenon and merits further attention and explanation. However, this material, taken as a whole, does not constitute

evidential support for the claims that all children at a certain age harbor incestuous wishes; that they are 'forced' to at least consciously relinquish them due to parental threats; and that these incestuous wishes persist at an unconscious level into adulthood.

7. Although the term "Oedipus complex" has been retained by them, a number of psychoanalytic theorists have essentially redefined it so that the original primacy of incestuous and hostile wishes is replaced by an emphasis on the individual's struggle to differentiate and achieve relative separation and autonomy.
8. A number of psychoanalytic theorists have proposed that phenomena attributed to the Oedipus complex, such as castration anxiety, are generated by familial dysfunction, including parental communications to the effect that the child's normal developmental strivings for separation, success, and relative autonomy are harmful to them.
9. In certain respects, the ways in which critiques and evidence in relation to the Oedipus complex have been dealt with in the psychoanalytic literature are representative of the nature of the development and change of psychoanalytic theory. The longevity and history of the hypothesis of a universal Oedipus complex presumably based on clinical reports of patients (e.g., the split between love and desire), Freud's self-analysis, and the Oedipus myth, reflects a serious problem in theory construction in psychoanalysis. They include the tendency to universalize from a limited number of instances and the tendency of analysts to always find confirming evidence in their patients' clinical productions.
10. The relinquishment of the Oedipus complex as a central factor in the development of neurosis, gender identity, superego development, and mate choice and its replacement by an emphasis on the issues of differentiation and separation–individuation raises questions that need to be addressed regarding the role of sexuality in a wide range of psychopathology. It also raises questions regarding the 'proper' role of sexuality in psychic life and its interactions with other motivational systems that need to be addressed.

## Notes

1 For an opposite view, see Friedman and Downey (1995) who argue that competitive–aggressive impulses toward the father or father figure are universal and have an innate basis. The evidence that they adduce is the prenatal neurendocrinological underpinnings for rough and tumble play in boys, which, they propose, is likely to influence the boys' fantasies. However, there is quite a leap from the prenatal neuroendrocrinological basis for rough and tumble play and the claim that specific competitive–aggressive impulses toward the father are innately based and universal, let alone that these impulses arise in the context of competition with father for sexual possession of mother. No evidence is presented in support of this latter claim.

2 Whereas the term "incest taboo" suggests a prohibition against something desired, the term "incest avoidance" does not carry that connotation.

3 One of the limitations of the Westermarck and neo-Westermarckian hypotheses is that they do not appear to distinguish between incestuous wishes toward peers and toward

caregiver. After all, it is generally mother, not sister, who provides the sensual pleasures through her ministrations. And it is these sensual pleasures, according to Freud, that result in the mother becoming the infant's and child's first libidinal object. Hence, a legitimate question that can be raised is the influence of these experiences of sensual pleasures at the hands of mother on the Westermarck effect. Do these experiences modify the Westermarck effect? One needs to keep in mind that all the empirical data testing the Westermarck hypothesis has been carried out with peer relationships, a situation in which the issue of prolonged provision of sensual pleasures does not arise. One could argue that whereas incest avoidance among siblings is accomplished through one type of mechanism (i.e., the Westermarck effect), incest avoidance in relation to the offspring-parent relationship is accomplished through another process, one closer to the Freudian conception of the Oedipus complex, that is, through a cultural taboo erected against incestuous wishes. I have not seen this issue addressed in discussions of the Westermarck effect of incestuous wishes.

4 I am grateful to Dr. Jerome Wakefield for bringing this book to my attention.

5 I am not at all sure that "romantic love" is the best term to describe adult attachment. For as Mitchell (2002) has noted, there is often relatively little romance in long-term adult attachments. Perhaps the more neutral terms "adult attachment" or "pair-bonding" are more accurate.

6 One could argue that similar to the insecurely attached individual, the securely attached individual is relating to his or her current figure in the same way that he or she related to the early parental figure. Therefore, why shouldn't the incest taboo also be equally triggered for the securely attached individual in relation to the current figure? I think the answer to this question lies in the consideration that because the securely attached individual has been more successful in internalizing a secure base, he or she is better able to achieve a greater degree of separation and individuation and therefore, greater freedom from early object ties and early modes of relating.

7 This remains the case despite Freud's (1914b) attempt, in response to Jung's rejection of what he viewed as Freud's pansexualism, to formulate narcissism in terms of distribution of libido.

# 4

# INNER CONFLICT

## Introduction

Ernst Kris (1947) commented that the subject matter of psychoanalysis is human behavior from the point of view of conflict. Indeed, the birth of psychoanalysis is marked by Breuer and Freud's (1893–1895) account of hysterical symptoms in terms of inner conflict, described as an "incompatibility . . . between the ego and some idea presented to it" (p. 122). Freud wrote that "defense hysteria" is the product of defense (repression) against an incompatibility between an idea and the ego. Thus, from the start, inner conflict and defense are the two primary concepts that mark the emergence of psychoanalysis. Further, these concepts continue to be central to Freudian theory as well as other psychoanalytic theories.

In the first section of the chapter, I present different psychoanalytic formulations of inner conflict, with a major emphasis on the views of Freud and Fairbairn. I believe that Freudian theory and Fairbairn's theory of endopsychic structure contain the most articulate and elaborated formulations of the role of inner conflict in psychological functioning. Hence, both theories are accorded lengthy discussions. However, I also devote a good deal of discussion to the role of conflict in Kleinian theory (e.g., Klein, 1975a,b); Kohut's (1984) self psychology theory; Loewald's (1966; 1979) formulation of inner conflict in relation to the achievement of individuation; Weiss and Sampson's (1986) formulation of a similar conflict; Kris' (e.g., 1988; 2017) distinction between convergent and divergent conflicts; Brenner's (2002) later formulation of mind in terms of conflict and compromise formation; Widlöcher's (2002) formulation of the conflict between infantile sexuality and object love; and the conflict between sexuality and attachment about which I have written elsewhere (Eagle, 2007b; 2013). In the course of discussing different views on the nature, origins, and inevitability of conflict, I also refer briefly to the work of the neo-Freudians, including Horney, Fromm, and Sullivan; and to the work of Rogers.

In discussing these various formulations, I focus on a number of interrelated issues, including the nature of our fundamental conflicts as identified in various psychoanalytic theories; the main determinants and origins of the conflicts we experience; the question of the inevitability of certain inner conflicts; and the implications of different conceptions of inner conflict for treatment. The next section of the chapter deals with selected empirical research on inner conflict; and the final section deals with the implications of the research findings as well as conceptual critiques for our understanding of the role of inner conflict in psychological functioning.

## Conflict in Freudian theory

### *Conflict between desire and one's self-image: Freud*

In the case studies in *Studies on Hysteria*, Freud (Breuer & Freud, 1893–1895) identified conflict between desires and fantasies harbored by the individual and her moral standards and sense of who she is. Therefore, the desires and fantasies need to be banned from conscious experience in order to protect her self-image. This early view remains a central perspective across psychoanalytic and non-psychoanalytic conceptions of inner conflict and defense. For example, the subtitle of Cramer's (2006) psychoanalytically oriented book on defense is "Protecting the Self", a perspective shared by non-psychoanalytic theorists such as Baumeister, Dale, and Sommer (1998) and Greenwald (1980) who have carried out research and have written about inner conflict and defense.

### *Conflict between the pleasure principle and the reality principle: Immediate versus delayed gratification: Freud*

According to Freud (1900), the conflict between the urge for immediate gratification and the need to delay gratification in the service of finding appropriate objects and carrying out appropriate actions that will provide gratification (e.g., the actual breast and sucking at the nipple actions) is fundamental and present at birth. Freud (1900) variously conceptualized this conflict as one between the pleasure principle and the reality principle, between primary and secondary processes, and later in his writings, with the emergence of drive theory, as one between the id and the ego (Freud, 1923).

The metapsychological formulation underlying these conflicts is the foundational assumption of the *constancy principle*, namely, that the basic function of the "mental apparatus" is to keep "the quantity of excitation present . . . as low as possible or at least to keep it constant" (Freud, 1920, p. 9). In one of his earliest statements of the constancy principle he writes that "in every individual there exists a tendency to diminish this sum of excitation . . . in order to preserve his health" (Freud, 1893, p. 36). In short, the basic function of the "mental apparatus" is to discharge excitation as a means of protecting the organism. Insofar as the discharge of excitation is roughly equivalent to gratification and pleasure and the build-up of excitation is roughly equivalent to lack of gratification and unpleasure, the conflict is between immediate and delayed gratification.

At the outset, the conflict between the urge for immediate gratification and the imperative to delay is not an inner conflict, but essentially one between the infant and the ineluctable nature of the world, namely, the fundamental and stark reality that gratification of certain needs (i.e., hunger) is not possible without a delay that allows commerce with actual external objects and without certain intentional actions being implemented. Simply wishing or fantasizing gratification will not do the job. In this sense, at this stage in life, the conflict is one between one's urges and the unyielding nature of physical reality (including the nature of how we are biologically constructed). The conflict between immediate and delayed gratification becomes an inner conflict when the nature of physical reality becomes internally represented in the psychic structure of the ego.

## *Conflict inherent in the "danger situations": Freud*

According to Freud (1926[1925]), inner conflict is also engendered by the "danger situations" of loss of the object, loss of the object's love, castration threats, and later, superego condemnation. That is, parental prohibitions, punishment, and threat of punishment in reaction to the child's expression of instinctual wishes, desires, and fantasies (e.g., incestuous wishes) generate conflict between the child's impulses and the fear of the "danger situations." Over time, this conflict between an inner wish and external dangers becomes internalized (e.g., in the form of expectation and anticipation of danger in association with an inner wish) with the result that the conflict becomes an inner conflict. Further, insofar as the prohibited wishes (e.g., incestuous wishes) are presumed to be inimical to family and society, one can say that from this more clinical and experience-near perspective too, there is a primary conflict between the id and the ego as well as the id and the superego.

## *Id–ego conflict: Freud*

It is only with the development and maturation of the ego, whose primary function is reality-testing, that the conflict between one's urges for immediate gratification and the need for delay becomes an inner conflict. With the emergence of drive theory, the fundamental conflict that dominated Freud's writings was the id–ego conflict, a conflict between different structures of the personality The link between the enduring conflict between the id and ego and the constancy principle becomes apparent when one keeps in mind that insofar as the tensions associated with drives constitute the major inner source of excitation (the greatest demand on the mind) and insofar as, also in accord with the constancy principle, undischarged excitation constitutes the greatest danger to the ego, it follows that the id is an inherent threat to the ego.

And, indeed, reflecting this reasoning, both Freud and Anna Freud formulate precisely this view. The following passages from Freud and Anna Freud express the inherent antagonism between the id and the ego in very clear terms. "What it is that the ego fears is of being overwhelmed or annihilated" (Freud, 1923, p. 57); "the majority of the instinctual demands of this infantile sexuality are treated by the ego as dangers and fended off as such" (Freud, 1926, p. 155).

"In the first place, an excessive strength of instinct can damage the ego in a similar way to an excessive 'stimulus' from the external world" (Freud, 1940[1938], p. 199). Anna Freud (1936/1966) sums matters up by stating that "the danger which threatens the ego is that it may be submerged by the instincts; what it dreads above all is the *quantity* of instinct" (p. 165). Indeed, so fundamental is the danger that the id represents, that according to A. Freud (1936/1966), strength of instinct is a casual factor in psychosis. To be noted here is the assumption, one that contrasts with the early case studies, that the id–ego conflict is *an inherent and inevitable one*, not contingent upon environmental vicissitudes such as historical era or societal attitudes, but rather endemic in the human condition. Or, to put it another way, insofar as civilization as well as physical reality require delay of gratification, there is an inherent antagonism between the id and the ego.

## Id–superego conflict: Freud

A trajectory paralleling the relationship between the individual and physical reality also characterizes the relationship between the individual and social reality. Early in life, the conflict is between inner demands and the external social reality of prohibitions and limitations. In the course of development, societal prohibitions and values, as transmitted through the socialization agents of parents, family, and educators, become internalized in the form of a superego structure. Thus, what starts out as a conflict between inner demands and external social reality becomes transformed into an inner conflict between different aspects of oneself, namely, instinctual urges and internalized values and prohibitions.

## Ego–superego conflict

According to Freud's model of the superego, parental disapproval and punishment of the child's expressions of sexual and aggressive wishes, most clearly during the oedipal stage, are internalized as a psychic structure. Thus, Freud (1923) writes that the superego is the heir to the Oedipus complex. Following internalization, instead of simply fearing external parental punishment, for example, in the form of loss of love and of castration threats, one now fears punishment from one's superego. Just as the child feared the external danger situations, one now fears internal dangers at the hands of the superego. As Freud (1923) puts it, the ego now fears "condemnation . . . by its critical agency" (p. 51). Thus, an external conflict is now transformed into an inner conflict.

Freud repeatedly refers to the closeness between the id and the superego. This is so in a number of ways: one, the superego appears to have greater access to id impulses than does the ego, as reflected in the presumed fact that repression is instigated at the behest of the superego – as indicated subjectively by the sense of being 'bad.' Two, in punishing the ego, the superego makes use of aggression and sadism and, in extreme situations, of the death instinct. Thus, Freud's description of ego–superego conflict is, in some respects, a description of id–superego conflict, with punishment of the ego as the fallout of this conflict. That is, the superego punishes the ego for allowing any expression of id impulses and perversely, employs the aggression and destructiveness of the id in carrying out its punishment.

## *Conflict between narcissism and object love: Freud*

Still another fundamental conflict identified by Freud (1914b) is that between narcissism and object love. According to Freud, because there is a limited quantity of libido, the greater the quantity of libido invested in the ego, the less available for the object, and vice versa. As Freud (1914b) puts it, "The more of the one is employed, the more the other becomes depleted" (p. 76). Hence, there is "an antithesis between ego-libido and object-libido" (p. 76). Further, Freud (1914b) writes:

> A strong egoism is a protection against falling ill, but in the last resort we must begin to love in order not to fall ill, and we are bound to fall ill if, in consequence of frustration, we are unable to love.
>
> (p. 85)

That is, in the course of normal development one must move from narcissism to object love.

However, Freud (1914b) also writes that there is "an original cathexis of the ego, [Freud is obviously referring here to primary narcissism] from which some is given off to objects" (p. 75). But this libidinal cathexis of the ego "fundamentally persists and is related to the object-cathexes much as the body of an amoeba is related to the pseudopodia which it puts out" (p.75). The idea that libidinal cathexis of the ego "fundamentally persists" as well as the pseudopodia analogy suggest that the individual is ever ready to withdraw libido from the object and return it to the ego, and is likely to do so under certain circumstances (e.g., illness). This suggests a chronic and fundamental potential for conflict between narcissism and object love.

Although the inner conflicts described above are the most general and fundamental ones, in the corpus of his writings Freud identifies a number of other inner conflicts that one finds in human behavior, including the following ones:

1. The conflict between "the affectionate and sensual currents" which is characteristic of an unresolved oedipal complex and is implicated in sexual difficulties such as inhibition of desire and "psychical impotence" (Freud, 1912c).

2. The conflict between heterosexuality and homosexuality, a product of our bisexual nature (Freud, 1937, p. 224).
3. The ego–superego conflict between seeking fulfillment of one's ambitions and fear of punishment implicated in the phenomenon of being "wrecked by success" (Freud, 1916, pp. 316–318). This conflict is seen by Freud as entailing guilt linked to the persistence of unresolved oedipal incestuous wishes.
4. The conflict between one's self-image and ego ideal.
5. The conflict within the ego between the "old peaceful ego" and the "new warlike [ego]" (p. 209) presumably central in "war neurosis" (Freud, 1919, pp. 208–213).[1]
6. The conflict between the sexual instinct and the ego or self-preservative instinct, which Freud (1910a, pp. 214–215) compares to love and hunger. It is not clear why these two instincts should conflict with each other until one recognizes that according to Freudian metapsychology, the tensions inherent in sexual instincts represent a potential threat of overwhelming the ego. In short, this is a variation of the id–ego conflict. This formulation also parallels the conflict between ego libido and object libido that Freud (1914b) posits in *On Narcissism*. According to this view, the more one cathects an object with libido, the less available for cathecting oneself; and vice versa. Hence, the conflict here parallels the one between narcissism and object love.
7. The conflict between renouncing satisfaction in the face of a danger from reality (e.g., threat of castration) and the disavowal of reality, along with the continued pursuit of satisfaction (e.g., masturbation). What is especially interesting about this form of conflict is that according to Freud (1940[1938]), both trends occur at the same time. Thus, as the title of Freud's paper makes clear, the result is "splitting of the ego in the process of defense" (see Chapter 5).
8. The overarching conflict between the "two primal instincts Eros and destructiveness" (Freud, 1937, p. 246) (derived from Empedocles' love and strife), which Freud introduced relatively late in his writings. On a less grand scale, Freud (1909, pp. 236–238) had already introduced the conflict between love and hate central to ambivalence and implicated in melancholia.

The fundamental and irreducible nature of conflict between Eros and Thanatos or the death instinct posited by Freud is probably the clearest expression of his views regarding the inescapable presence of an overarching conflict in psychological and biological life. Also, it seems to reflect his 'final view.' This conflict, which Freud viewed as fundamental to psychological and biological life, is formulated as an inter-instinctual conflict between two primary instincts rather than between id and ego. Indeed, this overarching conflict between Eros and the death instinct does not seem especially compatible with the id–ego model that had dominated Freudian theory. Further, there is an enormous distance between the highly abstract metapsychological formulation of a basic conflict between Eros and destructiveness or the death instinct and clinical work – a consideration that has led most analysts to essentially ignore this late version of inner conflict.

Despite this state of affairs, it is, I believe, useful to devote some discussion to the conflict between Eros and the death instinct in order to gain some insight into Freud's thinking, particularly the conception of the relationship between Freud's early formulations of the constancy principle as well as the 'mental apparatus' as a discharge mechanism and the positing of a death instinct. Freud's (1937) description of the aim of the death instinct as "the urge . . . to return to an inanimate state" (Freud, 1937, p. 246) reflects the continuing influence of the constancy principle in Freud's thinking. Recall that in accord with the constancy principle, the primary function of the 'mental apparatus' is to discharge excitation and thus keep the level of excitation at a zero level or as low as possible. As Freud (1924) puts it:

> [W]e have taken the view that the principle which governs all mental processes is a special case of Fechner's "tendency toward stability," and have accordingly attributed to the mental apparatus, the purpose of *reducing to nothing* [my emphasis], or at least keeping as low as possible, the sums of excitation which flow in upon it.
>
> (p. 159)

Freud (1924) borrows the term "Nirvana principle" from Low (1920) to describe this tendency and, taking his formulation to its logical conclusion, notes that the "Nirvana principle" "[belongs] . . . to the death instinct" (p. 160). For, reducing the sum of excitation to zero is, of course, equivalent to returning to an inanimate state, that is, death. Freud also recognizes that the metapsychological equation of unpleasure with increases in excitation and pleasure with the reduction of excitation ultimately also aligns the pleasure principle with the death instinct and grapples with what is to him the mysterious facts that increases in excitation can be pleasurable and that experiences of pleasure are not only a function of a "quantifiable factor," but also of a "qualitative characteristic" (p. 160) about which, he states, we know little. He also writes that although the Nirvana principle belongs to the death instinct, it "has undergone a modification in living organisms through which it has become the pleasure principle" (p. 160). And, Freud (1924) goes on to say, "the source of the modification" of the Nirvana principle "can only be the life instinct, the libido" (p. 160).

All this, in my view, is Freudian metapsychology at its most questionable and its most confused and confusing. What seems to be required is a thorough overhaul of the *general* conception of pleasure and unpleasure defined primarily in terms of decreases and increases in excitation, underlying which is the positing of the constancy principle, the Nirvana principle, and a conception of the primary function of the mental apparatus as discharge of excitation. The quantitative conception of pleasure in terms of decreases in excitation leads to a strange convergence between the primary function of the 'mental apparatus' and the aim of the death instinct. If one keeps in mind that, according to Freud, the essence of gratification of instinctual wishes and needs entails discharge of excitation, one is forced to also recognize the odd link between gratification and the death instinct in Freud's formulations. On this view, the individual is, so to speak, damned if he or she gratifies and damned if he or she does not. That is, failure to discharge excitation confronts the individual with the danger of excessive excitation; and carried to its extreme, the discharge of excitation entailed in gratification becomes equivalent to a return to an inanimate state, that is, the state that is the aim of the death instinct.

These odd convergences suggest still another reason that there is something profoundly amiss with the fundamental formulations of the constancy principle, the notion of the mind or nervous system as a discharge 'apparatus,' and the posited equivalence of gratification with discharge of excitation. At least some of these odd implications and links would be dealt with through the relatively simple steps of getting rid of the Nirvana principle and redefining the constancy principle entirely in terms of homeostasis rather than zero excitation.

Finally, Freud's conceptualization of Eros as a unifying force in psychic life does not appear to be compatible with the idea that instincts, including the sexual instinct – which is surely at least a distant cousin of Eros – is an implacable enemy of the ego. If, as Freud maintains, Eros is an instinct, then, along with other instinctual forces, it, too, should carry with it the threat of excessive excitation. However, it is clear that Freud does not view Eros as *that* kind of instinct. But, if that is so, the fundamental nature of at least some instincts is altered, now understood by Freud as a unifying force rather than one that is inherently in conflict with the ego.

## *Conflict, compromise formation, and psychopathology: Freud*

As is well known, Freud's theory of neurosis as well as slips, humor, and dreams, rests on the idea that all these phenomena entail *a compromise* between a wish and forces aligned against its expression in consciousness. The germ of this idea begins quite early in Freud's writings. Freud (Breuer & Freud, 1893–1895) writes that the "quota of affect" (pp. 213–214) accompanying every experience needs to be discharged. When adequate discharge of the "quota of affect" does not occur, through a process that Freud (1894, p. 60) acknowledged he did not understand, the affect is 'converted' into somatic symptoms. The result is that the individual is freed of conscious conflict, but is saddled with a hysterical symptom.

These early ideas were elaborated in his later work to include the propositions that instinct makes a demand upon the mind and that the tensions associated with instinctual wishes need to be discharged.[2] Given our psychobiological nature, the tensions generated by ungratified instinctual wishes do not disappear; they continue to exert pressure on the mind and 'seek' various means of discharge. If because of inner conflict, the forbidden instinctual wish cannot be gratified directly and an adequate discharge of instinctual tensions cannot occur, one can resort to disguised and partial gratification in the form of a compromise between the wish and the defense against it. As is well known, Freud (1901) identified 'normal' means of discharging instinctual tensions in a disguised and compromised way including dreams, humor, parapraxes, and fantasy, all of which he referred to as the "psychopathology of everyday life." The pathological form of a compromise 'solution' to an id–ego inner conflict is, of course, a neurotic symptom. Thus, Freud formulated a 'unified' theory in which a single process – compromise between a wish and defense against the wish – is hypothesized to underlie phenomena as different on the surface as neurotic symptoms, dreams, humor, slips, and fantasy.

### *Conflict between pleasure and unpleasure associated with childhood sexual and aggressive wishes and the role of compromise formation: Brenner*

For many years, Brenner (e.g.,1982, 1998, 2002) has taken the position that conflict and compromise formation are ubiquitous in mental life and that all behavior is the product of these two processes. Indeed, Brenner is the quintessential expositor of Kris' (1947) definition of psychoanalysis as the study of mind from the point of view of conflict. During the last number of years, in a series of influential papers, Brenner (e.g., 1998, 2002) has forcefully argued that the following long-held traditional ideas need to be abandoned because they are not supported by relevant data: (1) that the mind consists of separable systems or structures (e.g., id, ego, and superego); (2) that conflict and compromise formation are themselves pathological; and (3) that resolution of conflict is a realistic psychoanalytic aim. Brenner has some other interesting things to say, including his rejection of the ideas that the id is non-verbal, cut off from reality, and characterized exclusively by primary process, whereas the ego is verbal, is the 'organ' attuned to reality, characterized by secondary process, and can function in a relatively conflict-free way. However, in the present context, I want to focus on Brenner's conceptions of conflict and compromise formation. According to him, conflicts always arise "over the sexual and aggressive wishes of early childhood" (Brenner, 1998, p. 165). All behavior, according to Brenner (2002), is a "compromise formation originating in the pleasure-seeking wishes of childhood" (p. 402). For all individuals, "the problem is how to achieve as much pleasurable gratification as possible, while avoiding as much associated unpleasure as possible" (p. 404). The unpleasure associated with gratification of childhood wishes is directly linked to the child's experience of parental negative reactions to the child's expression of childhood sexual and aggressive wishes.

According to Brenner (1998), given the child's utter dependence on parents, it is important for the young child to:

> avoid parental wrath and punishment, *real and fantasied* [my emphasis], by whatever means are possible. One way to do so and win love and approval is to avoid wishing or doing what one's parents would disapprove of or would punish, especially anything that is incestuous, castrating, or parenticidal.
>
> (p. 177)

Further,

> ideas of parental punishment and wrath never disappear. They are defended against in one way or another, but they never disappear any more than does

> any other component of the conflicts over the sexual and aggressive wishes of childhood origin. They play an active role in mental functioning at the age of 60 as at the age of 6. They persist throughout life.
>
> (Brenner, 1998, p. 176)

The universal way of addressing this problem, according to Brenner (2002), is a compromise formation between these conflicting motives of seeking gratification of "a childhood, pleasure-seeking wish" (p. 404) and of avoiding the unpleasure associated with gratification of the wish. Such compromise formation, Brenner tells us, is not pathological, but ubiquitous. The difference between the 'normal' and the pathological, according to Brenner, is not that one is a compromise formation and the other is not, but rather a matter of the degree to which:

> compromise formation allows for enough in the way of pleasurable gratification, if it is not accompanied by too much unpleasure in the form of anxiety and depressive affect, if there is not too much inhibition of functions as a result of the defenses at work and not too much in the way of self-punishing and for self-destructive tendencies.
>
> (p. 404)

Thus, for Brenner (2002), the fundamental inner conflict is between a "pleasure-seeking wish" (p. 404) and the unpleasure associated with that wish. Further, according to Brenner, "the conflicts that are the most intense and fateful for mental functioning throughout the course of an individual's life are those that center on the sexual and aggressive wishes of early childhood," which "make their first identifiable appearance in mental life at about the age of three years" (p. 405). Brenner goes on to say that "the pleasure-seeking wishes in question are essentially the same as those that characterize the sexual lives of adults" (p. 405). Furthermore, from early childhood on:

> throughout the course of life, people's minds strive to achieve pleasurable gratification of the sexual and aggressive wishes in question, and at the same time, to avoid the associated unpleasure. Every thought, plan, fantasy, action, and so on is a compromise between these two imperatives, and every thought, plan, fantasy, and action must therefore be understood as such . . . Mental functioning beginning then and forever after is always a compromise between the two.
>
> (p. 406–407)

Despite Brenner's assertion that all behavior, including intellectual endeavors and projects, are a compromise formation, he apparently views his own formulation not as simply a compromise formation, influenced by childhood conflicts, but as an accurate assessment of how the mind works. That formulation, it appears, is due to the "important and obvious facts that render those concepts [id, ego, and superego] invalid" (p. 416). If every thought, plan, action, etc., is a compromise formation related to childhood conflictual sexual and aggressive wishes, why should one give Brenner's new formulation any greater credence than his presumed compromise formation reflected in his earlier advocacy of the structural theory? Brenner's own sweeping generalization regarding ubiquitous compromise formation leaves little room for evaluating a theory, including Brenner's new theory, based largely on evidence, on what he refers to as the "obvious facts."

Further, the 'facts' that are obvious to Brenner may not be obvious to others. As we have seen above, Brenner (2002) asserts, as if he were describing an indisputable fact, that "The conflicts that are most intense and fateful for mental functioning throughout the course of an individual's life are those that center on the sexual and aggressive wishes of early childhood" (p. 405). Further, he is even precise in identifying the appearance of these wishes at age three. These assertions are followed not by presentation of any evidence linked to observations of children, but by references to "Freud, (1905, 1926)" despite the statement in the Abstract that "evidence is put forth . . ." (p. 397). No evidence, clinical or non-clinical, is presented in the entire paper. There are only assertions followed by references to Freud and vague statements such as "In the light of our newer knowledge, . . ." (p. 405). That "newer knowledge" does not, apparently, include any research on the developmental impact of childhood experiences and conflicts *not* having to do with sexual and aggressive wishes.

Quite remarkably, Brenner writes as if there were no theoretical developments or empirical findings during, say, the last 50 or so years on psychological development and functioning to which he need refer. Thus, in a section on "The Preoedipal Period," Brenner asserts that although he sees:

> no reason to doubt the significance of what happens in the earliest years, . . . the evidence available to us supports the view that its importance lies in its effects upon the sexual conflicts and compromise formations that characterize the ages of three to six years.
>
> (p. 413)

Of course, Brenner does not specify the specific nature of the "evidence available to us." The closest he gets to addressing that question is his hypothetical example of "an adult patient with symptoms of depression, whose mother was emotionally unavailable during the patient's first and second years of life" (p. 413). According to Brenner (2002), "analysis . . . *will show in every such case* [my emphasis] that the patient's reactions to mother's absence can be understood only when the conflicts of the second three years of life are taken into account" (p. 413).

I think Brenner makes an important point in suggesting that the psychological impact of an event, including a traumatic event, is partly dependent on subsequent events and experiences. For example, Rutter (1971) has shown that the psychological effects of loss of a parent through divorce will be strongly influenced by later events such as the nature of the caregiving provided subsequent to the traumatic event. However, Brenner (2002) goes on to state with regard to the hypothetical patient:

> Such a patient may be convinced, for example, that mother did not love her/him because of the patient's "bad" sexual wishes, or because of his/her "bad" murderous impulses or jealousy, and that his/her punishment and/or penance included castration – wishes and fears that arose and flowered in the patient's mind during the ages of three to six years.
>
> (p. 413)

In other words, the effects of mother's emotional unavailability during the hypothetical patient's early years of life will be a function not just of a wide range of later events, but *only* of later oedipal sexual and aggressive conflicts. And the support for this assertion is that "analysis . . . *will show in every such case* [my emphasis] that the patient's reactions to mother's absence can be understood only when the conflicts of the second three years of life [i.e., oedipal conflicts] are taken into account" (p. 413). Brenner does not seem to entertain the possibility that what he believes "analysis . . . will show in every case" may have something to do with the analyst's theoretical lens.

As noted above, according to Brenner, "the conflicts that are the most intense and fateful for mental functioning throughout the course of an individual's life are those that center on the sexual and aggressive wishes of early childhood" (p. 405). In other words, oedipal wishes that presumably emerge from three to six years of age in the life of the child remain at the center of one's conflicts for the rest of one's life. Surely, Brenner is aware that adults (as well as children) may be conflicted about many things other than oedipal sexual and aggressive wishes (e.g., attachment needs; separation-individuation). However, according to his position, these conflicts are either less "intense and fateful for mental functioning" or can be understood as indirect expressions of oedipal sexual and aggressive wishes. Brenner provides no evidence for his sweeping and reductionistic generalization. Rather, it is based on the axiomatic theoretical assumption of the universality of the oedipal complex and its later sequellae, which in turn allows Brenner to find supportive evidence in every analytic case. I am reminded here of Peterfreund's (1983) distinction between a "stereotyped" versus a "heuristic" approach to data from the analytic situation.

After reviewing "Conceptions of conflict in psychoanalytic theory and practice," including Brenner's work, Smith (2003) writes:

> It is rare these days to hear analysts speak about analyzing the sexual and aggressive conflicts . . . might the phrase sexual and aggressive conflicts of childhood be so tinged that it can no longer be spoken? Or interpreted in so limited a fashion – artificially linked, perhaps, to an archaic view of drive theory – that we cannot acknowledge the childhood wishes it denotes?
>
> (pp. 88–89)

This is an odd plaint. The criticism against Brenner is not that children do not have sexual and aggressive wishes, but that, in Brenner's view, all other seemingly non-sexual and non-aggressive childhood wishes are not "fateful" in relation to later development, or are reducible to sexual and aggressive oedipal wishes. Such criticism is not based on "an archaic view of drive theory." Indeed, although Brenner rejects the structural theory, it is his insistence on the exclusive significance of oedipal wishes that can be seen as reflecting "an archaic view of drive theory."

## Conflict between life and death instincts (love and hate): Melanie Klein

In contrast to Freud's emphasis on sexuality, Klein accords overriding importance to aggression and hate. In Freudian theory, sexuality has been central, with aggression taking its place in the theory in later writings. Contrastingly, in Kleinian theory, aggression is central, with relatively little attention given to sexuality. For example, if one examines the index of Klein's *Envy and Gratitude*, one will find five pages referring to sex in a 341-page book. Further, half of those references are concerned with the child's observation of the primal scene. Hence, the Kleinian answer to the question of what we are conflicted about is that we are conflicted about love and hate. It should be noted that aggression and hate lend themselves to an emphasis on guilt insofar as they entail harm to others and thus call for repair.

Based on Freud's positing of Eros and Thanatos, Melanie Klein proposes that the fundamental conflict underlying psychic life from birth on is one between the life and death instincts or, at a different level of discourse, between love and hate. As Klein (1948/1975) writes, "We may assume that the struggle between life and death instincts already operates during birth" (p. 31). At the center of Klein's description of mental life are the vicissitudes of the conflict between love and hate, in particular, the processes of projection and introjection of hostility and love and the interaction of these processes with internal and actual object relational experiences in the world.

The following passages from Klein's writings summarize the process of projection and introjection with regard to the death instinct:

> The frustrating (bad) external breast becomes, owing to projection, the external representative of the death instinct; through introjection it reinforces the primary internal danger-situation; this leads to an increased urge on the part of the ego to deflect (project) internal dangers (primarily the activity of the death instinct) into the external world. There is therefore a constant fluctuation between the fear of internal and external bad objects, between the death instinct acting within outwards.
>
> (p. 32)

Further, according to Klein, "This interaction exists in some measure throughout life" (p. 32). As for the life instinct, Klein writes:

> Side by side with the deflection of the death instinct outwards, the life instinct – by means of the libido – attaches itself to the external object, the gratifying (good) breast, which becomes the external representative of the life instinct. The introjection of the good object reinforces the power of the life instinct within. The good internalized breast, which is felt to be the source of life, forms a vital part of the ego and its preservation becomes an imperative need. The introjection of this first loved object is therefore inextricably linked with all the processes engendered by the life instinct.
>
> (p. 32)

The impact of the above internal processes, according to Klein, interacts with external events. She writes that "innate aggressiveness is bound to be increased by unfavorable external circumstances and, conversely, is mitigated by the love and understanding that the young child receives" (Klein, 1959/1975, p. 249). Or, as she puts it more simply, "love develops in response to [mother's] love and care; hatred and aggression are stimulated by frustration and discomfort" (Klein, 1942/1975, p. 320). However, it should be noted, according to Klein, insofar as some degree of frustration is inevitable, some degree of hatred and aggression will always be stimulated by external events that will inevitably trigger processes of projection and introjection that, in turn, will have a major impact on psychological functioning.

Klein recognizes not only the influence of mother on baby, but also of baby on mother. As Klein (1963/1975) puts it, mother's behavior is "influenced by the infant's response to her" (p. 312). Thus, "a contented baby who sucks with enjoyment, allays his mother's anxiety," whereas "a child who has difficulties over feeding may arouse the mother's anxiety and guilt and thus unfavorably influence her relation to him" (Klein, 1963/1975, p. 312).

The impact of baby on mother will also partly depend "on the ways in which external influences are interpreted and assimilated by the child, and thus in turn largely depends on how strongly destructive impulses and persecutory and depressive anxieties are operative" (Klein, 1959/1975, p. 256). With regard to this last point, Klein is suggesting the role of constitutional factors, which she explicitly identifies when she writes that some "children have a stronger innate aggressiveness and greed than those infants whose occasional outbursts of rage are soon over" (p. 249). Thus, the intensity of conflict and "the ways in which external influences are interpreted and assimilated" (i.e., the child's psychic reality) will largely depend on constitutional factors, such as strength of "innate aggressiveness."

To sum up, according to Klein, the fundamental conflict that shapes our psychological functioning, one based on the innately based strength of life and death instincts, is the conflict between love and hate. Although external factors and constitutional predispositions may influence the intensity and impact of this conflict, it is a universal and inescapable one. Further, it is a conflict that is present at birth and continues during one's entire lifetime.

## *Conflict between ego structures: Fairbairn*

For Fairbairn, because there is no id structure, the fundamental inner conflict is not between id and ego, but between different ego structures. Whereas for Freud, a primary challenge confronting the individual is the achievement of drive gratification, for Fairbairn the primary challenge for the individual is, as Jones (1952) puts it in his preface to Fairbairn's (1952) book, for "the ego . . . to reach an object where it may find support" (p. v). Thus, it is in the arena of object relations, including internal object relations, that inner conflict is located.

As is the case with Freud's writings,[3] one can describe Fairbairn's views on inner conflict from the perspective of his complex metapsychology or from the perspective of his more experience-near descriptions. I will start with the former, Fairbairn's theoretical formulation of the "endopsychic structure of the personality," which can be murky and complex, and will then take up his more experience-near clinical descriptions. The emphasis in both sections will be on Fairbairn's view of inner conflict.

According to Fairbairn, under the impact of deprivation and frustration, the unitary ego is split into the sub-structures of the libidinal ego and the anti-libidinal ego. (The central ego is what remains of the original unitary ego.) As far as I understand Fairbairn's metapsychological scheme, the splitting of the unitary ego and the resulting multiplicity of egos comes about in the following way: because mother is both gratifying and frustrating, she becomes an ambivalent object for the infant:

> Since it proves intolerable to [the infant] to have a good object which is also bad, he seeks to alleviate the situation by splitting the figure of his mother into two objects. Then, in so far as she satisfies him libidinally, she is a 'good' object, and, in so far as she fails to satisfy him libidinally, she is a 'bad' object.
>
> (Fairbairn, 1952, p. 110)[4]

In order to better control the 'bad' object, the infant resorts to internalization of the object.[5] The 'bad' object, Fairbairn goes on to observe, has two facets: it frustrates as well as tempts and allures. Indeed, it is this very combination of frustration and allurement that renders the object 'bad.' In order to deal with this intolerable inner situation, the internal 'bad' object is split into its alluring and the exciting aspects and rejecting and frustrating aspects. Both the exciting and frustrating internal objects are then repressed by the central ego.[6] Because the ego "maintains libidinal attachment to the objects undergoing repression" (Fairbairn, 1952, p. 112), it, too, suffers the fate of division and is split into the libidinal ego and the anti-libidinal ego or internal saboteur. The central ego rejects these attachments to the internal 'bad' object, with the consequence that along with the internal exciting and frustrating objects, the subsidiary egos share the fate of repression.

I want to pause here to make a few comments regarding the above formulations. Whereas there is a good deal of evidence supporting Fairbairn's (1952) central claim that we are inherently object-seeking creatures, there is little evidence to support Fairbairn's formulations regarding the hypothesis that under the impact of deprivation and frustration, the infant or child splits the object into 'good' and 'bad' objects. Indeed, as is characteristic of many psychoanalytic theorists writing about psychological development, Fairbairn makes no reference to observations of infant or child behavior that would constitute evidence of such splitting.

There is also no observational evidence presented to support the idea that a consequence of deprivation and frustration are splits in the ego into libidinal and anti-libidinal ego structures. Indeed, one is confronted with the challenges of 'translating' these formulations into experience-near terms. For example, what kinds of feelings, thoughts, and behaviors would reflect these splits in the ego? It is a testimony to the evocative power and the sense that they capture something important about psychological functioning that Fairbairn's metapsychological formulations of endopsychic structure have had the influence they have had despite their turgid and complex nature and the host of unanswered questions they generate. For example, what is an internal object? How does internalizing the object enable the child to feel that he or she is better able to control the object? What kinds of experiences and behaviors would reflect these processes?

## *The internal object*

The concept of internalization has a long and fraught history in psychoanalytic theory, one that requires its own separate treatment (see, for example, Schafer (1968) and Meissner (1981)). What Fairbairn appears to mean by internalization of the 'bad' object is closer to the concept of introject than to ordinary identification. That is, it seems to refer to a process through which negative interactional experiences become part of oneself and yet not fully assimilated. The concept of superego can serve as a model of an internal object (indeed, Fairbairn (1952) wrote that this was, indeed, the case). In common parlance the superego is often depicted as a homunculus standing on one's shoulder telling one what to do, or, more often, what not to do. Such locutions as "my conscious tells me . . ." are quite common and capture the experience of harboring some attitudes, values, feelings, and thoughts that are part of oneself and yet, not fully part of oneself in the sense that they are experienced, to some degree, as emanating from an outside agency.[7]

Keeping in mind the superego as a quintessential example of an internal object, one can think of it in the following way: The child internalizes the rejecting attitudes of the caregiver toward himself or herself, not in the form of specific memories of being treated in a certain way by the caregiver (i.e., *I* was treated in such and such a way by *you*). Rather, internalizing an internal object is meant to convey the idea that these rejecting attitudes become parts of the child's personality structure. Over time, the feeling of oneself as 'bad,' that is, as worthy of rejection, becomes unlinked from specific experiences (e.g., rejection) at the hands of a 'bad' separate other. That is, the child now feels rejecting toward aspects of himself or herself. Indeed, the other can be consciously represented as idealized and 'good.'

The representation and experience of oneself as 'bad' is now a stable structure in the personality that is not linked to particular episodes or to specific interactional experiences, but is akin to what has been referred to as "procedural knowledge" (Eagle, 1987; Lyons-Ruth, 1999; Lyons-Ruth et al. 1998; Tulving, 1985). Although the internal object is a stable structure of the personality, it is not fully assimilated as an integral part of oneself and, like the superego, can be experienced as a persecutory presence or agent, i.e., as an introject. In this sense, it is unlike procedural knowledge. As we will see, it is the introject status of the internal object that leads Fairbairn (1952) to talk about "exorcising" the bad object.

The basic idea being captured here is that one has internalized a set of interactional experiences that, because they are too painful, cannot be fully assimilated as part of oneself and yet, in some way, are part of oneself. To use a concrete physical analogy, it is as if one had swallowed a piece of plastic that, although now inside one's body, rather than being digested and thereby becoming, employing Piaget's (1971) metaphoric term, "aliment" and part of one's body, remains undigested as a foreign body. The use of this metaphor in the psychological realm is captured by the expression "It sticks in my craw" to describe an experience that one cannot let go because one cannot fully assimilate it. One 'chews' on it over and over again. It is interesting to note the parallel between an experience that 'sticks in one's craw' and Freud's early concept of "strangulated affect." In both cases, the experience cannot be fully assimilated.

As both Rubens (1994) and Guntrip (1969) point out, experiences that are capable of being integrated into the personality result in memory, learning, and gradual alteration of the whole self. That is, they are fully assimilated and, as such, serve as 'aliment' for the growth of memory, learning, and self. When however, experiences are intolerable, they are split off from the central self. They become crystallized endopsychic structures or, one can say, split-off subsystems with their own aims and motivations that are not integrated into the rest of the personality.

Although splits in the ego as a consequence of the trauma of deprivation and rejection suggest a dissociative process, in Fairbairn's formulation, the split-off ego structures are in dynamic conflict with each other. Fairbairn was clearly aware of the fact that the notion of splits in the ego suggested the process of dissociation and bore a family resemblance to Janet's work as well as to Freud's early formulation of the etiology of hysteria. Indeed, with regard to the latter, he urged that we go "back to hysteria" (Fairbairn 1952, p. 92), by which he intended to convey the idea of the greater compatibility between Freud's early writings on hysteria and his theory of endopsychic structure of the personality. He notes that in contrast to the active nature of repression, "dissociation as described by Janet is, of course, essentially a passive process – a process of disintegration due to failure on the part of the cohesive function normally experienced by the ego" (Fairbairn, 1954, pp. 105–106). Further, he finds Janet's concept of dissociation wanting precisely because it is a passive process. He is drawn to Freud's concept of repression because it is an active process and therefore is more conducive to the development of a dynamic psychology.

Thus, both Freud and Fairbairn reject Janet's account of hysteria in terms of dissociation due to a weak ego being (passively) overwhelmed by trauma and propose instead an account that emphasizes active conflicting forces in the personality. More specifically, the libidinal ego and the anti-libidinal ego are not simply structures that, so to speak, exist passively side by side, dissociated from each other, but rather are in active dynamic conflict with each other. That is, the individual pursues aims that are not only different from each other, but also conflict with each other.[8]

## *Conflicts between different internal object relationships: Fairbairn*

There are a number of different and interrelated kinds of conflict one can identify in Fairbairn's theorizing. As we have seen, one kind of conflict is between the split-off ego structures of libidinal ego in an object relationship with the internal exciting or alluring object and the anti-libidinal ego in an object relationship with the internal rejecting object. In more clinical and experience-near terms, the conflict between libidinal ego in relationship to the exciting object and anti-libidinal ego in relationship to the rejecting object can be understood as different and conflicting aspects of oneself in affective relationships with different and conflicting aspects of representations of the other. One aspect of oneself, referred to by Fairbairn as the libidinal ego, is in an affective relationship with the exciting and alluring aspect of one's representation of the other; another aspect of oneself, the anti-libidinal ego, is in an affective relationship with the rejecting aspect of one's representation of the other. Thus, the two different aspects of oneself are not only split off from each other, but are in active conflict with each other. One aspect of the individual (libidinal ego) keeps attempting to gain the love of the exciting, but rejecting object, while another aspect of the individual has nothing but contempt for these needs and attempts (anti-libidinal ego).

Although it may be played out in an actual relationship with another, we are dealing with *inner conflict* between the individual's experienced wishes and needs and his or her contemptuous reactions to those wishes and needs. I refer, somewhat awkwardly, to a relationship with *representations* of the other because Fairbairn makes it clear that the relationship with an apparent actual external other is largely a stage for an *internal object relationship* between aspects of oneself and an internal object, which, in the present context, I roughly translate as a representation of the other. Further, insofar as an internal object is also an aspect of oneself (even if as an introject), one's object relationships can be seen as one aspect of oneself in a conflictual relationship with another aspect of oneself.

## *Conflict between primary identification and separation: Fairbairn*

Fairbairn (1952) identifies a fundamental conflict between "the regressive lure of identification and the progressive urge toward separation" (Fairbairn, 1952, p. 43).[9]

It is important to note that for Fairbairn, the progressive urge toward separation is not simply a matter of increasing independence from the object, but of "mature dependence" rather than "infantile dependence" (Fairbairn, 1952, p. 34) on the object. That is, healthy functioning always entails an object component, "the self in relation to another" (Rubens, 1994, p. 153). Further, Fairbairn (1952) tells us, the individual experiences "devotion" and "obstinate attachment" to internal objects, which are largely motivated by the fear that relinquishing these ties is equivalent to living in an empty, objectless inner world. Because the ego cannot survive without support from the object, relinquishment of these ties is experienced as equivalent to the loss of the ego. And Fairbairn (1952) writes, the "loss of the ego is the ultimate psychopathological disaster" (p. 52). Hence, we cling to our internal 'bad' objects as preferable to an empty inner world devoid of object relations. Even 'bad' object relations are preferable to no object relations. The latter is experienced as unsustainable. This dire fear associated with attempts to dissolve one's "devotion" and "obstinate attachment" to internal objects is for Fairbairn a critical factor in the maintenance of psychopathology and is a major clinical challenge in the treatment of certain patients.

As Armstrong-Perlman (1994) observes, some patients spend their lives "pursuing alluring but rejecting objects. . . [who] have remained elusive objects of desire" (p. 223). Despite the unsatisfying nature of these relationships – often not merely unsatisfying, but abusive and cruel – the patient finds it exceedingly difficult to relinquish them. The loss of the relationship and of the vital connection it provides are experienced as catastrophic, generating the fear of disintegration of the personality. Many of these patients experience an intense conflict between, on the one hand, the recognition of the unsatisfactory nature of the relationship and even the desire to leave the relationship and, on the other hand, the unbearable fear of loss of a connection to external and internal objects. As Armstrong-Perlman (1994) writes: "The fear is that loss will lead either to the disintegration of the self, or to a reclusive emptiness to which any state of connectedness, no matter how infused with suffering, is preferable" (p. 224).

My own clinical experiences, particularly with women in abusive relationships, are entirely in accord with Armstrong-Perlman's description. For a number of years, as part of a university community service program, I have been working with women who have been subjected to domestic violence. Whatever the differences among the life circumstances and life trajectories of these women, they share a set of dynamics that illustrate Fairbairn's formulations with remarkable clarity. They include: an abiding and chronic conflict between the conviction that they need to leave the relationship and the profound fear of inner emptiness and lack of connection that, they are convinced, leaving the relationship would bring about. That this fear may, in an important sense, be justified is made evident when even successful (and frequently short-lived) attempts to leave the relationship often result in profound depression, anxiety, suicidal impulses and utter despair. In one case, after exiting the relationship, one of the women in the group became utterly dysfunctional and could not even manage to get out of bed. Not surprisingly, she returned to the abusive relationship, which, indeed, is the norm in domestic violence. It is important to reiterate that for many abused women, leaving the relationship is experienced as giving up not only an actual external relationship, but also an internal affective connection, the loss of which is psychologically equivalent to inner emptiness and void and loss of the ego.

In understanding the experience of many of these women, we have found it useful to think in terms of addiction and affect regulation. That is, just as the individual with a drug addiction becomes dysregulated when the drug is not available, so similarly, do many of the abused women become dysregulated when they experience loss of connection to the object or, at times, even when they anticipate such loss.

Although I have been focusing on domestic violence, the dynamics I have described are also quite pronounced in other maladaptive relationships, particularly sado-masochistic relationships. Despite knowing otherwise at the rational cognitive level, many individuals in these relationships are generally unable to give up the fantasy that their partner will, at some point, meet their needs. They are often unable to accept at an emotional level the hopelessness of the relationship in this regard. When, at times, this reality becomes too emotionally evident, it is often followed by intolerable depression and despair, often followed by a reinstatement of the fantasy in order to dispel the intolerable depression and despair. This is a powerful barrier to any attempt at a realistic emotional engagement with the reality of the relationship (I am not addressing here the question of gratification inherent in sexual and moral masochism (Freud, 1905, p. 158)).

It is not uncommon for many abused women to respond with rage to their experience of humiliation and frustration. It is also not uncommon for such rage to be followed by ruefulness and shame, self-contempt, attempts to undo, and the conviction that the abuser's negative and contemptuous characterization of them is accurate. Expressions of rage are often followed by attempts to be 'good' in the hope that by being good, even saintly, they will earn the abuser's love. This dynamic is similar to Fairbairn's (1952) description of the child taking the badness into himself or herself in the hope that by reversing the badness and being good, he or she will earn the parents' love. As Fairbairn (1952) points out, to believe that one is not loved because of one's badness, a conditional fact, is preferable to feeling unloved *unconditionally*. The latter offers no hope that there is anything that one can do to earn parental love. As Fairbairn (1952) puts it, "it is better to be a sinner in a world ruled by God than to live in a world ruled by the devil" (pp. 66–67). The attempt to be unqualifiedly 'good' does not last, and episodes of rage, of course, recur. This triggers the vicious cycle of shame, self-recrimination, attempts to be good, failure, more rage, and so on.

I worked with a woman who repeatedly reacted to the realization that her fantasy in relation to her partner would not be fulfilled with the experience of depression, despair, and suicidal thoughts and feelings. She repeatedly dealt with these intolerable feelings by re-instating the hope and fantasy that the 'bad' object could be transformed into a 'good' one, only to be repeatedly severely disillusioned through her experience of her partner's abusive and demeaning behavior, and then confronted once again with the terrible reality that her fantasy and hope were futile. This would then lead once again to despair and suicidal impulses, a cycle that would be repeated over and over again. My patient would, at one level, recognize the futility of her hope and fantasy and, at the same time, at another level, disavow that terrible reality and continue to nurture the hope and fantasy that she could transform the 'bad' object into the 'good' object who would love her. As Freud (1940b) describes in his essay on "splitting the ego in the process of defense," her behavior and her psychic life reflected, at one and the same time, both the recognition and the disavowal of reality.

A common theme that emerges in work with abused women and that emerged with my patient is their puzzlement regarding their object choice. That is, they question why they are so frequently attracted to men who turn out to be abusive and, more generally, who are unable to be loving and caring. Many victims of domestic violence get emotionally involved with the same type of abusive partner over and over again. Why is this the case? I am not suggesting that this question can be answered in a definitive way. However, I think that some answers, implicit in Fairbairn's theorizing, are more useful and insightful than the vague and essentially non-explanatory concept of repetition compulsion. First, one must recall that, according to the perspective of Fairbairn's object relations theory, not only are we object-seeking creatures, but the kind of cognitive and affective connections we form with objects, including internal objects, define our very identity. Hence, to a significant extent, to paraphrase Rubens (1994, p. 158), a particularized relation of specific aspects of the self in relation with specific aspects of the object would define our identity and our way of being with an other. To put it another way, the early established template or schema of the subsidiary ego structures in a particular relationship to internal objects is experienced as a vital aspect of one's identity that, whatever suffering it may bring, is not readily relinquished. In short, object choice contributes to maintenance of one's identity.

There is another factor that is, I believe often involved in the object choice of abused women. I have described the futility of the patient's fantasy of transforming the 'bad' object into a 'good' object, with the implication that this is a futile and unrealistic hope because of the reality of who the object is (e.g., an abuser), that is, because of an unfortunate object choice. This, of course, may be true. Indeed, many of the abused women we have seen report not being at all attracted to or interested in men who are 'nice guys' and not likely to be abusive. However, there is often more subtle clinical evidence that the lack of interest in the 'nice guy' and the attraction to the potentially 'bad' object are also motivated by conflicts pertaining to intimacy and the accompanying fear of engulfment. Thus, although the patient I described above was, in fact, subject to a great deal of abusive behavior and suffered greatly under its impact, on the occasions when her partner seemed to make an effort to behave more positively toward her, she would frequently become provocative and behave in a way that was virtually certain to sooner or later reinstitute the usual abusive interactional pattern.

### *Conflict between fantasy and reality: Fairbairn*

Implicit in the above formulation are a number of conflicts, including the conflict between fantasy and reality. Indeed, for Fairbairn, a core feature of psychopathology, in particular, schizoid psychopathology,[10] is the individual's powerful tendency to live in a self-enclosed fantasy world in which one relates to the other largely as a stand-in for an internal object rather than to an actual external other. The individual is living in a fantasy world of internal objects and internal object relationships. Fairbairn (1952) also refers to the individual's "devotion" and "obstinate attachment" (Fairbairn, 1952, p. 103, 117) to early objects that conflict with his or her strivings to free himself or herself from these powerful ties to internal objects and find and relate to a real external object in the world. One can, in broad terms, also see this as a conflict between fantasy and reality.

So, for example, the issue with my patient was not entirely one of object choice, but also of her actively contributing to the constant re-creation of an interactional scenario that matched the template of her well-established inner world of object relationships. Thus, side by side with her fantasy that her partner could be transformed into a 'good' object and that they would live happily ever after was her actual behavior that served to repeatedly re-create and maintain the 'bad' object situation. My patient's *fantasies* of intimacy and closeness and living happily ever after were far more powerful in organizing her psychological life and sustaining her than any possibility of intimacy in the actual relationship. Indeed, the latter was repeatedly sabotaged.

Although Fairbairn's attribution of the gap between fantasy and reality to the patient's need to maintain connection to internal objects may be largely correct, I would suggest that the "devotion" to early objects and object relationship is also in the service of avoiding the dangers represented by actual intimacy and an actual 'good' object. Indeed, some of the women in our domestic violence program describe the experience of a 'normal' (i.e., non-abusive) relationship as boring and emotionally dead.

The above dynamics are not limited to domestic violence and outright abusive relationships, but are also present in other relationships. Consider individuals involved in affairs in which one individual is not fully available because he or she is married. The relationship is often sustained by the excitement of an illicit affair, but also, in some cases, by the fantasy of intimacy and love that will be forthcoming when the hitherto unavailable individual becomes fully available. It is not uncommon, however, in such cases for the excitement and intimacy to disappear once the situation changes and the unavailable individual becomes available. It becomes clear in these instances that the excitement and intimacy is sustained not only by the illicitness of the relationship, but also by a fantasy that cannot survive the reality of the object's actual availability. The degree of relatedness and intimacy activated in fantasy cannot be matched by the degree of relatedness and intimacy experienced in the actual relationship.

I recall a remarkable section of a film I saw some years ago. The film is set in a small Israeli village. One of the characters in the film comes out into the street every night when the moon appears and in a poignant lamentation, cries loudly, "Rachel. My Rachel." One has the immediate image of a terrible loss in the life of this poor soul. A few scenes later, we find the character in the grassy field of a mental hospital at dusk behind a metal fence. A woman walks up to the fence and our poor soul approaches the fence to greet her. The woman is none other than Rachel. They chat for a while in a mundane, relatively affectless way: "How are you? How have you been?", and so on. Soon the moon emerges in the sky and our character excuses himself, walks to the center of the field and bays at the moon: "Rachel. My Rachel." The scene brilliantly demonstrates that the object in our character's object relationship is an internal object, that his passion and affect are directed to the internal object, and that he is living in an inner fantasy world that has little or nothing to do with the actual Rachel. (One is reminded of Lacan's (1966/2002) distinction between the object that triggers desire and the actual object of desire.)

I am also reminded of the intense love affair between Fermina and Florentino in Gabriel Garcia Marquez's (1994/2014) *Love in the Time of Cholera*. The love affair was conducted solely via letters. When Fermina actually encountered Florentino in person, "She asked herself, appalled how she could have nurtured such a chimera in her heart for so long with so much ferocity." In responding to the question, 'what can literature teach us about love?' in the *New York Times* Book Review section (February 9, 2014), after citing the above passage from Marquez's novel, the reviewer David Levithan (2014) writes: "I have always been more in love with my fantasies of the woman I was with, not the beautiful and complicated human beings they actually were . . . true love . . . asks us . . . to truly see the people we love" (p. 18). I would add that from a Fairbairnian perspective, true object relationships with actual others make the same demand. It is interesting to observe the continuum – rather than a radical discontinuity – between the psychotic character in the Israeli film and both the literary character of Fermina and the actual character of David Levithan, along with the rest of us.

## *Conflict between need for closeness and fear of engulfment: Guntrip*

Guntrip (1969) has described a pattern that he refers to as an "in and out program" (p. 36) that some individuals adopt as a means of dealing with the conflict between the need for object relationships and the fear of being engulfed by them. Although his main focus is on schizoid phenomena, the dynamics he describes are more widely applicable. The dilemma to which the "in and out" pattern is a solution is the chronic conflict between desire and longing for closeness in a relationship with another and fear of being swallowed up and engulfed in the relationship. On the one hand, the individual cannot survive psychologically without some connection to the object, the absence of which produces the terror of isolation; and on the other hand, every object relationship is experienced as carrying the risk of engulfment and the loss of individuality. The risk is particularly intense when the object relationship is a symbiotic one, established on the basis of what Fairbairn (1952) refers to as primary identification.

Thus, the individual is damned if s/he does and damned if s/he does not. The compromise solution to this seemingly unresolvable conflict that the individual often reaches is the "in-out program" described by Guntrip (1969), which can be expressed in various ways and can take various forms. One form is alternating periods of literally being in and out of the relationship, that is, separations and reunions. This pattern is frequently seen in domestic violence couples – repeated break-ups and reunions. Another in–out pattern is remaining in the relationship, but without full commitment, with, emotionally speaking, one foot always out the door. Still another in–out pattern is chronically maintaining an optimal degree of distance that avoids both the terror of isolation and the fear of engulfment. This is probably the most stable form of the in–out pattern.

## *Conflict between individuation and parricide: Loewald*

Loewald (1979) essentially reinterprets the Oedipus complex by formulating it in terms of the conflict between strivings for autonomy and symbolic parricide (see Chapter 3). He writes that "in an important sense, by evolving our own autonomy, our own superego, and by engaging in nonincestuous object relations, we are killing our parents" (p. 758). He also writes:

> [I]n considering this from the particular angle I wish to emphasize, it is no exaggeration to say that the assumption of responsibility for one's own life and its conduct is in psychic reality tantamount to the murder of the parents, to the crime of parricide, and involves dealing with the guilt incurred thereby.
>
> (p. 757)

And in a very strong and pithy statement, Loewald writes that "without the guilty deed of parricide, there is no autonomous self" (p. 762).

## *Conflict between individuation and merger: Loewald*

Loewald reinterprets the Oedipus complex not only in terms of the conflict between individuation and parricide, but also in terms of the conflict between individuation and merger. He writes that "oedipal, incestuous object relations are characterized by hovering between the poles of identification and object cathexis, between merger and individuality" (Loewald, 1979, p. 771). According to Loewald (1979), there is an inherent and fundamental conflict between "merger and individuality" (p. 772). Further, according to him, although it may wane over time, what "remains with [all of us] is a "psychotic core" in which this fundamental conflict plays out.

The conflict between merger and individuation posited by Loewald has also been described as one between symbiosis and separation–individuation (Mahler,

1968) and also bears a strong family resemblance to the posited conflict between agency and communion (Bakan, 1966). In a more general context and in a more diluted form, it is also related to the presumed conflict between relatedness and self-definition.

### *Conflict between strivings for autonomy and guilt toward parents: Weiss and Sampson*

Weiss and Sampson and their colleagues (1986) have developed a mini-theory called Control–Mastery theory that focuses on the conflict between, on the one hand, the individual's strivings for autonomy and other related aims such as achieving success in one's ambitions and, on the other hand, guilt toward parental figures. These strivings for separation and autonomy may evoke guilt because these strivings are unconsciously (and sometimes consciously) experienced as equivalent to harming parents or incurring their wrath. Most important, according to Control–Mastery theory, these feelings of guilt are generated by *parental communications*, often subtle and disavowed, that indeed tend to equate the child's strivings for autonomy with harm to parents. Weiss and Sampson refer to this complex of feelings and psychic equivalences as constituting "unconscious pathogenic beliefs" that take the form of: 'If I pursue my ambitions, it will be at your expense and/or will harm you in some way or evoke your anger.'

### *Inner conflict in self psychology: Kohut*

Kohut (1982) rejects the Freudian view of human nature, which he dramatically describes in the following way: "man as an insufficiently and incompletely tamed animal, reluctant to give up his wish to live by the pleasure principle, unable to relinquish his innate destructiveness" (p. 401); and replaces it with an image of the individual struggling to "unfold his innermost self battling against external and internal obstacles" (p. 405). He writes: "We believe, in other words, that in the last analysis we are not dealing with an uninfluentiable [sic] conflict of basic opposing instincts (Thanatos battling Eros) but with, at least potentially interferences that impinge on normal development" (Kohut, 1982, pp. 401–402). He contrasts the "*Guilty Man*" of Freudian theory, who is "in hopeless conflict between the drives that spring from the biological bedrock of *homo natura* and the civilizing influences emanating from the social environment as embodied in the superego" with the "*Tragic Man*" of self psychology who is "attempting, and never quite succeeding to realize the programme laid down in his depth during the span of his life" (Kohut, 1982, p. 402).

Thus, Kohut does not accord much importance to inner conflict – what he refers to as "structural conflicts" – in his developmental formulations, his theory of the etiology of psychopathology, or in his description of clinical material. Indeed, he writes that "in the presence of a firm self, conflict per se is by no means deleterious" (Kohut, 1984, p. 45). His emphasis in both theory and clinical work is on self-defects and the impediments to the development of a cohesive self.

Despite Kohut's rejection of any fundamental role for conflict in psychological functioning, there appear to be implicit references to inner conflict in Kohut's theorizing. As noted, Kohut (1982) refers to individuals "battling against external and internal obstacles" in order to pursue and fulfill "their own nuclear programme and destiny" (p. 399). Also, as noted, Kohut writes that the individual never quite succeeds in the realization of his or her nuclear program – thus, the "Tragic Man" of self psychology. A number of considerations and questions arise. One, a battle against seemingly inevitable external and internal obstacles surely suggests some kind of unavoidable outer and inner conflict that bedevils the individual's pursuit to realize his or her nuclear program. Kohut, at least in his 1982 paper, does not articulate the nature of these obstacles, especially the "inner obstacles." However, the presence of inevitable *internal obstacles* to realizing one's nuclear program seems to suggest that there are 'forces' in the individual that work against such realization. But, if this is so, we are talking about something that surely bears a strong family resemblance to inner conflict. It would be very useful if self psychology theorists addressed more fully the nature of these "internal obstacles."

### Conflict between pursuing one's nuclear program and ties to objects: Fosshage

Even if he does not say in so many words, Fosshage (2017) has essentially addressed this issue in attempting to develop what he refers to as a relational self psychology perspective. According to Fosshage, from that perspective, the central conflict confronting the individual is one between pursuing his or her nuclear program and the threat to vital ties that such pursuit represents. Thus, in effect, Fosshage has identified what from his perspective are the primary "internal obstacles" alluded to by Kohut. They are the dangers of losing vital ties were one to pursue one's nuclear program. Fosshage (2017) writes that the child will "abdicate his or her own experience" (p. 13), and relinquish or thwart his or her pursuit of self-realization in order to maintain vitally needed ties, even if these ties are undermining. Brandchaft (2007) refers to the child's pathological accommodation and, to quote Fosshage (2017) again, "it is tantamount to selling one's soul in an effort to save it" (p. 13).

### Convergent and divergent inner conflicts: A. Kris

Kris (e.g., 1988) has distinguished between what he refers to as convergent versus divergent conflicts. The term "convergent conflict" is intended to convey the idea of opposing forces pushing against each other as in two football teams lined up against each other. Id–ego conflicts or drive–defense conflicts are examples of convergent conflicts. They are characterized by the conflict between expressing or experiencing a wish and repressing that wish because of the anxiety such expression would entail. As Kris (1988) notes, making the unconscious conscious (i.e., lifting repression) as a goal of psychoanalytic treatment would seem appropriate to dealing with this kind of conflict.

Divergent conflicts, as Kris describes them, are characterized by "conflicts of ambivalence" (Kris, 1985, p. 538) and entail painful choices. Kris refers to such conflicts as divergent because, in contrast to convergent conflicts, where the opposing elements push against each other, in divergent conflicts, the conflicting elements pull in opposite directions. If two opposing football teams lined up against each other serves as a metaphor for convergent conflicts, two teams engaged in a tug of war serves as a metaphor for divergent conflicts.

A quintessential example of a divergent conflict is precisely the kind of conflict described by Fairbairn (1952) between "the regressive lure of identification and the progressive urge of separation" (p. 43). It would be viewed as divergent by Kris because the individual faces a painful situation in which the pursuit of one aim is experienced as being carried out at the expense of the conflicting aim. Thus, the fear is that if one pursues developmental strivings, one will have to sacrifice object ties; and conversely, if one gives priority to maintaining object ties, one will have to relinquish the pursuit of developmental strivings. Insofar as either 'choice,' it is feared, entails the sacrifice of the alternative choice, any 'choice' is painful and involves the experience of loss. Thus, whereas the appropriate therapeutic approach to convergent conflicts is lifting repression and making the unconscious conscious, the appropriate therapeutic approach to divergent conflicts is helping the patient deal with these conflicts through "a process akin to mourning" (Kris, 1985, p. 554). Further, according to Kris (1985), in contrast to convergent conflicts, which entail repression and are unconscious, in divergent conflicts "the elements in conflict may both be conscious" (p. 555) – still another reason that lifting repression and making the unconscious conscious are not appropriate goals for divergent conflicts.

According to Kris (1985), "mourning does not mean giving up the love for a lost object. What is given up is the illusion of permanence" (p. 557). Kris (1985) goes on to say that in divergent conflicts "the characteristic misconception [is] that expression and satisfaction of one side necessarily means total loss of the other, that no satisfactory compromise can be reached" (p. 557) and states that this misconception "does yield, along with the resolution of the conflict in painful alternations" (p. 557).

Let us apply Kris' formulation of divergent conflicts to a further discussion of the seemingly quintessential divergent conflict between pursuing one's developmental strivings (the new) and maintaining ties to early objects (the old). According to Kris (1985), the individual enmeshed in this conflict assumes, often unconsciously, that this conflict is intractable in the sense that pursuing one aim entails the irredeemable loss of the other aim. Hence, either 'choice' seems unbearably painful. Kris tells us that this construal of the conflict as intractable is precisely the problem and overlooks the solutions that lie in a "process akin to mourning" and in "resolution of the conflict in painful alternations" of pursuing one aim and then the other.

The positing of these two solutions is confusing. On the one hand, mourning is a process that helps one come to terms with an irretrievable loss. On the other hand, resolution through alternatively pursuing one aim and then the other aim is a strategy that enables one to retain both conflicting aims and therefore, obviates the need for mourning an irretrievable loss. These two solutions, which Kris presents together as means of resolving divergent conflicts seem to contradict each other and themselves seem to constitute a divergent conflict. That is, relinquishing an aim and mourning the irretrievable loss constituted by such relinquishment and alternatively pursuing two conflicting aims without relinquishing either aim would seem to be two incompatible means of resolving a divergent conflict.

Consider the relationship between mourning and painful alternations of two seemingly conflicting aims as two solutions to divergent conflicts in the context of loss of a loved one. What do painful alternations mean in the context of loss of a loved one? Perhaps the answer lies in a phenomenon one frequently observes in the early response to death of a loved one, of alternations between accepting and denying the reality of loss. At times, these two contradictory responses also appear to exist side by side simultaneously rather than alternate with each other. In both cases, denial appears to allow the individual to titrate the severity of the trauma and give him or her time to accept the reality of the loss. Perhaps the early alternations between denial and acceptance allow the bereaved individual time to be capable of a process of mourning that is characterized by both acceptance of the loss and recognition that such acceptance does not preclude love for and a feeling of connection to the lost object.

According to Kris (1985), the individual does not realize "that mourning does not mean giving up the love for a lost object" (p. 567). It only means giving up "the illusion of permanence" (p. 557). What I understand Kris to be saying here is that although the loved one is, indeed, lost, one's love for the loved one can be continued and need not be lost. That is, one's *emotional connection* to the loved one need not be lost. If I understand Kris correctly, he is suggesting that recognition that one's love for the lost loved one can continue makes possible the process of mourning and helps the individual resolve the seemingly intractable divergent conflict between accepting the reality of the loss of the object and the unbearable pain that such acceptance entails.

## Conflict between auto-erotic fantasies of infantile sexuality and object love: Widlöcher

According to Widlöcher (2002), there is a fundamental conflict between the auto-erotic fantasies of infantile sexuality and object love. Widlöcher (2002) writes that "infantile sexuality takes form as a result of an internal demand and achieves satisfaction in psychic and/or autoerotic activity" (p. 13), which is entirely in the realm of fantasy and imagination. In such fantasies:

> [The object] is only the actor called upon to play a role in the imaginary scenario. It is interchangeable, and the same object can play different parts

> in the same scenario. Wish fulfillment . . . is the goal that is sought and the source of pleasure.
>
> (p. 13)

Further and most important in the present context, psychic life is characterized by a constant and "conflictual interweaving of love for the other and the quest for autoerotic pleasure" (p. 31). Indeed, for Widlöcher, psychoanalysis is primarily concerned with the residues of the fantasies of infantile sexuality, their persistence into adult psychic life, and their interference with the individual's capacity for object love, that is, the individual's ability to love a real and separate other (see Eagle, 2007; 2013).

## *The conflict between attachment and sexuality: Eagle*

There is a good deal of evidence that, although closely related to each other, sexuality and attachment are not only separable, but also in certain respects, antagonistic instinctual motivational systems. This can be seen in a number of ways. With regard to their distinctiveness or separability, as Bowlby (1969/1982) notes, "the activation of the two systems vary independently of each other" and "the class of objects toward which each is directed may be quite different" (p. 231). And, as both Holmes (2001) and Fonagy (2001) have noted, it is not uncommon to observe intense attachment without sexual interest and intense sexual interest without attachment.

Diamond (2003) has proposed that sexuality and attachment are governed by two different systems: sexuality "by the sexual mating system" (p. 174) and attachment by "the attachment or pair-bonding system . . . the goal of which is the maintenance of an enduring association" (p. 174). Or, as Hazan and Zeifman (1994) put it, sex brings partners together and attachment is the "psychological tether" that keeps them together. There is also a good deal of evidence that attachment and sexuality are mediated by different neurochemical systems (See Eagle, 2013, for a partial summary of such evidence).

There is also a good deal of evidence suggesting a partial antagonism or conflictual relationship between the two systems. Freud (1912c) observed clinically the conflictual relationship between "love and desire" or the "affectionate and sensual currents," which are roughly equivalent to attachment and sexuality. In his account of "psychical impotence," he wrote "where they love they do not desire and where they desire they cannot love" (p. 183). Freud also made clear that although this conflict was more pronounced in neurosis, it was widespread and virtually normative in "civilized man."

Freud attributed the split between love and desire to the persistence of oedipal incestuous wishes. However, I have argued (Eagle, 2007b, 2013) that the inherent features of the sexual and attachment systems go a long way in accounting for that split. There is overwhelming evidence that across a wide range of species, including humans, sexual interest and arousal are triggered by novelty and variety, whereas experiencing someone as an attachment figure requires familiarity and prolonged propinquity. As I have argued elsewhere (Eagle, 2013):

> Given the operation of these two systems, as one's current partner becomes one's attachment figure, sexual interest and excitement are likely to wane, a prediction that is generally supported by empirical evidence. This state of affairs presents the individual with an integrative challenge that is met by different individuals with varying degrees of success.
>
> (p. 126)

> In short, the split between love and desire, a phenomenon that for Freud was at the core of oedipal conflicts, can be profitably understood in terms of the general relation between the attachment and sexual systems as well as the individual vicissitudes in dealing with the competing pulls and demands of these two motivational systems.
>
> (p. 127)

Having reviewed some of the major formulations on inner conflict, let me address common themes that emerge as well as some divergences and convergences regarding the nature of our fundamental conflicts.

## The nature of our fundamental conflicts

One of the themes that emerges from the above different conceptions of conflict is a shift from an overriding emphasis on conflicts related to childhood sexual aggressive wishes culminating in the Oedipus complex to an emphasis on conflicts having to do with strivings for individuation. As we have seen, two fundamental conflicts have been posited in regard to such strivings: one, the conflict between individuation and both longings for and fear of merger; and two, the conflict between strivings for individuation and the guilt induced by these strivings. As we have also seen, there are different views regarding the source of such guilt, with Loewald arguing that guilt arises out of the individual's experience of strivings for individuation as psychically equivalent to parricide; and Weiss and Sampson arguing that the child's association of guilt with strivings for individuation and autonomy is mainly due to parental communications.

It is worth noting that implicit in Freud's account of the Oedipus complex and its resolution is a recognition of the issue of individuation. Thus, he writes that the persistence of incestuous wishes interferes with the individual's capacity to libidinally cathect an object outside the family, which, if successful, would surely constitute an expression of individuation. Indeed, as we have seen, Loewald essentially reconceptualizes the attempt to resolve the Oedipus complex as essentially a struggle to achieve individuation.

## *Anxiety and guilt*

Accompanying the shift from an emphasis on conflicts related to childhood sexual and aggressive wishes to conflicts concerned with individuation is a shift from an emphasis on the affect of anxiety to an emphasis on the affect of guilt. One can see the beginnings of this shift in Strachey's (1934) classic paper in which he places a great deal of stress on softening the guilt associated with a primitive and harsh superego as a central therapeutic goal. One can also see a similar trend in Klein's (1948, p. 34) formulation of the depressive position, with its emphasis on guilt and reparation; in Winnicott's (1969) discussion of the capacity for "ruth" in contrast to ruthlessness; and in Modell's (1965; 1971) discussion of "survivor guilt" and "separation guilt."

As one would expect in a discussion of guilt, in all these formulations the common emphasis is on the individual's reaction to the feeling that he or she has harmed someone (usually parental figures). Thus, one can understand why Klein and Winnicott would view the capacity for guilt and the accompanying desire to repair as a developmental achievement. Such feelings betoken a capacity to recognize that one has harmed another (or that one wishes to) as well as a capacity to care enough about the other so that one feels concern about the harm one has done (or wished to do). (See Friedman, 1985, for a very useful discussion of the nature of guilt as an affect.)

Given the role of the superego in Freudian theory, one would think that guilt would be at the center of inner conflict. But that is not the case. Although Freud frequently refers to guilt in relation to the workings of the superego, he does not make a clear distinction between guilt and anxiety and, indeed, emphasizes anxiety rather than guilt and/or assimilates guilt to anxiety. He repeatedly writes that the fear of superego condemnation is ultimately linked to castration anxiety. Freud's reasoning is that insofar as parental punishment, in particular the threat of castration, becomes internalized in the form of the superego, the essence of superego condemnation is castration anxiety. Thus, he locates the ultimate source of "the ego's dread of the super-ego" to castration anxiety (Freud, 1922, p. 57). He writes: "But if we ask ourselves what it is that the ego fears from the super-ego, we cannot but think that the punishment threatened by the latter must be an extension of the punishment of castration" (Freud, 1926a, p. 128). He also refers to "social and moral anxiety" and "conscience anxiety" (p. 128) rather than conscience guilt.

One of the problems with this assimilation of guilt into anxiety is that both subjectively and conceptually, anxiety and guilt are different and distinguishable affects. Further, in ordinary language, when we speak of conscience, the primary affect is guilt rather than anxiety. In contrast to the experience of anxiety, the experiential essence of guilt as a feeling is that it is a reaction to something one has done or desired that is experienced as constituting harm to someone. Of course, one may also experience anxiety in anticipation of punishment for what one has done or desired. For example, the strivings for individuation which, Loewald (1979) maintains, are experienced as equivalent to parricide are likely to generate not only guilt, but also fear of punishment and retribution. And, as Weiss and Sampson (1986) note, the experience of outdoing father may generate not only guilt, but also fear of incurring his wrath. And indeed, the fear of incurring the wrath of the gods through one's *hubris* is a common theme in Greek mythology. Thus, one can understand that guilt and anxiety often go together. However, they are different and distinguishable affects. Normally, the experience of danger and harm to oneself elicits fear and anxiety and reactions of fight or flight, whereas, if one possesses a conscience, the feeling that one has harmed someone tends to elicit guilt and the desire to repair in some way (Klein, 1975).

The distinction between anxiety and guilt is also seen in the different psychological and conceptual networks in which they are embedded. Under certain circumstances, the feeling of guilt attendant upon the belief that one has harmed someone has a natural connection to forgiveness from the person one feels one has harmed. And being forgiven by the harmed person goes some way to relieving guilt. This is far less the case with regard to the connection between forgiveness and anxiety.

The primacy of anxiety in Freudian theory is also seen in the metapsychological claim that underlying the danger situations of loss of the object, loss of the object's love and castration is the danger that the ego will be overwhelmed by excessive excitation, certainly a case of harm to oneself rather than harm to another. Also, in accord with Freud's metapsychological account, in contrast to guilt, anxiety entails the build-up of excitation and, indeed, is subjectively experienced that way. One can thus understand the centrality of anxiety in the context of Freud's metapsychological formulations and concepts, including the constancy principle, the conception of the function of the mental apparatus as discharge of excitation, the conception of the sexual drive in terms of build-up and discharge of excitation, and the equation of unpleasure with build-up of excitation and pleasure with discharge of excitation.[11]

Even when Freud does focus on guilt, it is in the context of self-punishment and self-destructive behavior, the motive for which is to atone for one's transgressions and thereby mitigate unconscious guilt. Further, atonement for guilt is directed toward placating an agency within oneself rather than making up for harm to another. This is also the case in Freud's (1923) observation that in psychopathology, particularly in obsessional neurosis and melancholia, "the ego ideal displays particular severity and often rages against the ego in a cruel fashion" (p. 51). Here, Freud focuses on the ego ideal aspect of the superego, which punishes the ego for not having lived up to an ideal. However, Freud does not make clear what affect is generated by one's not living up to one's conscious or unconscious ego ideal. It is not clear that it is primarily guilt or anxiety.

Modell's (1965, 1971) discussion of "survivor guilt" and "separation guilt"; Loewald's (1979) reformulation of the Oedipus complex in which the emphasis is on guilt linked to the psychic equivalence between individuation and parricide; and the central role of guilt in Weiss and Sampson's (1986) concept of unconscious pathogenic beliefs: these post-Freudian formulations are much closer to our ordinary understanding of guilt in their emphasis not on retaliation for transgression (which has to do with fear and anxiety and the reactions of fight or flight), but with concern for having harmed someone (which has to do with repair).

### *The conflict between self-definition and relatedness*

It is likely that when autonomy and relatedness are experienced as in conflict with each other, it is attributable to particular sets of experiences and the construals of autonomy and relatedness these experiences have generated. For example, in the "in and out" program described by Guntrip (1969), for the individual who subjectively experiences relatedness as engulfment, it would almost certainly be experienced as in conflict with separation and autonomy. But this is a pathogenic state of affairs, not the inherent relationship between relatedness and autonomy or self-definition.

### *The conflict between fantasy and relating to an actual object*

Despite the important difference that Fairbairn does not refer to the pleasure-seeking nature of autoerotic fantasy, there is, nevertheless, a somewhat surprising family resemblance between Widlöcher's (2002) and Fairbairn's (1952) views on the conflict between infantile fantasy and the individual's capacity for object love. The individual's relationship to 'imaginary' rather than real external objects emphasized in Widlöcher's formulation parallels Fairbairn's description of the relationship with internal objects. In both cases, the individual's relation to a fantasy object is a major impediment to his or her success in relating to a real separate other.

## The inevitability of inner conflicts

Are inner conflicts inevitable? If so, what is the nature of these conflicts? Before addressing these issues, I want to note that I am not posing the question of whether or not it is possible to avoid any experience of conflict. Undoubtedly, every life is marked by the experience of conflict of some kind, including conflicting choices and aims. Rather, in posing the question of whether inner conflicts are inevitable and inherent in human nature and in the human condition, I refer to the particular conflicts identified by the theorists I have discussed.

### *The conflict between desire and self-image*

The conflicts described in Freud's early case studies arise out of an incompatibility between certain desires and fantasies and the women's moral values, sense of duty, and self-image as in the case, for example, of Elisabeth von R. or out of the conflict between a fantasy and desire and the sense of one's unworthiness, as in the case of Lucy R. However, these unacceptable desires and fantasies are hardly *inherently* conflictual. Rather, they are rather tame and are experienced as conflictual and incompatible with the ego due to the attitudes and values of a particular society in a particular historical era that have been internalized by these women. It follows that were these women living in a different society and/or a different historical era, the same desires and fantasies would not necessarily be experienced as conflictual. In short, in Freud's early writings, the conflict between desire and the ego is not seen as inevitable, but contingent and due to environmental factors. However, once Freud formulates drive theory and the id–ego model, all this changes.

## *The inevitability of conflict between the id and the ego*

The assumption that inner conflict is inherent in the human condition and therefore inevitable is most clearly seen in Freud's and Anna Freud's metapsychological positing of a primary antagonism between the id and the ego. This assumption has been subject to cogent criticism by Apfelbaum (1966) in a classic paper, by Erikson (1946), Fenichel (1938), Loewald (1960). For example, Fenichel (1938) writes: "The ego is not by nature hostile to instincts. Its organization serves, on the contrary, to heighten the probability of instinctual satisfaction. Only in some situations do conflicts develop" (p. 74). And even Freud (1926a) himself contradicts his assertion of an inevitable conflict between the id and the ego. Freud (1926b) modified that account when he writes: "There is no natural opposition between id and ego; they belong together and under healthy conditions cannot in practice be distinguished from each other" (p. 201).

Freud's 1926b formulation suggests that his earlier widely accepted view (including accepted and endorsed by Anna Freud) of the inherent antagonism between the id and the ego is more descriptive of neurosis than "healthy conditions." If, however, the antagonism between the id and the ego is not inherent, but rather a product of neurosis, the question that arises is the nature of the factors that result in conflict between the id and the ego. Further, Freud does not discuss the contradiction between his 1926 view regarding the lack of opposition between the id and the ego in health and the background network of formulations and assumptions scaffolding the earlier view of an inherent antagonism between id and ego. I refer to the network of formulations and assumptions that include the principle of constancy, the conception of mind as a discharge apparatus, the conception of drives in terms of blind discharge and as representing the most powerful source of inner excitation confronting the ego, the oedipal complex, and generally, the canonical description of Freudian theory as a drive–defense model (roughly equivalent to an id–ego model), all of which imply an antagonistic relationship in which the expression of drive is met with by the need for defense. It is this network of assumptions and formulations that forms the background and logically supports the ideas that the id is a natural enemy of the ego and constitutes the greatest threat to the ego's integrity.

If Freudian theory on the relationship between the id and the ego is to be coherent, one cannot radically modify the earlier view of a primary antagonism between the id and the ego and, at the same time, expect that the set of formulations on which the assumption of a primary antagonism is made will necessarily remain intact. But this is just what Freud appears to do in his 1926 paper. That is, he radically revises his earlier formulation of the relationship between the id and the ego without addressing the implications of the revision for the set of formulations and assumptions on which the earlier account is based. This results in a patchwork of inconsistent and even logically contradictory formulations. As I have argued elsewhere (Eagle, 1987), a thorough overhaul of id–ego theory is required, including relinquishment of the conception of the id as a "cauldron, full of seething excitations" (Freud, 1933, p. 73) blindly pressing for discharge and cut off from reality, with the personality therefore requiring a separate organ and controlling structure, the ego, designed to mediate reality and to exert control over the blind seething cauldron.

The metapsychological assumption of a primary antagonism between the id and the ego is also somewhat softened in Freud's discussion of the "danger situations" insofar as there seems to be the implication that were parental responses to the child's sexual and aggressive wishes less disapproving and more benevolent, the child's conflicts in relation to these wishes would be ameliorated. However, as we have seen, this would be misleading. For, from a Freudian perspective, childhood sexual and aggressive wishes are not only at odds with the ego, but are also inimical to society. Hence, the necessary parental stance is disapproval, with the equally necessary aim of restraining expression of these wishes.

In a formulation similar to Freud's account of the "danger situations," Brenner (1998) maintains that a fundamental conflict is one between the pleasure linked to gratification of childhood sexual and aggressive wishes and the unpleasure associated with the child's experience of parental reactions, "real and fantasied" (Brenner, 1982, p. 122) to expressions of these wishes. In referring to "real and fantasied" parental reactions,he seems to suggest that, say, castration fears may be based not only on actual parental threats of castration, but on the child's construal of parental reactions as well as fantasies regarding the kind of punishment that is merited by his or her wishes – something like the punishment fitting the crime (e.g., if the child has incestuous wishes, he or she may have the fantasy that removing the offending organ is a just punishment). If one maintains, as Brenner does, that conflicts around childhood sexual and aggressive wishes are inevitable and universal, and if one further assumes that the conflict-inducing unpleasure associated with these wishes is not largely due to parental behavior, but also or perhaps mainly to the child's punitive fantasies, then in order for Brenner's assumption regarding the inevitability and universality of conflicts around childhood sexual and aggressive wishes to be viable, he also has to assume that punitive fantasies in regard to these wishes are also universal, quite independently of parental behavior.

Further, insofar as in Brenner's account, these punitive fantasies can be relatively independent of parental behavior, they cannot be attributed to the superego if one understands that concept in terms of the internalization of parental prohibitions and values. Therefore, one must assume that not only are childhood sexual and aggressive wishes universal in Brenner's account, but also that conflict-inducing punitive fantasies regarding these wishes are also universal. Without the latter assumption, it is not clear on what basis one would argue that conflicts in relation to childhood sexual and aggressive wishes are inevitable. About the only argument I can see Brenner making that could perhaps preserve his account would be an appeal to a universal taboo against incestuous wishes and parenticide as the source of the child's hard-wired punitive fantasies in relation to childhood sexual and aggressive wishes.

There is little doubt that throughout their lives, individuals experience conflict in regard to sexual temptations and urges as well as aggressive impulses. Recognition of this fact hardly requires the armamentarium of psychoanalytic theory. However, the distinctive claim made by Freud and Brenner is that these conflictual urges and impulses are linked to universal childhood incestuous and hostile wishes emanating from the Oedipus complex and continuing throughout life. It is this claim that can be called into question. As we have seen in Chapter 3, there is serious doubt about the claim of universal incestuous and hostile wishes that appear regularly at a particular stage of psychosexual development.

## *The inevitability of conflict in relation to strivings for individuation*

Although there is convergence on the idea that strivings for individuation are often embedded in conflict, there are differences regarding the theoretical formulations of the nature and origins of such conflict. For Loewald, strivings for individuation are inherently conflicted in at least two ways: one, these strivings conflict with what, according to Loewald (1962), are powerful and universal longings for merger. He identifies a "basic polarity inherent in human existence between individuation and primary narcissistic union" (p. 490–491). He also writes that the fundamental conflict "between merger and individuation," although it may wane over time, "remains with [all of us as] a psychotic core" at the center of which is this fundamental tendency toward merger (Loewald, 1979, p. 772).]

Two, according to Loewald (1979), strivings for individuation also conflict with the guilt attendant upon the individual's experience of these strivings as psychically equivalent to parricide. This conflict, too, according to Loewald, is an inevitable aspect of psychological development. He writes: "without the guilty deed of parricide, there is no autonomous self" (Loewald, 1979, p. 768). It is not clear on what basis Loewald assumes that strivings for individuation are always necessarily experienced as parricide and that in each of us there is a "psychotic core" characterized by the desire or pull for undifferentiated merger. Loewald merely asserts the universality and inevitability of these conflicts.

Although Fairbairn (1952) identifies a similar conflict (between the regressive lure of identification and the progressive urge toward separation), unlike Loewald, he does not locate the source of that conflict in presumably universal longings for merger) or in the presence of a universal "psychotic core"). Indeed, he does not posit any such longings at all. Rather, for Fairbairn, the conflict between separation and primary identification (Fairbairn's term that is closely related to the concept of merger) is rooted in the individual's fear of being without ego supports. That is, one remains "devoted" and "obstinately attached" to early internal objects because of one's fear of living in an inner world devoid of connections to objects. In contrast to Loewald, implicit in Fairbairn's formulation is the idea that under optimal circumstances, primary identification would hold little lure, and hence, there would be little conflict surrounding strivings for individuation. Thus, for Fairbairn, whereas individuation conflicts with "immature dependence" (one aspect of which is merger), it is entirely congruent with "mature dependence." Indeed, "mature dependence" is a hallmark of healthy development.

Also in contrast to Loewald's view, in which such guilt is linked to the psychic equivalence between strivings for individuation and parricide, Weiss and Sampson propose that the guilt towards parents that accompanies strivings for individuation (a core respect of what they refer to as "unconscious pathogenic beliefs") is not an inherent one, but attributable to parental communications that in effect equate strivings for separation and individuation with harm to parents. Thus, whereas for Loewald, this conflict is an inherent and inevitable aspect of the human condition, for Weiss and Sampson, it is a contingent one that is a function of environmental vicissitudes, in particular, parental reactions to the child's strivings. Indeed, implicit in Weiss and Sampson's theorizing is the very real possibility that when parents support and nurture the child's strivings for individuation, there is little guilt attached to these strivings and, hence, little conflict associated with them.

One can also add to the above Winnicott's (1965) distinction between the true self, that is, living in accord with one's organic impulses versus living in accord with the wishes of others; Lacan's (1966/2002) similar distinction between living one's life in accord with one's subjectivity versus living one's life in accord with the desire of the other; Rogers' (1951, 1960) distinction between pursuing self-realization and living in accord with "conditions of worth"; Fromm's (1941) distinction between freedom and embeddedness; and Greenberg's (1991) distinction between the pursuit of effectance and the pursuit of safety.

## *Are conflicts between relatedness and self-definition inevitable?*

One can trace the origin of the assumption of an inevitable conflict between relatedness and self-definition to a particular understanding of Freud's (1914) formulation of the relationship between narcissism and object love. As noted earlier, according to Freud (1914a), the more one directs libido to the ego, the less libido available to direct to objects, and vice versa. Hence, it appears that according to this formulation, the greater the investment in self-definition, the less available for investment in objects. On this view, the individual confronts, in effect, a zero sum choice between ego-libido and object-libido, that is, between narcissism and object love. This assumption leads Freud to the odd conclusions that falling in love depletes the ego and that the schizophrenic who withdraws libido from objects and cathects the ego suffers from excessive self-regard. As Blatt (1998) writes, "most theorists consider relatedness and self-definition to be independent processes; indeed, some (e.g., Freud, 1930) consider them antagonistic or contradictory forces" (pp. 727–728).

However, are relatedness and self-definition, in fact, antagonistic or contradictory aims? As Blatt (1998) has argued, it makes more sense to view self-definition and relatedness not as independent or antagonistic, but rather in terms "of a complex dialectical transaction between two . . . fundamental forces" (p. 727). As he observes:

> [T]he development of an increasingly differentiated, integrated, and mature sense of self . . . is contingent on establishing satisfying interpersonal relationships. Conversely, the development of increasingly mature, reciprocal, and satisfying interpersonal relationships depends on the development of a mature self-definition or identity.
>
> (p. 727)

An inevitable conflict between relatedness and self-definition may, indeed, be the case with regard to pathological and regressive modes of relating, such as in yielding to "the regressive lure of identification," in "infantile dependence," and anxiety-saturated merging fantasies. However, in healthy relatedness, such as "mature dependence" or reciprocal relationships, there is no inherent conflict between relatedness and self-definition.

Nowhere is the non-conflictual, and indeed, synergistic relationship between self-definition and autonomy and relatedness made clearer than in attachment theory and research. Thus, the relatively non-anxious and non-conflictual pursuit of exploration and autonomy *depends upon* the presence of a secure base, both an actual one and later in life, an internalized one. There is some fascinating research demonstrating that in both animals and children, the comfortableness and literal range of exploration are related not only to the physical presence of the caregiver but also, in children, to her emotional availability (e.g., Sorce & Emde, 1981). There is also evidence that the internalization of a secure base facilitates exploration and autonomy. In short, according to attachment theory and supported by much research, there is no inherent conflict but rather a dependent relationship between autonomy and relatedness.

The conflict between the two motivational trends of relatedness and self-definition occurs only in certain circumstances. The absence of a reliable and consistent secure base may also lead to an enmeshed/preoccupied pattern of attachment that is characterized by a chronic fear of abandonment and by the sacrifice of exploration to a compulsive preoccupation with one's attachment needs. Conversely, the absence of a secure base may lead to an avoidant attachment pattern, characterized by the sacrifice of attachment to exploration.

Implicit in the relationship between exploration and a secure base is the conclusion that absent certain hampering circumstances, such as parental rejection and inconsistency of parental communications, there is no obvious conflict between pursuing self-definition and maintaining object ties. Indeed, according to attachment theory, the exploratory motivational system that is implicated in the developmental striving for self-definition and separation–individuation *does not* conflict with the attachment motivational system. The experience and internalization of a secure base – which certainly constitutes an object tie – *facilitates* rather than interferes with exploratory behavior. From this perspective, there is no inherent conflict between maintaining early object ties and pursuing one's exploration of the world, a central component of striving for autonomy and self-definition.

Failure to provide a secure base may contribute to a vicious cycle in which particular kinds of relatedness (e.g. enmeshed/preoccupied attachment, over-dependency, infantile dependence, and so on) *do*, indeed, conflict with the pursuit of developmental strivings, including individuation and self-definition. For example, for an individual with an enmeshed/preoccupied attachment pattern, that is, someone who is preoccupied with fears of abandonment and who has not internalized a secure base, the nature of his or her object tie or relatedness *does* conflict with the exploration necessary for self-definition and for pursuing developmental strivings. A vicious cycle is created in which an environmental failure generates the kind of object tie that makes it difficult for the individual to take the very steps necessary to alter the nature of that object tie.

## *Another look at the conflict between narcissism and object love*

The theoretical starting point for Kohut's self psychology theory was his rejection of Freud's (1914b) positing of an inherent conflict between narcissism and object love and his insistence that in the course of normal and healthy development, one must move from narcissism to object love. According to Kohut (1971, 1977), narcissism itself is a developmental line, which in healthy development is characterized by the move from archaic to mature narcissism. Further, Kohut (1984) tells us that many a meaningful and even joyful life has been led without object love at its center. Thus, one of Kohut's main reasons for the rejection of Freud's insistence on the centrality of object love is that it does not provide adequate recognition of the importance of mature or healthy narcissism in leading a fulfilling life.

It is not clear that what Kohut means by the term narcissism is the same as what Freud means by that term. In the more clinical context of discussing narcissistic personality disorders, Kohut's conception of archaic narcissism focuses on lack of self-cohesiveness and certain observable clinical features such as grandiosity, poor regulation of self-esteem, susceptibility to fragmentation anxiety, and so on. Correspondingly, his conception of mature narcissism focuses on adequate self-cohesiveness and its reflection in such observable features as a realistic sense of one's abilities, adequate regulation of self-esteem, and pursuit of one's ambitions and ideals in accord with one's abilities and values.

In further elaboration of this notion, Kohut (1984) cites King's ideas regarding the importance of functioning in accord with one's design. Thus, although he does not use the term, what Kohut means by "mature narcissism" is very close to what Rogers (1960) refers to as "self realization" and what Maslow (1954) calls "self actualization." In the present context, the question is whether functioning in accord with one's design of pursuing one's nuclear life program or attempts to achieve self-realization inherently conflict with object love. It is clear from reading *On Narcissism* that for Freud (1914b) the core of narcissism is excessive investment in oneself at the expense of investment in objects outside oneself. He describes this state of affairs in the metapsychological language of "ego libido" versus "object libido." In more ordinary experience-near language, he is essentially describing excessive self-absorption at the expense of interest and investment in objects outside oneself. From Freud's perspective, object love is equivalent to libidinal investment in objects in the world. This understanding of narcissism is, after all, directly linked to the original myth in which Narcissus falls in love with his own reflection, thus taking his own bodily image as a sexual object. From this perspective, one can understand why Freud would identify excessive preoccupation with one's body in, for example, hypochondria, as a quintessential expression of narcissism.

For both Freud and Kohut, grandiosity (in Freud's terms, megalomania or excessive self-regard) would be viewed as an expression of narcissism. However, this convergence holds only for what Kohut refers to as archaic narcissism. The divergence between Freud and Kohut becomes apparent in Kohut's description of what he refers to as mature narcissism. As we have seen, for Kohut, a hallmark of mature narcissism is pursuing one's nuclear life program, which, as I have noted, is essentially equivalent to self-realization, that is, fully actualizing one's abilities in the pursuit of one's goals and ideals. It is clear that Kohut views this as a form of narcissism – albeit a mature form – because he understands such a pursuit as a focus on the self and its realization. But here is where, I believe, matters become confused. The fact is that in the pursuit of one's nuclear program or in self-realization, one's focus and libidinal investment are not on the self, but rather on an aspect of the world that has captured one's interest and passion and that provides an opportunity for the expression of one's talents and gifts. After all, narcissistic self-absorption does not produce poetry, music, paintings, or scientific theories. Indeed, it precludes these achievements insofar as self-absorption is antithetical to the state of absorption in the world outside oneself. This antithesis between the two is at the core of Freud's positing an opposition between narcissism and object love. From this perspective, the self is not realized through a focus on the self. Rather, self-realization is a by-product of one's interests and passions in something outside oneself.

Understood this way, what Kohut refers to as mature narcissism partakes in very little of what is for Freud an essential aspect of narcissism, namely, excessive self-absorption. Indeed, as I have tried to show, pursuit of one's nuclear program and self-realization, essential features of what Kohut refers to as mature narcissism, require a degree of freedom from the self-absorption that is a central feature of narcissism, as it is understood by Freud. Indeed, in a very real sense, pursuing one's interests and passions entails a *form of object relations* insofar as they involve oneself not in relation to oneself, but to objects in the world (Eagle, 1981). Where Freud is clearly wrong is his assumption that emotional investment in the object (object love) depletes the self. Indeed, the opposite is the case.

What this discussion points to are the conclusions, one, that what Kohut refers to as mature narcissism is not truly narcissistic, but in a very important sense, object-relational; and two, that whereas there is an inherent conflict between object relations (and object love) and what Freud (1914) refers to as primary narcissism, there is no inherent conflict between what Kohut refers to as mature narcissism and object relations (and object love). Indeed, as I have tried to show, pursuit of one's nuclear program and achievement of self-realization often entail passionate object relations in the sense of passionate engagement with objects outside oneself. Further, interests outside oneself as well as object love enhance rather than detract from the self.

Thus, it turns out, then, that what Kohut views as a separate line of development along the dimension of narcissism (i.e., from archaic to mature narcissism) can be meaningfully understood, at least to an important extent, in terms of a trajectory from narcissism (i.e., self-absorption, grandiosity, etc.) to an increasing capacity to turn to objects in the world. Or, stated in another way, what Kohut states as the developmental trajectory from archaic to mature narcissism essentially entails the move from self-absorption to an increasing capacity for self-realization through investment in objects in the world. Thus, in an important way, this formulation is essentially equivalent to Freud's (1914b) description of healthy development in terms of the move from narcissism to object love. Further, correctly understood, the conflict between narcissism and object love posited by Freud (1914) cannot rightly serve as a basis for the presumed conflict between individuation (one can substitute self-realization and self-definition here) and object relations or object love (one can substitute relatedness here). Indeed, to reiterate, individuation and self-realization are synergistic with object relations and object love in at least two ways: one, successful individuation requires a relational secure base; and two, individuation and self-realization are not characterized by self-absorption, but rather by absorption in objects in the world.

It is interesting to observe that Fairbairn (1952) contrasts "infantile dependence" not with independence, but with "*mature dependence*." Thus, for Fairbairn, as well as for Bowlby, there is no inherent conflict between ties to objects and pursuit of developmental strivings (what Fairbairn (1952) refers to as "the progressive urge toward separation"). Rather as noted, there is conflict between *certain kinds of ties to objects* and developmental strivings (For Fairbairn, 1952, it is object ties characterized by the "regressive lure of identification" (p. 43)). Further, the kinds of object ties that *do* conflict with the pursuit of one's developmental strivings or realizing one's nuclear program, according to attachment theory (as well as to self psychology, Control–Mastery theory, Stolorow and Atwood's intersubjective theory, and Mahler's symbiosis–separation–individuation theory) are those that are the product of particular kinds of environmental failures, for example, parental failure to provide a secure base, intergenerational envy, and parental communications conveying the message that strivings for autonomy entail harm to parents.

## *Inevitability of conflict between individuation and merger*

Loewald also posits a fundamental and inevitable conflict between strivings for individuation and regressive pulls for merger. What Loewald is suggesting here is that a universal aspect of the developmental process – again, quite independently of parental behavior – is not only a 'natural' striving for individuation, but an equally 'natural' regressive pull toward merger. This is what he calls the "psychotic core." I am exceedingly skeptical of any positing of a universal "psychotic core" for a number of reasons. For one thing, it equates a presumably universal and normal stage of development with psychosis. Second, it equates fantasies and desires for merger, which can be quite gratifying in, to use Pine's (1981) term, "moments" of experience such as the experience of sexual passion. Third, it makes little evolutionary sense to posit a universal and therefore, selected-for psychological structure that is inherently maladaptive. And finally, however dramatic the positing of a universal "psychotic core" may be, there is little evidence that such a structure exists.

The positing of a universal wish for merger seems to be based on the assumption of a longing to return to a presumed early developmental stage of symbiotic union and undifferentiated merger. However, all the research evidence on infants indicates that there is no such developmental stage, a consideration that undercuts the basis for the positing of a universal wish for merger. Hence, any wishes or pulls for merger that one does encounter clinically must be understood through the investigation of idiosyncratic processes and dynamics.

## *Are splits in the ego inevitable?*

Fairbairn's (1952) answer to the above question is that because some degree of experiences of rejection and deprivation is inevitable, internalization of the 'bad' object and consequent "splits in the ego" are inevitable. Hence, although Fairbairn appears to attribute splits in the ego to environmental failure, he also seems to be saying that some degree of pathology is inevitable due to the inevitable 'imperfections' of our early caregiving experiences in the form of frustration and deprivation. The implication is that were our early experiences utopian, that is, devoid of any experience of frustration and deprivation, there would be no "splits in the ego" or internalization of 'bad' objects and that we would retain the original "pristine" state of the ego and the unity of the personality.

The formulation that the original "pristine personality of the child" born with a "dynamic unitary ego" that cannot be sustained due to inevitable frustration and deprivation reads like a psychoanalytic version of the fall from grace. The infant's original purity is corrupted (in the form of splits in the ego) by the nature of the world. Thus, a confrontation with the world leads to the loss of our pristine nature and wholeness, in short, a fall from grace.

That Fairbairn's theory of endopsychic structure conjures up the biblical image of the fall from grace is not simply happenstance. Fairbairn had strong religious impulses. Some weeks after attending the 1910 Missionary Conference as an undergraduate student at the University of Edinburgh, Fairbairn wrote: "I have decided to devote my life to the cause of religion" (as cited in Hoffman & Hoffman, 2014, p. 75). And between 1912 and 1914 Fairbairn studied theology at various universities. As a number of commentators have noted, Fairbairn's religious interests and inclinations are reflected in his theoretical formulations. Skolnick and Scharff (1998) write that "For Fairbairn (1944) the establishment of the endopsychic structure, while universal and inevitable, represents a fall from grace" (p. 141). And Hoffman and Hoffman (2014) write: "The Judaic and Christian narrative portraying a pristine beginning, a shattering decline, and hope and redemption through healing love is the cadence that permeates Fairbairn's work" (p. 69).

That traumatic experiences in the form of deprivation and frustration are inevitable in the course of development indicates that Fairbairn's formulation of the endopsychic structure of the personality is a theory of the human condition rather than a theory of how particular and exceptional traumas influence personality development. That is, there is an inevitable conflict between the infant's demands[12] and the nature of the world, – which, in the course of development, becomes transformed into an inner conflict – a formulation remarkably similar to Freud's.

It is interesting to observe that whereas Fairbairn puts the emphasis on the inevitability of parental failure, Klein places the emphasis on the greediness of the infant, a degree of greediness so great that even perfect parenting could not satisfy. She writes: "it is part of the emotional life of the infant that he is greedy and desires more than even the best external situation can fulfill" (Klein, 1960/1975, p. 271).

## *Internal obstacles to pursuing one's nuclear program*

Although not explicitly stated, Kohut (1982) suggests that conflict surrounding pursuit of one's nuclear program is inevitable when he writes that due to internal obstacles (he also notes the presence of external obstacles), one never succeeds in its realization – thus, the "Tragic Man"of self psychology. Indeed, that fate is what renders him tragic. But why, according to Kohut, does one never quite succeed in realizing one's nuclear program? Why is some degree of failure inevitable? The inevitability of failure suggests that never quite succeeding in actualizing one's nuclear program is not primarily a contingent phenomenon, that is, is a product of environmental circumstances that one confronts. If failure were due to particular parental attitudes, for example, the implication would be that in more benevolent environments, one could realize one's nuclear program. The inevitability of failure due to internal obstacles, however, suggests instead that we are dealing with a non-contingent necessary product of human nature or, at the very least, a product of an inescapable aspect of the relationship between the individual and the family as well as the relationship between the individual and society. Another way to put it is to say that if the internal obstacles to realizing one's nuclear program is truly inevitable, it would suggest that it is intrinsic to human nature or at least, that it is an intrinsic aspect of the relationship between the individual and the world.

## *Conflict in neo-Freudian theories*

Without engaging in an extended discussion, I want to at least briefly note that in the formulations of Horney, Sullivan, Fromm, and Rogers, the source of inner conflict is also located in some kind of environmental failure. For Horney and Fromm, inner conflicts in the individual reflect conflicts and contradictions within society, whereas for Sullivan and Rogers, the source of inner conflicts lies in interpersonal relations. Further, for all these theorists, a central conflict posited is one between strivings for self-realization and autonomy and the forces opposing these strivings.

For Horney, the opposing forces include the "tyranny of the shoulds" and an unrealistic idealized self. Basing his formulations on the biblical allegory of Adam and Eve's exile from the Garden of Eden, Fromm (1941) locates the essential human conflict as one between embeddedness in nature, on the one hand, and consciousness of oneself as well as awareness of one's separateness and mortality, on the other hand. Fear of the latter often leads to relinquishing one's freedom and separateness and submitting to others. This offers a form of security, but at the expense of one's freedom and autonomy.

And implicit in Sullivan's (1953, 1956) concepts of the self as the product of "reflected appraisals" and the rigidity of the self system is the idea that individuals seek security and approval from significant others, even at the expense of enduring self stasis. The aim of security is mediated by the formation of a self-system that protects the individual from the experience of anxiety and threats to self-esteem largely through keeping incongruous and threatening material from being consciously experienced. Sullivan also writes about "personifications" of oneself and others that may have little to do with the reality of who one actually is and who others actually are. Implicit in Sullivan's formulations is the conflict between the rigidity of the self-system motivated by the need to avoid anxiety and disapproval from significant others, on the one hand, and developmental growth and openness to experience, on the other hand. In this sense, Sullivan's formulations can be seen as another variation on the theme of a basic conflict between stasis and growth, more specifically, between protecting the self and maintaining early object ties (in the form of seeking approval) on the one hand, and developmental growth on the other.

Rogers, too, has written about the conflict between self-realization and living one's life in accord with the evaluations and expectations of others described as "conditions of worth," and between the actual self and the idealized self, the latter organized in accord with "conditions of worth." One can also understand these conflicts as conflicts between status and a basic motivation for self-realization and growth.

Rogers (e.g., 1951; 1960) wrote that when parents make their love and acceptance contingent upon certain conditions being met rather than provided unconditionally, these "conditions of worth" are internalized such that one's self-regard and indeed, a wide range of experiences and behaviors are based on these parental evaluations and expectations rather than on one's organismic experiences. This sets up enduring conflicts – what Rogers referred to as an "incongruence" – between organizing experiences in accord with "conditions of worth" and the individual's actual organismic experiences organized in accord with movement towards growth that Rogers referred to as the "actualizing tendency." Such conflicts can also be understood in terms of the tension between living one's life and experiencing oneself and the world in accord with the expectations and desires of others versus organizing one's life in accord with one's self-actualizing tendency.

There are clear general parallels between Rogers' formulations and those of a number of psychoanalytic theorists. For example, among the 19 propositions that underlie his theory, there is one that states that experiences that are incompatible with the structures of the self are likely to be experienced as a threat (Rogers, 1951), a formulation that is quite similar to Sullivan's (e.g. 1953) description of the self-system and Freud's (1894) description of an incompatibility between an idea and the ego.

As another example, Rogers' discussion of the discrepancy between the actual and the idealized self (the self that is the product of "conditions of worth") brings to mind Winnicott's (1965) description of the "true self" versus the "false self" and Freud's discussion of the ideal self. As still another example, Rogers' idea that one restricts one's experiences in accord with "conditions of worth" bears a strong family resemblance to Stolorow, Atwood, and Orange's (2002) statement that "regions of experience" are sacrificed by the individual in order to maintain vital ties to objects.

As a final example that is especially interesting is the parallel between Rogers' description of the stultifying effects of living one's life in accord with "conditions of worth" and (Lacan's 1966/2002) location of pathology in the individual's tendency to live his or her life in accord with the desire of the other. There are many other examples one could cite, all of which argue for greater recognition of the relevance of Rogers' work to post-Freudian theoretical formulations.

## *Implications for treatment: Freud and Fairbairn*

Fairbairn describes the aims of treatment in a variety of interrelated ways, paralleling the different interrelated ways he describes the nature of inner conflict. According to Fairbairn, patients come to treatment with an inner world that is a closed system in which a relationship with external objects "is only possible in terms of transference" (Fairbairn, 1958, p. 381), that is, a system in which the external object is experienced as a stand-in for an internal object and in which object relationships, to a significant extent, are a stand-in for an internal object relationship. From this perspective a central aim of treatment is to enable the patient to experience and relate to external objects more fully in terms of who they are. One can partly understand this aim as attempting to tilt the conflict between a fantasy-saturated inner world and an inner world directed toward reality in the direction of the latter. In an important sense, implicit in Fairbairn's view of treatment is the aim of enhancing reality-testing when that is understood to include the domains of affect and object relations. Another way to put it is to say that an overarching aim of treatment is to transform the patient's solipsistic inner world in which object relationships are essentially relationships among different aspects of oneself to object relationships with actual objects in the world. As we have seen, although the theoretical constructs are quite different, this aim parallels Widlöcher's therapeutic goal of removing the barriers to object love represented by auto-erotic fantasies.

Another overarching aim of treatment from a Fairbairnian perspective is to enhance and enlarge the province of the central ego. This means lifting repression of internal objects and split-off ego structures and integrating them into the central ego, that is, achieving greater unity of the personality. However, the accomplishment of this aim runs up against strong barriers. These include the patient's resistance against re-experiencing the "bad object situation" once repression is relaxed, and perhaps most important, the patient's fear of experiencing the catastrophe of an empty objectless inner world were the patient to relinquish his or her "devotion" and "obstinate attachment" to internal objects.

Fairbairn also states as a goal of psychoanalytic treatment the implementation of:

> a process whereby infantile dependence upon the object gradually gives place to mature dependence upon the object. This process of development is characterized (a) by the gradual abandonment of an original object-relationship based upon primary identification; and (b) by the gradual adoption of an object-relationship based upon the differentiation of the object.
> (Fairbairn, 1952, p. 34)

What Fairbairn has in mind here is not an amelioration of 'over-dependency' as it is generally understood, but rather the gradual replacement of object relationships in which one is relating to an internal object with object relationships in which one is relating to real "differentiated" objects in the external world. As Ogden (1983) writes, from a Fairbairnian perspective, "one measure of psychological health is the degree to which internal object relations can be modified in the light of current experience" (fn. 6, p. 238).

For Fairbairn, the patient's success in abandoning ties to internal objects and in the resolution of conflicts between infantile dependence and mature dependence, between the regressive lure of identification and the progressive urge toward separation, between fantasy and reality, between the "devotion" and "obstinate attachment" to early internal objects and object relationships to actual objects, and between pursuing one's needs and self-contempt and shame in response to these needs all rest on the patient's experience of the therapist as a 'good' object. As Fairbairn (1952, p. 87) puts it, therapeutic success is a "function of establishing a special kind of object relationship with the therapist." This presumably makes it safe for the patient to lift repression and re-experience the 'bad object situation'; to "exorcise" the internal 'bad' object without the fear of living in an empty inner world; and to be better able to engage in object relationships with actual objects in the external world.

What is not made very clear in Fairbairn's writings are such issues as how the therapist comes to be experienced as a 'good' object, the specific routes to and processes involved in these achievements, or even what it means, specifically, for the therapist to be a 'good' object. What kind of characteristics, interventions, and interactions constitute being a 'good' object from Fairbairn's perspective. For example, how does the patient come to be capable of experiencing the therapist as an actual 'good' object rather than as largely a transference stand-in for an internal object? In classical theory, the answer to this question lies in the analysis of the transference; in Control–Mastery theory, it lies in the therapist's test-passing; in Alexander and French's (1946) theory it lies in corrective emotional experiences; and in Kohut's self psychology, it lies in empathic understanding and "optimal failure." Fairbairn's answer to this question is not entirely clear or specific. His writings are more concerned with descriptions of the nature of personality structure, particularly in psychopathology, than with specifics of therapeutic process and outcome.

Fairbairn (1952) writes that an important goal of treatment is to "exorcise" the 'bad' internal object. In effect, Fairbairn is stating that the patient needs to rid himself or herself of what under the impact of trauma, he or she defensively made part of the self. That is, he or she must re-externalize what was originally external and defensively internalized. This is in striking contrast to an important aim of treatment from a Freudian perspective – as expressed in the adage, where id was, there shall ego be – of re-internalizing (and integrating) aspects of one's psychobiological nature (e.g., instinctual wishes and urges) that were defensively rendered external. These differences reflect two sharply different views of human nature. For Freud, insofar as instinctual impulses are an intrinsic aspect of our psychobiological nature, even when defensively excluded from consciousness, they do not disappear and do not cease being aspects of our psychobiological nature and continue to make demands on the mind. Therefore, in order to achieve greater unity of functioning, they need to be reinternalized and assimilated into the personality. From this perspective, where id was, there shall ego be can be understood as what was defensively excluded and rendered an impersonal 'it' needs to be assimilated into a personal 'I'. In short, what was defensively excluded from one's experience of oneself needs to be included and become an assimilated part of oneself.

In sharp contrast, for Fairbairn, insofar as, the 'bad' object has defensively been made part of the self (as an internal object or introject), under the impact of environmental failure, the therapeutic task is for the patient to rid himself or herself of this not fully assimilated foreign body or what Fairbairn (1952) refers to as an "internal saboteur." In short, the patient needs to once again make external what was defensively made internal. To state the contrast in a somewhat different way, broadly speaking, whereas for Freud, a central therapeutic task is to transform the ego-alien (id) into the ego-syntonic (ego), for Fairbairn, a central therapeutic task is to transform the at least partly ego-syntonic (the internal 'bad' object) into the ego-alien ("exorcising" the 'bad' object so that it is no longer part of oneself).

Both Freud and Fairbairn agree on the importance of lifting repression in treatment. And both argue that the patient's resistance to the relaxation of repression is motivated by anxiety associated with what they fear would emerge once repression is lifted. However, whereas for Freud, the patients' feared contents are forbidden wishes associated with anxiety (e.g., incestuous and hostile impulses), for Fairbairn the feared contents have to do with re-experiencing the "bad object situation," that is, re-experiencing the trauma of rejection, deprivation, and frustration. However, the differences here between Freud and Fairbairn are not as deep as they appear. For Freud too, the anxiety associated with the emergence of forbidden wishes is, in an important respect, also linked to trauma, namely, the trauma of the "danger situations" of loss of the object, loss of the object's love, castration threats, and superego condemnation (Freud, 1926a, pp. 166–167).

Further, for both Freud and Fairbairn, due to transference, the therapist is associated with the traumatic "danger situations." However, despite this convergence, an important difference between Freud and Fairbairn remains. For Freud, certain repressed instinctual wishes (i.e., incestuous and hostile wishes) are inherently antithetical to living in a civilized society. Hence, for anyone who has been socialized, the means of resolving inner conflict available to the individual are mainly sublimation and renunciation of the inherently anti-social wishes (e.g. incestuous wishes).

For Fairbairn, there is no id and, therefore, no inherently anti-social wishes. Hence, there is no inevitable id–ego conflict. Rather, the needs and wishes that become enmeshed in conflict and are subjected to repression are not anti-social wishes, but developmentally appropriate needs and wishes for love and caring. It is these latter needs and wishes that, according to Fairbairn, are conflictual and anxiety-laden due to their association with the "bad object situation" of rejection and deprivation.

Implicit in Freud's theorizing is the idea that as socializing agents for society, a parental function is to instill anxiety in the child in relation to certain instinctual wishes, in particular, oedipal wishes. To not do so is to fail in one's parental function. Hence, the conflict inducing "danger situations" are not an aberration or an anomaly; they represent an important parental socializing function. This idea is not present in Fairbairn's theorizing. For Fairbairn, the main parental function is to provide love and caring and there is little in Fairbairn's writings that addresses the issue of parents as socializing agents for society. Hence, for Fairbairn, the main failure in parental function is the failure to provide love and caring rather than a failure to socialize inherently anti-social impulses.

## *Implications for treatment: Loewald and Weiss and Sampson*

Although understanding it in different ways, there is convergence between Loewald and Weiss and Sampson on the proposition that normal developmental strivings for individuation and separation are often embedded in conflict; and that the nature of the conflict includes guilt elicited by these strivings. However, as we have seen, there is a basic disagreement regarding the source of that guilt. For Loewald, guilt is inherent in the very strivings themselves insofar as they are experienced as equivalent to parricide. For Weiss and Sampson, however, guilt surrounding these strivings is the product of parental communications.

What are the implications for treatment for both these convergent and divergent views regarding the nature and source of the conflict over strivings for individuation? With regard to the former, what is striking about Weiss and Sampson's and, to some extent, Loewald's view is that it locates conflict not in forbidden infantile wishes, but rather in 'forbidden' *normal developmental strivings* that are subjectively associated with guilt. On this view, it is not infantile wishes that are repressed, but normal developmental strivings that are experienced as equivalent to harming parents (thus, cliciting guilt) or incurring their wrath (thus, eliciting anxiety).

Although this is a marked departure from Freudian theory regarding the nature of wishes that are subject to repression, it constitutes, in effect, a reversion to early Freud. Recall that in the early case studies it is not infantile wishes and fantasies that are repressed. Rather, for the most part, it is age-appropriate wishes such as Lucy R.'s wish to marry her employer or Elisabeth's von R.'s romantic fantasies about her brother-in-law.

Let me turn now to the implications for treatment of the divergent views of Loewald and Weiss and Sampson. As we have seen, Loewald maintains that strivings for individuation are necessarily experienced as psychically equivalent to parricide, whereas Weiss and Sampson attribute such equivalence, when it occurs, to parental communications that make that equivalence. Although Loewald posits the inherent nature of that equivalence, he does not appear to attribute *actual* death wishes to the individual, a clear departure from the Freudian theory of the Oedipus complex. Hence, neither Loewald nor Weiss and Sampson would expect to find repressed parricidal wishes in treatment. Rather, they would expect to uncover unconscious psychic equivalence between strivings for individuation and parricide or its equivalent (e.g., guilt in relation to harming parents in some way). However, in contrast to Loewald, Weiss and Sampson would expect to be able to uncover the connection between such psychic equivalence and memories of parental communications and would also expect to find a similar connection in the transference attributions made by the patient. It is not clear to me how someone taking Loewald's position would deal therapeutically with the patient's psychic equivalence between developmental strivings for individuation and parricide and the guilt that such equivalence elicits. Loewald suggests that such guilt is inevitable and needs to be worked through in some way in the course of development.

### *Implications for treatment: Kris*

As we have seen, the essence of divergent conflicts for Kris is the subjective feeling that in making choice A one necessarily experiences the loss of option B. Kris' approach to dealing with this kind of conflict consists in either helping the individual mourn the loss involved in foregoing choice B or helping him or her recognize the possibility of alternation between A and B. With regard to relatedness and self-definition, if, indeed, there is no inherent conflict between the two sets of aims, neither mourning nor alternation may be necessary. Rather, as Blatt (1998) suggests, integration between the two motivational trends is possible.

## Research on conflict

Let me turn now to selected research on conflict. I begin with the early research on conflict and psychosomatic illness and on experimental neurosis in animals.

### *Conflict and psychosomatic illness*

During the 1950s, the centrality of inner conflict in psychopathology was extended from an understanding of neurosis to the understanding of psychosomatic illnesses. Alexander and his colleagues proposed what has come to be known as a "specificity of conflict theory" in accounting for various psychosomatic illnesses (Taylor, 1987). According to Alexander (1959; 1954), psychosomatic patients' struggle with dependency conflicts, and how they deal with frustration of dependency needs, including what one might refer to as secondary conflicts, varies with different psychosomatic illnesses. For example, in one account, the physiological correlates of chronic unconscious wish to be fed, as an expression of unresolved conflicts about dependency, were hypothesized to be associated with peptic ulcer (Alexander, 1934).

In a study designed to test this hypothesis, Weiner, Thaler, Reiser, and Mirksy (1957) found that a psychological constellation presumably reflecting unresolved and persistent conflicts about dependency and oral gratification was able to distinguish hyper- and hypo-pepsinogen secretors. They concluded that:

> although neither a high rate of gastric secretion nor a specific psychodynamic constellation is independently responsible for development of peptic ulcer, together, however, these two parameters constitute the essential determinants in the precipitation of peptic ulcer on exposure to social situations noxious to the specific individual.
>
> (p. 1)

In other words, according to the authors, peptic ulcer is the product of the predisposing factors of unresolved dependency conflicts and a high rate of gastric secretion interacting with precipitating stress factors.

As another example of "specificity of conflict" theory, essential hypertension was hypothesized to be associated with conflict over expression of aggression, which, in turn, would risk frustration of the individual's dependency needs (e.g., Alexander, 1939). That is, expressing aggression toward the one on whom one is dependent risks not having one's dependency needs met. As other examples, the asthmatic child was presumably struggling with conflict between the wish to be held and to cry and the fear of rejection. The dynamics in neurodermatitis were understood in terms of repressed hostility toward father figures handled through attacking oneself through the skin (Miller, 1948). And as a final example, Johnson, Shapiro, and Alexander (1947) proposed that individuals with rheumatoid arthritis were characterized by "a chronic inhibited hostile aggressive state as a reaction to the earliest masochistic dependence on the mother that is carried over to the father and all human relationships, including the sexual" (p. 299).

As Taylor (1987) makes clear, Alexander viewed the specific conflicts he identified as only one factor that, when interacting with other factors, generated the illness. He finally rejected the concept of specificity and maintained that it should be limited to "specific organ vulnerability" (Alexander, 1962, p. 20). The specificity of conflict theory of psychosomatic illness has been pretty much abandoned, largely because of lack of empirical support. However, the role of conflict and stress in a wide range of illness has been incorporated into a holistic view of psychological and physical health and illness.

## *Conflict and experimental neurosis in animals*

During the 1930s–1950s, a great deal of animal research was carried out on the role of conflict in the development of "experimental neurosis."This area of research was initiated by Pavlov (e.g., 1941). According to a new biography of Pavlov, he began thinking about neurosis in dogs after reading about the case of Anna O. (Todes, 2014). Although originating in the work of Pavlov (1941), experimental neurosis caught the interest of a number of psychoanalysts and psychoanalytically oriented theorists, including Alexander's colleague French (e.g., 1933), and Masserman (e.g., 1944, 1950, 1953). What was of special interest about experimental neurosis was the demonstration that environmentally induced conflict alone could induce neurotic behavior (e.g., rigidity, stereotypy). For a period of time, some analysts as well as behavior theorists envisaged the possibility of integration between ideas and formulations from behavior theory and psychoanalytic theory, at the center of which was the importance of conflict in both perspectives. From the side of behavior theory, this culminated in a widely read volume entitled *Personality and Psychotherapy* (Dollard & Miller, 1950), which essentially translated Freudian ideas into behavior theory terms.

Remarkably enough, the Editorial Board of Psychosomatic Medicine Monographs in the 1940s included Alexander and the behaviorist Clark Hull. And the Advisory Board included animal researchers such as Liddell and psychoanalysts including Karl Menninger, Felix Deutsch, and Lawrence Kubie. The monograph series was underwritten by the Committee on Neurotic Disorders of the National Research Council Division of Anthropological Psychology. An assumption shared by these disparate types that formed the basis for their working together was that unresolvable conflict was at the center of neurosis and the experimental neurosis in animals could serve as a valid analogue for human neurosis.

Unlike the focus on *inner* conflict entailing unacceptability of a wish or need in psychosomatic research, the conflict in the experimental neurosis research is one presented by the external environment. That is, the pathological behavior (i.e., the experimental neurosis) induced by this kind of conflict arises when the animal's choice behavior becomes increasingly problematic due to the increasing difficulty in discriminating stimuli. For example, say the animal is rewarded when responding to a square stimulus and shocked when responding to a circle stimulus. Experimental neurosis is induced when through making these stimuli more similar to each other, it becomes increasingly difficult for the animal to discriminate between them. Although one could argue that the animal experiences an inner conflict regarding what response to make, the fact is that insofar as the experimental neurosis paradigm does not entail a conflict between a wish and a defense against the wish, one can question whether this paradigm constitutes an ecologically valid analogue of neurosis. One can argue, however, that being confronted with a seemingly unresolvable conflict *of any kind* tends to trigger the kind of pathological rigidity and stereotypy of behavior that one sees both in experimental neurosis in animals and in human neurosis.

Bizarre infant behavior such as freezing or twirling during the reunion phase of the Strange Situation, which is classified as disoriented/disorganized attachment, has features that are similar to experimental neurosis behavior, in particular, the feature of being confronted with a conflict that has no solution. There is evidence that the disorganized behavior of the child is associated with a history of infant–mother interactions in which mother is frightened/frightening or shows other anomalous behavior (e.g., Hesse & Main, 2006; Lyons-Ruth & Jacobvitz, 2008; Main & Hesse, 1990). In this situation, the infant is confronted with a dilemma similar to the one that triggers experimental neurosis behavior in the animal. Normally, when an infant or child is distressed, he or she turns to the attachment figure for soothing and comforting. However, when the attachment figure herself is frightened or frightening, that is, when she herself is the source of the distress, there is no adaptive response available to the infant or child. Like the animal in the experimental neurosis situation, the child is faced with "a conflict without solution" The result is bizarre and stereotyped behavior (e.g., freezing, twirling, walking backward, and so on) similar to the stereotyped behavior seen in experimental neurosis.

## *Research on conflict between immediate and delayed gratification*

A fundamental conflict posited by Freud (1900), one that he believed is inherent in the human condition is one between the pleasure principle and the reality principle. Stated in more concrete terms, Freud identified the conflict between the demand for immediate gratification and the need to plan and delay both for the sake of one's welfare and ironically, in order to achieve actual gratification in the real world. This fundamental conflict, Freud tells us, directly confronts the individual early in life and continues to do so in perhaps more complex and subtle forms throughout one's life.

In the Freud (1900) scheme, after experiencing gratification of hunger at the breast, the next time hunger is experienced, the infant hallucinates the breast – a quintessential example of the operation of a primary process mode of functioning. It is only in response to the reality that hallucination of the breast fails to relieve hunger that, Freud tells us, the infant is forced to turn to actual objects, to recognition of means–ends relations, and to thinking, which Freud views as experimental actions. The infant learns that wishing will not make it so, and that there is a necessary temporal and instrumental gap between the need and its gratification that is occupied by certain events that must occur if gratification in the real world is to take place. Recognition of this 'gap' between the need (or wish or desire) and its gratification is a central marker of reality-testing and is expressed in the individual's ability to delay gratification in order to fill the 'gap' with necessary planning and action.

Thus, the capacity to delay gratification as well as to tolerate frustration can be viewed as an important indication of adequate ego functioning. In the course of normal development, the reality principle gradually predominates over the pleasure principle. That is, the infant learns that immediate gratification is not always possible and therefore, he or she must learn to delay. However, Freud (1900) tells us, the reality principle never fully replaces the pleasure principle. That is, the tendency to seek immediate gratification never disappears from psychological life. Under certain circumstances the insistence on 'I want what I want when I want it' can readily emerge.

The balance between the pleasure principle and the reality principle varies not only with circumstances, but also among individuals, a rich source of research in this area. That is, there are individual differences in capacity to delay gratification. Further, this is one aspect of the individual's *self-regulating function* that includes the capacity to tolerate tension and noxious affects and to engage in planning, pursuit of goals over long periods of time, and self-protective management of risk and danger.

A good deal of research on delay of gratification has been carried out over a more than 50 year period by personality psychologists. Early studies on the correlates of individual differences in children's ability to delay gratification, which make reference to the concepts of the pleasure principle and the reality principle, were carried out in the 1960s, largely by Mischel and his colleagues and have continued since that time.

The basic design of the delay of gratification studies involves smaller rewards (e.g., a bar of candy) for immediate gratification or larger rewards (e.g., two bars of candy) for delayed gratification. Much of the research in this area is concerned with the correlates of these individual differences in ability to delay gratification. In an early study with 12–14 year old children, Mischel (1961b) reported that compared to children who chose a delayed but larger reward, children who chose a smaller but immediate reward, scored lower on a social responsibility scale. From that early study to the present day, there have been probably hundreds of investigations linking ability to delay gratification to personality variables and to situational factors that either facilitate or hamper delay of gratification. The personality and situational variations have included deployment of attention (Mischel, 1970; Mischel, Ebbeson, & Zeiss, 1972; Peake, Hebl, & Mischel, 2002; Sethi, Mischel, Aber, Shoda, & Rodriguez, 2000) focusing on actual versus symbolic reward (Mischel & Moore, 1973), father absence (Mischel, 1961b), maternal limit-setting (Houck & Lecuyer- Mauss, 2004), obesity (Schlam, Wilson, Shoda, Mischel, & Ayduk, 2013), maternal separation (Sethi et al., 2000), focusing on "hot" versus "cool" thoughts (Ayduk, Mischel, & Downey, 2002; Metcalfe & Mischel, 1999), attachment patterns (Chisholm, Burbank, Coall, & Gemmiti, 2005; Jacobsen, Huss, Fendrich, Kruesi, & Ziegenhain, 1997), need for achievement (Mischel, 1961c), cognitive and social competence (Mischel, Shoda & Rodriguez, 1989; Shoda, Mischel, & Peake, 1990), neural networks (Berman et al., 2013; Casey et al., 2011), ego resilience (Funder & Block, 1989), borderline personality disorder (Ayduk et al., 2008), cultural factors (Mischel, 1961c), social responsibility (Mischel, 1961b), age (Mischel & Metzer, 1962), gender (Bjorklund & Kipp, 1996; Silverman, 2003), rejection sensitivity (Ayduk et al., 2000), ability to perform an inhibitory task (Eigsti et al., 2006), and conditions during the waiting period (Mischel & Grusec, 1967).

There are too many studies to cover; instead I will summarize some representative studies and will focus on those especially relevant to psychoanalysis. A number of early studies have focused on concurrent relationships between ability to delay and other variables. For example, significant associations have been found between ability to delay gratification among 11–14 year old children and achievement on the Thematic Apperception Test (TAT) (Mischel, 1961c); social responsibility (Mischel, 1961b); and father absence (Mischel, 1961b). Significant associations have also been reported between ability to delay gratification and severity of psychological disturbance (Shybut, 1968).

Tangney, Baumeister, and Boone (2004) reported that self-control was associated with better academic performance, fewer reports of psychopathology, higher self-esteem, less binge and alcohol abuse, secure attachment, and better interpersonal skills.

A number of studies have experimentally manipulated various factors that either facilitate or hinder the individual's capacity to delay gratification. There is evidence that whereas experimental manipulations that directed the participant's attention to the reward shortened the delay time, distractions lengthened delay times (Mischel & Ebbesen, 1970; Mischel et al., 1972). In one study, during the waiting period, children from three and a half to five years and five months in age were exposed either to *images* relevant or irrelevant to the reward (of either two marshmallows and a pretzel or two pennies and a token). The results showed significantly longer delay for the relevant as compared to the irrelevant image condition. What is especially interesting about these findings is that they are precisely the opposite of results showing shorter delay when children are exposed to the *actual* reward objects (Mischel & Ebbesen, 1970; Mischel et al., 1972. Especially interesting is the contrast in results between the effect on delay of instructing children to think about the reward objects (Mischel et al., 1972) that resulted in shorter delay, and the effect of presenting images of the reward objects that resulted in longer delay.

There is evidence that the ability to delay gratification is related to other aspects of self-regulation. Sethi et al. (2000) reported that toddlers' use of attentional distractions strategies during a brief separation from mother predicted greater delay of gratification at age five. Thus it appears that attentional distraction is an effective self-regulating strategy that enables the child to tolerate various forms of frustration.

In a study with adults, Ayduk et al. (2002) instructed participants to imagine a rejection experience. Half the participants were instructed to focus on their physiological and emotional reactions (the "hot focus") and half were instructed to focus on the physical setting of the experience (the "cool focus"). The results showed that fewer hostile thoughts and feelings linked to the imagined rejection experience were reported in the "cool focus" compared to the "hot focus" condition. The authors conclude that a "cooling strategy" is adaptive "under hot, arousing conditions that otherwise elicit automatic, hot-system responses" (p. 443).

I want to pause here for a moment to remind ourselves of the relevance of the above studies on delay of gratification and self-regulation to the issue of inner conflict. One can think of delay of gratification as reflecting a capacity to tolerate the frustration and sustain the conflict between the impulse to act in a way that achieves immediate gratification (and brings an immediate end to the conflict and the frustration it entails) and the recognition that delaying gratification and sustaining the conflict will result in greater reward. Thus, the ability to delay gratification can be understood as reflecting the capacity to tolerate and sustain a fundamental 'generic' inner conflict for adaptive purposes.

The capacity to delay can be reflected not only in the context of gratification, which can be thought of as an id–ego conflict (i.e., conflict between an impulse and reality considerations), but also in the context of an id–superego conflict. That is, the capacity to delay is also manifested in one's ability to resist a temptation that, if acted on, would bring immediate gratification, but that insofar as it violates one's values, would also generate guilt. Thus, the capacity to delay immediate gratification is called upon not only in exchange for a greater reward associated with delay, but also in the context of renunciation of gratification in order to maintain one's self-esteem and one's sense of values. As far as I know, there is little work in this area. It represents a ripe area for future research. One can also distinguish between ability to tolerate frustration in the context of delaying gratification of a pleasurable experience (as in the Mischel 'marshmallow' studies) and ability to tolerate frustration in the context of coping with negative affect and tension states.

### *Longitudinal studies on delay of gratification*

Especially interesting and germane to psychoanalytic theory are a set of longitudinal studies demonstrating the long-term predictive value of individual differences in delay of gratification. In one study by Mischel, Shoda, and Peake (1988), children who showed a high ability to delay gratification were rated by their parents as academically and socially competent, verbally fluent, rational, attentive, playful, and able to deal with frustration and stress at ages 4 and 5.

In a remarkable study carried out by Berman et al. (2013), children who were first tested for delay of gratification at age four were re-examined 40 years later on a task that required control over the contents of working memory. The findings showed that low delayers "recruit significantly higher-dimensional neural networks when performing the task compared with higher delayers" (p. 2). Berman et al. (2013) also reported the remarkable finding that from the pattern of the neural data experimenters could predict with 71% accuracy whether a participant was a high or low delayer.

With the same sample as the above study, Casey et al. (2011) found that ability to delay gratification at age 4 was lawfully associated with capacity for inhibition of response in a no-go go task. This association was found for "hot" and alluring stimuli (a happy face), but not for "cool" neutral and negative faces. Further, "whereas the prefrontal cortex differentiated between no-go and go trials to a high extent in high delayers, the ventral striatum showed exaggerated recruitment in low delayers" (p. 1499).

In another longitudinal study, Schlam et al. (2013) reported that performance on a delay of gratification task at age 4 accounted for a significant portion of variance in body mass index 30 years later. And finally, as another example of a longitudinal study, Eigsti et al. (2006) found that:

> the proportion of time preschoolers directed their attention away from rewarding stimuli during a delay of gratification task was positively associated with efficiency (greater speed without reduced accuracy) in responding to targets in a go/no-go task more than 10 years later.
>
> (p. 478)

These findings indicate that capacity to inhibit action in the context of delay of gratification (through an attentional deployment strategy) in childhood is predictive of cognitive control in adolescence. Many of these studies can be understood as shedding light on the relationship between early ego functioning and later behavior.

It is interesting to observe that in a non-psychoanalytic context, among the capacities that comprise "executive functioning" are "response inhibition" as well as the capacity to "suppress unwanted information from awareness" (Schmeidel & Tang, 2015, p. 93), capacities that parallel the ego functions of ability to delay and ability to defend against unwanted information. Schmeidel and Tang (2015) also report that "mild negative affect has been found to improve inhibitory control, whereas more intense negative affect undermines it" (p. 93). From a psychoanalytic perspective, this finding can be understood as indicating that signal anxiety (i.e., a mild negative affect) triggers the ego functions of delay and defense, whereas, traumatic anxiety (i.e., more intense negative affect) reflects the relative failure of ego functions.

## *Research on conflict between relatedness and self-definition*

There is a good deal of evidence that, in both young animals and children, the availability of a secure base enhances the range, and in children also the degree of comfort, of exploratory behavior, a central component of development of autonomy (e.g., Rajecki, Lamb, & Obmascher, 1978). Passman and Erck (1977) and Passman and Longeway (1982) have reported that the mere presence of a photograph of mother increased the child's exploratory behavior. And Sorce and Emde (1981) reported that over and above physical availability, mother's emotional availability increased exploratory activity. There is also evidence that in adults who are in dire circumstances (e.g. prisoner of war camp), a sense of connectedness to someone or something outside oneself is a protective factor in maintaining psychological integrity (see Eagle, 1981).

There is also evidence in a sample of college students that the subjects' degree of autonomy was significantly positively related to positive and honest interactions with parents as well as interactions with other male and female individuals (Hodgins, Koestner, & Duncan, 1996). The authors conclude:

> the studies support our position that autonomy neither negates nor conflicts with the human need for relatedness . . . One is not required to choose between satisfying one's need for autonomy and one's need for relatedness; fulfilling one appears to heighten the probability that the second will also be fulfilled.
>
> (p. 235)

In a recent study of Chinese student sojourners who had temporarily moved to Belgium, the authors found "that the basic psychological needs for autonomy, relatedness, and competence are positively interrelated" and that the satisfaction of each of these needs predicts unique variance in the students' psychological well-being, vitality, and depression (Vansteenkiste, Lens, Soenens, & Luyckx, 2006, p. 273). In short, as is predicted by attachment theory and supported by much research, there is no inherent conflict, but rather a dependent relationship between autonomy and relatedness.

## *Research on core conflicts*

For many years, Luborsky and his colleagues have carried out research on core conflict relationship themes (CCRTs) emerging in relationship episodes reported in psychotherapy sessions as well as interviews (e.g., Luborsky & Crits-Christoph, 1998). These themes consist of wishes (W), expected and experienced response of the other (RO), and subsequent response of the self (RS). The main findings that have been reported include: (1) the pervasiveness and consistency of particular themes across different relationships for a given individual; (2) the partial overlap between CCRTs in relation to the therapist and other significant figures; (3) the parallels between CCRTs from therapy sessions and dreams; and (4) the relationship between therapeutic outcome and interpretations addressing the patient's CCRTs. In general, the research findings employing the CCRT method support the psychoanalytic idea that individuals struggle with conflicts that are consistent over time and, to some limited extent, pervasive across significant relationships.

### *Research on unconscious pathogenic beliefs*

As noted earlier, according to Control–Mastery theory, patients often experience conflict in the form of guilt associated with certain strivings. Weiss and Sampson and their colleagues (1986) have proposed that the guilt is largely induced by parental communications that convey the message that these strivings inflict harm on parents and/or incur their anger. They have further proposed that patients tend to expect that the therapist will respond in the same way as parental figures did. Accordingly, patients will present tests to their therapist to determine whether or not he or she will respond in the same way as their parents did (which constitutes test failure) or will respond in a different way (which constitutes test-passing).

What distinguishes Control–Mastery theory from other psychoanalytic theories is the fact that systematic clinical data has been provided in support of its hypotheses. For example, Silberschatz et al. (1986) reported that interpretations that were congruent with the patient's unconscious plan were associated with greater therapeutic progress. Silberschatz, Curtis, and Nathan (1989) and Silberschatz and Curtis (1993) also found similar results in regard to interventions (i.e., passing tests or planning compatible interpretations) that helped the patient disconfirm pathogenic beliefs (see also Fretter, Bucci, Broitman, Silberschatz, & Curtis, 1994). One of the main findings that have emerged from the research of Weiss and Sampson and their colleagues (1986) is that test failures on the part of the therapist, as rated by clinical judges, are reliably followed by defensive behavior and lack of therapeutic progress, whereas test-passing is more likely to be followed by signs of therapeutic progress such as emergence of warded-off themes, greater flexibility of defenses, and reduced anxiety. A reasonable way of interpreting these results is that the 'conditions of safety' constituted by test-passing serve to disconfirm the patient's unconscious pathogenic beliefs and thereby help to ameliorate the conflict between the patient's strivings and the guilt these strivings have elicited. (See Silberschatz, 2005, for a more recent and excellent presentation of Control–Mastery theory.)

## Some conclusions

### *1. Infantile versus age-appropriate strivings*

As we have seen, psychoanalytic theories differ with regard to one, the conflicts that are viewed as fundamental; and two, whether the conflicts identified are assumed to be universal and inherent in the human condition or contingent upon environmental conditions. With regard to the first issue, one can contrast the emphasis on conflicts surrounding childhood sexual and aggressive wishes with an emphasis on conflicts concerning strivings for individuation and autonomy. This is a major difference insofar as, according to the latter view, it is not primarily *infantile* anti-social wishes that are embedded in conflict and subject to defense, but *normal developmental strivings*, in particular, strivings for separation, individuation, and self-realization.

### *2. Inherent versus environmentally induced conflict*

As for the second issue, the contrast is between those theorists, such as Loewald, who believe that developmental strivings for individuation are necessarily conflictual, and theorists, such as Weiss and Sampson, who attribute such conflict to particular parental communications and attitudes. It seems to me that the evidence available supports the latter position. A view similar to Weiss and Sampson's is expressed by Kohut (1984) who writes that the child's "normal oedipal self that should be the center of affectionate and assertive initiative" (p. 22) becomes pathological as a consequence of parental seductiveness and competitive hostile behavior. It is only under these circumstances, Kohut maintains, that the child's incestuous and hostile wishes posited by Freud become prominent. Further, Kohut argues that these wishes are a fragmentation product of parental failure to provide empathic mirroring.

### *3. From anxiety to guilt*

Interestingly, the shift from an emphasis on childhood sexual and aggressive wishes to one on individuation has been accompanied by a corresponding emphasis on guilt as well as anxiety as primary affects fueling conflict. This shift rests on the following consideration: according to classical theory, as articulated in the description of the "danger situations," the child fears parental punishment and retaliation in response to his or her sexual and aggressive wishes – hence, anxiety is the dominant affect. Contrastingly, although attributing it to different sources, according to both Loewald and Weiss and Sampson, the child experiences his or her developmental strivings for individuation as equivalent to harming parents – hence, guilt is the dominant affect.

### *4. Actual incestuous and parricidal wishes versus symbolic equivalence*

Another way to contrast the two perspectives is to note that whereas in classical theory the child harbors actual incestuous and hostile wishes, according to both

Loewald and Weiss and Sampson, the child does not necessarily have actual parricidal wishes. Rather, his or her developmental strivings for individuation are experienced as symbolically equivalent to parricide, that is, *as if* they constituted parricide. Thus, whereas in classical theory, the anxiety experienced by the child constitutes punishment that, so to speak, fits the 'crime,' according to Loewald and Weiss and Sampson, there may or may not be any 'crime,' that is, the child does not necessarily harbor actual death wishes.

## 5. Delay of gratification; precursors

According to Freudian theory, the conflict between the infant's demand for immediate gratification (hallucinatory wish fulfillment) and the need for delay of gratification is a fundamental and early one and never fully disappears. Further, the infant's and child's increasing capacity to delay gratification is not only an early expression of the development of a critical ego function, but also, later in life, a sign of ego strength. What is striking about the research findings of Mischel and his colleagues, as well as that of the others I have discussed is the degree to which they provide support for Freud's early and foundational formulations regarding the nature and importance of the early ego function of capacity to delay gratification. What is especially interesting and important about research on ability to delay gratification is its potential applicability to the issue of coping with similar conflicts in a variety of different content areas, for example, sexual temptations, aggressive behavior, oral gratification, impulsive decisions of various kinds, and inability to plan for long-term goals – all of which are influenced by the individual's ego strength, as expressed in the capacity to endure the conflict between immediate and delayed gratification.

The research on the ability to delay gratification has not included much attention to the developmental determinants and origins of that ability. From a psychoanalytic perspective, one would hypothesize that, in addition to temperamental factors, the child who is able to tolerate the frustration entailed in delay of gratification is likely to have had a history of having his or her early needs met which, in turn, nurtures "basic trust" (Erikson, 1950) and "confident expectation" of gratification (Benedek, 1938).

An obvious question that can be investigated is whether confident expectation in the availability of the caregiver as reflected in secure attachment is predictive of the child's ability to delay gratification. There is, indeed, a good deal of research indicating that ability to delay gratification is positively associated with secure attachment and negatively associated with insecure attachment (e.g., Olson, Bates, & Bayles, 1990). There are also interesting additional findings. For example, in one study (Jacobsen et al., 1997), avoidantly attached children with high cognitive functioning did not differ in waiting times from securely attached children. In a longitudinal study, Olson et al. (1990) reported that cognitive competence and secure attachment at two years of age predicted impulse control at six years of age.

### *6. Capacity to experience gratification*

From a psychoanalytic perspective, ego strength is seen not only in the ability to delay gratification, but also in the individual's capacity to experience gratification. This raises the question of whether there is a continuum of delay of gratification and whether there are some individuals who appear to be what one may think of as *excessively* capable of delayed gratification, and whose ability to experience gratification is inhibited or impaired by virtue of it being embedded in conflict.

Akhtar (2015) describes individuals who are capable of "chronic waiting" (p. 101) and in relation to whom, "one senses that there is something excessive about such tolerance of delay" (p. 101). He suggests that underlying this excessive tolerance of delay are "someday" fantasies in which some future miraculous event will lead to great happiness. One is reminded of Henry James' (1903) novella *Beast in the Jungle* in which the protagonist, year after year, is constantly telling his loyal and admiring female companion about the great things in store for him, including the appearance of a great love. Someday the beast in the jungle will spring. Time passes and the great love, his loving companion has been there all along, unrecognized and unappreciated. His life has been one of "chronic waiting" and of remarkable tolerance of delay of gratification, made possible and sustained by 'someday' fantasies. Such delay is no longer ego strength, but rather ego pathology sustained by fantasy. One sees this "chronic waiting" and "someday" way of life as an iatrogenic product in some analytic patients who, through collusion with their analyst, remain in analysis for an excessively long period of time waiting for some beast in the jungle to spring. Excessive delay would be an interesting area for future research.

## Epilogue

Although inner conflict was 'nominated' as a core psychoanalytic concept with great frequency, and although Kris (1947) defined psychoanalysis as a discipline that views human behavior from the perspective of inner conflict, the fact is that the concept of inner conflict has become increasingly less central in much contemporary psychoanalytic thinking. This is reflected in the persistent decline in the number of references to "conflict" in the *Journal of the American Psychoanalytic Association* from the 1980s to 2010 (the final year of the data collection), as reported by Dent and Christian (2014). Dent and Christian also found strong negative correlations in the years from 1985 to 2010 between the terms "conflict" and "attachment" and "relational" words, leading them to conclude that the increased interest in attachment and relational theories may have contributed to decline of interest in conflict theory.

We see two trends with regard to the concept of inner conflict: one, *within* discussions of conflict, there is an increasing emphasis on conflicts related to individuation relative to an emphasis on conflicts about sexual and aggressive wishes; and two, as Dent and Christian (2014) have shown, an overall decline in references to conflict in general. Further, the decreasing focus on conflict has been accompanied by an increasing clinical and theoretical emphasis on defects, deficits, and developmental arrests. A clear expression of this trend is seen in the centrality of self defects in Kohut's (1971; 1977; 1984) self psychology, in Stolorow and Lachmann's (1980) *Psychoanalysis of Developmental Arrests: Theory and Treatment*; in Kernberg's (e.g., 1976) formulation of the role of splitting in borderline personality disorder; and in the recent emphasis on impairments in mentalization as a central feature of borderline personality disorder (e.g., Bateman & Fonagy, 2006). With regard to the latter, although Fonagy and his colleagues (e.g., 2002) suggest that the borderline patient's difficulties with mentalization may be partly due to dynamic conflict factors, such as the patient's fear of knowing about what goes on in the other's mind, greater attention is given to failures in mentalization as a developmental defect.

In my 1984 book, *Recent Developments in Psychoanalysis: A Critical Evaluation*, I devoted a chapter to "developmental defect versus dynamic conflict" and argued against dichotomizing the two. I continue to take that position. However, it may be the case that although inner conflicts are present in all psychopathology, as Kohut (1977) maintained, defects and deficits of one sort or another are at the center of many current forms of psychopathology. If this is the case, it would perhaps follow that the centrality of the traditional psychoanalytic aims of making the unconscious conscious and ameliorating id–ego and id–superego conflicts may be applicable primarily to a relatively narrow range of problems, where one's aim, to quote Allan Stone (1997), is to discover the "otherness of oneself" (p. 36). Thus, although inner conflict may be ubiquitous, it may not be at the core of a wide range of psychopathology.

I refer here not only to forms of psychopathology in which defects and deficits are at the center, but also to ones that are linked to maladaptive representational patterns. Regarding the latter, consider for example, an extreme form of an enmeshed/preoccupied attachment pattern, in which the individual's reaction to current actual and potential attachment figures is saturated with chronic fears and expectations of abandonment. There is undoubtedly a conflict between anger at the attachment figure in reaction to expected abandonment. However, It is not at all clear that that is the primary issue here. Rather, the core problem here would seem to be the acquisition of maladaptive representations and expectations based on early experiences such as rejection and unpredictability on the part of the caregiver. That is, the individual thinks, feels, and interacts as if s/he were, to use Freud's (1926) phrase, in the original "danger situation." Further, the therapeutic focus in such cases would appear to be as much on altering maladaptive representations and expectations as on uncovering and resolving inner conflict.

This shift to an emphasis on altering maladaptive representations is seen in the emergence of one form or another of corrective emotional experience as a critical therapeutic factor, beginning with Alexander and French's (1946) formulation and expressed in such concepts as therapist test-passing (Weiss & Sampson, 1985); provision of an empathic bond (Kohut, 1984); and the therapist as a "good" object

(Fairbairn, 1952). The main emphasis in all those formulations is not on making the unconscious conflicts conscious and resolving them, but essentially on modification of maladaptive representations and expectations and replacing them with more adaptive representations and expectations. Also, even when the focus is on the traditional aim of making the unconscious conscious, the emphasis is not necessarily on unconscious inner conflict, but on unconscious or implicit maladaptive representations (i.e., expectations of rejection, pathogenic beliefs, maladaptive internal working models) that need to be made conscious so that they can be subject to examination and reflection.

Although, as we have seen, there is a good deal of evidence from the experimental neurosis literature that conflict can engender maladaptive behavior, that evidence does not speak to the inner conflict with which psychoanalysis is mainly concerned. Indeed, given its axiomatic status in classical psychoanalytic theory, there is surprisingly little evidence that inner conflict plays a central role in a wide range of psychopathology, including borderline conditions, other personality disorders, major depression, bipolar conditions, and various psychotic conditions. This consideration is clearly what Alan Stone (1997) had in mind when he argued that a psychoanalytic treatment approach is not especially appropriate to major mental illness, but is likely to be useful for discovering the "otherness of oneself," a psychological state of affairs in which the conflictual nature of the "otherness" is at the center of one's difficulties. In contrast to Leo Stone (1954) who wrote about the "expanded scope" of psychoanalysis, Alan Stone (1997), in effect, is calling for a *narrowed* scope of psychoanalytic treatment, that is, limited to a range of life difficulties in which conflict is at the center.

This is not to say that psychoanalytic formulations and insights cannot be relevant and useful in cases of major mental illness. Michael Stone (2012) presented a case in which a schizophrenic man murdered his pregnant girlfriend as a solution to his conflict between the feeling that he was not capable of providing for her and the coming baby and his need to preserve his self-image. However, a formulation limited to the man's conflicts and motivations without taking account of his major deficits would hardly be adequate. The claim, exemplified in the work of Brenner (e.g., 2002), that the entire range of psychological functioning, including that seen in severe psychopathology, can be accounted for by reference to conflictual childhood sexual and aggressive wishes and compromise formations governed by the pleasure principle, is simply untenable and is a quintessential instance of the overreach of classical psychoanalytic theorizing.

As the advent of ego psychology has tended to show, in order to adequately understand a wide range of psychopathology, one needs to extend one's perspective beyond the arena of inner conflict and include an assessment of ego functions, a central consideration in all psychopathology, but especially in severe psychopathology. Ego dysfunctions can include, for example, deficiencies in synthetic or executive function, in reality testing, in defense functioning, in affect regulation, in self-cohesiveness, in regulation of self-esteem, in proneness to traumatic anxiety, and so on. From the perspective of ego psychology, inner conflict is one factor that places an extra load on the ego and therefore may interfere with ego functioning. Resolution or amelioration of inner conflict may serve to strengthen ego functioning through reducing that extra load. However, there are also likely to be other factors and interventions that strengthen ego functioning, for example, emotional support, provision of a holding environment, feeling understood and experiencing an empathic bond, having the sense that one is represented in the other's mind, enhanced reflective capacity, experiencing meaning via interpretation in hitherto incomprehensible thoughts and feelings, and so on.

The possible impact of these interventions on ego functioning can be seen as an instructive example of the interplay of what one might refer to as meaning and mechanism (Ricoeur, 1970), a central feature of Freudian theorizing. That is, in contrast to experiencing chaotic and incomprehensible feelings and thoughts, the experience of meaning and purpose can serve to lessen catastrophic anxiety and the sense of chaos, and thereby strengthen ego functioning and keep it from unraveling. In my clinical experience, especially with more disturbed patients, often the primary therapeutic importance of insight-enhancing interpretations lies not only or even primarily in their contribution to awareness and self-knowledge, but also, and perhaps largely, in the ego-enhancing effect of transforming the experience of meaninglessness into meaning. Thus, an experience of *meaning* has an impact on the *mechanisms* of ego functioning (including reduced anxiety, greater affect regulation, and a sense of structural integrity).

One of the challenges facing psychoanalysis that a focus on defects represents is that whereas the classical psychoanalytic theory of treatment speaks the language of inner conflict, including its identification, analysis, and resolution, it does not have a nuanced and adequate language for defects and deficits. Indeed, from the very start, Freud (1894) rejected Janet's emphasis on constitutional defects and replaced it with the centrality of inner conflict and defense (i.e., "defense hysteria," p. 47). This distinction between conflicts and defects became blurred with the advent of ego psychology, which opened the door to a consideration of ego strengths and ego defects. Thus, the notion of defects entered psychoanalytic theorizing, even if the nature of the defects was not limited to constitutional weakness. Indeed, in contrast to Janet's focus on constitutional weakness, from a psychoanalytic perspective, defects in ego functioning could be attributed to early negative experiences, or perhaps in a more nuanced formulation, to an interaction between constitutional predispositions and early experiences (a diathesis–stress model). Thus, not only did the concept of defects enter psychoanalytic theorizing, but also the importance of early trauma generating defects. In effect, ego psychology now bore more of a family resemblance to a modified form of Janetian theory. One can also point to the family resemblance between ego psychology and Fairbairn's attribution of "splits in the ego" (certainly an instance of ego defects) to the trauma of early deprivation and rejection.

Pursuing the red thread, we come to the explicit primacy of defects attributable to early trauma (i.e., traumatic lack of empathic mirroring) in Kohut's self psychology. Were it not for what one might refer to as the narcissism of theory building, the notion of self-defects could easily be accommodated under the rubric of ego defects. However, insofar as ego psychology retained conceptual and historical links to aspects of classical theory (i.e., drive theory, id–ego conflict) a new theoretical language appeared to Kohut to be necessary. One consequence of that new theoretical language was the exclusion of any prominent role for inner conflict. Thus, whereas from an ego psychology perspective, one can understand that resolution of inner conflict can be ego strengthening, this possibility finds no prominent place in self psychology. Indeed, inner conflict plays virtually no role at all in Kohut's (1984) later writings.

But if, as self psychology theory suggests, the resolution of inner conflict is not an important route to self or ego strengthening, what other route or routes are available? After all, whereas from a traditional psychoanalytic perspective, we know or think we know how to deal with unconscious inner conflicts, how do we deal with defects that are presumably relatively independent of inner conflicts? Kohut's answer to this question quite fittingly employs the metaphor of repair. Thus, whereas conflicts call for compromise and resolution, defects call for repair or put more crudely, broken things need to be fixed. But just how do defects get repaired? And going beyond metaphor, what does it mean to repair psychological defects?

Kohut's response to these questions lies in his discussion of "optimal failure" or "optimal frustration" and "transmuting internalization." That is, through repeated experiences of less than perfect mirroring and through a process of "transmuting internalization," there is an accretion of structure and an enhancement of self-cohesiveness. Although suggestive, this account is vague and fails to clarify the specific processes that presumably lead to repair of self defects and enhancement of self-cohesiveness. For example, what identifiable psychological processes are involved in "transmuting internalization"?

Although the prominence of reference to defects, deficits, and developmental arrest and the concomitant de-emphasis on conflict is relatively recent, the shift began some time ago in the context of an ego psychology perspective on severe psychopathology. This is seen relatively clearly for example, in Federn's (1950) *Ego Psychology and the Psychoses*. He refers to psychosis as "an ego disease" and attributes it to a "deficient ego" (p. 157). He also writes that "it is one of the fundamental and unshakable tenets of Freud that neuroses are mainly defense phenomena, while psychoses are mainly defect phenomena, of the ego" (p. 169).[13] Although Federn minimizes the role of inner conflict in psychosis, he also observes that, along with other factors, its presence can play a potential role in the precipitation of psychosis. Thus, he writes that "everything which, since the beginning of life, has traumatized the individual or has produced a chronic conflict adds to the danger of psychosis" (p. 195). Although Federn refers to the psychoanalysis of psychosis, in his description of such treatment, the major psychoanalytic tenets are no longer present. For example, he calls for ego-strengthening interventions rather than analysis of resistance; and he suggests that the analyst refrain from transference interpretations or interpretation of conflict. (It is not clear what makes such treatment psychoanalytic.)

One should note the implicit logic of Federn's view of psychosis as an "ego disease." Given that everyone is confronted with some degree and form of inner conflict, its mere presence could not be the primary factor in psychopathology, particularly severe psychopathology. To the extent that inner conflict *is* involved in the etiology of psychopathology, its significance lies in the fact that it is still another burden with which an already compromised ego must deal. How much of a burden it constitutes is a function of such factors as its intensity and chronicity and how one copes with conflict. But – and this is a critical point – how one deals with conflict and its effect on one's overall functioning are precisely matters of intactness of ego functions, that is, degree of ego strength.

I am reminded of my early training in Rorschach assessment. It was very tempting to try to use the *content* of Rorschach responses to identify the nature of the individual's conflicts (e.g., dependency conflict; gender identity conflicts; conflicts over aggression and sexuality). But those of us trained in the Rapaport tradition soon learned that this approach was not very useful – after all, everyone had some form of conflicts. If the Rorschach was to be maximally useful, we were taught, we needed to focus on *formal* features of the Rorschach responses, which would shed light on the individual's manner and adequacy of ego functioning (see Holt's, 2008, work on measuring primary process in Rorschach responses). Underlying this focus was the assumption that adequacy of ego functioning, as reflected in the formal features of the Rorschach responses, represented a more useful index of personality functioning than identifying the content of inner conflicts.

To sum up, with the increasing dominance of ego psychology over many years, along with the "expanded scope" of psychoanalysis, as we have seen from the Dent and Christian (2014) survey, the primacy of inner conflict in the psychoanalytic literature began to recede. This was so for a number of reasons. One, the recognition that issues of ego strength and ego weakness and their significance for integrative capacity were central factors in understanding the more severe psychopathology encompassed by the "expanded scope" of psychoanalysis; two, the recognition that, although to a lesser degree, even in neurotic psychopathology, issues of ego weakness and ego strength are relevant; and three, the recognition that, in all cases the therapeutic importance of resolution or of amelioration of inner conflict lies, at least in large part, not only in its contribution to self-awareness and self-knowledge, but in its ego-strengthening effects. One way to put this is to say that insight and self-awareness that lead to amelioration of inner conflict (or to its recognition so that some coping steps can be taken) are ego enhancing. Thus, on this view, self-knowledge and awareness of one's conflicts may be therapeutic largely to the extent that they enhance ego functioning.

Finally, although inner conflict may play a less central role in more severe forms of psychopathology, it remains a central factor in neurosis as well as in the broad context of the quests for discovering the "otherness of oneself" and for achieving a greater degree of unity of personality – quests that have always been at the heart of the psychoanalytic project.

## Notes

1 I cannot refrain from noting here that Freud's jargon of conflict between "peaceful ego" and "warlike ego" simply amounts to the statement that the soldier is conflicted between wanting to save his life and not wanting to view himself and be viewed by others as cowardly and unpatriotic.

2 I have wondered whether the idea that sexual tensions need to be discharged if one is to preserve one's health is partly rooted in folk beliefs. I recall hearing on a number of occasions when I grew up the comment accompanied by a knowing look that a particular woman's problems, ranging from acne to 'nervousness,' would be ameliorated once she married. On one occasion, during my teenage years, the father of a friend of ours who had returned home after being hospitalized during a psychotic episode, approached a group of us with the request that we find a prostitute for his son. It was clear that he thought that this would be curative. I do not know of any literature that links Freud's hydraulic model to folk beliefs.

3 Recall the distinction made between Freudian metapsychology and clinical theory made among others, by Gill (1976), Holt (1976), and Klein (1976) who argued that it is the clinical theory rather than the metapsychology that is at the heart of psychoanalysis. However, see also Eagle (1980) and Rubinstein (1976) who question the validity of a sharp distinction between the two perspectives.

4 See Kernberg's (1987) discussion of self representation, object representation, and affect unit, which is clearly based on Fairbairn's formulations.

5 Fairbairn (1952) observes that:

> it is always the 'bad' object . . . that is internalized in the first instance; for . . . I find it difficult to attach any meaning to the primary internalization of a 'good' object which is both satisfying and amenable from the infant's point of view. (pp. 110–111)

However, at a later point, Fairbairn allows for the possibility of the internalization of 'good' objects based on a complex and turgid argument that, I must confess, I do not fully understand.

6 In trying to understand Fairbairn's often convoluted formulation and place it in a language that is more comprehensible, I take Fairbairn to be saying that through a motivated process, the individual lacks conscious access to certain representations of the object.

7 It is useful to make a distinction between the concept of superego, which implies a more archaic structure, and the concept of mature conscience. The distinction between the two would be apparent in the different language employed. The experience of a homunculus sitting on one's shoulder or the locution "my conscience tells me . . ." associated with the concept of superego can be contrasted with the language, reflecting one's fully ego-syntonic values, of "I believe" or "I feel."

8 The topic of Fairbairn's (1929) MD thesis was "The relationship of dissociation and repression considered from the point of view of medical psychology." In that thesis, he views dissociation as the more general process and repression as a special instance of the more general category of dissociation.

9 Fairbairn (1952) makes clear that he is not referring to ordinary identification, but rather to what he refers to as "primary identification," the hallmark of which is failure to distinguish between self and other.

10 Fairbairn's focus is often on schizoid psychopathology, which may give one the impression that he is referring to a specific category of psychopathology. However, it becomes clear in reading Fairbairn's work that he believes that at the core of all psychopathology is the schizoid condition. One finds a similar pattern in Kohut's work. In his early book (1971), Kohut writes that whereas self psychology is appropriate for a pathology of self-defects (e.g., narcissistic personality disorder), classical theory is appropriate for "structural conflicts." However, by the time that his 1984 book appears, Kohut now argues that at the core of all psychopathology are self-defects.

11 It is not clear why Kohut (1984) refers to the "Guilty Man" of Freudian theory (in contrast to the "Tragic Man" of self psychology). The fact is that the affect of anxiety plays a far more central role than guilt in Freudian theory.

12 Does the inevitability of deprivation and frustration are inevitable lie in the nature of the infant's needs or demands? What are these needs and demands? Are they demands for immediate gratification, even if what is assumed to be gratified is different from Freud's assumptions. If so, Fairbairn's apparent environmental failure theory essentially becomes, like Freud's theory, a theory of human nature in which inner conflict is inevitable due to the human condition.

13 I doubt that this distinction is one of Freud's fundamental and unshakable tenets. See, for example, Freud's (1911) discussion of the Schreber case. I think that Federn puts it this way as a way of lending Freud's authority to the reduced emphasis on inner conflict.

# 5

# THE CONCEPT OF DEFENSE

## Introduction

The concept of defense is without question one of the core concepts of psychoanalytic theory, both in an historical and conceptual sense. Along with unconscious processes, it was the most frequent response to my query regarding the identification of core psychoanalytic concepts. There is little doubt that the concept of defense represents one of the most robust and enduring contributions psychoanalytic theory has made to an understanding of mind. Also, perhaps more than any other psychoanalytic concept, the concept of defense has been assimilated into non-psychoanalytic theories and has exerted a strong influence on psychological theory and practice as well as empirical research. Indeed, the existence of a large body of research on defences makes it possible to examine the empirical status of this concept and to address the many issues and questions that have arisen since Freud introduced the concept of repression.

Freud's introduction of the "cornerstone" concept of repression marks the birth of psychoanalysis. Prior to that point, Freud essentially agreed with Janet's account of hysteria. Breuer and Freud (1893–1895) write:

> The longer we have been occupied with these phenomena the more we have become convinced that the splitting of consciousness which is so striking in the well-known cases under the form of 'double conscience' [dual consciousness] *is present to a rudimentary degree in every hysteric and that a tendency to such a dissociation, and with it the emergence of abnormal states of consciousness (which we shall bring together under the term 'hypnoid') is the basic phenomenom of this neurosis.* In these views we concur with Binet and the two Janets.
>
> (p. 12, emphasis in original)

However, there is one central point on which Breuer and Freud (1893–1895) disagree with Janet. They write:

> It is not the case that the splitting of consciousness occurs because the patients are weak-minded; they appear to be weak-minded because their mental activity is divided and only a part of its capacity is at the disposal of the conscious thought. We cannot regard mental weakness as the *typus hystericus*, as the essence of the disposition to hysteria.
>
> (p. 231, emphasis in original)

What, then, is the essence of the disposition to hysteria? Breuer and Freud's (1893–1895) answer: "It turns out to be a *sine qua non* for the acquisition of hysteria that an incompatibility should develop between the ego and some idea presented to it" (p. 122). In what Freud (1893–1895) refers to as "defense hysteria," he claims that he "was repeatedly able to show that the splitting of consciousness is *the result of an act of will on the part of the patient*" (p. 46, emphasis in original). This "act of will" is nothing less than repression, which in these early writings was viewed as voluntary and conscious. Thus, Freud refers to an hysterical patient's recall of her intention of "pushing the thing away" (p. 47). The essence of repression, then, is the motivated banishment of unacceptable mental contents (i.e., incompatible with the ego) from consciousness in order to avoid distressing affect.

## Definition of repression

In his later 1915 essay on repression Freud writes that "the essence of repression lies simply in turning something away, and keeping it at a distance, from the conscious" (p. 147). Freud makes clear in his ensuing discussion that the 'something' that is turned away from conscious awareness is: (1) an idea (*Vorstellung*) or "ideational representative" of an instinct; (2) ideas that have become associatively connected with the repressed idea; and (3) the affective element of the instinctual representative. As for the motive for repression, it is always some form of unpleasure that would be experienced were the repressed mental contents to enter consciousness. Indeed, for Freud, repression of mental contents linked to the danger of unpleasure is analogous to flight in relation to painful and/or dangerous external situations.

Although other defenses have been posited since Freud's introduction of the concept of repression, the fact is that essential to the concept of defense is the idea of keeping unacceptable thoughts and/or feelings (e.g., anxiety-provoking threats to self-esteem) from being consciously experienced and/or from being acknowledged as part of oneself.

## The nature of defense: what is one defending against?

The essence of defense is protection of the individual. Protection against what? In his early work, Freud's answer to this question, as reflected in the early case studies, was essentially that defense operates to protect the individual's self-image. That is, any thought or feeling that threatened one's self-image could be defended against through repression. Later responses to the question of what one is defending against included a metapsychological one based on the constancy principle, and a more experience-near clinical one. From the perspective of the former, the constancy principle, the greatest danger to the ego is being overwhelmed with excessive excitation. Further, insofar as undischarged instinctual impulses (id) constitute the greatest internal source of excitation and therefore the greatest threat of overwhelming the ego with excessive excitation, they are seen by Freud (as well as Anna Freud) as the natural enemy of the ego, against which ego defenses need to be erected. As A. Freud (1966, p. 157) puts it, there is a primary antagonism between the id and the ego.

Freud's (1926) more clinical and experience-near response to the question of what one is defending against is that because sexual and aggressive mental contents trigger anxiety linked to the "danger situations" (p. 129) (of loss of the object, loss of the object's love, castration anxiety, and superego condemnation), they are banished from consciousness. That is, the child removes from conscious experience those thoughts and feelings that are associated with parental disapproval and punishment and that he or she experiences as threatening vitally needed ties to parents.

Freud essentially reduced this experience-near account to his metapsychological formulation by stating that the ultimate danger constituted by each of the "danger situations" – loss of the object, loss of the object's love, castration anxiety, and superego condemnation – is that the child is left at the mercy of undischarged and excessive excitation. On this view, it is not the loss of the object, etc. per se that constitutes the threat or danger, but rather that this loss results in the ego being left at the mercy of undischarged tensions and excitations. That this view was taken quite seriously by later Freudians is seen in Spitz and Wolf's (1946) attribution of the marasmus he observed in orphaned infants to the fact that there was no available object through which they could discharge sexual and aggressive tensions.

In Freud's later formulation, the affective state from which one is protected by defense is mainly the threat of anxiety. Since Freud, this formulation has been extended to include other negative affective states such as guilt (e.g., Weiss & Sampson, 1986), shame (e.g., Morrison, 1989), depression (e.g., Brenner, 1991) and threats to one's self-image and to loss of self-esteem (e.g., Fenichel, 1945; Kohut, 1971, 1977, 1984). Indeed, with regard to the latter, the title of a book by a major psychoanalytically oriented researcher on defenses is *Protecting the Self* (Cramer, 2006). And Baumeister et al. (1998) define defense simply as "protection of self-esteem against threat" (p. 1081).

To the extent that affect states such as depression, shame, guilt, and loss of self-esteem do not readily lend themselves to be understood in terms of build-up of excitation, Freud's central metapsychological idea that the primary function of defense is to prevent the build-up of ego-threatening excessive excitation becomes less tenable. What remains as a plausible and important implication of that formulation is the idea that, when effective, defenses serve, through different means, *to regulate negative affect*. Thus, what anxiety, guilt, shame, depression, threats to one's self-image and to one's self-esteem all have in common is negative affect and the function that all defenses have in common is the regulation of such negative affect.[1] Indeed, although often obscured by different theoretical contexts and different theoretical terms, this conception of defense cuts across different psychoanalytic theories and 'schools,' as well as non-psychoanalytic theories.

Freud's linking of defense to the "danger situations" is essentially identical to a number of contemporary psychoanalytic formulations, at the center of which is the idea that the child removes from conscious experience *those thoughts and feelings that are experienced as threatening to vitally needed object ties*. Although stated in different theoretical languages, there is a clear convergence among Freud's description of the "danger situations"; Stolorow et al.'s (2002) idea that "regions of experience . . . are sacrificed to safeguard the needed tie" (p. 47); Stern's (2003) claim that the relational field "structures the possibility of knowing – the potential for what we can say and think and what we cannot" (p. 31); Winnicott's (1965) concept of the "false self" understood as the child's compliance with parental demands and removal from his or her realm of experience vital aspects of his or her personality; and Fairbairn's (1952) formulation that the threat of living in an empty objectless inner world is the "ultimate psychopathological disaster" (p. 52) against which one needs to defend oneself.[2]

Implicit in all these formulations is the central idea that the experienced threat to vitally needed object ties represents the most potent source of negative affect, against which one needs to defend oneself. Thus, despite Freud's emphasis on the constancy principle and his theoretical assumption that instinctual impulses represent the greatest danger to the ego (because of their potential to overwhelm the ego with excessive excitation), according to the logic of his formulation of the "danger situations," it would follow that *any* thoughts and feelings the conscious experience and expression of which would threaten ties to the object and risk bringing about the "danger situations" would be defended against.

To sum up, there seems to be wide agreement both within psychoanalysis and, as we shall see, outside the psychoanalytic context, that the primary function of defense is protection against such noxious affective experiences as anxiety, guilt, depression, emptiness, shame, low self-esteem, self-fragmentation, threats to one's self-image, and loss of identity. Furthermore, there is also at least implicit agreement that threatened disruptions of vital object ties represent a major (but not the only) source of generating these noxious affects. However, also implicit in a wide range of theories is the proposition that *any set of experiences* that threaten to bring about these noxious affects will be defended against. I think it is fair to say that this 'expansion' of the range of applicability of the concept of defense characterizes contemporary work both within and outside the psychoanalytic context.

## *How do defenses operate?*

I begin with Freud's account of how repression operates. In effect, Freud essentially proposes a negative feedback thermostat-like system characterized by the following components: (1) a forbidden mental content threatens to reach consciousness; (2) this elicits a small dose of anxiety that Freud (1926) refers to as a "signal of anxiety" (p. 125), that is, a signal of danger; (3) the small dose of "signal anxiety" triggers the repressive defense of keeping the forbidden content from reaching consciousness – or, if it has momentarily reached consciousness, it is banished from consciousness; and (4) when the forbidden content is removed from consciousness, "signal anxiety" abates. Thus, this is a thermostat-like process in which the forbidden content elicits signal anxiety, which triggers repressive removal of the forbidden mental content, which then reduces signal anxiety. When defenses fail, "signal anxiety" becomes transformed into traumatic anxiety. Understood this way, it is clear that defenses constitute a form of affect regulation.

In the above schematic outline of how repression operates, I have simplified somewhat the structure of Freud's concept of repressive defenses by omitting the following features: (1) the ego as censor can banish from consciousness not only the specific forbidden content, but also mental contents that are associated with a forbidden wish or desire; (2) the forbidden mental content may elude the censor and reach consciousness in a disguised form[3] – hence, the distinction between manifest and latent content, in which the former is a disguised expression of the latter; and (3) because a repressed wish continues to exert pressure to reach consciousness, a constant counterforce is required to maintain repression. As Freud (1915b) puts it, repression entails "an uninterrupted expenditure of force" (p. 151). Hence, it follows that the excessive use of repression not only constricts the individual's range and depth of experience, but also may deplete the ego; and modulating the need for repression not only increases the individual's range and depth of experience, but also increases the quantity of energy available to the ego.

## Are defenses conscious or unconscious?

When Freud (Breuer & Freud, 1893–1895) introduced the concept of repression, as noted earlier and as Erdelyi (1990) has emphasized, he appears to have conceptualized it as conscious and volitional. He refers to an "act of will" and "pushing the thing away." Thus, in Freud's early writings, there is little or no real distinction between what we refer to today as repression and suppression. Erdelyi (1990) argues that Freud continued to view repression as conscious in his later work and that it was Anna Freud and others who conceptualized repression as an unconscious process. However, the evidence, I believe, is decisive that Freud, too, came to view repression as an unconscious process. Recall that Freud's discomfort with a topographical model in which conscious is equated with ego and unconscious with instinctual wishes was motivated by his recognition that ego functions, including ego defenses, can be and often are unconscious. Hence, ego could no longer be equated with conscious processes. What was required was a *structural* model of id, ego, and superego that at least partly replaced or at least supplemented the topographical model. In the present context, the important point is that if, Erdelyi argues, Freud continued to think of the ego function of repression (and other defenses) as conscious, the topographical model would suffice and there would be little need for a structural model.

One also needs to note that if Freud thought of repression as a conscious process, it would make little sense to identify lifting repression as a central therapeutic process aim and making the unconscious conscious as an overall process and outcome therapeutic goal. Also, what would talk about analyzing resistance and analysis of defense mean in the context of Erdelyi's proposal? In any case, most psychoanalytic theorists would undoubtedly accept Cramer's (2006) definition of defenses as "*unconscious* mental mechanisms" (p. 7) (my emphasis). Furthermore, according to Cramer, "defenses are effective because they function outside of awareness – that is, they are unconscious; the awareness of the functioning of a defense should render it ineffective" (p. 18). I want to make it clear that at this point I am not arguing that, in fact, defenses are always and necessarily unconscious or that this is the best way to think of defenses. As we will see, that is a complex issue, partly a matter of empirical data and partly a matter of definition and conceptualization. What I am saying is that in the context of classical psychoanalytic theory, defenses are understood as essentially unconscious processes.

## *The homunculus problem*

As we have seen in Chapter 2, positing of unconscious processes raises the homunculus issue. This also applies to the positing of unconscious defences. A question that arises is how the ego can identify forbidden and dangerous content against which a defense is required before the conscious individual can do so. The classic problem here is the one of seeming to postulate a homunculus (i.e., the ego) that appears to possess all the capacities and level of intelligence that a conscious person does.[4]

A number of ways of dealing with this issue have been proposed. One proposal, implicit in the negative feedback model of Freud's concept of repression outlined above, is that what triggers "signal anxiety" and subsequent defense is a momentary and fleeting awareness of a particular forbidden thought or feeling rather than a fully formed and fully articulated desire or wish. As we will see, this formulation is made explicit in the work of Sartre (1956), Fingarette (1963), and Stern (2003).

Quite apart from the question of what Freud intended, this construal of repression that allows for the possibility of a fleeting or momentary awareness of the repressed content tends to support a version of Erdelyi's proposal that defense need not be fully unconscious. Indeed, as we saw in Chapter 2, Sandler and Anna Freud (1985) essentially acknowledge the likelihood of momentary awareness of the forbidden impulse against which the individual is defending.

Another way of meeting the homunculus criticism is the idea that defenses can be triggered by partial cues such as 'this is new and unfamiliar,' or a vague sense that there is something scary or sexual or aggressive here, which leads to selective inattention or failure to process further.

## *Alternative conceptions of defense: not spelling out*

One of the early criticisms of Freud's concept of repression was made by Sartre (1956) who argued that viewing repression and other defenses essentially as subpersonal mechanisms bypassed the issue of the individual's choices and responsibilities. He proposed that the act of repression is an expression of "bad faith" ("mauvaise foi") – a form of *self-deception* – carried out by a person rather than implemented by a subpersonal mechanism. Sartre's critique has been taken up and elaborated by Fingarette (1963; 1969) and later by Stern (2003).

According to Fingarette (1969), many of the phenomena described in terms of repression are more meaningfully understood as evidence of "avoidance of becoming explicitly conscious of our engagement, [and avoidance of] becoming explicitly conscious that we are avoiding it" (p. 42). That is, we do not *"spell out"* "some feature of (our) engagement in the world" (p. 46). Furthermore, as in the case of all defenses, not spelling out is motivated by the aim of avoiding anxiety, guilt, and other noxious affects and experiences.

Fingarette presents an example of someone who has been a failure in realizing a particular ambition and then adopts the policy of not spelling out this assessment of the situation, as well as of having adopted the policy of not spelling it out. Sartre (1956) provides an example of a married woman who, seemingly unaware of the import of her behavior, permits her hand to remain in the hands of a man who is trying to seduce her. When his intention is made more explicit (in part because he is encouraged by her apparently acquiescent behavior), she reacts with surprise and outrage. Sartre describes the combination of the woman allowing her hand to remain in the man's hand and reacting with surprise and outrage as being in bad faith. From Fingarette's point of view, the woman has failed to spell out both her partial acquiescence to the seduction and her policy to not spell out her acquiescence.

Although Fingarette does not make it fully explicit, implicit in his (and Sartre's) criticisms of the repression concept is the assumption that the man's realization of his failure and the woman's acquiescence in the seduction are not fully articulated thoughts and feelings that have been repressed and are therefore unconscious and waiting to be uncovered through the lifting of repression. Rather, both the man's realization and the woman's acquiescence are vaguely felt and *not spelled out*. Hence, the defensive operations consist mainly in keeping the vaguely felt as vague (i.e., not spelled out) rather than banishing from consciousness a thought or feeling that has already been fully processed and articulated.[5]

Fingarette's suggestion is that it is not so much that the vaguely felt thought or feeling is unconscious or completely unavailable to conscious experience, but rather that it remains unarticulated and vague. Indeed, in the above examples, the sense of failure or acquiescence in a seduction may be fleetingly experienced at the periphery of consciousness, but not further spelled out. As noted in Chapter 2, something like this process seems to aptly describe the case of Lucy R., whose awareness of her fantasy of marrying her employer was just below the surface of her awareness.

### *Defense as failing to formulate unformulated experiences*

Fingarette's formulation has been elaborated and developed by Stern (2003) who conceptualizes defense as the motivated failure to further formulate vague unformulated experiences. According to Stern, unformulated experiences are characterized by "feelings of tendency," "indefinable, extremely rapid sensations" (James, 1890), "felt meanings" (Gendlin, 1962); and defense consists in not formulating these experiences any further. Further, according to Stern, the primary means of formulating unformulated experiences is through *language*, that is, through giving them words. As Stern puts it, in contrast to the Freudian view of defense in which formulated material has been ejected from consciousness, "unformulated experience is material that has never been brought into consciousness" (p. xii).

Further, unlike the Freudian view in which repressed material has a determinate structure, according to Stern, "the form [unconscious experience] will eventually take in words is not predetermined by its own structure" (p. xi). Thus, for Stern, the essence of defense is the failure to give words to wordless raw experience. In one respect, Stern takes a direction – in my view a problematic one – not shared by Sartre or Fingarette. He views unformulated experiences as essentially uninterpreted and indeterminate in their meaning, subject to many possible formulations, primarily as a function of the relational context of these unformulated experiences. As I have noted elsewhere (Eagle, 2011; see also Eagle, Wolitzky, & Wakefield, 2001):

> If unformulated experiences are indeterminate, entirely uninterpreted, never created, and subject to many different possible formulations or conceptions, why would they elicit a defensively motivated failure to formulate? There must be some determinate content – whether characterized as "feelings of tendency" (James, 1890) or "felt meanings" (Gendlin, 1962) – that, at some level, the individual experiences as threatening in order for the unformulated material to trigger a defensively motivated failure to formulate further. To respond to a vague felt feeling as threatening, as something requiring the defense of refusing to formulate further already indicates some interpretation of the experience, some determinate content. . . . if the unformulated experience is so utterly vague and so without determinate threat that it can be completed or formulated or coconstructed in virtually an indefinite variety of ways, then why talk about formulating or completing a *particular* unformulated experience? Why talk about refusal to formulate as a defense? What content is being defended against?
>
> (p. 117)

Consider again Sartre's woman who does not spell out her acquiescence in a seduction and Fingarette's man who does not spell out his failure to realize his ambition. In both cases, what is not spelled out – or in Stern's terms, what is not formulated – is a *determinate* content, namely, interest in the seduction in the one case, and a sense of failure in the other. Were this not the case, what would each of them be defending against? In short, for each of them to defensively fail to spell out or formulate, there must be some determinate mental content – even if it is fleeting or "felt meanings" or "feelings of tendency" – against which each of them is defending by not spelling out or further formulating the fleeting experience.

## *The role of attention in defense*

According to Freud (1950/1895), "primary *thought-defense* arises, which, . . . takes the release of unpleasure as a signal . . . to leave a particular pathway – that is, to direct the cathexis of attention *elsewhere*" (p. 382) (emphasis in the original). Freud (1900) also writes that "the act of becoming conscious depends upon a definite psychic function – attention – being brought to bear" (p. 529). On this view, attention cathexis is necessary to render a mental content conscious. Hence, one of the means through which defense operates is withdrawal of attention cathexis or failure to deploy attention. Sullivan's (1956) concept of "selective inattention" clearly captures this aspect of defense. (See Rapaport, 1967, for an elaboration of Freud's ideas on the relationship among consciousness, attention, and repression.)

In both Freud's and Sullivan's formulations, attention is withdrawn from or not deployed to certain mental contents (i.e., thoughts and feelings) that have been encoded to some appreciable degree. One can, however, also fail to deploy attention in order to prevent further encoding of unarticulated and unformulated mental contents, with the result that they remain in a vague form. For example, a vaguely sensed feeling of failure or acquiescence in a seduction remains vague and fleeting because attention is deployed away from these fleeting and vaguely sensed thoughts and feelings. Consequently, they do not get encoded beyond a certain point. Thus, despite convergence on the role of attention mechanisms, there appear to be important differences between Freud and Rapaport, on the one hand and Fingarette and Stern, on the other with regard to the relationship between attention and defense. According to Freud and Rapaport, defense operates by deploying attention away from mental contents that have been encoded to a significant degree, whereas for Fingarette and Stern, defense operates by short-circuiting the encoding process itself by deployment of attention away from it.

Implicit in Freud's and Rapaport's position is the idea that relatively full encoding of a mental content (e.g., I desire X) can occur without attention or consciousness. After all, it is Freud (Breuer & Freud, 1893–1895, p. 223) who maintained that the major part of mental life goes on outside of awareness and who maintained that the only difference between conscious and unconscious mental contents is the absence of consciousness in the latter. Contrastingly, at least Stern seems to suggest that encoding (i.e., formulating) requires attention in order to take place. Without attention, experience remains not only unformulated, but indeterminate in its meaning. As I understand Fingarette's position, although the individual may not spell out or fully articulate his or her experience or, more to the point, his or her feelings, thoughts, desires, and aims, what is not spelled out has determinate content and meaning – for example, a vague sense of failure or a seemingly passive acquiescence in a seduction. Hence, *some* degree of attention is directed toward the experience and *some* degree of encoding has taken place, but not a sufficient degree necessary for a clear spelling out or articulating.

Thus, one can contrast Fingarette and Stern by noting that whereas for Fingarette, defense is directed against further encoding or spelling out of experience that has been given some determinate meaning, for Stern, defense is directed against the encoding or formulating of any determinate meaning. In short, different theorists place defense at different levels of the encoding–retrieval process: In Freudian theory, defense is directed at the retrieval process; for Finagarette, it is somewhere between initial and full encoding; and for Stern, it is very early in the encoding process.

## *Failure to understand personal import and to make connections*

G. S. Klein (1976) has identified the failure to make connections among different mental contents and to understand the personal import of certain experiences as central aspects of defense. According to this view, although certain experiences may be conscious and fully encoded, what is defended against is the connections among the experiences and their personal import. That is, the individual defends against becoming aware of the personal meanings to which these connections point. This view of defense bears certain similarities to Fingarette's emphasis on not spelling out the project in which one is engaged, to Fonagy's formulations having to do with the capacity for mentalization, and to Sullivan's (1956) discussion of "undeveloped implications" (p. 58) of experiences that are themselves in conscious awareness. He notes that these "undeveloped implications" are not easily accessible "because [they are] not well tied into the general tissue of your life" (p. 58). Thus, although particular thoughts and feelings may be in awareness, the individual does not make those connections among these thoughts and feelings that would provide a reliable guide to vital aspects of the individual's psychological life, his or her attitudes, fears, aspirations that are implicit in the connections among these thoughts and feelings.

Let me briefly provide a concrete example. A patient, F.L., who had been very competent and successful, reacted to certain difficulties in his business by feeling panicky and dysfunctional to a degree that puzzled and frightened him. I had learned from F.L. that he felt puny in his childhood and teens and that the dominant feeling he thought his parents had toward him was pity. He was also told by his father, who was himself a business man, that he would never make a successful business man. Thus, the memory of feeling puny, the experience of being the object of pity, and the current panic and feelings of being dysfunctional were all in awareness. What was not in awareness was the *connections* among these different mental contents. The current business crisis triggered feelings of being puny (i.e., helpless), pitiful, and a poor business man. Being able to make that connection was extremely useful in enabling F.L. to deal with the current situation in his usual competent way.

To be noted is that F.L did not recover a repressed memory or become aware of an unconscious wish or desire. Rather, in making the connections between his early feelings of puniness and memories of being pitied and his current feelings of panic and not being able to cope, he was able to acquire a new perspective regarding his current state. I am reminded here of Friedman's (1991) comment that the analyst brings the good news that the "danger situations" are no longer dangerous.

One can cite many other examples in which what is brought into awareness is not a repressed memory or wish, but rather connections among fully conscious material. For example, in the Control–Mastery theory literature, one finds many examples in which although patients are aware of their fears and anxieties as well as early parental communications, they come to recognize the connections between the two sets of experiences and thus develop a new perspective toward their fears and anxieties.

One can think of analysis of the transference in terms of helping the patient make connections between his or her expectations and responses to a current figure and his or her expectations and responses to an early figure. For example, the patient may expect that the therapist will be as disapproving of or as ambivalent about the former's successes as his or her parents were. Success in making such a connection may generate a new perspective toward the patient's experience of the therapist.

In the present context of discussing defense, an important question that arises is: what prevents the individual from making the connections among different experiences? According to G. S. Klein (1976), it is mainly the operation of defense that prevents connections from being made. But what is one defending against when one fails to make connections? Or, to put it another way, what are the dangers that would emerge were one to make certain connections? The answer to these questions is not always evident.[6] However, if, as Klein maintains, failure to make connections is a form of defense, it must be a *motivated* failure rather than simply an incapacity (an issue that also comes up in regard to failure to mentalize). In the case of F.L., the failure to make connections may have been motivated by the desire to avoid the distressing affect triggered by memories of feeling puny and pitiful. In other cases, the motive force may be avoidance of other distressing affects. But the general motive of protecting oneself against some danger and distressing affect must be present if one is to view the failure to make connections as a defense.

One of the mechanisms proposed by Sullivan through which implications are left undeveloped is "selective inattention." One simply does not attend or think about threatening implications. Sullivan (1953) also posits a self-system that bars anxiety-laden material threatening to the integrity of the self from awareness. The self-system and its function are obviously analogous to the Freudian ego and its censorship function. However, an additional emphasis in Sullivan's formulation is the tendency of the self-system to protect and maintain itself by resisting change of any kind. One might say that implicit in Sullivan's account is the idea that information or experiences that imply radical change or discontinuity of any kind is threatening to the self and therefore is defensively barred from the self system.

### *Defense against acknowledging thoughts and feelings as part of oneself*

Where the goal of psychoanalysis is making unconscious contents conscious, it is natural to understand defense as the mechanism or process that bars these contents from being experienced in conscious awareness; and analysis of defense is understood as the analytic work that lifts these barriers. However, the picture changes when the goal of psychoanalysis is formulated as "where id was, there shall ego be" (Freud, 1933[1932]), p. 80), particularly when the latinized id and ego are translated from the original German of "das Es" and "das Ich" as respectively, "the it" and "I" (Brandt, 1966; Eagle, 1987). In this latter framework, the goal of psychoanalysis becomes 'where impersonal it was, there shall personal I be.' Or to state it more fully, those aspects of oneself that were defensively excluded and rendered as impersonal it shall be acknowledged as part of oneself and integrated in one's personality and one's sense of self.

What is critical in this process is not simply making certain unconscious contents conscious, but *acknowledging and avowing* them as one's own, as part of oneself. Of course, one cannot acknowledge or avow something of which one is unaware. In that sense, access to consciousness may be necessary but not sufficient for personal ownership (see Kihlstrom, 1987). However, one can consciously experience a thought or feeling as *ego-alien*, as really not one's own. For example, one can have an ego-alien unbidden and obsessive thought that is fully conscious and yet experience it as not part of oneself, as coming from outside oneself. Here, the defense operates not to ban the thought from consciousness, but to prevent personal ownership, which, in common with all defenses, serves to maintain and protect one's self-image.

### *Cognitive biases as defense*

In a classic paper entitled "The totalitarian ego: Fabrication and revision of personal history," Greenwald (1980) describes "cognitive biases" – which, in the present context, can be, essentially understood as defenses insofar as they serve to enhance one's self-image and to maintain the stability of one's ego or self organization. These biases include *egocentricity* characterized by exaggeratedly viewing oneself as a central player in events; "*beneffectance*" defined as the readiness to view oneself as the origin of good effects and the reluctance to view oneself as the origin of bad effects; and *cognitive conservatism* understood as the resistance to cognitive changes and the tendency to preserve existing cognitive structures. As noted, all these cognitive biases serve to preserve one's self-organization, enhance one's self-image, and raise one's self-esteem or at least reduce threats to one's self-esteem. Greenwald argues that although these cognitive biases may distort reality, discourage growth, and in the long run, may be disadvantageous, they nevertheless may also serve adaptive purposes of promoting perseverence. In the present context, I want to emphasize the defensive function of these cognitive biases in protecting the self from self-devaluation and its accompanying negative affects.

## Defense and the interpersonal situation

Let me turn to what can be referred to as the interpersonal or relational aspect of defense that is implicit in both Freud's formulation as well as contemporary psychoanalytic formulations and that should be made explicit. Surprisingly, this aspect of defense has not been explicitly addressed in the relational psychoanalytic theory of Mitchell and his colleagues. However, as we will see, it does play a central role – even if also not made explicit – in Control–Mastery theory.

The early context for the development of defense in Freud's theorizing is an *interpersonal* one. That is, according to Freud, certain thoughts and feelings are defended against because they are associated with parental prohibitions and punishment in the form of the "danger situations" of loss of the object, loss of the object's love, castration threats, and later, superego condemnation. Implicit in this formulation is the idea that defense operates not only to keep oneself unaware of certain mental contents, *but also to keep others from becoming aware of them.*

An assumption made in Freudian theory is that early parental responses become internalized in the form of stable intrapsychic structures. The superego is an obvious example of such a structure. The relationship between signal anxiety and defense is another example of the internalization of originally external dangers. That is, once the "danger situations" become internalized, they are transformed into internal dangers, with the result that mental contents associated with the "danger situations" trigger signal anxiety, which then triggers defense. Thus, although originally based on external dangers, with the formation of intrapsychic structure, particularly the superego, the danger is now from within in the form of anxiety, guilt, and self-punishment rather than primarily anticipated punishment from the other. In short, in Freud's understanding, despite its origin in early interpersonal interactions, once developed, defense is essentially an intrapsychic mechanism that determines which mental contents will be permitted access to consciousness and which will be restricted access.[7] Little attention is given to the role of the contemporary other in influencing what is permitted and not permitted to enter consciousness.[8]

In contrast to this view, in at least some contemporary psychoanalytic theories, what is permitted to reach consciousness and what is barred from consciousness is not simply a function of defenses acquired early in life in the course of interactions with parental figures, but is dynamically influenced by interactions with contemporary significant figures. Thus, according to the latter view, one's "horizons of awareness" and "regions of experience" are shaped not only by early parental invalidation and validation, but also by current interpersonal interactions and experiences of validation and invalidation. Thus, it is not only the child, but also the adult who sacrifices areas of conscious experience in order to safeguard vitally needed ties. As Stolorow et al. (2002) put it, "regions of experience are sacrificed to safeguard the needed tie" (p. 47).

This extension or articulation of what is implicit in the Freudian theory of defense is especially evident in the contemporary emphasis on transference as an interactional process (Gill, 1984). That is, insofar as the essence of transference entails responding to a current other in terms of early expectation and patterns established with parental figures, one would surely expect that the individual's early experience of the "danger situations" would influence his or her expectations in relation to current others, including the therapist. More specifically, he or she would fear loss of the object, loss of the object's love, etc. as a consequence of allowing the expression of certain thoughts and feelings. Further, just as was the case in childhood, the individual's defensive response to these fears would include not only banishing certain mental contents from consciousness, but also great reluctance to *communicate* any semblance of these mental contents that do not reach consciousness to the other lest one be traumatized – even if these mental contents are fleetingly available to oneself.

Thus, what is kept from consciousness is not simply a function of inner conflict (i.e., one's self-condemnation of one's mental contents), but also of one's interactional experiences and construals of cues emitted by the other. Nowhere is this more evident than in the proposal of Control–Mastery theory (for which supportive research evidence is available – see Chapter 1) that the patient's judgment as to whether conditions of safety obtain, defined by the other's passing of tests, strongly influence whether or not warded-off contents will emerge into conscious awareness.

This idea is also implicit in a number of other formulations, including Winnicott's (1965) distinction between "true self" and "false self" (i.e., a self of social compliance), Donnell Stern's suggestion that the relational field structures the possibility for knowing – "the potential for what we can say and think and what we cannot" (p. 31), and Rogers' (1951, 1959) idea that "conditions of worth" influence whether or not fleeting visceral feelings will be attended to and brought to full consciousness or permitted to fade away. It is also reflected in the reconceptualization of transference from projections on to a blank screen to construals of and responses to cues emitted by the analyst (Gill, 1984, 1994).

In short, what is barred from consciousness and what is 'permitted' to reach consciousness are strongly influenced by one's judgments and expectations, both conscious and unconscious, regarding the other's likely response to one's expression of certain mental contents. This entails a striking extension of the concepts of defense. That is, on this view, defenses operate not only to keep oneself unaware of certain mental contents, but also to keep others from becoming aware of them.

Despite this increasing trend toward the 'interpersonalizing' of defense, most theories, including Control–Mastery theory, do not spell out its full implications. Thus, in accord with traditional theory, Weiss and Sampson appear to assume that prior to test-passing and subsequent relaxation of defense, warded-off contents are repressed and unconscious, that is, thoroughly unavailable to conscious experience. They do not appear to consider the possibility, in my view, the likelihood, that at least some of the time, the issue is not simply that warded-off contents are not available to consciousness; there is also the patient's reluctance to *communicate* certain thoughts and feelings that may be available to consciousness, even if fleetingly and not fully spelled out. I would suggest – and I would like to believe this jibes with others' clinical experience – that a good part of the time the patient is at least fleetingly aware (and, at times, more fully aware) of certain mental contents, but in anticipation of a negative reaction, is reluctant to communicate them to the analyst.

From this perspective, one can say that defense operates not only in regard to what one will tell oneself, but also in regard to what one will tell others. Furthermore, there may not always be a hard and fast distinction between the two. Over time, much of what one will not tell others is also what one will not tell oneself. Indeed, one effective way of keeping things from others is self-deception. And, as Fingarette has observed, one effective means of deceiving oneself is not articulating or spelling out certain thoughts, feelings, and interactions to oneself.

I think it is useful to think of defense as operating in the context of an ongoing dynamic interplay between the interpersonal and the intrapsychic.[9] The expected negative reaction from the other not only discourages communication of these mental contents to the other, but also serves to reinforce the defense against further articulating and spelling out these mental contents to oneself. As Gray (1990) observes, the anxiety associated with the defended-against conflictual contents is "crucially heightened by a fantasy [read pathogenic belief], that to put into words what comes to mind in the presence of the analyst is to *create some kind of risk – some consequence which will arise from or within the analyst*" (p. 1086, my emphasis). As Gray also observes, this fantasy is nothing less than the transference-based fear that the early "danger situations" (Freud, 1926, p. 129) will be repeated in the treatment situation. (If one omits Gray's assumption that defended-against mental contents are necessarily drive derivatives, Gray's formulation here is virtually identical in structure to basic Control–Mastery theory formulations.) (See Wachtel, 2014, who cogently argues that psychoanalytic theories tend to overlook the role of contextual factors in psychological functioning.)

This dynamic interplay between the interpersonal and the intrapsychic is somewhat more complex. For the determinants of the expected and sometimes experienced negative reaction from the other may include a complex combination of one's projections, cues emitted by the other, and one's idiosyncratic construals of those cues. The point I want to emphasize here is the contrast between the idea of defense in terms of deeply buried repressed unconscious mental contents and the conception of defense in terms of fleetingly available mental contents that are not communicated to the other and are not further articulated to oneself. I think a good part of our clinical work is concerned with phenomena at this preconscious level of awareness.

To return to the case of Lucy R., there are aspects of her experience that Freud notes, but does not make much of, and that should be further addressed. We know that Lucy R. harbors the fantasy that her employer has romantic feelings toward her and the wish that eventually he will offer to marry her. Freud tells Lucy R. in this regard, "And then we must remember the sensitiveness you now feel towards the servants, after having lived with them peacefully for years. You're afraid of their having some inkling of your hopes and making fun of you" (p. 117). And Lucy R. states: "People would laugh at me if they had any idea of it" (p. 117). It would be quite surprising if Lucy R.'s fear that people would laugh at her were they to have some inkling of her hopes and fantasies did not also extend to her analyst and did not play a role in Lucy R.'s failure to communicate these hopes and fantasies to Freud, even though they were just below the surface. However, Freud does not address this issue.

I do not want to suggest a sharp dichotomy between what one tells oneself and what one tells others or that one is fully aware of certain thoughts and feelings, but hesitates in a deliberative fashion to communicate them to others although it is, of course, commonplace to think and feel certain things that, for a number of reasons, one deliberately decides not to communicate. However, that is not always the case. The interpersonal context can influence not only what one will say to another, but what one will say to oneself, that is, what one will permit oneself to think and feel, based on implicit judgments of how the other will likely react. (See Mead's (1934) seminal idea that even in thinking, one implicitly addresses a generalized other.)

### *Defense against mentalizing*

The interpersonal aspect of defense is also seen in Fonagy et al.'s (2002) hypothesis that the failure to mentalize is directed not only against one's own thoughts and feelings, but also against knowing or examining the other's thoughts and feelings. As Fonagy et al. (2002) suggest, this defense is motivated by the sensed danger that a clear awareness of the other's thoughts and feelings in relation to oneself would be too painful to experience. One sees inferential evidence of the operation of this defense in the parental idealization that is an important criterion for the avoidant–dismissive attachment classification on the Adult Attachment Interview (AAI) (George, Kaplan, & Main, 1984). The evidence that such idealization is defensive is provided by two sets of facts: (1) the association between avoidant–dismissive attachment and parental rejection; and (2) the inability of the narrator to provide concrete instantiations of interactions with parents that support the idealization and/or to provide specific episodes that contradict the general idealization.

## Are defences adaptive or maladaptive?

### *The maladaptive nature of defense*

Repression was viewed by Freud in his early writings as pathogenic in a number of ways. In his early formulation of defense, in particular, repression, it was seen as playing a causal role in psychopathology, namely, hysteria. Indeed, as the term "defense hysteria" (Freud, 1894, p. 47) suggests, hysteria was seen as being brought about by the repression of ideas incompatible with the ego. According to Freud

(Breuer & Freud, 1893–1895, p. 9), because the "quota of affect" accompanying certain ideas cannot be discharged due to repression, the affect remains in a strangulated state and is 'converted' into somatic hysterical symptoms. Also, according to Freud, insofar as a mental content is repressed, it becomes *isolated* from the rest of the personality and functions as a powerful pathogen. This basic idea that a mental content isolated from the rest of the personality functions as a pathogen is also prominent in Janet's and Charcot's writings. In his discussion of hysteria, Charcot refers to "a coherent group of associated ideas, which become lodged in the mind in the manner of a parasite, remaining isolated from all the rest" (as cited in Macmillan, 1991, pp. 64–65). And Janet dramatically writes:

> One would have to go through all the mental pathology and part of the physical pathology to show the disturbances produced by an idea excluded from personal consciousness . . . The idea, like a virus, develops in a corner of the personality inaccessible to the subject, works subconsciously, and brings about all disorders of hysteria and of mental disease.
>
> (Ellenberger, 1970, p. 149)

Echoing Charcot's reference to a parasite, Freud (Breuer & Freud, 1893–1895) writes that although repression succeeds in freeing the ego from a contradiction, "it has burdened itself with a mnemic symbol lodged in consciousness like a sort of parasite" (p. 49).

Other pathogenic consequences of repression that Freud (1915b) later identifies include depletion of the ego because repression requires a "constant expenditure of energy" (p. 151) and the fact that repression of instinctual wishes endows them with increased power in the individual's fantasy life. He writes with regard to the latter: the "repressed instinct-presentation . . . develops in a more unchecked and luxuriant fashion. It ramifies like a fungus, so to speak, in the dark and takes on extreme forms of expressions" that are anxiety-provoking "due to the way in which they reflect an extraordinary strength of instinct. This illusory strength of instinct is the result of an uninhibited development of it in phantasy and of the damming-up consequent on lack of real satisfaction" (p. 149).

As I have noted elsewhere (Eagle, 2011a):

> This passage is . . . one of few occasions in which Freud suggests that the experienced "strength of instinct" may be partly illusory, the result of a fantasy that is unchecked and not exposed to the light of reality because it has been subject to repression.
>
> (p. 13)

This idea of the *illusory* strength of instinct does not fit well with Freud's basic metapsychological assumption that the primary 'inner' source of the real not fantasied danger is that of the ego being overwhelmed with excessive excitation, the source of which is instincts. It is, after all, this basic assumption that led Anna Freud (1966) to posit the "id's primary antagonism to the ego" (p. 157) and to attribute at least certain forms of psychosis to the ego being overwhelmed by the strength of instinct.

## *The adaptive function of defense*

Although early on Freud focused on the pathogenic consequences of repression (and, by implication, of other similar defences), his theory of defenses continued to develop and included adaptive functions of defense. Indeed, a hint of the adaptive aspect of repression is already present in Freud's early writings. Recall Freud's (Breuer & Freud, 1893–1895) observation that although repression burdens the ego with a parasite-like mnemic symbol lodged in consciousness, it succeeds in freeing the ego from a contradiction. In its latter function, repression *protects* the individual from the conscious experience of being driven by contradictory aspects of himself or herself, that is, by inner conflict. Thus, from early on and in rudimentary form, the logic of Freud's formulation of defense identifies its benefits as well as its costs, its adaptive as well as its maladaptive consequences.

The adaptive aspects of defense are also implicit in Freud's (1896) emphasis on the return of the repressed as a consequence of *failure* of defense as the critical factor in the development of neurosis. Although repression itself, he writes, leads to "the formation of a primary symptom" (p. 222), it is when "the repressed ideas return, . . . [that] new symptoms are formed which are those of the illness proper" (p. 222). As Freud (1950[1892–1899]) also notes, the symptoms of the "illness proper" are compromise formations between the forces of repression and the pressures of the repressed. Strachey observes in a footnote that this account "might be called the standard formula for the development of a neurosis" that "is implied in discussions of neurosis throughout Freud's writings, even in quite late ones" (Freud 1896, p. 222). One may sum up Freud's view by saying that although repression exacts a cost, it also protects the individual from conscious experience of anxiety and other negative consequences. Indeed, it is the failure of repression that is the critical factor in neurosis. As we will see, the costs and benefits of repressive defenses are a focus of much empirical research.

Cramer (2006) writes that "defense mechanisms are part of normal development – in fact, are essential to normal development" (p. 10). She cites Freud's (1937) comment that it is "doubtful whether the ego could do without them altogether during its development" (p. 237). Cramer then distinguishes between "the use of defenses within a normative frequency [which] is essential for daily healthy adaptation" and an "unusually heavy reliance on defense mechanisms [which] may signal psychopathology" (p. 10). She also distinguishes between "some forms of defense [that] fall outside the range of normality, whereas other forms are normatively appropriate" (p. 10). The conception of defenses as adaptive and normative is further illustrated by the following two comments: "Defenses are phenomena serving to protect the integrity of ego organization. Thus, their formation is implicitly one of adaptation" (Loewenstein, 1967, p. 800). "We can regard the defense mechanisms as being directed towards the maintenance of well-being, rather than specifically directed against the emergence of anxiety" (Sandler & Joffe, 1967, p. 513).

One of the issues that arises with regard to the adaptiveness of defense is the *kind* of defense the individual employs. As we will see, distinction is made between immature and mature defenses (e.g., denial versus intellectualization or splitting versus repression), with the implication that immature defenses are more pathogenic. However, as we will also see, the *context* of defense is extremely important in assessing its pathogenicity. A defense, such as denial, may be pathogenic in one context and quite adaptive in another context.

## Freud on defense and society

Freud also gives a prominent role to the adaptive aspects of repression not only in regard to intrapsychic functioning, but also in his formulation of the relationship between the individual and society, in particular, in his account of what we understand as the socialization process. He writes that "civilization has been built up at the cost of the sexual trends which, being inhibited by society, are partly, it is true, repressed but have partly been made usable for other aims" (Freud, 1933, p. 110) (Freud is referring here to sublimation). He also observes that "what we have come to see about the sexual instincts, applies equally and still more to the other ones, the aggressive instincts" (p. 110). In *Civilization and its Discontents*, Freud (1930) writes that "it is impossible to overlook the extent to which civilization is built up upon a renunciation of instinct . . . (by suppression, repression, or some other means?) of powerful instincts" (p. 97).

It is interesting to observe that in the context of socialization, the function of defense is not limited to the intrapsychic one of protecting the individual from anxiety and other negative consequences (e.g., threats to one's self-image), but also includes the enabling of the adequate functioning of society and civilization through the repression of 'untamed' instincts. Further, the frequent instigator of defense, the superego, is a structure comprised of internalized societal prohibitions and values that have been transmitted through the family. One can say that whereas the intrapsychic function of defense is to protect the self or ego, the societal function of defense is, so to speak, to protect society, or, at least, make it possible for society to exist and function. This latter function of defense rests on the assumption that there is an inherent incompatibility between the individual – or at least the individual's sexual and aggressive impulses – and society. Without this assumption, there is little reason to focus on the societal function of defense or to provide a prominent place for defense in formulations of the socialization process (see Marcuse, 1966) for an extended discussion of the relationship among instincts, repression and civilization).

Let me turn next to empirical research on defensive processes.

## Research on defenses

### *Studies on repression*

There are an enormous number of empirical studies on defense in the experimental psychology literature. Much of the early work, which focused on attempting to demonstrate repression in the experimental laboratory, had very little relationship to how repression was understood in psychoanalytic theory and was therefore deservedly ignored by psychoanalytic clinicians and theorists. Experimental tests of repression included studies such as determining whether nonsense syllables associated with mild electric shock were more poorly remembered than nonsense syllables not associated with mild electric shock (Levinger & Clark, 1961).

In 1974, Holmes wrote that after years of research, no experimental evidence emerged demonstrating the existence of repression. And in 1991, he wrote that nothing had emerged that would lead him to change his verdict. And in a more recent paper entitled "Does repression exist?", Rofé (2008) reviews and evaluates the evidence for the following aspects of repression: (1) repression of memory for traumatic events (e.g., sexual abuse); (2) the pathogenic effects of repression (e.g., development of neurosis); (3) "the existence of a dynamic and sophisticated unconscious entity" necessitated by the concept of repression (p. 72); and (4) the therapeutic effects of lifting repression. Rofé concludes that the preponderance of the evidence does not support any of the above claims regarding repression.

Although Rofé's conclusions may be warranted by the evidence he cites, there are a number of problems with Rofé's critique. One such problem is Rofé's exclusive emphasis on repression of *memory for traumatic events*. The fact is that following Freud's earliest papers, it is repression of ideas associated with forbidden wishes, desires, and fantasies that is given primary clinical and theoretical attention. Rofé is aware of this fact. He writes: "Some investigators claim that studies that examine the memory component are irrelevant for evaluating the psychoanalytic concept of repression, as S. Freud (1915a) altered the focus of repression from memory to the inhibition of instinct" (p. 64). He also cites Fonagy's (1999) observation that "Some still appear to believe that the recovery of memory is part of the therapeutic action of the treatment. There is no evidence and in my view to cling to this idea is damaging to the field" (p. 215). Nevertheless, Rofé defends his focus on memory for traumatic events "because in the recent years the debate regarding the existence of repression has been focused almost entirely on the motivation of forgetting trauma" (p. 64). The debate to which Rofé is referring is mainly the false memory debate. But if the findings generated by studies on motivation for forgetting trauma are not most directly relevant to the question of the existence of repression, the fact that that issue has been the focus of the debate is beside the point. It has been a misplaced focus – somewhat like the drunkard who looks for his lost keys where the light is rather than where he lost the keys.

The other limitation of Rofé's argument has to do with the question of ecological validity. As Erdelyi and Goldberg (1979) have observed, not every psychological phenomenon can be successfully demonstrated in the experimental laboratory. That a particular phenomenon cannot be demonstrated in this way hardly means that it does not exist. To make this assumption is not science but scientism – as is the carrying out of studies that are based on operational definitions of concepts that have little ecological validity insofar as they bear little relationship to either real-life phenomena or the theory from which the concepts are taken (See Kazdin, 2006).

The limitations of Rofé's arguments notwithstanding, in my view, there is little strong evidence that repression, defined as an unconscious process (1) regularly occurs in relation to conflctual impulses and desires. As I have argued, I believe that there is a continuum between suppression and repression rather than a clear distinction; (2) that the effects of repression and other related defences are largely pathogenic; and (3) that the main mechanism of therapeutic action consists in lifting repression. With regard to the issue of the continuum between suppression and repression, in a critique of Erdelyi's (e.g., 2006) view that repression should be understood as voluntary forgetting, McNally (2006) writes that "Freud did not earn his reputation as a bold and original thinker by blandly affirming that people sometimes try not to think about unpleasant things" (p. 526). The import and significance of McNally's statement is more rhetorical than substantive. The issues here do not have to do with how Freud earned his reputation for boldness and originality or how blandly versus excitedly Freud affirmed this or that. The substantive issues have to do with how we go about disavowing aspects of oneself – what Stone (1997) refers to as the "otherness of oneself" – and the impact of these disavowals, however, they come about, on our functioning and our sense of who we are.

More recent work on defense, including research on "repressive style" (which I will discuss later), does not suffer from the severe limitations of the early work on repression and, accordingly, has a great deal more of ecological validity. Although repression is not defined in precisely the way that Freud used the term, in recent work on "repressive style" and other related research, the way in which it is operationally defined has sufficient ecological validity to make the research meaningful to psychoanalytic theorists and clinicians. For one thing, rather than attempt to demonstrate repression in the experimental laboratory, – which often severely compromises ecological validity – more recent research focuses on more ecologically valid contexts such as therapeutic sessions or treats repression as a personality variable and studies correlates of individual differences in that variable.

Let me describe some representative examples of research on repression or, more accurately, on 'something like' repression. As noted in Chapter 2, Luborsky (1973) showed that the patient's "momentary forgetting" in therapeutic sessions was reliably preceded by contents independently judged to be conflictual and anxiety-provoking. Given the momentariness of the forgetting, this is hardly a cogent instance of repression in the sense of keeping mental contents out of consciousness over an extended period of time. Also, one can plausibly attribute the momentary forgetting to the disruptive effects of anxiety rather than to a motivated defense.

However, a plausible explanation is that momentary forgetting may be attributable to 'something like' repression.

Luborsky and his colleagues (Luborsky et al., 1990) carried out another study that is relevant to the question of the specific behaviors that underlie repression. Participants were presented with ten TAT-like pictures, some of which were sexual and aggressive in content. Various measures of the participants' defensive style were also independently obtained, based on the Rorschach Index of Repressive Style (RIRS) (Levine & Spivak, 1963, 1964), the Holzman Rorschach Measure of Repression (Gardner, Holzman, Klein, Linton, & Spence, 1959), and the Weinberger Questionnaire Measure of Repression (Weinberger, Schwartz, & Davidson, 1979). The results showed that the higher the score on the RIRS measure of repressive style, the less looking about in inspecting the pictures as measured by the scatter of eye fixations. This pattern was stronger for the sexual and aggressive pictures. The RIRS measure also correlated with less recall and postponment of recall for sexual pictures.

The above findings point to the wisdom of Singer and Sincoff's (1990) suggestion that the term "repression" be broadened – to describe "systematic styles of avoiding thought or self-awareness of potentially troublesome life issues or who actively avoid situations that might remind them of such issues" (p. 494). As they note, in processing and responding to both the external environment and inner cues, we select and filter what occupies our conscious experience. The strategies for selecting and filtering include "selective attention, avoidance of labelling, avoidance of reminiscence and rehearsal, distraction through physical and social activity, and ruminative thoughts about trivialities" (p. 494). One can undoubtedly add additional strategies to this list.

As Singer and Sincoff also note, with repeated use these strategies become habitual and automatized so that they are carried out without awareness and without a sense of volitional intention. One can say that these strategies are unconscious, not primarily in a dynamic sense, but in the sense that all habitual and automatized activity is unconscious. However, although this may be true, I do not think it is the full story. There is also, I believe, a motivated investment in keeping the strategies automatic and unexamined. I think this is something of what Fingarette has in mind when he writes about the individual not only not articulating or spelling out the project in which he or she is engaged, but also not articulating or spelling out his or her *policy* to not spell out or articulate this strategy. Many defensive strategies are sustained both by their habitual and automatized nature as well as the implicit and motivated policy to not reflect on or examine the role they play in one's life. In short, although the unconscious status of some defensive strategies may, in part, be attributable to habit and automatization, it is also sustained by keeping them habitual and automatic, that is, by keeping them out of conscious awareness and failing to reflect on them.

However, it is possible that at least some mental contents that are kept out of conscious awareness through the use of automatic defensive strategies are unconscious not primarily as a consequence of repression, that is, of an active banishment from consciousness, but as a result of habitual strategies such as restricted attention (as in the Luborsky et al., 1990 study), keeping oneself constantly distracted, keeping experiences vague and not spelled out, and so on.

### *Defense and the rebound effect*

Freud (1915b) stated that repression requires a "persistent expenditure of force" (p. 151) to keep the repressed material from reaching consciousness. He attributed this to the individual's need to deal with the constant pressure of the repressed impulse to reach consciousness and gain control of motility. An interesting additional explanation of why one must engage in sustained mental effort to keep suppressed material from conscious experience is provided by the research of Wegner (e.g., 1994) on suppressing thoughts. In brief, the efforts to suppress such thoughts paradoxically lowers their activation threshold, with the result that one needs to engage in a continuing effort to keep them from occupying conscious experience.

## Research on "repressive style"

"Repressive style" is defined in the following way: (1) report of low anxiety on an anxiety questionnaire; (2) high score on defensiveness as measured by the Crowne-Marlowe Social Desirability Scale (Crowne & Marlow, 1960) – that is, denial of unpleasant and anti-social thoughts; and (3) despite report of low anxiety, a high level of physiological arousal, particularly under conditions of stress (Asendorpf & Scherer, 1983; Weinberger et al., 1979). Tomarken and Davidson (1994) have characterized individuals with a repressive style as showing an "impaired memory for negative self-relevant feedback . . . and a relative inability to consciously perceive negative affective stimuli under specific conditions" (p. 340).

Other measures of repressive style have included clinical judgments based on interviews (Vaillant, 1976); the Repression-Sensitization Scale (Byrne, Barry, & Nelson, 1963); Holzman Rorschach Measure of Repression and Isolation (Holzman, 1962); Rorschach Index of Repressive Style (RIRS) (Levine & Spivak, 1964); and Weinberger Questionnaire Measure of Repression (Weinberger, 1990). Some of the results that have emerged employing these different measures include repressors' poor recall of childhood memories (Davis, & Schwartz, 1986); later age of recalled childhood memories (Luborsky et al., 1990); less looking at sexual features of a stimulus (Luborsky et al., 1990); relative failure to retrieve words relevant to anger and fear (Davis, 1990); greater conventionality (Bonanno & Singer, 1990); better performance on a dichotic listening task, which requires shutting out information from the non-shadowed ear (Bonanno & Singer, 1990); and repressor patients' poorer retention of information related to lifestyle risk factors of heart attack (Shaw, Cohen, Doyle, & Palasky, 1985). These and other results suggest a pattern in which negative information, negative affect, and negative thoughts are less accessible to the conscious experience of those with a repressive style.[10]

## Costs and benefits of repression and avoidant defenses

Although much of the psychoanalytic literature focuses on the pathogenic aspects of repression, as noted above, from his earliest writings, Freud referred both to its benefits as well as its costs. To review, this is seen in a number of ways. For one thing, it is the return of the repressed rather than repression per se that is most closely tied to the eruption of psychopathology. Two, Freud (1894) points to the adaptive function of repression when he comments that when someone "decide(s) to forget an incompatible idea, the 'distressing affect' that is aroused by the 'occurrence of incompatibility' is no longer experienced" (p. 47). "However, although the ego has freed itself of a contradiction, it has burdened itself with a mnemic symbol 'lodged in consciousness', like a sort of parasite" (Freud, 1894, p. 49). Three, although repression relieves the individual of distressing affect, it may be conducive to the development of somatic symptoms seen in hysteria. And four, the costs and benefits are reflected in the facts that society necessitates "restrictions and repression of the sexual instinct" (Freud, 1913, p. 209), the cost of which is an inevitable degree of neurosis.

I want to emphasize again the fundamental point that according to the psychoanalytic conception of defense, although certain costs may be exacted, when defense is intact it serves to shield the individual from the conscious experience of anxiety and other distressing affects. And when defenses fail, these distressing affects erupt into consciousness. So, the evidence that repressive defenses are associated with costs and benefits is entirely compatible with the psychoanalytic theory of defense. It will be important to keep this conclusion in mind in a later discussion of this issue.

Let me now turn to some of that evidence. The benefits of a repressive style include less experience of conscious anxiety and other negative affects and a decreased likelihood of being diagnosed with a psychiatric disorder (Lane, Quinlan, Schwartz, Walker, & Zeitlin, 1990). These results are congruent with the psychoanalytic formulation that when defenses are intact they succeed in warding off anxiety and other negative affects associated with psychiatric disturbance. These results are also consistent with some findings on the relationship between attachment patterns and psychopathology. Thus, Adam, Sheldon-Keller, and West (1995) reported that individuals with an avoidant attachment pattern that bears a strong family resemblance to repressive style are at a decreased risk (compared to those with an enmeshed/preoccupied attachment pattern) for suicide attempts, and presumably also for experiencing the intense affective distress associated with suicide attempts.

The costs of a repressive style that have been reported include a decreased immune response under stress (Schwartz, 1990), heightened systolic blood pressure (King, Taylor, Albright, & Haskell, 1990), increased salivary cortisol levels (Brown et al., 1996), greater serum glucose levels (Jamner, Schwartz, & Leigh, 1988), and a heightened susceptibility to a variety of somatic conditions, including hypertension and ulcers (Schwartz, 1990).

Why should use of a repressive style entail somatic costs? One account identifies heightened autonomic activity associated with the inhibition of negative affect that is characteristic of repressive style (Gross & Levenson, 1993; Koriat Melkman, Averill, & Lazarus, 1972). For example, Esterling, Antoni, Kumar, & Schneiderman (1990) write "that to inhibit ongoing behavior, thoughts, and feelings, physiological work must be performed" that "may serve as a low level chronic stressor which has the potential of long-term cumulative damage" (p. 507). Similarly, Schore (1994) speculates that a "chronic stressful state of [both] heightened excitation and heightened inhibition . . . may characterize the psychobiology of repression" (p. 325). To be noted here is the similarity of these accounts to Freud's (1915b) hypothesis that repression entails a "persistent expenditure of force" (p. 151).

The above neat picture of the costs and benefits of repressive style is upset by other findings suggesting that repressive and avoidant defenses are associated mainly with benefits and show little evidence of costs. Thus, Coifman et al. (2007) reported that repressive coping in both a bereaved and non-bereaved sample was associated with *fewer* somatic complaints; and in the bereaved sample was associated with fewer symptoms of psychopathology. They argue that their own and similar findings contradict the presumably Freudian claim that defensive avoidance of negative affect is maladaptive and conclude that the evidence "suggests the idea that repressive coping may serve as a protective buffer from emotional disorders, particularly in the context of adverse life events" (p. 755). These findings appear to be especially challenging insofar as increased somatic susceptibilities is assumed by Freudian and other theories to be one of the maladaptive costs of repressive coping.

Other studies, however, have reported findings that seem to be at odds with Coifman et al.'s (2007) findings. Thus, Cousineau and Shedler (2006) reported that individuals who show a discrepancy between explicit self-report and implicit measures of well-being and distress – a pattern characteristic of repressive style – show a significantly greater number of visits to the university health center and significantly greater number of verified illnesses, as indicated by the attending nurse's judgment that the health problems reported were sufficiently serious to warrant a consultation with a physician.

How can one account for these apparently discrepant findings? There are a number of possibilities. One possibility is that they are due to the different ways of measuring somatic symptoms. In the Coifman et al. (2007) study, data on somatic symptoms were obtained from a self-report check list, whereas in the Cousineau and Shedler (2006) study, health status was objectively assessed through independent records maintained by the campus health center. Given the repressor's tendency to avoid negative affect as well as memory of negative events, it may be that the self-report check list responses are an under-estimation of actual somatic problems. Contrastingly, the measures of somatic problems, such as immune response, blood pressure, etc., employed in the earlier discussed repressive style research, as well as visits to the campus health center, are objective. Hence, they are less likely to be 'contaminated' by the individual's defense style. At present, we await further clarification of these discrepant findings.

## Attachment patterns and defense

The story gets even more complex. An avoidant attachment pattern or strategy can be thought of as a defensive strategy insofar as it succeeds in banishing from consciousness painful thoughts and feelings related to attachment needs and experiences. Hence, research on the correlates and consequences of avoidant attachment is quite relevant to understanding the costs and benefits of defense. The defensive function of an avoidant attachment pattern is seen in the evidence that individuals high in avoidance show limited access to negative traits (Mikulincer, 1995); high levels of self-reported self-esteem (Bartholomew & Horowitz, 1991; Brennan & Morris, 1997); tend to inflate positive self-appraisal in response to threatening events (Mikulincer, 1998); and tend to project negative self-traits on to others (Mikulincer & Horesch, 1999).

There is also evidence that avoidant attachment individuals are more successful at suppressing negative thoughts as well as their physiological accompaniments. Thus, Fraley and Shaver (1997) reported that avoidant individuals not only showed a weaker rebound effect when asked to suppress thoughts about a painful breakup of a close relationship, but also a lower galvanic skin response (GSR). This last finding is especially noteworthy insofar as it suggests that, in contrast to the findings on "repressive style," avoidant individuals do not necessarily show dissociation between verbal report and physiological response and may not show the 'cost' of physiological activation associated with keeping painful thoughts out of consciousness. Of course, it is possible that physiological indices other than GSR might reveal evidence of physiological activation. For example, Sroufe and Waters (1977) found increased heart rate associated with an avoidant/dismissive attachment pattern. It is also possible, that at least some avoidant individuals might show a pattern more similar to the repressive style pattern. Further research is needed in this area.

The above findings speak to what one may refer to as the adaptive benefits of an avoidant pattern, as seen in high levels of conscious self-esteem, positive self-appraisal, greater ability to suppress negative thoughts apparently without incurring a physiological cost, although there are inconsistent findings in this area. The adaptive benefits of an avoidant pattern are also reflected in the frequent finding that compared to a preoccupied attachment pattern, individuals with an avoidant and secure attachment pattern are generally more difficult to distinguish from each other on various measures of adaptive functioning. This suggests that at least within a certain range, an avoidant pattern reflects relatively intact defenses whereas a preoccupied pattern reflects a relative failure of defense (Eagle, 2011a). After all, whatever else it may entail, the function of defense is to present the conscious experience of distressing feelings and thoughts. For the most part, avoidant individuals are better able to achieve this than preoccupied individuals.

There is also evidence, however, regarding the costs or maladaptive aspects of an avoidant pattern. Thus, Mikulincer, Horesh, Eilati, and Kotler (1999) found that an avoidant pattern was positively associated with severity of psychiatric symptoms among Israeli settlers living in territory controlled by the Palestine Authority. This suggests that the costs and benefits of an avoidant pattern may be a function of contextual factors such as degree of stress and cognitive–affective demands placed on the individual. And indeed, Mikulincer et al. (2004) carried out a series of studies to test the hypothesis that the capacity of avoidant individuals to block conscious experience of distressing thought will be influenced by degree of cognitive load imposed on them. In Study 1, participants were asked to think of a painful breakup and write a brief description of it, followed by a 5-minute stream of consciousness task. Half of the participants were assigned to the suppression condition (don't think about the relationship) and half were given no instructions. All the participants were asked to place a checkmark every time they thought about the relationship and all were given a Stroop task consisting of separation, neutral, and negative words under low cognitive load (repeat from memory a one digit number) and high cognitive load (repeat from memory a seven digit number).

Of the many findings reported, I will focus on those that are most germane in the current context. Employing the Experience of Close Relationships (ECR) measure (Brennan, Clark, & Shaver, 1998), Mikulincer, Dolev, and Shaver (2004) reported the following results:

1. Although low avoidance subjects reported fewer separation thoughts in the suppression versus control condition, high avoidance subjects reported fewer separation thoughts in both suppression and control conditions. In other words, even when not instructed to suppress separation thoughts, they did so anyway.
2. In the Stroop task,[11] as evidenced by the longer reaction times, avoidant subjects showed greater access of separation words under high than low cognitive load conditions, which suggests that an increased cognitive load reduces the effectiveness of the avoidant defense.

Further evidence that a high cognitive load compromises the effectiveness of an avoidant defense was found in Study 2. In a suppression thought condition, avoidance was associated with longer reaction times on the Stroop to negative self traits in the high versus low cognitive load condition. The results of Study 1 and 2 taken together suggest that whereas under low cognitive load conditions, an avoidant defense may succeed in keeping 'negative' mental contents (i.e., painful separation thoughts and negative self traits) from consciousness, it is less successful under conditions of high cognitive load. These findings are congruent with Freud's (1915b) hypothesis that repression (and, by implication, other avoidant defense strategies) entails a "persistent expenditure of force" (p. 151). Thus, whereas the "expenditure of energy" required may not compromise the defense under conditions of low cognitive load – the defense may appear to operate automatically – the 'extra' effort required under a high cognitive load condition appears to weaken the defense, as evidenced by the greater access of negative thoughts in the Stroop task and their more frequent appearance in consciousness.

I have devoted all this space to the Mikulincer et al. (1999) study because it addresses interesting and important issues having to do with the nature of defense. Most importantly, their findings suggest that in assessing the operation and consequences of defense, one should take account of the context in which the defense is operating. For good theoretical reasons, Mikulincer et al. (1999) focus on low versus high cognitive load. However, as we have seen in the earlier discussion, there are undoubtedly other contexts (e.g., serious illness; dire external circumstances) that are likely to influence the operation of defense.

## Empirical research on different defense mechanisms

Baumeister et al. (1998) have written one of the more interesting and useful papers on empirical research on defense mechanisms. They observe that modern personality and social psychology propose that defense mechanisms are directed not primarily to "disguis[ing] one's sexual and aggressive impulses," but rather are "designed to protect self-esteem" (p. 1082), an idea, they note, already suggested by Fenichel (1945). I would add that this idea is already present in Freud's early writings. Thus, in his early case histories (Breuer & Freud, 1893–1895), certain thoughts and feelings, including sexual ones, are defended against (repressed) because they violate the individual's moral standards and her sense of who she is.

Baumeister et al. (1998) summarize research on various defense mechanisms, including reaction formation, projection, displacement, undoing, sublimation, and denial. They report empirical evidence for reaction formation, undoing, denial, and a revised version of projection. Of special interest are the operational definitions of different defense mechanisms in the various studies and the findings that are interpreted as supporting or failing to support the existence of these defense mechanisms. Consider as an example, the defense of reaction formation, which Baumeister "loosely" defines "as a means of defending against esteem threat by exhibiting an exaggerated or extreme reaction in the opposite direction" (p. 1089). As examples of research on reaction formation, Baumeister et al. (1998) refer to a number of studies, including one in which homophobic men reported low levels of sexual arousal in response to observing videotapes of a homosexual scene, whereas their physiological responses were higher than non-homophobic men (Adams et al., 1996). In another study, white individuals who viewed themselves as nonprejudiced were given false physiological data suggesting that they were racist. When the participants left the study, they were approached by confederate White or Black panhandlers. Participants who were led to believe that they were racist gave significantly more money to the Black panhandler than participants who were not given the false information.

One can question whether the above behaviors and experimental situations capture reaction formation as it is understood in psychoanalytic theory – although the latter study seems to get close to it. However, by noting that they are "loosely" defining the concept, Baumeister et al. (1998) would likely argue that these studies capture something like reaction formation. The other question that arises is whether the participants in the above studies were entirely unaware of the motives for their defensive behaviors. That is, were the defensive motives for these behaviors unconscious, for some, a necessary feature of a "defense mechanism" (e.g., Cramer, 2006). This issue came up earlier in the chapter in a discussion of the work of Fingarette and Sartre, who conceptualize the self-deception inherent in defense in terms of not "spelling out" the meaning of their behavior rather than in terms of entirely unconscious mechanisms. In the context of the studies described by Baumeister et al. (1998), it is entirely possible – in my view likely – that the participants had at least a fleeting awareness of the defensive nature of their behavior. It certainly cannot be ruled out.

Baumeister et al. (1998) present an interesting discussion of the defense of projection. However, I am reserving discussion of projection for the discussion of the projective mode of thought, projection as a defense, and the concept of projective identification.

## Neural and physiological correlates of defense

During the era of perceptual defense research a number of studies demonstrated not only that the recognition thresholds of taboo words were higher than non-taboo words, but that prior to recognition, SCRs discriminated between taboo words and non-taboo words (e.g., McGinnies, 1949). As indicated by the term "perceptual defense," these findings were interpreted by some as reflecting the operation of defense in delaying the conscious recognition of threatening words. After about the 1960s, for a variety of reasons, perceptual defense studies came to a halt. (For a description of studies on perceptual defense, see Eriksen, 1954.)

With the advent of fMRI technology, there has been an explosion of research on neural correlates of psychological processes, including defensive processes. I will discuss a few representative studies. Most studies on neural correlates of repression have defined it in terms of fully conscious and voluntary suppression (e.g., Depue, Curran, & Banich, 2007), which makes it less relevant to psychoanalytic theory. In a recent study, in an attempt to investigate repression as it is understood in psychoanalytic theory, Schmeing et al. (2013) conceptualized it as an unconscious process that comes into play in relation to internal conflicts. In Study 1, they found that associations to words that were subsequently forgotten were accompanied by activation of the anterior cingulate cortex (ACC), increases in SCR, and longer reaction times (RTs). The authors interpret these findings as "consistent with the hypothesis that these associations were repressed because they elicited internal conflicts" (p. 1).

In Study 2, participants were instructed to associate the first three words that came to mind, followed by a period of free association to sentences that were either neutral, negative but unrelated to conflict, or related to "typical conflicts regarding desire for care versus autarchy or self-value" (p. 3). Compared to associations to non-conflict-related sentences, associations to conflict-related sentences were more likely to be forgotten and were accompanied by enhanced activation of the

ACC, deactivation of the hippocampus and hippocampal cortex, and increase in SCRs and RTs.

The authors conclude that "these results are consistent with the hypothesis that during repression, explicit memory systems are down-regulated by the anterior cingulate cortex" (p. 1) and further observe that "this pattern of results fits exactly to the psychodynamic theory of repression as a mechanism for avoiding conscious access to conflict-related material" (p. 9). As the authors note, it would be important to carry out similar research with stimuli that are designed to match participants' specific conflict areas.

In a fascinating single case study, Kanaan, Craig, Wessely, and David (2007) reported the case of a woman with an unexplained right-hand paralysis and with no recall of the stressful event that presumably played a role in the precipitation of the conversion disorder. Compared with an equally stressful event from the patient's past, cued recall of the repressed event "was associated with regional brain activations characteristic of emotional arousal, including the amygdala and right inferior frontal lobe," as well as "with decreased motor activity in the area corresponding to the subjectively paralyzed limb" (p. 202).

## Research on positive illusions

There is evidence that positive illusions, defined as falsely positive views, whether of one's medical condition or of one's personal abilities, are associated with greater physical and mental health as well as longevity (e.g., Taylor, 1989; Taylor, Kemeny, Reed, Bower, & Gruenewald, 2000; Taylor, Klein, Gruenewald, Gurung, & Fernandes-Taylor, 2003a; Taylor, Lerner, Sherman, Sage, & McDowell, 2003b). For example in one study, Taylor et al. (2000) found that HIV-positive "individuals who held positive illusions about the likely course of their illness remained asymptomatic longer than those who were more realistic about their condition" (Taylor et al., 2003a, p. 613). A good deal of the work on positive illusions deals, not only with responses to external trauma such as serious illness, but with illusory self-enhancement, that is, the tendency to view oneself in a more positive light than is objectively the case. In one study Taylor et al. (2003b) found that individuals with high self-enhancement, including illusory self-enhancement as defined by discrepancy between their own and a friend's ratings, "had lower cardiovascular responses to stress, more rapid cardiovascular recovery, and lower baseline cortisol levels" (p. 605).

There is conflicting evidence as to whether this sort of positive illusion is associated with measurable costs. For one thing, Taylor et al. (2003) failed to replicate the findings of Shedler, Mayman, and Manis (1993) that individuals who falsely present themselves in a positive light (i.e., as mentally healthy) show a heightened autonomic response to stress. Contrary to Shedler et al.'s (1993) findings, there were no differences on autonomic response between individuals clinically judged to be genuinely mentally healthy and those judged to report illusory (and presumably defensive) mental health. There is also evidence that positive illusions about oneself are a protective factor against experience of depression and that being realistic about oneself has been associated with proneness to depression, a pattern labelled "depressive realism" (Alloy & Abramson, 1988). However, it is important to note that there is evidence of a curvilinear relationship between positive illusions and adjustment in children (Brendgen, Vitaro, Turgeon, Poulin, & Wanner, 2004). Thus, only an optimal degree of positive illusions appear to be adaptive. Beyond that degree, positive illusions appear to be maladaptive.

Insofar as positive illusions can be seen as a form of defense in the service of maintaining self-esteem and avoiding negative affect, research on positive illusions is quite relevant to understanding the nature, function, and consequences of defense. In particular, the research on positive illusions is relevant to the issue of the adaptive versus maladaptive consequences of defense.

In seeming congruence with Taylor and her colleagues' findings, Freud (1917 [1915]) wrote with regard to individuals suffering from depression (melancholia):

> [I]t is merely that he has a keener eye for the truth than other people who are not melancholic . . . in his heightened self-criticism . . . it may be, so far as we know that he has come pretty near to understanding himself; we only wonder why a man has to be ill before he can be accessible to a truth of this kind.
>
> (p. 246)

Thus, like Taylor and her colleagues, Freud, too, seems to be saying that being utterly realistic about oneself is associated with depression and hence, is maladaptive.

In other contexts, such as in his discussion of the function of religion, he recognizes the role of illusion in protecting the individual from the experiences of fear and intolerable anxiety related to mortality. However, despite its comforts, Freud (1927) variously described religious beliefs as wishful "illusions" (p. 30), "the universal obsessional neurosis of humanity" (p. 43), a "narcotic" (p. 49), and a delusional expression of "psychical infantilism" (Freud 1930, p. 85). Thus, despite the comfort religion offers, Freud viewed it essentially as a mass neurotic failure to confront and accept reality. In the present context, one can understand Freud's view of religious beliefs as a massive, culturally shared defense designed to ward off intense anxiety (e.g., attendant upon dread of one's mortality). From Freud's psychoanalytic perspective, the ideal path of psychological development is to relinquish one's wishful and defensive infantile fantasies and become increasingly capable of accepting reality. A question raised by Freud's view is whether the goal of relinquishing defensive illusions that are comforting is a Weltanschauung presenting itself as a clinical aim (see Eagle, 2011).

Although like Taylor, Freud links depression to lack of illusions about oneself, given his attitudes toward illusions, including comforting illusions, he seems to be saying in *Mourning and Melancholia*, not that such lack of illusions *leads to* depression, but, rather that someone who is already depressed in reaction to loss, for example, is more likely to have a stark and unadorned view of himself or herself. In other words, in contrast to those who argue that being realistic about oneself or being without positive illusions plays a causal role in depression, Freud appears to reverse the causal direction by suggesting that the state of depression itself in response to loss entails the stripping away of illusions about oneself.[12] That is, when in that state, one assiduously directs one's attention to one's faults and shortcomings.

This account, in effect, offers an explanation of the relationship between depression and 'self realism' as a form of *state dependent cognition* (e.g. Bower, 1981). That is, when in a depressed mood or state, one selectively focuses on negative aspects of oneself as well as of the world. Furthermore, a central motive for such self-scrutiny is not the quest for self-knowledge and honest self-appraisal but *self-punishment*. Thus, Freud's recognition that self-knowledge can be used as a weapon against oneself does not threaten the legitimacy of self-knowledge as a marker of mental health as well as a central therapeutic aim.

There is some evidence that at least partly supports Freud's view. As Persons and Miranda (1992) argue, there is evidence against the theory that it is only or primarily stable trait-like beliefs that predispose the individual to depression. Rather, the evidence suggests that although there may, indeed, be stable cognitions that predispose individuals to depression, these cognitions "are accessible only during negative mood states" (p. 485). Persons and Miranda refer to this formulation as the "mood-state hypothesis," which, of course, can be understood as a variant of state dependent cognition and affect. In support of this hypothesis, Abramson, Metalsky, and Alloy (1989) found that compared to nonvulnerable subjects, vulnerable subjects reported increased negative mood and increased dysfunctional attitudes after viewing a negative mood induction film. Interestingly and unexpectedly, nonvulnerable subjects who reported increased negative mood after viewing the film reported decreased dysfunctional attitudes. In another study, Miranda, Persons, and Byers (1990) found that endorsement of dysfunctional beliefs varied with spontaneous mood fluctuations in both depressed psychiatric patients and a sample of asymptomatic patients. Further, reports of dysfunctional beliefs varied as a function of mood states in subjects who had experienced a depressive episode, but not in subjects who had never been depressed.

In further support of the hypothesis that dysfunctional attitudes related to depression are mood-state dependent, Miranda and Persons (1988) found that although subjects who reported previous episodes of depression showed more dysfunctional attitudes than subjects without a history of depression, "this effect occurred only for subjects who were in a negative mood state when their dysfunctional attitudes were assessed" (p. 76). These results indicate that although individuals with a history of depression are predisposed to have dysfunctional attitudes, these attitudes become manifest mainly when the individual is in a negative mood state (i.e., already depressed). As we have seen in the Abramson et al. (1989) study, individuals who do not have a history of depression do not show increased dysfunctional attitudes even when in a negative mood state. Indeed, they show a decrease in dysfunctional attitudes. In short, it is clear that the link between depression and dysfunctional attitudes is the product of an interaction between a predisposition to dysfunctional attitudes and negative mood states. The important point here is that individuals with a history of depression do not chronically express manifest dysfunctional attitudes and cognitions, but rather do so when already in a negative mood state. These findings suggest that the model in which depression is causally linked to chronic dysfunctional attitudes is an overly simplistic one; and tend to at least partly support Freud's (1917[1915]) claim that once depressed, one tends to generate dysfunctional attitudes about oneself.

## *Denial and situational context*

The costs and benefits of avoidant defenses as well as the role of context are shown in the finding that, compared to low deniers, coronary patients scoring high on the Levine Denial of Illness Scale spent fewer days in intensive care and showed fewer signs of cardiac dysfunction during the acute period of their illness. However, compared to low deniers, high deniers fared more poorly in the year following discharge from the hospital as shown by their greater noncompliance with medical recommendations and requiring more days of rehospitalization. In other words, denial was adaptive in one context, the acute period of illness, and maladaptive during another context, the period of recovery (Levine et al., 1987).

As a striking example of the importance of context and type of external trauma, consider the consequences of denial in different situations. As has been reported by survivors, the denial of one's extremely slim chances of survival in the concentration camps of Nazi Germany was an absolute necessity if one was to have any chance of survival. However, denial of other more subtle realities in the concentration camps such as the consequences of reporting illness or denial by escaping into a world of fantasy, were virtually death sentences.

The importance of context is also illustrated on a less extreme level by the evidence that whereas denial of the seriousness of one's illness following a heart attack or coronary bypass surgery is adaptive, as indicated by fewer days in intensive care and fewer signs of cardiac dysfunction, it is highly maladaptive in the year following hospitalization, as expressed in greater medical noncompliance and more days of rehospitalization. Esteve et al. (1992) reported that among myocardial infarction patients, high deniers "showed less anxiety and depressive reactions in the coronary unit and one month later, and also presented less psychopathology in general" (p. 491).

The above findings reveal an interesting pattern of the costs and benefits of denial. Whereas short-term denial of the seriousness of one's illness bestows benefits in the form of reduced anxiety and depression, in the longer term insofar as it is associated with relative failure to take the necessary lifestyle steps to reduce one's future risks of a heart attack, denial exacts serious costs. Interestingly, a low level of denial seems to be associated mainly with costs and few benefits. Thus, in a 3–5 year follow-up study, Havik and Maeland (1988) found that a low level of denial "was associated with more problems related to work, sexual life and physical activities, and with a higher mortality rate" (p. 145). Higher levels of denial of the impact of the illness were associated with better emotional outcome and were weakly associated with increased mortality.

In the course of working on this chapter, I came across a *New York Times* Sunday Review article about a brilliant US major who sustained multiple head injuries in Iraq. As the author of the article writes, "Yet Richard's intellect almost exacerbates his suffering for it better equips him to monitor his mental deterioration" (Kristof, 2012, p. 1). As is the case with the characters in *The Iceman Cometh* and *The Wild Duck*, one cannot help feeling that Major Richards would be better off with the illusions and defenses against awareness of his condition described by Taylor and her colleagues.

As Lazarus (1983) notes, what is referred to as denial is not a unitary and simple concept. For example, there is a legitimate distinction between denial of the terminal nature of one's illness and avoidance of talking and thinking about it. Also, denial can be partial rather than complete. For example, many patients who appear to deny that they are dying do in fact seem to appear to know at some level (Weisman, 1972). There is also a distinction between first-order denial of facts and second-order denial of the implications of these facts (Weisman, 1972). As Lazarus also points out, the adaptive versus maladaptive value of denial varies with whether anything, such as effective action, can be gained by awareness and realistic assessment. For example, he notes the usefulness of denial and questions the value of realistic self-assessment for stroke victims for whom little can be done.

One can observe the phenomenon of 'partial denial,' as well as its adaptive value, following the sudden death of a loved one. In certain respects, the bereaved person appears to deny the reality of the loss, as manifested in such behaviours as 'hearing' his or her spouse's footsteps or expecting him or her to be coming home from work. However, at another level, the individual does not deny the reality of the loss. Thus, there is both denial and non-denial. The adaptive value of the 'partial denial' is to allow the bereaved individual to titrate the full awareness of the loss, thus making coping more possible. (See Freud's (1940[1938]) discussion of avowing and disavowing at the same time, thus "splitting of the ego in the process of defense" – the title of one of Freud's late essays.)

Nowhere is the defense of 'partial denial' more apparent than in "denial of death" (Becker, 1973). We all know that we are mortal and that death is inevitable. And yet, most of us live our lives as if this were not the case. At the very least, we engage in systematic and enduringly avoidant 'not thinking about it.' It is interesting, as Hoffman (1998) has observed, that psychoanalytic theory has little to say regarding anxiety about death; and when it does comment on it, it interprets it as an expression of a presumably more fundamental fear, such as separation anxiety or castration anxiety. It is as if psychoanalytic theory itself engages in denial regarding the reality of anxiety about death. Perhaps this is so because unlike separation anxiety or castration anxiety, there is little either psychoanalytic theory or practice has to offer in relation to this fundamental source of anxiety.

## Changes in defense and psychotherapy

As we have seen, analysis of defense is viewed as a major ingredient of therapeutic action, particularly in classical and ego psychology psychoanalytic approaches. An important question that arises is to what degree defenses change in psychoanalytic and psychodynamic treatment as well as in the course of development. A number of studies have investigated this question in a number of ways. Vaillant (1976) followed a sample of 95 men for 30 years and found defensive functioning matured over this period of time without any therapeutic intervention. Ablon, Carlson, and Goodwin (1974) reported that a large percentage of patients with primary affective disorders who were hospitalized for an average of four months and treated with medication and psychotherapy showed decreasing use of immature defenses and increasing use of mature defenses. Cramer and Blatt (1990) reported a significant decrease in the use of denial, projection, and identification after 15 months of inpatient treatment in a psychoanalytically oriented hospital facility. Akkerman, Carr, and Lewin (1992) reported a significant decrease in the use of immature defenses accompanying recovery from depression among inpatients. Perry (2001) found an improvement in defensive functioning following twelve months of once or twice a week psychodynamic psychotherapy, a finding also reported by Perry and Bond (2012) after six months of psychodynamic psychotherapy.

In a study of long-term psychodynamic psychotherapy, Perry and Bond (2012) approached the question of defensive functioning by conceptualizing defenses hierarchically based on their level of adaptiveness and then determining patients' shifts in the level of adaptiveness of their defenses as an outcome of treatment. Examples of highly adaptive defenses include humor, suppression, and sublimation; below that level, neurotic defenses such as obsessional and hysterical ones; below that, narcissistic defenses and disavowal; and below that major image-distorting and acting-out. Based on the above scheme, ratings of level of adaptiveness of defenses were made based on transcripts of psychotherapy sessions at different points in treatment.

The major findings of the study included a decrease in lower level defenses and an increase in high adaptive level defenses by 2.5 years of treatment; and a slower rate of change in defenses for those showing a greater number of lifetime and current Axis I disorders. Child sexual abuse and witnessing violence were significant negative predictors. Quite important for the question of the ecological validity of change in defense as an outcome marker, improvement in defensive functioning was associated with improvement in symptoms and in overall longer-term functioning.

As the authors note, given the naturalistic nature of the study, one cannot determine the direction of causal influence. Improvement in symptoms and level of functioning may lead to changes in defense rather than the other way around; or a third variable may lead to changes in defenses and improvement in symptoms, and level of functioning. Whether change in defense precedes symptomatic improvement and level of functioning needs to be addressed in future research.

However, the findings reported by Perry and Bond (2012) suggest that level of defensive functioning should be included as an outcome variable in psychotherapy research, particularly in research on psychodynamic psychotherapy. The Perry and Bond study as well as other studies (e.g., Perry, Petraglia, Olson, Presniak, & Metzger, 2012; Winston, Winston, Samstag, & Muran, 1994) also suggest that just as has been hypothesized in classical and ego psychology theories of psychodynamic treatment (e.g., Gray, 2005), positive changes in defensive functioning are an outcome of successful psychodynamic treatment. The implicit assumption is that higher level defences are more adaptive than lower level defenses.

Roy, Perry, Banon, and Luborsky (2009) investigated changes in defensive functioning based on archived tape-recordings of 17 completed psychoanalyses, the duration of which ranged from 141 to 1,162 sessions. As in the Perry and Bond (2012) study, Roy et al. (2009) found statistically significant pre–post changes in overall defensive functioning (ODF) and reported that 71% of the patients showed improvement in ODF by the termination of treatment, as defined by the use of fewer immature defenses and more adaptive defenses. However, athough the results were statistically significant, there is some question as to how meaningful they are in a real-life context. The percentage of adaptive defenses increased from 4.95 to 5.10; the percentage of immature defenses decreased from 26.75 to 23.20; and there was no change in neurotic level defenses. Given the special focus of psychoanalysis on analysis of defense, these results do not suggest a robust effect in altering defensive patterns. We also do not know how the magnitude of the changes in defensive functioning following psychoanalysis compare with such changes in brief and long-term psychodynamic psychotherapy. Do the more frequent sessions, the longer duration, and other features of the psychoanalytic situation make a difference with regard to level of defensive functioning?

A limitation of the methodology of the Roy et al. (2009) study, along with other similar ones, one that speaks to the question of ecological validity, is the sole reliance on psychotherapy sessions to measure defensive functioning. We do not know how these in-session measures relate to defensive functioning in the course of the individual's life outside psychotherapy. A related limitation of relying solely on psychotherapy sessions is that it precludes addressing the question of whether changes observed at the end of treatment *remain at follow-up*. Further, there can be no follow-up when measures of defensive functioning are based only on therapeutic sessions.

Finally, an additional serious limitation of the Roy et al. (2009) and other similar studies is that they do not deal with the clinically and theoretically interesting and important question of what one should except when level of defensive functioning changes in particular ways. Psychoanalytic theory has much of interest and importance to say about the role of defense in psychological functioning, including pathological functioning as well as the hypothesized consequences in the individual's life of changes in defensive functioning. It is these expected consequences and repercussions of adaptive and maladaptive defenses for the individual's psychological life that constitute the motivation for investigating levels of defensive functioning and their changes in treatment in the first place. Psychoanalytic theory does not just predict changes in defensive functioning in the course of successful treatment. It predicts that certain other consequences will occur (e.g., greater insight and awareness, more adaptive behavior, change in symptomatology, improved relationship patterns) as a function of changes in defensive functioning. Without investigating these associated consequences, it is not clear why one would want to study changes in defensive functioning. At this point, we do not know the extent to which changes in defensive functioning are causally linked to the kinds of other changes predicted by psychoanalytic theory.

## Issues raised by research findings

### *Defense against external trauma versus defense against internal mental contents*

One of the difficulties in assessing the research on the costs and benefits of defenses lies in the fact that different studies focus on different sources of threat against which the individual is defending. For example, the Coifman et al. (2007) study deals with defense against negative affect triggered by the external trauma of bereavement.[13] And much, although not all, of the research on positive illusions that I will discuss later also deals with the external trauma of serious illness. Contrastingly, the Cosineau and Shedler (2006) study, as well as the studies on repressive style, deal with avoidant-repressive defenses against experience of anxiety and threats to one's self-image as a general personality style. One cannot assume that defenses erected against mental contents related to external trauma will have the same adaptive or maladaptive consequences as similar defenses erected against mental contents linked to conflictual wishes and desires.

There is one place in Freud's early writings where he does not clearly distinguish between conflictual desires and external trauma and where one might understandably come to the conclusion that according to Freudian theory, defensive avoidance of negative affect is maladaptive. I refer here to Freud's (Breuer & Freud, 1893–1895) concept of "strangulated affect" (p. 17). According to his formulation, every experience is accompanied by a "quota of affect" (an interesting idea that can be understood as referring to the affective component of every experience; see Damasio, 2000). Normally, this "quota of affect" is discharged through ordinary means – for example, consciously experiencing the affect, talking about it, and so on. However, when one's affective reaction is repressed, the "quota of affect" is not discharged and in the case of hysteria, the affect becomes "strangulated" and is converted into somatic symptoms – through a process Freud acknowledged he did not understand.

The above formulation constituted the theoretical underpinning and rationale for the proposal that the abreaction of "strangulated affect" (achieved with the aid of hypnosis) was the main ingredient in treating hysteria. Without going into the details of early psychoanalytic history, suffice it to say that it soon became clear that abreaction – as well as hypnosis – was not therapeutically effective in the long run. In response to this realization, Freud moved on to other therapeutic approaches and techniques – free association, interpretation, etc. – with which we are all familiar. My point here is that the proposition that "defensive avoidance of negative affect is maladaptive" is very early Freud and largely applies to external trauma. This proposition was then made more complex and nuanced, if not relinquished, by later theoretical developments, some of which I have already noted.

The fact is that although abreaction of "strangulated affect" has figured prominently in histories of the early psychoanalytic theory of treatment, even in his early writings Freud (Breuer & Freud, 1893–1895, p. 9) placed at least as great an emphasis on the therapeutic importance of what can be called "rectification by other ideas"; that is, the process through which traumatic ideas are placed alongside the individual's "dominant mass of ideas" or associative network and are thereby more readily reintegrated into one's personality. The emphasis here is not on abreaction of strangulated affect, but on achieving integration into one's personality of hitherto defensively isolated mental contents (see Eagle, 2011). Although the concept of associative modification of isolated mental contents was initially discussed in the context of external trauma, it was later applied to conflictual wishes, desires, and fantasies that were isolated from the rest of the personaltiy by virtue of defense. It is this later perspective that served as the basis for the classical psychoanalytic theory of treatment, with its emphasis on analysis of defense and integration of defended against wishes and desires rather than abreaction of negative affect.

The therapeutic goal of "where id was, there shall ego be" (Freud, 1933), p. 80) expresses this emphasis on integration succinctly. And yet, critics of Freudian theory continue to target Freud's early emphasis on abreaction of negative affect and continue to argue that results demonstrating no clearly measurable maladaptive effects of failing to express negative affect contradict Freudian theory. In short, the perhaps misplaced emphasis on the importance of abreaction of negative affect in dealing with external trauma and the contemporary rush to debriefing interventions following external trauma cannot legitimately be derived from psychoanalytic theory in any straightforward way – although one must acknowledge that at least some psychodynamically oriented clinicians appear to interpret – perhaps one should say misinterpret – psychoanalytic theory as if abreaction were still a main therapeutic process goal.

It is likely that the adaptiveness or maladaptiveness of defense will vary with, among other things, situational context, such as whether it is directed toward reactions to external trauma (e.g., loss, illness) or thoughts and feelings linked to one's desires, wishes, and impulses. Also we do not know whether the individual employs the same defenses in both situations. This would be an interesting area for future research. Most important, one needs to keep in mind that the Freudian theory of defenses refers primarily to the latter, not the former.

It may well be the case that although say, repressive-avoidant defenses may be highly adaptive in regard to external trauma such as loss or life-threatening illness, they be less so in regard to conflictual wishes and desires. A basic assumption of

Freudian theory is that wishes and desires are often linked to one's psychobiological nature and therefore do not simply disappear when they are defended against by being pushed out of conscious experience. Rather, they remain active and continue to influence our thoughts, feelings, and behavior. Hence, defenses against wishes and desires may have different consequences for psychological functioning.

The distinction between defense against external trauma and defense against inner mental contents gets somewhat blurred when one notes that some external trauma may especially elicit and trigger conflictual inner mental contents. Thus, whereas the prototypical external trauma with which Charcot and Janet were concerned was railway accidents, Freud focused on dramatic and fraught external trauma such as rejection in love, the struggle between filial loyalty and romantic desires, and so on, which are especially likely to trigger conflictual inner mental contents and defenses against them.

In the latter case, confronting one's negative affects in regard to 'forbidden' mental contents may be adaptive insofar as it may lead to the recognition that as an adult these negative affects are no longer fully warranted. As Friedman (2008) puts it, the analyst brings the "good news" that the "danger situations" are no longer dangerous. If the triggering of conflictual mental contents is not a major issue and if the individual has managed to deal with external trauma through avoidant-repressive defenses, one may ask what is to be gained by encouraging the individual to confront or experience presumably defended against negative affect.

The assumption often made by many mental health workers, including psychodynamically oriented ones, is that some form of confrontation with or working-through of negative affect associated with trauma is therapeutically necessary. However, this may not always be the case. Indeed there is evidence that debriefing interventions following exernal trauma can be harmful (Wortman & Silver, 1989; Rose, Brewin, Andrews, & Kirk, 1999). The rush to such interventions seems to reflect, in part, the early and abandoned emphasis on abreaction of "strangulated affect." There are, undoubtedly, important individual differences here that are overlooked by a one size fits all theory. Therapists are likely to see individuals who have not been successful in adequately managing the effects of trauma through the reliance on avoidant-repressive defenses and may assume that this is true of all individuals.

It is interesting to note that Janet (1907) who attributed the precipitating trigger of hysterical symptoms to external trauma, treated these symptoms through hypnotically replacing the traumatic event with a benevolent one. In essence, he was hypnotically strengthening his patients' avoidant defenses – precisely the opposite of Freud's early efforts to bring material to conscious experience through hypnosis. These different approaches appear to reflect Janet's assumption that his patient's hysterical symptoms were precipitated by external trauma, whereas Freud generally attributed the onset of his patient's hysterical symptoms to defenses against the anxiety aroused by conflictual wishes and desires. It may well be that they were dealing with different types of patients.

A classic example of the distinction between the individual's reaction to the external trauma of loss in the form of normal mourning and the reaction in the form of pathological depression is seen in Freud's (1917[1915]) *Mourning and Melancholia.* Without getting into a discussion of the merits of Freud's specific formulation, the point I want to call attention to in Freud's account is the distinction between a, so to speak, average expectable reaction to an external trauma of loss and a reaction in which the external trauma triggers conflictual unconscious mental contents such as hostile impulses and ambivalence that need to be defended against.

In addition to drawing a distinction between defense against external trauma and defense against inner mental contents, it may also be important to distinguish among different kinds of external trauma. Not all external traumas are the same. The effects of, as well as adequate means of coping with external traumas are likely to be different among, for example, a life-threatening accident, the trauma of war, loss of a job, a lover's rejection, loss of a spouse, physical or sexual abuse in childhood, and so on. It is also possible that effective interventions may vary with the type of trauma experienced by the individual.

## Know thyself versus positive illusions: Weltanschauung or clinical theory?

Despite Freud's recognition of the relationship being relatively illusionless about oneself and depression, the research I have described does potentially represent a challenge to the psychoanalytic emphasis on insight, awareness, and self-knowledge. For example, Lazarus (1983) states that he no longer believes "that we must always be in touch with our feelings" and states that "one can argue, in fact, that illusion is necessary to positive mental health" (p. 1). And, unfortunately, he simplistically attributes to Freud the equation of "having illusions with being crazy" (p. 2). As we have seen, the logic of the Freudian theory of defense does not suggest that defensive avoidance of negative affect is uniformly maladaptive, irrespective of context. Neither does it deny that defensive avoidance can, in certain circumstances, be adaptive.

However, notwithstanding Lazarus' over-simplification of the Freudian theory of defense, it seems to me that there is a tension – and even possible contradiction – between the Freudian theory of defense, particularly its recognition, on the one hand, of the adaptive aspects of defense, and its overall equation of mental health with the Enlightenment goals of knowing the truth about oneself and living without illusions, and, on the other hand, the strong emphasis, perhaps also embedded in the Enlightenment vision, on the role of defense in psychopathology and on the curative power of knowing the truth about oneself. One can understand why Coifman et al. (2007), Lazarus (1983), and others read Freudian theory the way they do. And one can also understand why research demonstrating that illusions about oneself are a protective factor against the experience of depression and that being realistic about oneself has been associated with proneness to depression are interpreted as contradicting the significance of valuing of self-knowledge and shedding illusions as marks of mental health as well as an emphasis on the therapeutic or curative power of lifting defenses and achieving insight about oneself.

It is clear that Freud believed that self-knowledge and knowing the truth about oneself (i.e., one's wishes, desires, and fantasies and the defenses against them) was not only an Enlightenment value but also the path to clinical cure. The very birth of psychoanalysis is marked by the claims that repression (i.e., not knowing about oneself) is pathogenic and that lifting repression (i.e., knowing about oneself) is the road to clinical cure, in particular, the removal of hysterical symptoms. Remarkably, the Enlightenment vision and clinical necessity appeared to converge. Indeed, despite Freud's insistence that psychoanalysis was not a Weltanschauung, but a scientifically grounded theory of human nature, the image of an analyzed person seemed to be an ideal representative of living in accord with the Enlightenment imperative to know thyself.

Thus, from the perspective of psychoanalytic theory (as well, to a certain extent, from other perspectives, such as cognitive behavioral therapy (CBT), Gestalt therapy, and Rogerian theory), the ideally healthy person is someone who realistically knows himself or herself, including his or her irrationalities and weaknesses as well as strengths, and is in touch with his or her 'true' thoughts and feelings. But, as we have seen, this overall view appears to be challenged by a set of findings that raise the question of whether there really is a legitimate convergence between the Enlightenment value of living without illusions and clinical cure or, more broadly, between these values and mental health. Or, to repeat the question I posed earlier, Freud's disclaimer notwithstanding, do the psychoanalytic goals of knowing oneself and living without illusions constitute a Weltanschauung parading as clinical necessities? It seems to me that these questions pose a serious challenge to, at least, certain aspects of classical psychoanalytic theory.

## *Analysis of defense and the Enlightenment vision*

Despite other changes in psychoanalytic theory, the analysis of defense remains an essential process goal of psychoanalysis. Indeed, with the advent of ego psychology, the primary focus of interpretation has been the patient's defenses rather than – or, at least, in addition to – repressed mental contents. This has become even more the case largely through the influence of Gray (e.g., 2005) and his colleagues. In Gray's approach, referred to as "close process monitoring" the analyst is attentive to disturbances in the patient's free associations (e.g., pauses, hesitations, blanks, etc.) and interprets their defensive source (e.g., anxiety triggered by aggressive thoughts).

More recently, Gray's colleagues have essentially defined the primary function of this kind of analytic work as helping the patient better understand how his or her mind works rather than uncovering specific repressed mental contents (Busch, 2009; Sugarman, 2006). Thus, say a break in the flow of associations is a marker of anxiety triggered by unconscious aggressive thoughts or feelings toward the analyst. The interpretive focus on the part of Busch or Sugarman would not be primarily on uncovering the aggressive contents, but on helping the patient understand and gain insight into what happens to his or her thinking when he or she is anxious and conflicted.

It will be noted that this emphasis on helping the patient understand how his or her mind works is a new and perhaps more robust version of the fundamental belief that self-knowledge is curative. As such, it continues to reflect the assumption of a convergence between the Enlightenment vision and clinical cure. According to this view, the ideally mentally healthy or the successfully analyzed person is an ideal representative of one who is living in accord with the Enlightenment imperative to know oneself, that is, being in touch with how one's mind works.

## *Mentalization and defense analysis*

There is somewhat of a family resemblance between Gray's "close process monitoring" and the emphasis on enhancing mentalization and reflective function (e.g., Bateman & Fonagy, 2006) insofar as the focus in both approaches is on reflection on one's mental contents and on helping the individual better understand how his or her mind works (with both approaches linked to the classical psychoanalytic process goal of enhancing the observing function of the ego). However, there are also important differences, even if subtle ones, between the two approaches. Gray's "close process monitoring" is clearly a particular form of defense analysis; the analyst's communication is something like: "let us look at what you do when you are anxious" (which, Gray assumes, is usually triggered by an unacceptable – usually, aggressive – thought).

Although mentalization also entails reflection on one's feelings and thoughts, the emphasis is not necessarily on defense analysis. That is, it is not 'look at what you do when you are anxious.' Rather, the focus is on enhancing reflection whether or not the failure to reflect is due to defense. Further, and this is an important feature of the mentalization approach, the emphasis is on enhancing reflection on the other's state of mind as on one's state of mind. Thus, the communication is something like: "let us look not only at your feelings and thoughts, but let us also reflect on what you assume the other person's feelings, thoughts, and intentions are, as well as on the basis of your assumptions about the other person's feelings, thoughts, and intentions." Although failure to reflect on one's own and the other's mental state may be motivated by defense (one does not want to know the other's feelings and attitudes toward oneself), that is not always the case.

Quite apart from the issue of defense, in a number of contexts, a high level of reflective capacity is associated with desirable outcomes. For example, high risk mothers (i.e., single mothers living in poverty and overcrowded conditions) with a high level of reflective capacity are more likely to have securely attached infants than high risk mothers with a low level of reflective capacity (Fonagy, Steele, & Steele, 1991; Fonagy et al., 1995). This is likely to be at least partly due to the high reflective functioning mother being better able to 'read' her infant's mental state and therefore be better attuned to her infant.

Finally, a high level of reflective capacity is associated with more adequate affect regulation, whereas a low level of reflective capacity is associated with a low threshold for affect dysregulation. Thus, there is a consensus that in borderline personality disorder (BPD) patients "affect dysregulation and impaired mentalization interact in a vicious circle" (Allen, Fonagy, & Bateman, 2008, p. 263). However, dysregulated affect such as in an experience of narcisisstic injury and consequent rage is likely to be modulated if one has the capacity to step back from these feelings and reflect on one's reactions, including one's automatic and unquestioned construals of the other's attitudes and intentions. Hence, the use of Mentalization Based Treatment (MBT) for BPD patients.

Returning to the issue of defense, two critical questions arise: one, in view of the research on defense I have described (as well as clinical experiences regarding the therapeutic limitations of insight, awareness, and self-knowledge – see Eagle, 2011a,b,), to what extent is the belief in the clinical value of knowing how one's mind works an Enlightenment value parading as a clinical proposition? And two, if defense is largely adaptive, why the primacy of analysis of defense, whether it is understood as uncovering repressed mental contents or understanding how one's mind works?

As we know, Freud articulated the central goal of psychoanalytic treatment as "making the unconscious conscious" (Freud, 1917[1916–1917]), p. 436). According to classical theory as well as ego psychology, the primary factor that keeps the unconscious from becoming conscious and that maintains the split between id and ego is defense. Given this goal, it is perfectly understandable that at the center of analytic work is analysis of defense. But if defenses are largely adaptive and directed toward the maintenance of well-being, why do they need to be analyzed and, so to speak, overcome? Insofar as it is mainly defense that keeps mental contents unconscious, implicit in the primacy of analysis of defense as well as the goal of making the unconscious conscious is the inherent maladaptive nature of defense. The very term "defense" suggests an inner threat against which a defense is erected.

Ideally, one's wishes, desires, ideas, and feelings would not be experienced as threats that require defense. Another way to put this is to say that because one would experience safety rather than danger and anxiety in relation to one's thoughts, feelings, and impulses, there would be little or no need for defense. In this state of health, as Freud (1926b) observes, it would be difficult to distinguish between the id and the ego. He writes that the ego and the id "belong together, and under healthy conditions cannot in practice be distinguished from each other" (p. 201).[14] The individual would have achieved a unity of the personality, which is an age-old ideal (see Apfelbaum, 1966). One is reminded of Confucius' statement that at the age of 70, the dictates of his heart and his sense of right and wrong were one and the same.

I am aware that I have described an ideal state rather than a realistic goal. However, I do so to highlight the logic of the conception of mental health in psychoanalytic theory and the place of defense in that conception. In particular, one needs to address such questions as the rationale for the primacy of the analysis of defense if defenses are primarily adaptive and directed towards maintenance of well-being? Just as the function and adaptive value of defense varies with context and the use to which the defense is put, so similarly, is this likely to be true of the function and adaptive value of self-knowledge and living without illusions. The value of illusions and, as a corollary, the maladaptive and destructive uses to which self-knowledge and the truth can be put, is a salient theme in the modern classics of O'Neill's *The Iceman Cometh* and Ibsen's *The Wild Duck*. In both plays, the truth is pressed on the characters with destructive intent and certainly with destructive consequences. In the former play, the characters' sense that they could continue to survive psychologically returns only when the truth is abandoned and the characters return to their illusions, or as O'Neill puts it, to their "pipe dreams."[15]

In accord with the theme of both plays, Rank (1936) writes:

> with the truth, one cannot live. To be able to live one needs illusions . . . The more a man can take reality as truth, appearance as essence, the sounder, the better adjusted, the happier he will be . . . this constantly effective process of self-deceiving, pretending, and blundering, is not a psychopathological mechanism.
>
> (pp. 251–252)

This is an extraordinary statement from a major psychoanalytic theorist.

Perhaps one can no longer assume that knowing oneself and clinical 'cure' necessarily converge. One may need to consider the possibility that, at least in some cases, what is taken to be a successful analysis perhaps is more likely to lead more to enhanced self-knowledge than to clinical 'cure.' Indeed, Stone (1997) suggests that although unmatched as a way of coming to know what he refers to as the 'otherness' of oneself, psychoanalysis is not especially suitable as a method of treating at least serious mental illness.

Of course, what analysis does and does not accomplish is an empirical question. At the core of the issue here is the relationship between self-knowledge and well-being. The empirical evidence suggests that the two may not converge and may, indeed, in certain circumstances, diverge. It may well be that if forced to choose, some individuals – it is very likely that Freud was one such individual – would opt for self-knowledge over a well-being that entails self-deception and illusions. However, the possibility that the two do not necessarily converge represents a serious challenge to a therapeutic approach or more broadly, to a system of thought that identifies health and well-being with self-knowledge and the relative absence of self-deception and defensive illusions.

Some psychoanalytic theorists have lessened the emphasis on analysis of defense and have stressed the importance of extinguishing maladaptive schemas and generating more adaptive ones through the provision of more benevolent experiences with the therapist.[16] The most notable historical example of that development is, of course, seen in Alexander and French's (1946) concept of corrective emotional experiences. Variations and elaboration of that concept have been formulated in a number of contemporary psychoanalytic theories, including self psychology, Control-Mastery theory, and the formulations of, among others, Lyons-Ruth, Fairbairn, and Winnicott.

An element common to these different formulations is the assumption that independently of analysis of defense, some form of corrective emotional experience will itself be therapeutic. Thus, for Kohut, the empathic bond between patient and therapist is the primary therapeutic ingredient. Weiss and Sampson and their colleagues have shown that test-passing and conditions of safety themselves, without interpretation, are therapeutic and serve to facilitate the reduction of symptoms and the emergence of warded-off contents (see Eagle, 1993a). Fairbairn's emphasis on the therapist as a 'good' object, Lyons-Ruth's concept of "implicit relational knowing," and Winnicott's concept of a holding environment (1956) are further examples of a decreasing emphasis on analysis of defense and a concomitant increasing emphasis on corrective emotional experiences provided by the therapeutic relationship.

Although there is a convergence on the importance of corrective emotional experiences, there are interesting differences among different theories worth noting regarding their therapeutic role. Alexander and French (1946) essentially hypothesized that corrective emotional experiences serve to *extinguish* maladaptive schemas and expectations and to facilitate new learning. For Kohut, corrective emotional experiences in the form of "optimal frustration" and an empathic bond contribute to accretions in self-cohesiveness through the process of "transmuting internalization". Neither Alexander and French nor Kohut suggest that defenses need to be lifted in order for these therapeutic outcomes to occur. Contrastingly, although with Alexander and French and Kohut, Weiss and Sampson and their colleagues maintain (and demonstrate) that analysis of defense may not be necessary for therapeutic progress to occur, they nevertheless continue to emphasize the importance of relaxation of defenses in order to facilitate the emergence into awareness of warded-off mental contents. That is, although relaxation of defenses does not necessarily require direct interpretation and can come about through corrective emotional experiences (i.e., test-passing and conditions of safety), it remains a central process goal of treatment. And this is so because, as Weiss and Sampson and their colleagues have shown, relaxation of defenses facilitates the emergence into awareness of warded-off contents, in particular, one's unconscious pathogenic beliefs. Thus, whereas relaxation of defenses and the consequent emergence into awareness play little or no role for Alexander and French and Kohut, these factors continue to play a central role in Control–Mastery theory.

## Summary and conclusions

The concept of defense is a quintessential example of a psychoanalytic concept that clearly merits being retained. This key psychoanalytic concept has had extraordinary heuristic value and has stimulated an enormous amount of research, from the New Look research of the 1940s and 1950s to more current research on different aspects of defense. Just as clearly, the concept of defense needs to be modified in a number of ways. What can one conclude regarding the concept of defense in the light of the above discussion and research findings? Let me consider some of the issues and questions addressed in this chapter:

1. What is one defending against? It seems clear that Freud's idea that defense operates primarily against sexual and aggressive impulses largely because they represent the threat of excessive excitation requires modification. As the evidence suggests and as Freud himself observed in his early writings, the primary functions of defense are: (1) in Cramer's (2006) words, to protect the self; (2) to ward off negative affects; and (3) to protect vital ties to objects. The first function includes protecting the stability of self-organization, one's sense of oneself, and self-esteem. The second includes protection not only against experience of anxiety, but also other negative affects such as depression, shame, guilt, and humiliation (see Brenner, 1991). And the third function includes protection of relational ties that are experienced as vital to one's psychological survival. Insofar as threats to vital ties also threaten the self and generate intense negative affects, this third function of defense can be understood as a derivative of the first two functions of defense.

2. Are defenses conscious or unconscious? Among the "seven pillars of defense mechanism theory" Cramer (2008) lists as pillar 1: "Defense mechanisms are cognitive operations that operate outside of awareness" (p. 1964). According to the logic of Freudian theory, repression and other defenses operate at an unconscious level. A common assumption made, reflected in Cramer's (2008) statement, is that defenses could not effectively operate as defenses were we aware that we are employing them. Such awareness would, so to speak, spill the beans regarding what we are engaged in and therefore defeat the very purpose of defense, namely, to keep us unaware of both the fact that we are engaging in defense and what we are defending against.

I think the evidence suggests that things are more complex. As we have seen, in Freud's (Breuer & Freud, 1893–1895) own example of repression in the case of Lucy R., it is clear that she is aware, even if fleetingly, of being in love with her employer, and entertaining fantasies about him, but decides to push such thoughts out of her mind. And, as we have also seen in Chapter 1, Anna Freud and Sandler (Sandler & Freud, 1985) entertain the idea that the individual has a momentary and fleeting awareness of the mental content being defended against. We have also seen evidence that in certain forms of denial, the individual knows at some level what is being denied and makes a quasi-volitional decision to avoid and not think about certain contents.

It seems clear that cognitive operations that qualify as defense on functional grounds are not necessarily fully unconscious. A dichotomy between conscious and unconscious or between awareness and unawareness does not do justice to the nuanced nature of certain defenses. More generally, more attention needs to be given to *dimensions* of consciousness, including *gradations or degrees of awareness,*

# 6

# SOME CONCLUDING COMMENTS

## Introduction

I want to do two things in this concluding chapter: provide a summary of some conclusions warranted by the material presented in the previous chapters; and two, briefly discuss and elaborate on some topics that were not given prominence in the previous chapters, but merit further discussion.

The concepts of unconscious processes, inner conflicts, defense, and the Oedipus complex covered in this volume constitute the core interlocking elements of the classical psychoanalytic theory of psychological functioning. And, indeed, with the exception of the Oedipus complex, they were 'nominated' with the greatest frequency by respondents as the core concepts of psychoanalytic theory. In the light of the research findings, clinical evidence, and conceptual critiques discussed in the foregoing chapters, what are some conclusions warranted regarding the current status of these concepts? To begin with the overall general conclusion, whereas some fundamental ideas remain relatively intact, little remains unchanged.

What remain relatively intact are the central ideas that our behavior, thoughts, and feelings are influenced by factors outside our conscious awareness. This is the case in a number of senses: (1) as the subliminal research findings demonstrate, we can be influenced by external stimuli outside conscious awareness; (2) as the work of Bargh and his colleagues and Nisbett and Wilson demonstrates, we are not always aware of the specific ways that external stimuli available to conscious awareness influence our behavior; (3) we are often not aware of the dimensions and categories according to which we organize external stimuli that are available to conscious awareness; and (4) we are often not fully aware of the ways in which we avoid conscious experience of certain conflictual mental contents that would generate distressing affect and threats to one's self-image and self-esteem were they to enter conscious awareness. This central formulation contains the core concepts of inner conflict and defense and constitutes the essence of Freud's conception of the "dynamic unconscious."

There is little doubt that we indulge in a great deal of defensive and self-deceptive behavior and entertain illusions that are motivated by the desire to avoid distressing affect and threats to our self-image. There is much evidence for the psychoanalytic claim that the ubiquitous presence of inner conflict and defense culminates, in the language of ordinary discourse, in a state of self-deception or more broadly, what Ricoeur (1970) refers to as "false consciousness," which is essentially the claim that, in important respects, consciousness is dissimulating and therefore may not always constitute a reliable guide, indeed, may deceive us, with regard to the full range of who we are, including the wishes, desires, and fantasies that comprise who we are.[1] Further, although there are important differences regarding the mental contents about which we are conflicted and that are subject to defense and self-deception, the basic ideas of inner conflict and defense cut across different psychoanalytic theories.[2]

## Unconscious processes

There is also an enormous amount of evidence supporting the hypothesis of unconscious mental processing, far more evidence than even Freud might have expected and certainly far more than those who equated the mental with what is conscious could possibly have imagined. This evidence, however, largely supports Freud's formulation of the "descriptive unconscious," which was mainly intended as a prolegomenon for his primary focus, namely, the so-called "dynamic unconscious." That is, he intended to first demonstrate the viability of the concept of unconscious mental processes as a means of paving the way for his primary interest, the "dynamic unconscious." The solid and wide support for unconscious processing, while important, is not directly relevant to the distinctly psychoanalytic claims contained in the concept of the dynamic unconscious.[3]

Virtually all the studies providing evidence for unconscious mental processes discussed in Chapter 2 deal with the effects of *external* stimuli of which we are unaware rather than inner wishes, desires, and fantasies. Hence, the finding, for example, that subliminal stimuli can be processed at a semantic level and can have effects on cognition would seem to have limited relevance to psychoanalytic theory, at least those aspects of psychoanalytic theory having to do with inner conflict, defense, and the "dynamic unconscious."

More relevant to psychoanalytic theory, in particular to a theory of primary and secondary process, is the demonstration that stimuli out of awareness are processed differently than stimuli in conscious awareness. This was shown in the Pine (1960; 1961) and Marcel (1980) studies as well as by Turvey and Fertig's (1970) demonstration that not only can we be unaware of the dimensions along which we encode external stimuli but also that these dimensions may not be accessible to conscious experience. One way of interpreting the findings reported by Bargh and his colleagues, discussed in Chapter 2, on the effects of external stimuli on our behavior and cognition (e.g., our judgments) without our awareness that we are being influenced by these stimuli – assuming their replicability – is that they, in effect, demonstrate primary process cognition. Consider, for example, the finding that holding a cup of hot coffee leads to assessing someone as having a warm personality. From the perspective of the psychoanalytic theory of primary and secondary process, this finding can be understood as an instance of concretistic thinking in which a feeling of bodily warmth primes an attribution of warmth to someone's personality. Most individuals would certainly not consciously accept as rational the proposition that holding a cup of hot coffee should influence one's assessment of someone's personality. Thus, the particular priming effect reported would appear to depend on the fact that the influence of the external stimuli occurs outside awareness.

There is remarkably little research reported that is directly relevant to the "dynamic unconscious" when that is understood in the context of Freudian drive theory. The few studies that have been carried out support the central idea that we do, indeed, tend to engage in defensive operations that are intended to avoid distressing affect, in particular, negative affect associated with threats to one's self-image. Beyond this general support, there is little evidence for other features attributed to the "dynamic unconscious," including the claim that our fundamental inner conflicts center on a "cauldron full of seething excitations" (Freud, 1933, p. 73) in which infantile sexual aggressive wishes (i.e., Oedipal wishes) that are pressing for discharge and access to conscious awareness and motility, are barred from doing so by unconscious counter forces, and have decisive influences on psychological development. There is much wrong with this picture on a number of grounds, including the likelihood that unconscious mental contents are often fragmentary, unformulated (Stern, 2003), and not spelled out (Fingarette, 1963) rather than a fully formed "hidden reality" (Fingerette, 1969) or, in Mitchell's (1998) metaphor, analogous to insects under a rock that have been there all along and are uncovered once the rock is lifted.

A major change in psychoanalytic theorizing about unconscious processes that has emerged is reflected in the shift from the conception of the "unconscious" as a "cauldron full of seething excitations" to an unconscious of 'rules,' representations, and schemas largely formed in childhood, and often relatively resistant to change. The unconscious of contemporary psychoanalytic theories is 'populated' by internal working models (IWMs), internal objects and internal object relationships, pathogenic beliefs, relational configurations, and representations of self, other, and prototypic self–other interactions. Further, to an important extent, these beliefs, configurations, and representations are unconscious not necessarily by virtue of repression, but rather by virtue of having been acquired early in life, often non-verbally. They can be described as implicit and part of one's procedural knowledge. In this sense, beliefs, configurations, and representations are implicit structures that can be more readily understood as aspects of a descriptive rather than a dynamic unconscious.

However, this is only partly the case insofar as these representations are often also embedded in a dynamic context of conflict and defense. That is, to some extent, the unconscious status of the representations emphasized in contemporary psychoanalytic theory can be motivated by the avoidance of distressing effects. For example, as Bowlby (1980) has observed and as research on the Adult Attachment Interview (AAI) has suggested, an individual's conscious internal working model may be quite different from his or her inferred unconscious internal working model, the latter reflecting the individual's motives to avoid painful experiences (e.g., experience of rejection by the caregiver) and to retain a benevolent image of the caregiver. Indeed, this is essentially how the category of avoidant–dismissive attachment is operationally defined in AAI research.

Thus, one can say that central aspects of a dynamic unconscious, defined as the product of inner conflict and defense, is retained in attachment theory. However, in the context of attachment theory, inner conflict and defense are not related to infantile sexual and aggressive wishes and impulses, but rather to mental contents having to do with the vicissitudes of one's one's attachment needs and one's need to retain a benevolent representation of one's caregiver. Thus, by defending against the conscious experience of his or her attachment needs, the avoidantly attached individual avoids the conscious experience of painful rejection experiences, which also enables him or her to retain a benevolent and idealized representation of the caregiver.

This conception of a dynamic unconscious does away with various elements of the classical conception of the dynamic unconscious, including such ideas as timeless infantile wishes pressing for discharge, the build-up of excitation due to the failure to discharge drive impulses as an inherent threat to the ego, and so on. The dynamic unconscious in the context of attachment theory (as well as other contemporary psychoanalytic theories to the extent that there is a dynamic unconscious) is not primarily characterized as the repository of inherently unacceptable and infantile asocial or anti-social wishes, but includes legitimate and vital lifelong needs, such as the need for a secure base as well as the need to separate and individuate, needs that do not defy societal requirements and standards. These needs and wishes are rendered conflictual, unacceptable, distressing and subject to defense, not by virtue of their inherent anti-social nature, but by virtue of parental communication (often implicit), demands, and pressures.

In certain respects, the structure of Freud's (1926a) account of the "danger situations," which can be understood relatively independently of his metapsychological construal of them (i.e., in terms of their prevention of discharge of excitation), is quite compatible with the above model of the dynamic unconscious. It will be recalled that in Freud's description of the "danger situations," the child's fear of loss of the object and loss of the object's love is associated with his or her expression of sexual and aggressive impulses. An analogous account is implicit in what I refer to as the attachment theory version of the dynamic unconscious. However, in the latter version, the wishes and needs that trigger the "danger situations," are not infantile sexual and aggressive wishes, but rather attachment needs that are met with caregiver rejection, inconcsistency, or anger, caregiver behaviors that can be seen as quintessential instances of a "danger situation." Further, as is the case in Freud's description of the "danger situations," in at least one attachment pattern of reaction to the "danger situations," in order to avoid the caregiver's inconsistency, rejection, or anger, the child learns to refrain from making attachment overtures to the caregiver and to ban the experience of attachment needs from consciousness, the latter referred to by Bowlby (1988) as "defensive exclusion" (pp. 33–35).

Although the above account of the dynamic unconscious in the context of attachment theory works quite well in regard to avoidant–dismissive attachment, it does not readily fit the pattern of either anxious/ambivalent or disorganized attachment. Thus, rather than excluding attachment needs from consciousness, the anxious/ambivalent child is preoccupied with these needs and with fears of abandonment. In the discourse of attachment theory, there is a tendency for hyper-activation of the attachment system. As for disorganized attachment, it is understood more as a breakdown of any 'strategy' (or defense) rather than an expression of a coherent strategy. Although the process of "defensive exclusion" (Bowlby, 1988), characteristic of avoidant/dismissive attachment, implies both inner conflict and defense, this is less apparent in the case of the anxious/ambivalent child or the enmeshed/preoccupied adult. A conscious or preconscious preoccupation with fear of abandonment characteristic of enmeshed/preoccupied attachment, suggests more the *failure* of defense than the functioning of intact defenses. Indeed, this conclusion is buttressed by the evidence, one, that enmeshed/preoccupied attachment is over-represented in borderline personality disorder; and two, that in a number of studies, avoidant and secure individuals are more similar to each other in a number of areas of functioning than either is to enmeshed/preoccupied individuals.

## Inner conflict, the Oedipus complex, and defense

Although Freud made a major contribution in recognizing the role of defense in psychological life, there is little evidence that defenses, including repressive defenses, necessarily operate at a fully unconscious level. Rather, a plausible case has been made for the proposition that defenses operate at what one might refer to as a preconscious level (or alternatively, at the fringe of consciousness) characterized by not spelling out and not articulating the projects in which one is engaged, not fully formulating the unformulated, not making connections among experiences, distraction, not focusing attention, not avowing certain mental contents as part of oneself, and not experiencing affect. In short, there is often a thin and blurry line between suppression and repression. As we have seen in the case of Lucy R., Freud's supposed account of repression of wishes and fantasies turns out to be an instance of fleeting awareness and conscious suppression, a process akin to what Freud referred to as the preconscious.

There is also little evidence that how we resolve or fail to resolve conflicts around infantile sexual and aggressive wishes (including oedipal wishes) has a decisive influence on psychological development and functioning and plays a determinative role in neurosis, gender identity, object choice, and superego formation. Although this formulation is taken as canonical and has been taught at psychoanalytic institutes as received wisdom for many years, it is based not on clinical evidence or longitudinal developmental studies, but on Freud's writings on the Oedipus complex. However, as we have seen, there is little evidence for the existence of a universal Oedipus complex, let alone for the claim that the vicissitudes of its resolution have a vital influence on psychological development.

As we have also seen, although the term "Oedipus complex" is retained, it has essentially been reconceptualized out of existence. That is, it is employed as a metaphor for the conflicts variously referred to as merger versus individuation, symbiosis versus separation–individuation, and the regressive lure of identification versus the progressive urge for separation. In much post-Freudian theorizing, some variation of these inner conflicts is believed to play a primary role in psychological development, including the development of various forms of psychopathology. That is, many post-Freudian theorists propose that how the individual deals with the primary conflict between regression and stasis, on the one hand, and progression and growth, on the other hand, whether he or she will be able to achieve "mature dependence" (Fairbairn, 1952, p. 34), rather than how he or she resolves the Oedipus complex, will play a fateful role in his or her life.

Although employing a different language, implicit in attachment theory is an emphasis on the importance of negotiating the conflicts between what Fairbairn (1952) refers to as "immature dependence" and individuation, the latter roughly equivalent to his concept of "mature dependence." Thus, in the context of attachment theory, secure attachment entails the capacity to make use of a secure base (and eventually, to internalize a secure base) for support in the process of exploring the world and oneself, critical factors in the developmental process of separation and individuation. The securely attached individual can individuate while retaining ties, indeed, depending on ties, to the object. Contrastingly, insecurely attached individuals tend to negotiate the conflicts surrounding individuation by either finding it difficult to move beyond "immature dependence" (as in an enmeshed/preoccupied attachment pattern) or by adopting a defensive independence (as in dismissive/avoidant attachment).

It could perhaps be argued that the shift from the centrality of infantile sexual and aggressive wishes to the contemporary emphasis on issues of separation–individuation is simply a new theoretical 'fashion' reflecting cultural changes – similar to the argument proposed by Cushman (1990) that the emergence of a self psychology reflects what he refers to as the "empty self" in American culture. However, the plausibility of this argument is vitiated by the consideration that although their particular expression may vary, attachment and individuation processes are transhistorical, transcultural, and transspecies phenomena, embedded in evolutionary selection. Although vastly different in shape and expression, attachment processes and the progress toward individuation, as manifested in some degree of separation from parents, exploring and learning about the physical and social world, and acquiring various skills are as relevant for survival and prospering to the lion cub or to the young chimp as to the human infant and child. Similarly, although different in expression and shape, issues of attachment and individuation confront children from different cultures, including so-called collectivist cultures. Hence, it is likely that psychological functioning and personality development, including the development of psychopathology, will be powerfully influenced by the vicissitudes of attachment and individuation. And, of course, there is much evidence that this is the case.

There is no doubt that sexuality and aggression are also transhistorical, transcultural, and transspecies phenomena. Indeed, Freud's emphasis on the role of sexuality in psychic life was largely motivated by its embeddedness in biology and evolutionary processes. However, the question is whether conflicts and defenses centering on infantile sexual wishes (e.g., incestuous wishes) and infantile aggressive impulses (e.g., death wishes toward the same sex parent) play a determinative role in psychological development. Similarly, with regard to Kleinian theory, the question is whether fundamental aspects of psychological development are a product of the vicissitudes of conflicts surrounding an inborn death instinct and the battle between love and hate toward the object. However dramatic and evocative these formulations may be, they stand on extremely thin evidential grounds.

Some findings of research on defense constitute a challenge to certain aspects of a psychoanalytic theory of defense. One, there is little evidence that defenses are primarily directed against infantile sexual and aggressive wishes. Rather, they are directed against any mental contents that are likely to threaten one's self-image and to generate distressing affect. Two, defenses are not necessarily unconscious; one can be fleetingly aware of employing them. Further, defenses are normally implemented through ordinary everyday processes such as the voluntary deployment of attention, seeking distraction, not spelling out, not formulating, and not making connections among consciously available experiences. Three, there is evidence that contrary to received wisdom, being consciously aware of employing defenses does not necessarily vitiate their effectiveness (Rosenzweig, 2016). Four, defenses are not uniformly pathogenic: there are both costs and benefits to the use of defense. Five, the adaptive or maladaptive consequences of defense vary with the particular defense employed and, most important, with the situational context in which it is employed. Six, defense is not always only an intrapsychic process, but may include interpersonal and interactional aspects. That is, an important motive for defense may be the need to keep others as well as oneself from knowing aspects of oneself. Thus, defense is instigated not only in reaction to signals of internal danger (e.g., anxiety, guilt and superego condemnation), but also in reaction to signals of external danger, in particular, to indications of whether conditions of safety obtain. Seven, an essential means of defense lies not primarily in keeping unacceptable mental contents from conscious awareness, but in disavowal of these mental contents as part of oneself. Barring mental contents from conscious awareness is only one means, although a major one, of preventing the avowal or acknowledging certain mental contents as really a part of oneself. (One cannot disavow what is out of awareness.) That is the major function of defense. And it is this need to disavow and not acknowledge certain unacceptable aspects of oneself as, indeed, part of oneself, that is a major source of resistance – a consideration that helps one understand why making the unconscious conscious is, most frequently, not sufficient for therapeutic change (see Moran, 2001, for an excellent discussion of avowal as a critical aspect of first-person knowledge).

## Ego functions and personality development

Although not identified as a core concept by the respondents to my query, the importance of ego functions in personality development and behavior has emerged as a significant general finding. One of Freud's central insights that has received much empirical support is the relationship between the capacity to delay gratification and central aspects of psychological functioning. This insight has been well supported by findings on concurrent associations between delay of gratification and such aspects of psychological functioning as impulsivity, negative emotionality, over-control, development of conscience in children (Mittal et al., 2013). There is also evidence that separate neural systems mediate immediate and delayed gratification behavior. Decisions involving immediate gratification (of monetary rewards) correspond to preferential activation of "parts of the limbic system associated with the midbrain dopamine system, including paralimbic systems" (p. 503), whereas greater fronto-parietal cortical activation is associated with decisions for delayed receipt of monetary rewards (McClure et al., 2004).

In addition to concurrent relationships, the extraordinary predictive associations between early capacity to delay gratification and later adaptive behavior suggest that we are dealing with a basic aspect of personality functioning, one related to affect regulation and more broadly, to what is referred to as "executive function" in the cognitive psychology literature. The concept of executive function clearly parallels the concept of ego functions in psychoanalytic theory. Much of the research evidence on delay of gratification discussed in Chapter 4 can be profitably understood in terms of the role of a vital ego function (i.e., capacity to delay gratification; affect regulation) in behavior and in the trajectory of one's life patterns. Further, placing these findings in the context of ego functions and the broader theoretical framework in which an understanding of ego functions is embedded can enrich future research in this area and can expand such research to include important questions highlighted by a psychoanalytic perspective. For example, there is little or no research on topics such as the reverse of failure to inhibit delay, namely, excessive ego inhibition, over-control, and executive delay expressed as the relative inability to experience gratification and pleasure; the role of inner conflict in ability to delay gratification; the relationship between capacity to reflect on one's own and others' mental states and ability to delay gratification in various areas; and the question of whether one's capacity to delay gratification cuts across different content domains such as oral gratification, monetary rewards, and sexual and aggressive impulses. This latter question speaks to the issue of the trait-like or interactional (i.e., traits interacting with situation or content domain) nature of the ability to delay gratification.

The long-term predictive power of individual differences in the capacity to delay gratification highlights the enduring importance of viewing various aspects of behavior from the perspective of the ego functions, particularly, inhibitory capacity. The importance of a perspective that identifies and focuses on the vital role of ego function in psychological life, particularly its role in affect regulation seems to have been lost sight of or at least minimized in some contemporary psychoanalytic theories that reject a so-called one-person psychology. One perhaps widely shared current attitude toward psychoanalytic ego psychology is that it has had its day and that that day has passed and has been replaced by other theories and perspectives. That is unfortunate and reflects a problematic aspect of the nature of theory change in psychoanalysis (see Eagle, 1993b). The fact is that the importance and heuristic value of viewing behavior from the perspective of the nature and adequacy of the individual's ego functions has received a great deal of support from research evidence on delay of gratification, affect regulation, and executive functions.

I want to devote a brief discussion to a few issues that have been over-shadowed by more familiar concepts and formulations, and therefore have not been given much attention. In the foregoing chapters, indeed, not a single respondent identified them as core concepts or formulations of psychoanalytic theory. However, an assessment of psychoanalytic theory would not be complete without at least some mention of these ideas. Indeed, I believe that they constitute the heart of the psychoanalytic project, at least, the heart of its fundamental values.

I refer to the following central values that underlie at least clinical psychoanalytic theory: one, the valuing of ego autonomy in the sense of the experience of agency as contrasted with the experience of drivenness and compulsion.[4] The idea of ego autonomy is not limited to the ego's freedom from the id, but, as Rapaport (1967) emphasized, also includes relative freedom from the environment. That is, ego autonomy refers to freedom from drivenness and compulsion from any source, id, superego, and the environment, the latter including stimulus-boundedness in regard to external stimuli (Goldstein, 1983) and the pressures related to interpersonal social conformity.[5]

There are experiences, certainly not pathological, such as falling in love and being absorbed in creative work, in which one may perhaps feel driven and carried along almost without one's will. Anyone who has been fortunate enough to have these experiences can testify to their vital and life-affirming quality. Why are these experiences, seemingly characterized by a diminution of agency, not pathological? I think the answer to this question lies in the following considerations: what these and other similar experiences have in common is the seemingly paradoxical idea that the apparent yielding of one's autonomy is itself an ego-syntonic act of autonomy – in contrast to the ego-alien experience of being torn by conflict. That is, one relinquishes control wholeheartedly. Kris (1936/1952) tried to capture these experiences with his concept of "regression in the service of the ego" (p. 173). Although the term "regression" is unfortunate, what Kris was trying to convey was the central idea that in regression in the service of the ego, yielding rational control is itself an act of the ego and an expression of agency rather than an instance of the ego being overwhelmed by inner or outer forces.

Implicit in the concept of "regression in the service of the ego" is the idea that ego autonomy is not equivalent to ego control, but, indeed, includes the individual's ability to relinquish control, similar to what Ghent (1990) refers to as "surrender," which he describes as "letting down defensive barriers" (p. 108).

As noted in Chapter 4, another central value related to autonomy that underlies the psychoanalytic project, is the unity of the personality as a fundamental ideal. This may not be not apparent, given the classical psychoanalytic emphasis on inner conflict, the positing of a primary antagonism between the id and the ego, the presumed need for renunciation of infantile wishes, and so on. And, indeed, the idea that achievement of unity of the personality is a fundamental psychoanalytic ideal would likely be rejected by some psychoanalytic theorists as unattainable, including Brenner (e.g., 2002) who argues not only that inner conflict is inevitable, but also that resolution of conflict is an unrealistic aim and that all one can achieve are more adaptive or less adaptive compromise formations (which, of course, may constitute a step toward achieving at least some degree of unity of the personality). And yet, although Brenner may be right from a practical perspective, I think it can be shown that unity of personality is, indeed, a fundamental ideal in the writings of Freud – although, as an ideal, it may never be fully achieved, but only approached to varying degrees.

As I discussed in Chapter 1, early in his writings, Freud (Breuer & Freud, 1893–1895) identified two means of dealing with hysterical symptoms brought about by trauma: the abreaction of "strangulated affect" and the normal process through which the isolated traumatic idea enters "the great complex of associations and allows "rectification by other ideas" (p. 9). The latter idea of assimilation of mental contents into the dominant mass of ideas clearly anticipates the later "where id was, there shall ego be" (Freud, 1933, p. 80) as an overriding psychoanalytic goal. Whether formulated as assimilating isolated mental contents into the "dominant mass of ideas" or as "where id was, there shall ego be," the fundamental emphasis is on *integrating* into the personality those mental contents that for defensive reasons have remained *unintegrated* – or, to put it another way, on experiencing as part of oneself, as an 'I,' those mental contents (i.e., wishes, desires, and fantasies) that have been disavowed as not part of oneself (i.e., that have been relegated to an 'it' status).

The replacement or at least supplementation of making the unconscious conscious with where id was, there shall ego be, not only reflects the recognition that bringing an unconscious mental content into consciousness does not guarantee its integration, but also the overriding importance for Freud of the goal of unity of the personality. That is, the goal of psychoanalytic treatment becomes where 'it' was, there shall 'I' be. Insofar as 'I' is expanded to included what was hitherto excluded from it, the personality is now a more unified one.

As noted earlier, in seemingly obvious contradiction to the positing of an inevitable and inherent antagonism between the id and the ego, as we have seen Freud (1915) writes that in health one cannot distinguish between the ego and the id. In other words, there is a seamless unity between them. In proposing an instinct of Eros (Freud, 1930), the theme of unity is also expressed not only in an intrapsychic context of integration or unity among the different structures within the personality, but also on the gender scale of unity among individuals (the guiding principle of Eros).

It has been customary to identify self-knowledge as *the* fundamental value of psychoanalysis and thus locate psychoanalytic theory squarely in the center of the Enlightenment vision (see Eagle, 2011). However, as I have tried to show, one also finds in Freud's writings, as well as implicit in the logic of aspects of psychoanalytic theory, an emphasis on the importance of unity and integration. From this latter perspective, what becomes deeply valued is not simply, or perhaps primarily, expansion of self-knowledge in the sense of gaining information about oneself, but such attributes as wholeheartedness and the overcoming of ambivalence, self-deception, and conflict.

When self-knowledge is thought of in terms of becoming conscious of aspects of oneself that were unconscious, it essentially becomes equivalent to something like gaining information and achieving knowledge about oneself. This is especially the case when the information one gains comes through another's interpretations. To put it more generally, self-knowledge is thought of essentially as an epistemological achievement. However, as Moran (2001) has importantly pointed out, self-knowledge can take the form of third-person or first-person knowledge; and it is only third-person knowledge that is primarily an epistemological phenomenon. The emphasis is on gaining knowledge or information about oneself in a way that is not essentially different from how one gains information or knowledge about a third person. And just as one does not expect one's knowledge about a third person per se to change the person, one perhaps similarly should not expect the acquisition of information about oneself per se to change oneself.

In contrast to third-person knowledge, first-person knowledge, as Moran (2001) formulates it, is not a matter of gaining information about oneself as one would about another person, but primarily a matter of affirming and avowing who one is and standing behind that avowal.[6] Another way to put it is to talk about that acknowledging unacknowledged aspects of oneself and avowing them as part of oneself changes who one is, including one's identity, feelings, thoughts, understandings, and behaviors. Thus, as Moran (2001) points out, first-person self-knowledge is not primarily an epistemological phenomenon or achievement, but essentially a question of authenticity in the sense that it entails commitment to one's avowals and readiness to take actions that stand behind them.

We have traveled a long way only to return to the early seminal idea that unintegrated or isolated mental contents (in Freud's version, isolated by virtue of conflict and defense) erode the unity of the personality. On the path we have traveled, we have seen that disunity of the personality, which, in one context, can be understood as what one might refer to as sickness of the soul, can be contrasted with unity of the personality as a spiritual and moral ideal; and in another context, can be understood in terms of the contrast between neurosis and mental health.

## Implications for treatment

The altered conceptions of unconscious processes and of inner conflict and defense discussed in the previous chapters have important implications for the nature of treatment. Although these implications have been identified in the previous chapters, they bear repeating and extending here. When one thinks of psychopathology mainly in terms of the consequences of repressed conflictual wishes and impulses, it is understandable that a central aim of psychoanalytic treatment would be making the unconscious conscious. However, if one's emphasis in one's understanding psychopathology is on the role of early acquisition of maladaptive representations, it would follow that a central aim of treatment would be the alteration of these representations. Further, although becoming aware of one's representations and of their influence on one's behavior, feelings, and thoughts may be therapeutic, it is not always necessary. Rather, as we have seen, maladaptive representations may be altered through the therapeutic relationship itself, often without interpretation and insight.

Although an emphasis on the therapeutic relationship has its roots in earlier work (e.g., the writings of Ferenczi), Alexander and French's (1946) concept of "corrective emotional experience" represents an early and explicit statement of the therapeutic primacy of the therapeutic relationship. Although rejected by the psychoanalytic community at the time of its introduction, some variation of the importance of corrective emotional experience in psychoanalytic treatment has taken center stage in various psychoanalytic theories, including self psychology (empathic mirroring and understanding), Control–Mastery theory (test-passing), Fairbairn's object relative theory (the analyst as good object), and Winnicott's concepts of the facilitating and holding environment.

The findings, conceptual critiques and theoretical formulations discussed in the foregoing chapters raise important questions regarding the central role given to defense analysis in psychoanalytic treatment. Put most broadly, if defenses can be adaptive as well as maladaptive, it is not clear why defense analysis should be given canonical status in psychoanalytic treatment. The received wisdom, which begins with Freud's (Breuer & Freud, 1893–1895) positing of "defense hysteria" is that because, for at least neurotic patients, defense plays a primary causal role in psychopathology, it needs to be analyzed if therapeutic progress is to occur. (However, as Freud, 1896, p. 172; 1950[1892–1899], p. 222, also noted, symptoms appear as a consequence of the failure of defense – see Eagle, 2000.)

The meaning of analysis of defense varies with theoretical context. Thus, as noted above, in classical theory, defense is understood as directed against specific unconscious wishes, and analysis of defense essentially consists in interpretations that, to one degree or another, remove the defensive barriers to the full conscious experience of these wishes. Thus, from this perspective, knowing oneself is essentially knowing one's unacknowledged wishes and desires. However, as also noted, in contrast to this view, in the writings of Gray, Sugarman, and other contemporary ego psychologists, analysis of defense consists in knowing the defenses one employs and is directed to helping the patient better understand how his or her mind works rather than to uncovering specific repressed wishes. Relatedly, enhancing mentalization and reflective capacity is posited as an important goal of treatment in the contemporary psychoanalytic literature that, in turn, may serve to contribute to other important therapeutic goals such as an improved capacity to regulate affect.

Thus, in a broader conception of self-knowledge it is not limited to awareness of the particular mental contents barred from awareness, but also includes the characteristic ways in which one fails to reflect on one's own mental states and those of others. Further, the emphasis on enhancing mentalization and reflective capacity can be understood as one expression of the overriding goal of strengthening ego functions, particularly functions that play a central role in affect regulation. From a broad perspective, affect regulation, in turn, can be understood as an expression of the replacement of drivenness and compulsion with an increased sense of autonomy and agency. Although self-knowledge may play an important role in the achievement of these goals, in contrast to classical theory's situation of self-knowledge in the Enlightenment vision, implicit in some contemporary formulations is the idea that self-knowledge is a means to certain ends rather than an overriding end in itself.

The limits of at least third-person self-knowledge in bringing about therapeutic change has long been recognized in the psychoanalytic literature (e.g., the contrast between intellectual and emotional insight). This recognition has been expressed, for example, in a shift from primary emphasis on insight and awareness to the "corrective emotional" aspects of the therapeutic relationship. However, the psychoanalytic theory of therapeutic change can benefit from an increased recognition of the importance of strengthening ego functions (e.g., enhancing capacity for reflective functioning) in positive therapeutic outcome.

Freud's (1933) disclaimer notwithstanding, the primacy of certain fundamental values in classical theory suggests that, in certain respects, psychoanalysis *is* a Weltanschauung as well as a body of empirical claims. In order to counter what to Freud was the former unwelcome characterization, he often conflated values issues with empirical claims. For example, the centrality of self-knowledge in psychoanalysis was justified by Freud not as a central Enlightenment value, but as a clinical necessity, formulated in the clinical terms of repression, symptomatology, and lifting repression.

In short, classical psychoanalytic theory is an odd mixture of empirical claims and a Weltanschauung often conflated with each other and, therefore, often difficult to distinguish. As we have seen, at least many of the empirical claims are testable whereas the question of testability is far less relevant with regard to the Weltanschauung. For the latter, the primary issue is how meaningful and compelling these values are to a given individual. Thus, although lack of self-knowledge may not be equivalent to pathology, the acquisition of self-knowledge to health (the latter described by Stone, 1997, as confronting the otherness of oneself) may be a central value in an individual's life. And similarly, although relative absence of autonomy may not be entirely equivalent to pathology and autonomy to health in any simple way, it may constitute a primary value to be pursued in an individual life.

In ending this chapter, I want to make a final comment regarding the testability of some psychoanalytic claims that I could not 'fit in' in the other chapters. Many psychoanalytic empirical claims regarding human nature or psychological functioning are quite testable. However, the most appropriate model for testability is not the null hypothesis or the crucial experiment. As we have seen, for example, there is little convincing evidence for the hypothesis of a universal Oedipus complex and a good deal of evidence supporting alternative views (e.g., the neo-Westermarck hypothesis). However, the conclusions that a universal Oedipus complex does not exist is not based on a crucial experiment or on a number of experiments, crucial or otherwise. Rather, the conclusion is based on an accumulating and convincing body of evidence from a variety of disciplines (e.g., ethology, sociology, anthropology) and conceptual critiques that render the hypothesis of a universal Oedipus complex untenable and that provide support for alternative hypotheses. This approach to testing the empirical, often complex, claims of various aspects of psychoanalytic theory is, I believe, an appropriate one also applicable to testing the claims inherent in the concepts of the dynamic unconscious, inner conflict, and defense. If one puts all the previous chapters together, one has, in effect, a reformulation of the core elements of classical psychoanalytic theory. In brief, although the importance of the incest taboo remains, the Oedipus complex has been essentially re-conceptualized out of existence and replaced by the primacy of issues related to separation–individuation. Similarly, the nature of unconscious processes has been significantly modified, as have been ideas regarding what we are primarily conflicted about, the inner dangers against which we defend, and the processes through which we go about carrying out these defenses.

## Notes

1 It is important to distinguish between simply not being aware of the factors that influence and determine our conscious experience, many of which are inherently inaccessible to consciousness (e.g., impenetrable computational processes) and "false consciousness," which implies intentional and motivated dissimulation in the service of avoiding distressing affect or preserving a particular self-image. The latter is a motivated or intentional not knowing.

2 An important exception is self psychology theory, where there is little emphasis on inner conflict, defense, and unconscious mental processes.

3 The evidence for unconscious processing is often taken, mistakenly, as providing support for Freud's claims regarding the dynamic unconscious. For example, in a recent paper entitled "The neural basis of the dynamic unconscious" Berlin (2011) provides much evidence for unconscious mental processing, but virtually no evidence for the specific claims of the dynamic unconscious (see Eagle, 2011).

4 It is important to reiterate that, understood this way, autonomy is not in conflict with relatedness.

5 In this conception of autonomy, it is equivalent to what we normally mean by integrity.

6 The distinction in the psychoanalysis literature between intellectual and emotional insight, which has a long history in the psychoanalytic literature (e.g., Valenstein, 1962; Hatcher,

1973; Rosenblatt, 2004), has been the means of addressing some of the same issues and phenomena Moran (2001) identifies in his distinction between first-person and third-person self-knowledge. However, it is not at all clear that the presence or absence of emotion adequately accounts for the phenomena that both the distinctions between intellectual and emotional insight and third-person versus first-person self-knowledge are intended to address.

# REFERENCES

Ablon, S. L., Carlson, G. A., & Goodwin, F. K. (1974). Ego defense patterns in manic-depressive illness. *American Journal of Psychiatry, 131*, 803–807.
Abraham, K. (1913). A constitutional basis of locomotor activity. In *Selected papers* (pp. 235–243). New York: Basic Books, 1953.
Abrams, R. L., & Greenwald, A. G. (2000). Parts outweigh the whole (word) in unconscious analysis of meaning. *Psychological Science, 11*, 118–124.
Abramson, L. A., Metalsky, G. I., & Alloy, L. B. (1989). Hopelessness depression: A theory-based subtype of depression. *Psychological Review, 96*, 358–372.
Acker, F. (2008). New findings on unconscious versus conscious thought in decision making: Additional empirical data and meta-analysis. *Judgment and Decision Making, 3*(4), 292–303.
Ackerman, J. M., Nocera, C. C., & Bargh, J. A. (2010). Incidental haptic sensations influence social judgments and decisions. *Science, 328*, 1712–1715.
Adam, K. S., Sheldon-Keller, A. E., & West, M. (1996). Attachment organization and history of suicidal behavior in clinical adolescents. *Journal of Consulting and Clinical Psychology, 64*(2), 264–272.
Adams, H. E., Wright, L. W., & Lohr, B. A. (1996). Is homophobia associated with homosexual arousal? *Journal of Abnormal Psychology, 105*(3), 440–445.
Akhtar, S. (2015). Patience. *Psychoanalytic Review, 102*(1), 93–122.
Akkerman, K., Carr, V., & Lewin, R. (1992). Changes in ego defenses with recovery of depression. *Journal of Nervous and Mental Disease, 180*, 634–638.
Alexander, F. (1934). The influence of psychologic factors upon gastro-intestinal disturbances: A symposium. I. General principles, objectives, and preliminary results. *Psychoanalytic Quarterly, 3*, 501–539.
Alexander, F. (1939). Emotional factors in essential hypertension: Presentation of a tentative hypothesis. *Psychosomatic Medicine, 1*, 175–179.
Alexander, F. (1954). Psychoanalysis and psychotherapy. *Journal of the American Psychoanalytic Association, 2*, 722–733.
Alexander, F. (1959). Current problems in dynamic psychotherapy in its relationship to psychoanalysis. *American Journal of Psychiatry, 116*, 322–325.
Alexander, F. (1962). The development of psychosomatic medicine. *Journal of Psychosomatic Medicine, 23*, 13–24.

Alexander, F. G., & French, T. M. (1946). *Psychoanalytic therapy: Principles and applications.* New York: Ronald.

Allen, E. S., & Baucom, D. H. (2004). Adult attachment and patterns of extra dyadic involvement. *Family Process, 43*, 467–488.

Allen, J., & Fonagy, P. (2006). *The handbook of mentalization-based treatment.* New York: Wiley.

Allen, J. G., Fonagy, P., & Bateman, A. W. (2008). *Mentalizing in clinical practice.* Washington, DC: American Psychiatric Publishing.

Alloy, L. B., & Abramson, L. Y. (1988). Depressive realism: Four theoretical perspectives. In L. B. Alloy (Ed.), *Cognitive processes in depression* (pp. 223–265). New York: Guilford Press.

Amthauer, R., Brocke, B., Liepmann, D., & Beauducel, A. (1999). *Intelligence structure test.* Goettingen, Germany: Hogrefe.

Andersen, S. M., & Cole, S. (1990). Do I know you?: The role of significant others in general social perception. *Journal of Personality and Social Psychology*, 59, 384–399.

Anderson, A. K., Christoff, K., Panitz, D., DeRosa, E., & Gabrieli, J. D. E. (2003). Neural correlates of the automatic processing of threat facial signals. *Journal of Neuroscience, 23*, 5627–5633.

Anderson, C. M., & Bielert, C. (1990). Adolescent/adult copulatory behavior in nonhuman primates. In J. R. Feierman (Ed.), *Pedophilia: Biosocial dimensions* (pp. 176–200). New York: Springer-Verlag.

Andino, S. L., Menendez, R. G. A., Landis, T., & Pegna, A. J. (2009). Electrophysiological correlates of affective blindsight. *NeuroImage, 44*(2), 581–589.

Apfelbaum, B. (1966). On ego psychology: A critique of the structural approach to psychoanalytic theory. *International Journal of Psychoanalysis, 47*, 451–475.

Arendt, H. (1963). *Eichmann in Jerusalem: A report on the banality of evil.* New York: Penguin Books.

Arlow, J. A. (1969). Unconscious fantasy and disturbances of conscious experience. *Psychoanalytic Quarterly, 38*, 1–27.

Armstrong-Perlman, E. (1994). The allure of the bad object.In J. S. Grotstein, & D. B. Rinsley (Eds.). *Fairbairn and the origins of object relations* (pp. 222–233). London: Free Association.

Ascherman, L. I. & Safier, E. J. (1990). Sibling incest: Consequence of individual and family dysfunction. *Bulletin of the Menninger Clinic, 54*(3), 311–323.

Asendorpf, J. B., & Scherer, K. R. (1983). The discrepant repressor: Differentiation between low anxiety, high anxiety, and repression of anxiety by autonomic-facial-verbal patterns of behavior. *Journal of Personality and Social Psychology, 45*(6), 1334–1346.

Atwood, G. E., & Storolow, R. D. (1984). *Structures of subjectivity: Explorations in psychoanalytic phenomenology.* Hillsdale, NJ: Analytic Press.

Averbach, E., & Sperling, G. (1961). Short term storage of information in vision. In C. Cherry (Ed.), *Information theory* (pp. 196–211). Washington, DC: Butterworth.

Ayduk, O., Mendoza-Denton, R., Mischel, W., Downey, G., Peake, P., & Rodriguez, M. (2000). Regulating the interpersonal self: Strategic self-regulation for coping with rejection sensitivity. *Journal of Personality and Social Psychology, 79*, 776–792.

Ayduk, O., Mischel, W., & Downey, G. (2002). Attentional mechanisms linking rejection to hostile reactivity: The role of "hot" vs. "cool" focus. *Psychological Science, 13*, 443–448.

Ayduk, O., Zayas, V., Downey, G., Cole, A. B., Shoda, Y., & Mischel, W. (2008). Rejection sensitivity and executive control: joint predictors of borderline personality features. *Research in Personality, 42*, 151–168.

Bakan, D. (1966). *The duality of human existence: Isolation and communion in western man.* Boston, MA: Beacon Press.

Banfield, J. F., Pendry, L. F., Mewse, A. J., & Edwards, M. G. (2003). The effects of an elderly stereotype prime on reaching and grasping actions. *Social Cognition, 21*, 299–319.

Barelli, C., Heistermann, M., Boesch, C., & Reichard, U. H. (2007). Sexual swellings in wild white-handed gibbon females (Hylobateslar) indicate the probability of ovulation. *Hormones and Behavior, 51*, 221–230.

Bargh, J. A., Chen, M., & Burrows, L. (1996). Automaticity of social behavior: Direct effects of trait construct and stereotype activation on action. *Journal of Personality and Social Psychology, 71*(2), 230–244.

Barnard, C. J., and Fitzsimons, J. (1988). Kin recognition and mate choice in mice: The effects of kinship familiarity and social interaction on intersexual interaction. *Animal Behaviour, 36*, 1078–1090.

Barnard, C. J., & Aldhous, P. (1991). Kinship, kin discrimination, and mate choice. In P. G. Hepper (Ed.), *Kin recognition* (pp. 125–147). Cambridge, UK: Cambridge University Press.

Bartholomew, K., & Horowitz, L. M. (1991). Attachment styles among young adults: A test of a four-category model. *Journal of Personality and Social Psychology, 61*, 226–244.

Bateman, A. & Fonagy, P. (2006). *Mentalization-based treatment of borderline personality disorder.* New York: Oxford University Press.

Bateson, P. (1983). Optimal outbreeding. In P. Bateson (Ed.), *Mate choice* (pp. 257–277). Cambridge, UK: Cambridge University Press.

Bateson, P. (2004). Inbreeding avoidance and incest taboos. In A. P. Wolf & W. H. Durham (Eds.), *Inbreeding, incest, and the incest taboo: The state of knowledge at the turn of the century* (pp. 34–37). Stanford, CA: Stanford University Press.

Bateson, P. P. G. (1982). Preferences for cousins in Japanese quail. *Nature, 295*, 236–237.

Baumeister, R. F., Dale, K., & Sommer, K. L. (1998). Freudian defense mechanisms and empirical findings in modern social psychology: Reaction formation, projection, displacement, undoing, isolation, sublimation, and denial. *Journal of Personality, 66*(6), 1081–1124.

Becker, E. (1973). *The denial of death.* New York: Simon & Schuster.

Beebe, B., & Lachmann, F. (2002). *Infant research and adult treatment: Co-constructing interactions.* Hillsdale, NJ: Analytic Press.

Benedek, T. (1938). Adaptation to reality in early infancy. *Psychoanalytic Quarterly, 7*, 200–215.

Bentham, J. (1789/1907). *An introduction to the principles of morals and legislation.* Oxford: Clarendon.

Bereczkei , T., Gyuris, P., Koves, P., & Bernath, L. (2002). Homogamy, genetic similarity, and imprinting: Parental influence on mate choice preferences. *Personality and Individual Differences, 33*, 677–690.

Bereczkei, T., Gyuris, P., & Weisfeld, G. E. (2004). Sexual imprinting in human mate choice. *Proceedings of the Royal Society of London B, 271*, 1129–1134.

Berlin, H. A. (2011). The neural basis of the dynamic unconscious. *Neuropsychoanalysis, 13*(1), 5–31.

Berman, M. G., Yourganov, G., Askren, M. K., Ayduk, O., Casey, B. J., Gotlib, I. H., . . . Jonides, J. (2013). Dimensionality of brain networks linked to life-long individual differences in self-control. *Nature Communication, 4*(1373), 1–7.

Bermant, G. (1976). Sexual behavior: Hard times with the Coolidge effect. In M. H. Siegel & H. P. Zeigler (Eds.), *Psychological research: The inside story.* New York: Harper & Row.

Bernat, E., Shevrin, H., & Snodgrass, M. (2001). Subliminal visual oddball stimuli evoke a P300 component. *Journal of Clinical Neurophysiology, 112*, 159–171.

Bion, W. R. (1959). Attacks on linking. *International Journal of Psychoanalysis, 40*, 308–315.

Bixler, R. H. (1981). Mechanisms for the avoidance of incest. *Psychological Reports, 48*, 978.

Bjorklund, D. E., & Kipp, K. (1996). Parental investment theory and gender differences in the evolution of inhibition mechanisms.*Psychological Bulletin, 120*, 163–188.

Black, M. (1967). Review of A. R. Couch's explanation and human action. *American Journal of Psychology, 80*, 655–656.

Blatt, S. J. (1998). Contributions of psychoanalysis to the understanding and treatment of depression. *Journal of the American Psychoanalytic Association, 46*, 722–752.

Bonanno, G. A., & Singer, J. L. (1990). Repressive personality style: Theoretical and methodological implications for health and pathology. In J. L. Singer (Ed.), *Repression and dissociation* (pp. 435–470). Chicago, IL: University of Chicago Press.

Bower, G. H. (1981). Mood and memory. *American Psychologist, 36*, 129–148.

Bowers, K. S. (1984). On being unconsciously influenced and informed. In K. S. Bowers & D. Meichenbaum (Eds.), The unconscious reconsidered (pp. 227–272). New York: John Wiley.

Bowers, K. S. (1987). Revisioning the unconscious. *Canadian Psychology, 28*, 93–104.

Bowlby, J. (1969/1982). *Attachment and loss,* Vol. 1: *Attachment* (2nd ed.). New York: Basic Books (original work published 1969).

Bowlby, J. (1980). *Attachment and loss,* Vol. 3: *Loss: Sadness and depression*. New York: Basic Books.

Bowlby, J. (1988). *A secure base: Clinical applications of attachment theory*. London: Routledge.

Brandchaft, B. (2007). Systems of pathological accommodation and change in analysis. *Psychoanalytic Psychology, 24*, 667–687.

Brandt, L. W. (1966). Process or structure? *Psychoanalytic Review, 53*, 50–54.

Brendgen, M., Vitaro, F., Turgeon, L., Poulin, F., & Wanner, B. (2004). Is there a dark side of positive illusions? Overestimation of social competence and subsequent adjustment in aggressive and nonaggressive children. *Journal of Abnormal Child Psychology, 32*(3), 305–320.

Brennan, K. A., Clark, C. L., & Shaver, P. R. (1998). Self-report measurement of adult romantic attachment: An integrative overview. In J. A. Simpson, & W. S. Rholes (Eds.), *Attachment theory and close relationships*. New York, NY: Guilford.

Brennan, K. A., & Morris, K. A. (1997). Attachment styles, self-esteem, and patterns of seeking feedback from romantic partners. *Personality and Social Psychology Bulletin, 23*, 23–31.

Brenner, C. (1982). *The mind in conflict*. New York: International Universities Press.

Brenner, C. (1991). A psychoanalytic perspective on depression. *Journal of the American Psychological association, 39*(1), 25–43.

Brenner, C. (1998). Beyond the ego and the id revisited. *Journal of Clinical Psychoanalysis, 7*, 165–180.

Brenner, C. (2002). Conflict, compromise formation, and structural theory. *Psychoanalytic Quarterly, 71*(3), 397–417.

Breuer, J., & Freud, S. (1893–1895). *Studies on hysteria. Standard Edition*, Vol. 2. London: Hogarth Press, 1955.

Briffault, R. (1928). The mothers. *Journal of Philosophical Studies, 3*(11), 392–395.

Broadbent, D. E., & Broadbent, M. H. (1987). From detection to identification: Response to multiple targets in rapid serial visual presentation. *Perceptual Psychophysics, 42*(2), 105–113.

Broadbent, D. E., FitzGerald, P., & Broadbent, M. H. P. (1986). Implicit and explicit knowledge in the control of complex systems. *British Journal of Psychology, 77*, 33–50.

Brown, L. L., Tomarken, A., Orth, D., Loosen, R., Kalin, N., & Davidson, R. (1996). Individual differences in repressive-defensiveness predict basal salivary cortisol levels. *Journal of Personality and Social Psychology, 70*, 362–371.

Burston, D. (1986). The cognitive and dynamic unconscious: A critical and historical perspective. *Contemporary Psychoanalysis, 22*, 133–157.

Busch, F. (2009). On creating a psychoanalytic mind: Psychoanalytic knowledge as a process. *Scandinavian Psychoanalytic Review*, *32*, 85–92.

Buss, D. M. (1984). *The evolution of desire: Strategies of human mating*. New York: Basic Books.

Byrne, D., Barry, J., & Nelson, D. (1963). Relation of the revised Repression-Sensitization Scale to measures of self-description. *Psychological Reports*, *13*, 323–334.

Call, V., Sprecher, S., & Schwartz, P. (1995). The incidence and frequency of marital sex in a national sample. *Journal of Marriage and Family*, *57*, 639–652.

Calvillo, D. P., & Penaloza, A. (2009). Are complex decisions better left to the unconscious? Further failed replications of the deliberation-without-attention effect. *Judgment and Decision Making*, *4*, 509–517.

Casey, B., Somerville, L., Gotlib, I., Ayduk, O., Franklin, N., Askren, M., . . . Shoda, Y. (2011). Behavioral and neural correlates of delay gratification 40 years later. *Proceedings of the National Academy of Sciences of America*, *108*(36), 14998–15003.

Chen, H., & Wylie, B. (2015). Amnesia for object attributes: Failure to report attended information that had just reached conscious awareness. *Psychological Science*, *26*(2), 203–210.

Chisholm, J. S., Burbank, V. K., Coall, D. A., & Gemmiti, F. (2005). Early stress: Perspectives from developmental evolutionary ecology. In B. J. Ellis, & D. F. Bjorklund (Eds.), *Origins of the social mind: Evolutionary psychology and child development* (pp. 76–107). New York: Guilford Press.

Chomsky, N. (1965). *Aspects of the theory of syntax*. Cambridge, MA: MIT Press.

Clark, C. E. G. (1977). Mating patterns and reproductive strategies in a community of wild chimpanzees. *Behavioral Ecology and Sociobiology*, *6*, 29–38.

Cohen, A. B. (2005). The relation of attachment to infidelity in romantic relationships: An exploration of attachment style, perception of partner's attachment style, relationship satisfaction, relationship quality and gender differences in sexual behaviors (Unpublished dissertation). Adelphi University, Long Island, New York.

Coifman, K. G., Bonanno, G. A., Ray, R. D., & Gross, J. J. (2007). Does repressive coping promote resilience? Affective-autonomic response discrepancy during bereavement. *Journal of Personality and Social Psychology*, *92*, 745–758.

Cousineau, T. M., & Shedler, J. (2006). Predicting physical health: Implicit mental health measures versus self-report scales. *Journal of Nervous and Mental Disease*, *194*(6), 427–432.

Craik, F. I. M., & Lockhart, R. S. (1972). Levels of processing: A framework for memory research. *Journal of Verbal Learning and Verbal Behavior*, *11*, 671–684.

Cramer, P. (2006). *Protecting the self: Defense mechanisms in action*. New York: Guilford Press.

Cramer, P. (2008). Seven pillars of defense mechanism theory. *Social and Personality Psychology Compass*, *2*, 1963–1981.

Cramer, P., & Blatt, S. J. (1990). Use of the TAT to measure change in defense mechanisms following intensive psychotherapy. *Journal of Personality Assessment*, *54*(1–2), 236–251.

Crews, F. C. (1995). *The memory wars: Freud's legacy in dispute*. New York: New York Review of Books.

Crews F. C. (1996). The verdict on Freud. *Psychological Science*, 7(2), 63–68.

Crowne, D. P., & Marlowe, D. (1960). A new scale of social desirability independent of psychopathology. *Journal of Consulting Psychology*, *24*, 349–354.

Cushman, P. (1990). Why the self is empty: Toward a historically situated psychology. *American Psychologist*, *45*(5), 599–611.

Damasio, A. (2000). *The feeling of what happens: Body and emotion in the making of consciousness*. New York: Houghton Mifflin Harcourt.

Davis, D., Shaw, P. R., & Vernon, M. L. (2004). Attachment style and subjective motivations for sex. *Personality & Social Bulletin, 30*(8), 1076–1090.

Davis, P. J. (1990). Repression and the inaccessibility of emotional memories. In J. L. Singer (Ed.), *Repression and dissociation* (pp. 387–403). Chicago, IL: University of Chicago Press.

Davis, P. J., & Schwartz, G. E. (1986). *Repression and the inaccessibility of affective memories: Relationship to temperature laterality and muscle activity of the face.* Yale University, Transcript.

Davison, W., Pray, M., & Bristol, C. (1990). Mutative interpretation and close psychoanalytic monitoring. *Psychoanalytic Quarterly, 59*, 599–628.

de Waal, F. B. M. (1990). Sociosexual behavior used for tension regulation in all ages and sex combinations among bonobos. In J. R. Feierman (Ed.), *Pedophilia: Biosocial dimensions* (pp. 378–393). New York: Springer-Verlag.

de Waal, F. B. M. (2007). *Chimpanzee politics: Power and sex among apes.* Baltimore, MD: Johns Hopkins University Press (original work published 1982).

DeBruine, L. M. (2002). Facial resemblance enhances trust. *Proceedings of the Royal Society of London B, 269*, 1307–1312.

Dennett, C. (1969). *Content and consciousness.* New York: Humanities Press; London: Routledge & Kegan Paul.

Dennett, D. C. (1978). Toward a cognitive theory of consciousness. In D. C. Dennett (Ed.), *Brainstorms* (pp. 149–173). New York: Bradford Books.

Dent, L., & Christian, C. (2014). The rise and fall of psychic conflict: A corpus-based exploratory study of psychoanalytic literature. Poster presented at 2014 Spring Meeting of the Division 39 (April 23–27). New York.

Depue, B. E., Curran, T., & Banich, M. T. (2007). Prefrontal regions orchestrate suppression of emotional memories via a two-phase process. *Science, 317*, 215–219.

Descartes, R. ([1640]1996). *Meditations on first philosophy*, Trans. John Cottingham. Cambridge: Cambridge University Press.

Deutsch, H. (1929). The genesis of agoraphobia. *International Journal of Psychoanalysis, 10*, 51–69.

Deutsch, J., & Deutsch, D. (1963). Attention: Some theoretical considerations. *Psychological Review*, 70, 80–90.

Diamond, L. (2003). What does sexual orientation orient? A biobehavioral model in distinguishing romantic love and sexual desire. *Psychological Review, 110* (1), 173–192.

Dijksterhuis, A. (2004). Think different: The merits of unconscious thought in preference development and decision making. *Journal of Personality and Social Psychology*, 87, 586–598.

Dijksterhuis, A., & Meurs, T. (2006). Where creativity resides: The generative power of unconscious thought. *Consciousness and Cognition, 15*(1), 135–146.

Dijksterhuis, A., & Nordgren, L.F. (2006). A theory of unconscious thought. *Perspectives on Psychological Science*, 1, 95–109.

Dijksterhuis, A., & van Knippenberg, A. V. (1998). The relation between perception and behavior, or how to win a game of trivial pursuit. *Journal of Personality and Social Psychology, 74*(4), 865–877.

Dijksterhuis, A., & van Olden, Z. (2006). On the benefits of thinking unconsciously: Unconscious thought increases post-choice satisfaction. *Journal of Experimental Social Psychology, 42*, 627–631.

Dixson, A. F. (1983). Observations on the evolution and behavioral significance of "sexual skin" in female primates. *Advances in the Study of Behavior, 13*, 63–106.

Dollard, J., & Miller, N. E. (1950). *Personality and psychotherapy.* New York: McGraw-Hill.

Doyen, S., Klein, O., Pichon, C.-L., & Cleeremans, A. (2012). Behavioral priming: It's all in the mind, but whose mind? *PLoS ONE*, 7(1): e29081.

Duhem, P. ([1914]1954). *The aim and structure of physical theory* (Trans., P. P. Wiener). Princeton, NJ: Princeton University Press.

Eagle, M. (1959). The effects of subliminal stimuli of aggressive content upon conscious cognition. *Journal of Personality, 27*, 578–600.

Eagle, M. (1962). Personality correlates of sensitivity to subliminal stimulation. *Journal of Nervous and Mental Disease, 134*(19), 1–17.

Eagle, M. N. (1973). Validation of motivational formulations: Acknowledgement as a criterion. In B. B. Rubinstein (Ed.), *Psychoanalysis and Contemporary Science* (Vol. 2, pp. 265–275). New York: Macmillan.

Eagle, M. N. (1980). A critical examination of motivational explanation in psychoanalysis. *Psychoanalysis and Contemporary Thought, 3*, 329–380.

Eagle, M. N. (1981). Interests as object relations. *Psychoanalysis and contemporary thought, 4*, 527–565. (Also Eagle, M.N. [1982]. In J. Masling (Ed.). *Empirical studies in psychoanalytic theories* (Vol. 1, pp. 159–188). Hillsdale, NJ: Erlbaum.

Eagle, M. (1982). Privileged access and the status of self-knowledge in Cartesian and Freudian conceptions of the mental. *Philosophy of the Social Sciences, 12*, 349–373.

Eagle, M. N. (1984). *Recent developments in psychoanalysis: A critical examination*. New York: McGraw-Hill.

Eagle, M. N. (1987). The psychoanalytic and the cognitive unconscious. In R. Stern (Ed.), *Theories of the unconscious and theories of the self* (pp. 155–189). Hillsdale, NJ: Analytic Press.

Eagle, M. N. (1993a). Enactments, transference, and symptomatic cure: A case history. *Psychoanalytic Dialogues, 3*(1), 93–110.

Eagle, M. N. (1993b). The dynamics of theory change in psychoanalysis. In J. Earman, A. I. Janis, G. J. Massey, & N. Rescher (Eds.), *Philosophical problems of the internal and external worlds: Essays on the philosophy of Adolf Grunbaum*. Pittsburg, PA: University of Pittsburg Press.

Eagle, M. N. (2000). A critical evaluation of current conceptions of transference and countertransference. *Psychoanalytic Psychology, 17*(1), 24–37.

Eagle, M. N. (2001). Interests as object relations. *Psychoanalysis and Contemporary Thought, 4*, 527–565.

Eagle, M. N. (2007a). Psychoanalysis and its critics. *Psychoanalytic Psychology, 24*(1), 10–24.

Eagle, M. N. (2007b). Attachment and sexuality. In D. Diamond, S. Blatt, & J. Lichtenberg (Eds.), *Attachment and sexuality* (pp. 27–50). New York: Analytic Press.

Eagle, M. N. (2009). Agoraphobia: A case study. Franz Alexander lecture presented to the New Center for Psychoanalysis. March, Los Angeles.

Eagle, M. N. (2011a). *From classical to contemporary psychoanalysis: A critique and integration*. New York: Routledge.

Eagle, M. N. (2011b). Psychoanalysis and the Enlightenment vision: An overview. Plenary address given at annual spring meeting of the American Psychoanalytic Association, San Francisco, June 9 (also published in *Journal of the American Psychoanalytic Association, 59*(6), 1099–1118).

Eagle, M. N. (2011c). Interpretation and the therapeutic relationship: An attempt at integration. *Clinical Social Work Journal, 39*(2), 139–150.

Eagle, M. N. (2013). *Attachment and psychoanalysis: Theory, research, and clinical implications*. New York: Guilford Press.

Eagle, M. N., & Ortof, E. (1967). The effect of levels of attention upon "phonetic" recognition errors. *Journal of Verbal Learning and Verbal Behavior, 6*, 226–231.

Eagle, M. N., Wolitzky, D. L., & Klein, G. S. (1966). Imagery: Effect of a concealed figure in a stimulus. *Science, 151*(3712), 837–839.

Eagle, M. N., Wolitzky, D. L., & Wakefield, J. C. (2001). The analyst's knowledge and authority: A critique of the "new view" in psychoanalysis. *Journal of the American Psychoanalytic Association, 9*, 457–488.

Edelstein, R. S., Chopik, W. T., & Kean, E. L. (2011). Sociosexuality moderates the association between testosterone and relationship status in men and women. *Hormones and Behavior, 60*, 248–255.

Egid, K., & Brown, J. L. (1989). The major histocompatibility complex and female mating preferences in mice. *Animal Behavior, 38*(3), 548–549.

Eigen, M. (1993). *The psychotic core*. Northvale, NJ: Jason Aronson.

Eigsti, I. M., Zayas, V., Mischel, W., Shoda, Y., Ayduk, O., Dadlani, M. B., Casey, B. J. (2006). Predicting cognitive control from preschool to late adolescence and young adulthood. *Psychological Science, 17*(6), 478–484.

Elise, D. (2012). The danger in deception: Oedipal betrayal and the assault on truth. *Journal of the American Psychoanalytic Association, 60*, 679–705.

Ellenberger, H. (1970). *The discovery of the unconscious: The history and evolution of dynamic psychiatry*. New York: Basic Books.

Elliot, A. J., & Niesta, D. (2008). Romantic red: Red enhances men's attraction to women. *Journal of Personality and Social Psychology, 95*(5), 1150–1164.

Erdelyi, M. H. (1990). Repression, reconstruction, and defense: History and integration of psychoanalytic and experimental frameworks. In J. L. Singer (Ed.), *Repression and dissociation: Defense mechanisms and personality styles: Current theory and research* (pp. 1–31). Chicago, IL: University of Chicago Press.

Erdelyi, M. H. (2006).The unified theory of repression. *Behavioral and Brain Sciences, 29*, 499–511.

Erdelyi, M. H. & Goldberg, B. (1990). Let's not sweep repression under the rug. In J. F. Kihlstrom & F. J. Evans (Eds.). *Functional disorders of memory* (pp. 355–402). Hillsdale, NJ: Erlbaum.

Ericson, M. (1993). Rethinking Oedipus: An evolutionary perspective of incest avoidance. *American Journal of Psychiatry, 150*, 411–416.

Eriksen, C. W. (1954). The case for perceptual defense. *Psychological Review, 61*(3), 175–182.

Erikson, E. (1946). Ego development and historical change: Clinical notes. *Psychoanalytic Study of the Child, 2*, 379–389.

Erikson, E. (1950). *Childhood and society*. New York: W. W. Norton.

Erreich, A. (2003). A modest proposal: (Re)defining unconscious fantasy. *Psychoanalytic Quarterly, 72*(3), 541–574.

Erreich, A. (2015). Unconscious fantasy as a special class of mental representation: A contribution to a model of mind. *Journal of the American Psychoanalytic Association, 63*(2), 247–270.

Esterling, B. A., Antoni, M., Kumar, M., & Schneiderman, N. (1990). Emotional repression, stress disclosure responses, and Epstein–Barr viral capsid antigen titers. *Psychosomatic Medicine, 52*, 397–410.

Esteve, L. G., Valdes, M., Immaculada, M. R., & Jodar, T. D. (1992). Denial mechanisms in myocardial infarction: Their relations with psychological variables and short-term outcome. *Journal of Psychosomatic Research, 36*(5), 491–496.

Esteves, F., Dimberg, U., & Öhman, A. (1994). Automatically elicited fear: Conditioned skin conductance responses to masked facial expressions. *Cognition and Emotion, 8*, 393–413.

Etkin, A., Klemenhagen, K. C., Dudman, J. T., Rogan, M. T., Hen, R., Kandel, E. R., & Hirsch, J. (2004). Individual differences in trait anxiety predict the response of the basolateral amygdala to unconsciously processed fearful faces. *Neuron, 44*, 1043–1055.

Fairbairn, W. R. D. (1929). Dissociation and repression. Doctoral thesis. In E. F. Birtles, & D. E. Scharff (Eds.), *From instinct to self*, Vol. 2 (pp. 13–79). Northvale, NJ: Jason Aronson.

Fairbairn, W. R. D. (1952). *Psychological studies of the personality*. London: Tavistock, Routledge & Kegan Paul.

Fairbairn, W. R. D. (1954). *An object-relations theory of the personality*. New York: Basic Books.

Fairbairn, W. R. D. (1958). On the nature and aims of psychoanalytical treatment. *International Journal of Psycho-Analysis, 39*, 374–383.

Farooqui, A. A., & Manly, T. (2015). Anticipatory control through associative learning of subliminal relations. *Psychological Science, 26*, 325–334.

Farrugia, C., & Hogans, L. (1998). *Conceptualized the pair-bond: Attachment, caregiving, and sexuality as predictors of intimacy in adult romantic relationships*. Paper given at Sixth Australian Institute of Family Studies conference. Melbourne, Nov. 25–27, 1998.

Federn, P. (1950). *Ego psychology and the psychoses*. New York: International Universities Press.

Feeney, J.A., & Noller, P. (1990). Attachment style as a predictor of adult romantic relationships. *Journal of Personality and Social Psychology, 58*, 281–291.

Fenichel, O. (1938). The drive to amass wealth. In H. Fenichel & D. Rapaport (Eds.), *The collected papers of Otto Fenichel* (2nd ed.) (pp. 89–108). New York: Norton.

Fenichel, O. (1945). *The psychoanalytic theory of neurosis*. New York: W. W. Norton.

Field, G. C., Averling, F., & Laird, J. (1922). Is the conception of the unconscious of value in psychology? A symposium. *Mind, 31*, 413–442.

Fingarette, H. (1963). *The self in transformation: Psychoanalysis, philosophy and the life of the spirit*. New York: Harper & Row.

Fingarette, H. (1969). *Self-deception*. London: Routledge & Kegan Paul.

Fisher, C. (1954). Further observations on the Pötzl phenomenon: The effects of subliminal visual stimulation on dreams, images, and hallucinations. In H. Shevrin (Ed.), *Subliminal explorations of perception, dreams, and fantasies: The pioneering contributions of Charles Fisher*. Madison, CT: International Universities Press, 2003, Psychological Issues, Monograph 64.

Fisher, C., & Paul, I. H. (1959). The effect of subliminal stimulation on imagery and dreams: A validation study. *Journal of the American Psychoanalytic Association*, 7, 35–83.

Fisher, H. E. (1998). Lust, attraction, and attachment in mammalism reproduction. *Human Nature, 9*, 23–52.

Fiske, S. T., & Neuberg, S. L. (1990). A continuum model of impression formation, from category-based to individuating processes: Influence of information and motivation on attention and interpretation. In M. P. Zanna (Ed.), *Advances in experimental social psychology* (Vol. 23, pp. 1–74). New York: Academic Press.

Flores, R. Z., Mattos, L. F., & Salzano, F. M. (1998). Incest frequency, predisposition factors, and effect in a Brazilian population. *Current Anthropology*, 39, 554–558.

Fodor, J. A. (1983). *The modularity of mind: An essay on faculty psychology*. Cambridge, MA: MIT Press.

Fonagy, P. (1999). Memory and therapeutic action. *International Journal of Psychoanalysis, 80*, 215–223.

Fonagy, P. (2001). *Attachment theory and psychoanalysis*. New York: Other Press.

Fonagy, P., Gergely, G., Jurist, E. L., & Target, M. (2002). *Affect regulation, mentalization, and the development of the self*. New York: Other Press.

Fonagy, P., Steele, H., & Steele, M. (1991). Maternal representation during pregnancy predict the organization of infant mother attachment at one-year of age. *Child Development, 62*, 891–905.

Fonagy, P., Steele, M., Steele, H., Leigh, T., Kennedy, R., Mattoon, G., & Target, M. (1995). Attachment, the reflective self, and borderline states. The predictive specificity of the Adult Attachment Interview and pathological and emotional development. In S. Goldberg, R. Muir, & J. Kerr (Eds.). *Attachment research: Social, developmental and clinical perspectives* (pp. 233–278). Hillsdale, NJ: Analytic Press.

Fosshage, J. (2017). Emergence of conflict during the development of self: A relational self psychology perspective. In C. Christian, M. N. Eagle, & D. L. Wolitzky (Eds.), *Conflict and psychoanalysis*. New York: Routledge.

Fox, R. (1980). *The red lamp of incest: What the taboo can tell us about who we are and how we got that way*. London: Dutton.

Fraley, R. C., & Marks, M. J. (2010). Westermarck, Freud, and the incest taboo: Does familial resemblance activate sexual attraction? *Personality and Social Psychology Bulletin, 36*, 1202–1212.

Fraley, R. C., & Shaver, P. R. (1997). Adult attachment and the suppression of unwanted thoughts. *Journal of Personality and Social Psychology, 73*, 1080–1091.

French, T. (1933). Interrelations between psychoanalysis and the experimental work of Pavlov. *American Journal of Psychiatry, 89*, 1165–1203.

Fretter, P. B., Bucci, W., Broitman, J., Silberschatz, G., & Curtis, J. T. (1994). How the patient's plan relates to the concept of transference. *Psychotherapy Research, 4*, 58–72.

Freud, A. (1936). *The ego and the mechanisms of defense*. New York: International Universities Press, 1966 (Rev. ed.).

Freud, A. (1966). The ego and the mechanisms of defense. In C. Baines (Ed. and Trans.), *The writings of Anna Freud* (Vol. 2). New York: International Universities Press (original work published 1936).

Freud, S. (1887/1902). The origins of psychoanalysis. In M. Bonaparte, A. Freud, & E. Kris (Eds.) *Sigmund Freud's letters: Letters, drafts and notes to Wilhelm Fliess (1897–1902)*. (Trans. E. Mosbacher). London: Imago.

Freud, S. (1893). On the psychical mechanisms of hysterical phenomena. *Standard Edition*, Vol. 3, pp. 25–39. London: Hogarth Press, 1962.

Freud, S. (1894). The neuro-psychoses of defense. *Standard Edition*, Vol. 3, pp. 41–68. London: Hogarth Press.

Freud, S. (1896). The aetiology of hysteria. In J. Riviere (Trans.), *Sigmund Freud: Collected papers* (Vol. 1). New York: Basic Books.

Freud, S. (1900). The interpretation of dreams. *Standard Edition*,Vols. 4, 5. London: Hogarth Press, 1953.

Freud, S. (1901). The psychopathology of everyday life. *Standard Edition*, Vol. 6, pp. 1–279. London: Hogarth Press. 1960.

Freud, S. (1905). Three essays on the theory of sexuality. *Standard Edition*, Vol. 7, pp. 123–245. London: Hogarth Press, 1953.

Freud, S. (1908). Hysterical fantasies and their relation to bisexuality. *Standard Edition*, Vol. 9, pp. 155–166. London: Hogarth Press.

Freud, S. (1909). Notes upon a case of obsessional neurosis.*Standard Edition*,Vol. 10, pp. 5–149. London: Hogarth Press, 1978.

Freud, S. (1910a). *The origin and development of psychoanalysis*. New York: Henry Regnery (Gateway Editions), 1965.

Freud, S. (1910b). A special type of object choice made by men. *Standard Edition*, Vol. 11, pp. 165–176. London: Hogarth Press.

Freud, S. (1911). Psychoanalytic notes on an autobiographical account of a case of paranoia (dementia paranoides). *Standard Edition*, Vol. 12, pp. 2–82. London: Hogarth Press, 1958.

Freud, S. (1912a). The dynamics of transference. *Standard Edition*, Vol. 12, pp. 97–108. London: Hogarth Press.

Freud, S. (1912b). Recommendations to physicians practising psychoanalysis. *Standard Edition*, Vol. 12, pp. 109–120. London: Hogarth Press.
Freud, S. (1912c). On the universal tendency to debasement in the sphere of love (Contributions to the psychology of love II). *Standard Edition*, Vol. 11, pp. 177–190. London: Hogarth Press, 1957.
Freud, S. (1912d). Types of onset. *Standard Edition*, Vol. 12, pp. 231–238. London: Hogarth Press.
Freud, S. (1913). On psycho-analysis. *Standard Edition*, Vol. 12, pp. 205–212. London: Hogarth Press.
Freud, S. (1914a). On the history of the psychoanalytic movement. *Standard Edition*, Vol. 14, pp. 2–66. London: Hogarth Press, 1957.
Freud, S. (1914b). On narcissism: An introduction. *Standard Edition*, Vol. 14, pp. 67–102. London: Hogarth Press, 1957.
Freud, S. (1915a). Instincts and their vicissitudes. *Standard Edition*, Vol. 14, pp. 117–140. London: Hogarth Press.
Freud, S. (1915b). Repression. *Standard Edition*, Vol. 14, pp. 146–158. London: Hogarth Press.
Freud, S. (1916). Some character types met with in psycho-analytic work. *Standard Edition*, Vol. 14, pp. 311–333. London: Hogarth Press.
Freud, S. (1916–1917). Introductory lectures on psycho-analysis. *Standard Edition*, Vol. 15–16, pp. 1–482. London: Hogarth Press, 1961.
Freud, S. (1917 [1915]). Mourning and melancholia. *Standard Edition*, Vol. 14, pp. 204–258. London: Hogarth Press.
Freud, S. (1917 [1916–1917]). General theory of the neuroses. *Standard Edition*, Vol. 16, pp. 243–256. London: Hogarth Press.
Freud, S. (1919a). Introduction to psychoanalysis and the war neuroses. *Standard Edition*, Vol. 17, pp. 205–216. London: Hogarth Press, 1955.
Freud, S. (1919b). "A child is being beaten": A contribution to the study of the origin of sexual perversions. *Standard Edition*, Vol. 17, pp. 179–204. London: Hogarth Press.
Freud, S. (1920). Beyond the pleasure principle. *Standard Edition*, Vol. 18, pp. 7–64. London: Hogarth Press, 1955.
Freud, S. (1922). Neurotic mechanisms in jealousy, paranoia and homosexuality. *Standard Edition*, Vol. 18, pp. 223–232. London: Hogarth Press.
Freud, S. (1923). The ego and the id. *Standard Edition*, Vol. 19, pp. 12–66. London: Hogarth Press, 1961.
Freud, S. (1924). The economic problem of masochism. *Standard Edition*, Vol. 19, pp. 155–170. London: Hogarth Press, 1961.
Freud, S. (1925). Some physical consequences of the anatomical distinction between the sexes. *Standard Edition*, Vol. 19, pp. 241–258. London: Hogarth Press, 1961.
Freud, S. (1926a). An autobiographical study: Inhibitions, symptoms, and anxiety. *Standard Edition*, Vol. 20, pp. 77–174. London: Hogarth Press, 1959.
Freud, S. (1926b). The question of lay analysis. *Standard Edition*, Vol. 20, pp. 183–258. London: Hogarth Press.
Freud, S. (1927). The future of an illusion. *Standard Edition*, Vol. 21, London: Hogarth, pp. 3–56.
Freud, S. (1930). Civilization and its discontents.*Standard Edition*, Vol. 21, pp. 57–146. London: Hogarth Press, 1961.
Freud, S. (1933). New introductory lectures on psycho-analysis. *Standard Edition*, Vol. 22, pp. 1–182. London: Hogarth Press.
Freud, S. (1937). Analysis terminable and interminable. *Standard Edition*, Vol. 23, pp. 209–253. London: Hogarth Press, 1964.

Freud, S. (1940 [1938]). An outline of psycho-analysis. *Standard Edition*, Vol. 23, pp. 139–207. London: Hogarth Press. 1964.
Freud, S. (1940a). An outline of psycho-analysis. *International Journal of Psychoanalysis, 21*, 27–84.
Freud. S. (1940b). Splitting of the ego in the process of defence. *Standard Edition*, Vol. 23, pp. 271–278. London: Hogarth Press.
Freud, S. (1950[1892–1899]). Extracts from the Fliess papers. Draft K: The neuroses of defense (A Christmas fairy tale), January 1, 1896, p. 222. *Standard Edition*, Vol.1. London: Hogarth Press, 1966.
Freud, S. (1950/1895). Project for a scientific psychology. *Standard Edition*, Vol. 1, pp. 295–391. London: Hogarth Press.
Friedman, L. (2008). A renaissance for Freud's papers on technique. *Psychoanalytic Quarterly, 77*, 1031–1044.
Friedman, M. (1985). Toward a reconceptualization of guilt. *Contemporary Psychoanalysis, 21*, 501–547.
Friedman, R. C., & Downey, J. I. (1985). Biology and the Oedipus complex. *Psychoanalytic Quarterly, 64*, 234–264.
Fromm, E. (1941). *Escape from freedom*. New York: Avon Books.
Funder, D. C., & Block, J. (1989).The role of ego-control, ego-resiliency, and IQ in delay of gratification in adolescence. *Journal of Personality and Social Psychology, 57*, 1041–1050.
Gabbard, G., Litowitz, B. E, & Williams, P. (2012). *Textbook of psychoanalysis*, 2nd ed. Washington, DC: American Psychiatric Association.
Gardner, P., Holzman, P., Klein, G., Linton, H., & Spence, D. (1959). Cognitive control: A study of individual consistencies in cognitive behavior. *Psychological Issues, 4*, 1–186.
Gedo, J. (1968). Freud's self-analysis and his scientific ideas. *American Imago, 25*(2), 99.
Geha, R. E. (1984). On psychoanalytic history and the "real" story of fictitious lives. *International Forum for Psychoanalysis, 1*, 221–229.
Gendlin, E. T. (1962). *Experiencing and the creation of meaning*. Glencoe, IL: Free Press.
George, C., Kaplan, N., & Main, M. (1984). Adult Attachment Interview protocol. Unpublished manuscript, University of California, Berkeley at Berkeley, CA.
Gettler, L. T, McDade, T. W., Agustin, S. S., & Kuzawa, C. W. (2011). Short-term changes in fathers' hormones during father–child play: Impacts of paternal attitudes and experience. *Hormones and Behavior, 60*(5), 599–606.
Ghent, E. (1990). Masochism, submission, surrender. *Contemporary Psychoanalysis, 26*(1), 108–136.
Gilbert, D. T., & Hixon, J. G. (1991). The trouble of thinking: Activation and application of stereotypic beliefs. *Journal of Personality and Social Psychology, 60*, 509–517.
Gill, M. M. (1976). Metapsychology is not psychology. In M. M. Gill, & P. S. Holzman (Eds.), *Psychology vs. metapsychology: Essays in memory of George S. Klein*. New York: International Universities Press.
Gill, M. M. (1984). Transference: A change in conception or only in emphasis? *Psychoanalytic Inquiry, 4*(3), 489–523.
Gill, M. M. (1994). *Psychoanalysis in transition*. Hillsdale, NJ: Analytic Press.
Gitelson, M. (1963). On the problem of character neurosis. *Journal of the Hillside Hospital, 12*, 3–17.
Goldstein, K. (1983). *The organism: A holistic approach to biology derived from pathological data in man*. Salt Lake City, UT: American Book Publishing.
González-Vallejo, C., & Phillips, N. D. (2010). Predicting soccer matches: A reassessment of the benefit of unconscious thinking. *Judgment and Decision Making, 5*, 200–206.
Gray, P. (1990). The nature of therapeutic action in psychoanalysis. *Journal of the American Psychoanlaytic Association, 38*(4), 1083–1097.

Gray, P. (2005). *The ego and analysis of defense*. Oxford: Rowman & Littlefield.
Green, A. (1995). Has sexuality anything to do with psychoanalysis? *International Journal of Psychoanalysis*, *76*, 871–883.
Greenberg, J. (1991). *Oedipus and beyond: A clinical theory*. Cambridge, MA: Harvard University Press.
Greenson, R. R. (1967). *The technique and practice of psychoanalysis*. New York: International Universities Press.
Greenwald, A. G. (1980). The totalitarian ego: Fabrication and revision of personal history. *American Psychologist*, *35*, 603–618.
Greenwald, A. G. (1992). New Look 3: Unconscious cognition re-claimed. *American Psychologist*, *47*, 776–779.
Groddeck, G. (1923). *Das Buch vom Es: Psychoanalytische Briefe an eine Freundin*. Vienna: Internationaler Psychoanalytischer Verlag; Wiesbaden: Limes, 1961 (English translation: *The Book of the It*. New York: International Universities Press, 1976).
Gross, J. J., & Levenson, R. W. (1993). Emotional suppression: Physiology, self-report, and expressive behavior. *Journal of Personality and Social Psychology*, *64*, 970–986.
Grossman, L., & Eagle, M. (1970). Synonymity, anonymity, and association in false recognition responses. *Journal of Experimental Psychology*, *83*(2, Pt. 1), 244–248.
Grunbaum, A. (1990). "Meaning" connections and causal connections in the human sciences: The poverty of hermeneutic philosophy. *Journal of the American Psychoanalytic Association*, *38*, 559–577.
Guntrip, H. (1969). *Schizoid phenomena, object relations and the self*. New York: International Universities Press.
Hamilton, V. (1982). *Narcissus and Oedipus: The children of psychoanalysis*. London: Routledge & Kegan Paul.
Hannula, D. E., Simons, D. J., & Cohen, N. J. (2005). Imaging implicit perception: Promise and pitfalls. *Nature Reviews Neuroscience*, *6*, 247–255.
Hatcher, R. (1973). Insight and self-observation. *Journal of the American Psychoanalytic Association*, *21*, 377–398.
Havik, O. E., & Maeland, J. G. (1988). Verbal denial and outcome in myocardial infarction patients. *Journal of Psychosomatic Research*, *32*, 145–157.
Hazan, C., & Zeifman, D. (1994). Sex and the psychological tether. In D. Perlman, & K. Bartholomew (Eds.), *Advances in personal relationships* (Vol. 5, pp. 151–180). London: Jessica Kingsley.
Helmholtz, H. (1867/1968). Connecting the perceptions in general. In W. Warren, & R. Warren (Eds.), *Helmholtz on perception: Its physiology and development*. New York: Wiley.
Helmholtz, H. (1868/1971). The recent progress in the theory of vision. In R. Kahl (Ed.), *Selected writings of Hermann von Helmholtz*, pp. 144–222. Middletown, CT: Wesleyan University Press.
Hendrickx, H., De Houwer, J., Baeyens, F., Eelen, P., & Van Avermaet, E. (1997). Hidden covariation detection might be very hidden indeed. *Journal of Experimental Psychology: Learning, Memory, and Cognition*, *23*, 201–220.
Hepler, J., & Albarracin, D. (2013). Complete unconscious control: Using (in)action primes to demonstrate completely unconscious activation of inhibitory control mechanisms. *Cognition*, *128*(3), 271–279.
Hesse, E. (2008). The Adult Attachment Interview: Protocol, method of analysis, and empirical studies. In J. Cassidy, & P. R. Shaver (Eds.), *Handbook of attachment: Theory, research, and clinical implications*, 2nd ed. (pp. 552–598). New York: Guilford Press.
Hesse, E., & Main, M. (2006). Frightened, threatening, and dissociative parental behavior in low risk samples: Description, discussion, and interpretation. *Development & Psychopathology*, *18*, 309–343.

Hodgins, H. S., Koestner, R., & Duncan, N. (1996). On the compatibility of autonomy and relatedness. *Personality and Social Psychology Bulletin, 22*, 227–237.

Hoffman, I. Z. (1998). *Death, anxiety, and adaptation to mortality in psychoanalytic theory: Ritual and spontaneity in the psychoanalytic process*. Hillsdale, NJ: Analytic Press.

Hoffman, I. Z. (2009). Doublethinking our way to "scientific" legitimacy: The desiccation of human Schatzman experience. *Journal of the American Psychoanalytic Association, 57*, 1043–1069.

Hoffman, M., & Hoffman, L. (2014). Religion in the life and work of W. R. D. Fairbairn. In G. Clarke, & D. Scharff (Eds.), *Fairbairn and the object relations tradition* (pp. 69–85). London: Karnac.

Holender, D. (1986). Semantic activation without conscious identification in dichotic listening, parafoveal vision, and visual masking: A survey and appraisal. *Behavior and Brain Science, 9*, 1–23.

Holland, R. W., Hendriks, M., & Aarts, H. (2005). Smells like clean spirit: Nonconscious effects of scent on cognition and behavior. *Psychological Science, 16*(9), 689–693.

Holmes, D. S. (1974). Investigations of repression: Differential recall of material experimentally or naturally associated with ego threat. *Psychological Bulletin, 81*(10), 632–653.

Holmes, J. (2001). *The search for the secure base: Attachment theory and psychotherapy*. New York: Brunner-Routledge.

Holt, R. R. (1976). Drive or wish? A reconsideration of the psychoanalytic theory of motivation. In M. M. Gill, & P. S. Holzman (Eds.), *Psychology versus metapsychology: Essays in memory of George S. Klein*. New York: International Universities Press.

Holt, R. R. (2008). *Primary process thinking: Theory, measurement, research*. New York: Jason Aronson.

Holzman, P. (1962). Repression and cognitive style. *Bulletin of the Menninger Clinic, 26*, 273–282.

Houck, G. M., & Lecuyer-Maus, E. A. (2004). Maternal limit setting during toddlerhood, delay of gratification, and behavior problems at age 5. *Infant Mental Health Journal, 25*, 28–46.

Howe, R. B. K. (1991). Introspection: A reassessment. *New Ideas in Psychology, 9*(1), 25–44.

Hull, C. L. (1943). *Principles of behavior: An introduction to behavior theory*. Oxford: Appleton-Century.

Hull, C. L. (1951). *Essentials of behavior*. New Haven, CT: Yale University Press.

Ingham, J. M., & Spain, D. H. (2005). Sensual attachment and incest avoidance in human evolution and child development. *Journal of the Royal Anthropological Institute, 11*(4), 667–701.

Insel, T. R., & Young, L. J. (2001). The neurobiology of attachment. *Nature Reviews Neuroscience, 2*, 129–136.

Israëls, H., & Schatzman, M. (1993). The seduction theory. *History of Psychiatry, 4*(13), 23–59.

Jacobsen, T., Huss, M., Fendrich, M., Kruesi, M., & Ziegenhain, U. (1997). Children's ability to delay gratification: Longitudinal relations to mother-child attachment. *Journal of Genetic Psychology, 158*, 411–426.

James, H. (1903). *Beast in the jungle and other stories*. New York: Dover Publications.

James, W. (1890). *The principles of psychology* (Vols. 1–2). New York: Holt.

James, W. H. (1981). The honeymoon effect on marital coitus. *Journal of Sex Research, 17*, 114–123.

Jamner, L. D., Schwartz, G. E., & Leigh, H. (1988). The relationship between repressive and defensive coping styles and monocyte, eosinophile, and serum glucose levels: Support for the opioid peptide hypothesis of repression. *Psychosomatic Medicine, 50*, 567–575.

Janet, P. (1907). *The major symptoms of hysteria*. New York: Macmillan.
Johnson, A., Shapiro, L. B., & Alexander, F. (1947). Preliminary report on a psychosomatic study of rheumatoid arthritis. *Psychosomatic Medicine, 9*, 295–300.
Johnson, A. W., & Price-Williams, D. (1996). *Oedipus ubiquitous: The family complex in world folk literature*. Stanford, CA: Stanford University Press.
Jones, E. (1952). Preface. *Psychoanalytic studies of the personality*. London: Tavistock, Routledge & Kegan Paul.
Jones, E. (1953). *Sigmund Freud: Life and work*, Vol. 1. London: Hogarth Press.
Josephs, L. (2006). The impulse to infidelity and oedipal splitting. *International Journal of Psychoanalysis*, 87, 423–437.
Josephs, L. (2010). The evolved function of the oedipal conflict. *International Journal of Psychoanalysis, 91*(4), 937–958.
Josephs, L. (2011). The primal scene in cross-species and cross-cultural perspectives. *International Journal of Psychoanalysis, 92*(5), 1263–1287.
Jung, C. (1920). Studies in word association. *Journal of Nervous and Mental Disease, 54*(6), 593–611.
Kanaan, R. A., Craig, T. K., Wessely, S. C., & David, A. S. (2007). Imaging repressed memories in motor conversion disorder. *Psychosomatic Medicine, 69*(2), 202–205.
Kandel, E. (2007). *In search of memory: The emergence of a new science of mind*. New York: W. W. Norton.
Kardiner, A. (1939). *The individual and his society*. New York: Columbia University Press.
Kay, A. C., Wheeler, S. C., Bargh, J. A., & Ross, L. (2004). Material priming: The influence of mundane physical objects on situational construal and competitive behavioral choice. *Organizational Behavior and Human Decision Processes, 95*, 83–96.
Kemp-Wheeler, S. M., & Hill, A. B. (1992). Semantic and emotional priming below objective detection threshold. *Cognition and Emotion, 6*(2), 113–128.
Kernberg, O. F. (1976). Technical considerations re borderline personality organization. *Journal of the American Psychoanalytic Association, 24*, 795–830.
Kernberg, O. F. (1984). *Severe personality disorders*. New Haven, CT: Yale University Press.
Kernberg, O. F. (1987). Projection and projective identification: Developmental and clinical aspects. *Journal of the American Psychoanalytic Association, 35*, 795–819.
Kernberg, O. F. (1995). *Love relations: Normality and pathology*. New Haven, CT: Yale University Press.
Kierkegaard, S. (1886/1948). *Purity of heart is to will one thing*. (Trans. D. V. Steere). New York: Harper.
Kihlstrom, J. F. (1987). The cognitive unconscious. *Science, 237*(4821), 1445–1452.
King, A. C., Taylor, C. B., Albright, C. L., & Haskell, W. L. (1990). The relationship between repressive and defensive coping styles and blood pressure responses in healthy, middle-aged men and women. *Journal of Psychosomatic Research, 34*, 461–471.
Kinsey, A. C., Pomeroy, W. B., & Martin, C. E. (1948). *Sexual behavior in the human male*. Oxford: Saunders.
Klein, G. S. (1959). Consciousness in psychoanalytic theory: Some implications for current research in perception. *Journal of the American Psychoanalytic Association, 4*, 5–48.
Klein, G. S. (1976). Freud's two theories of sexuality. In M. M. Gill, & P. S. Holzman (Eds.), *Psychology versus metapsychology: Psychoanalytic essays in memory of G. S. Klein* (pp. 14–70). New York: International Universities Press.
Klein, G. S., Spence, D. P., Holt, R. R., & Gourevitch, S. (1958). Cognition without awareness: Subliminal influence upon conscious thought. *Journal of Abnormal and Social Psychology, 57*, 255–266.

Klein, M. (1942). Some psychological considerations: A comment. Reprinted in *Envy and gratitude and other works 1946–1963: The writings of Melanie Klein* (Vol. 4). London: Hogarth Press and the Institute of Psycho-Analysis, 1975.
Klein, M. (1948). On the theory of anxiety and guilt. Reprinted in *Envy and gratitude and other works 1946–1963: The writings of Melanie Klein* (Vol. 4). London: Hogarth Press and the Institute of Psycho-Analysis, 1975.
Klein, M. (1959). Our adult world and its roots in infancy. Reprinted in *Envy and gratitude and other works 1946–1963: The writings of Melanie Klein,* (Vol. 4). London: Hogarth Press and the Institute of Psycho-Analysis, 1975.
Klein, M. (1960). On mental health. In *Envy and gratitude and other works (1946–1963).* New York: Dell, 1975.
Klein, M. (1963). On the sense of loneliness. Reprinted in *Envy and gratitude and other works 1946–1963: The writings of Melanie Klein,* (Vol. 4). London: Hogarth Press and the Institute of Psycho-Analysis, 1975.
Klein, M. (1975a). *Love, guilt and reparation and other works 1921–1945.* London: Hogarth Press.
Klein, M. (1975b[1946]). *Love, guilt and reparation and other works 1921–1*945. London: Hogarth Press.
Klein, M. (1981). On Mahler's autistic and symbiotic phases: An exposition and evaluation. *Psychoanalytic Contemporary Thought, 4,* 69–105.
Klein, M. I., & Tribich, D. (1982). Blame the child: Freud's blindness to the damaging influence of parents' personalities. *The Sciences, 22*(8), 14–20.
Kluckhohn, C., Murray, H. A., & Schneider, D. M. (Eds.) (1953). *Personality in nature, culture, and society* (2nd ed.). Oxford, UK: Alfred A. Knopf.
Kogan, I. (2012). From psychic holes to psychic representations. Retrieved from http://internationalpsychoanalysis.net/2012/03/19/filling-in-the-painful-spaces-by-ilany-kogan/
Kohut, H. (1971). *The analysis of the self.* New York: International Universities Press.
Kohut, H. (1977). *The restoration of the self.* New York: International Universities Press.
Kohut, H. (1982). Introspection, empathy, and the semi-circle of mental health. *International Journal of Psycho-Analysis, 63,* 395–407.
Kohut, H. (1984). *How does analysis cure?* Chicago, IL: University of Chicago Press.
Koriat, A., Melkman, R., Averill, J. R., & Lazarus, R. S. (1972). The self-control of emotional reactions to a stressful film. *Journal of Personality, 40,* 601–619.
Kotler, T. (1985). Security and autonomy within marriage. *Human Relations, 38*(4), 299–321.
Kris, A. O. (1985). Resistance in convergent and in divergent conflicts. *Psychoanalytic Quarterly, 54,* 537–568.
Kris, A. O. (1988). Some clinical applications of the distinction between divergent and convergent conflicts. *The Bulletin of the Anna Freud Centre, 10,* 99–117.
Kris, A. (2017). Divergent and convergent conflicts. In C. Christian, M. N. Eagle, & D. L. Wolitzky (Eds.). *Psychoanalytic perspectives on conflict.* New York: Routledge.
Kris, E. (1936). The psychology of caricature. In E. Kris (Ed.), *Psychoanalytic Explorations in Art* (pp. 173–188). New York: International Universities Press.
Kris, E. (1947). The nature of psychoanalytic propositions and their validation. In S. Hook and M. R. Konvits (Eds.). *Freedom and Experience.* Essays presented to Horace Kallen (pp. 239–259). Ithaca, NY: Cornell University Press.
Kris, E. (1950). The significance of Freud's earliest discoveries. *International Journal of Psychoanalysis, 31,* 108–116.
Kristof, N. (2012). War wounds. *New York Times,* August 10, pp. 1–3.
Krosnick, J. A., Betz, A. L., Jussim, L. J., & Lynn, A. R. (1992). Subliminal conditioning of attitudes. *Personality and Social Psychology Bulletin, 18*(2), 152–162.

Kuzawa, C. W., Gettler, L. T., Muller, M. N., McDade, T. W., & Feranil, A. B. (2009). Fatherhood, pairbonding, and testosterone in the Philippines. *Hormones and Behavior, 56*, 429–435.

Kuzawa, C. W., Gettler, L. T., Huang, Y., & McDade, T. W. (2010). Mothers have lower testosterone than non-mothers: Evidence from the Philippines. *Hormones and Behavior, 4–5*, 441–447.

Lacan, J. (1966/2002). Ecrits: A selection. In B. Fink (Trans.), *Ecrits*. New York: W. W. Norton.

Lakoff, G., & Johnson, M. (1999). *Philosophy in the flesh: The embodied mind and its challenge to western thought.* New York: Basic Books.

Lane, R. D., Quinlan, D. M., Schwartz, G. E., Walker, P. A., & Zeitlin, S. B. (1990). The Levels of Emotional Awareness Scale: A cognitive-developmental measure of emotion. *Journal of Personality Assessment, 55*, 124–134.

Latchaw, A. (2010). The relationship between attachment style and degree of unresolved oedipal conflicts (Unpublished dissertation). Adelphi University, Long Island, NY.

Lau, D. C. (1979) Trans. *Confucius: The analects.* New York: Penguin Books.

Lazarus, R. S. (1983). The costs and benefits of denial. In S. Breznitz (Ed.), *The denial of stress* (pp. 1–30). New York: International Universities Press.

Lear, J. (1995). The shrink is in. *The New Republic*, 213, 18–25.

LeDoux, J. E. (2000). Emotion circuits in the brain. *Annual Review Neuroscience, 23*(1), 155–184.

Lee, S. Y., Kang, J. I., Lee, E., Namkoong, K., & An, S. K. (2011). Differential priming effect for subliminal fear and disgust facial expressions. *Attention, Perception, and Psychophysics, 73*(2), 473–481.

Lévi-Strauss, C. (1949/1969). *Elementary structures of kinship.* Boston, MA: Beacon Press.

Levine, J., Warrenburg, S., Kerns, R., Schwartz, G., Delaney, R., Fontana, A., . . . Cascione, R. (1987).The role of denial in recovery from coronary heart disease. *Psychosomatic Medicine, 49*, 109–117.

Levine, M., & Spivak, G. (1963). The Rorshach index of ideational repression: Application to quantitative sequence analysis. *Journal of Projective Techniques, 27*, 73–78.

Levine, M., & Spivak, G. (1964). *The Rorschach index of repressive style.* Springfield, IL: Thomas.

Levinger, G., & Clark, J. (1961). Emotional factors in the forgetting of word associations. *Journal of Abnormal Social Psychology, 62*, 99–105.

Levithan, D. (2014). Review of Marquez. *New York Times Book Review*, February 9.

Lewicki, P., Hill, T., & Czyzewska, M. (1992). Nonconscious acquisition of information. *American Psychologist, 47*, 796–801.

Lewicki, P., Hill, T., & Czyzewska, M. (1997). Hidden covariation detection: A fundamental and ubiquitous phenomenon. *Journal of Experimental Psychology: Learning, Memory, and Cognition, 23*(1), 221–228.

Lichtenberg, J. D. (1989). *Psychoanalysis and motivation.* Hillsdale, NJ: Analytic Press.

Liddell, B. J., Brown, K. B., Kemp, A. H., Barton, M. J., Das, P., Peduto, A., . . . Williams, L. M. (2005). A direct brainstem–amygdala–cortical 'alarm' system for subliminal signals of fear. *Neuroimaging*, 24, 235–243.

Liddell, B. J., Williams, L. M., Rathjen, J., Shevrin, H., & Gordon, E. (2004). A temporal dissociation of subliminal versus supraliminal fear perception: An event-related potential study. *Journal of Cognitive Neuroscience, 16*(3), 479–486.

Lieberman, D., Tooby, J., & Cosmides, L. (2003). Does morality have a biological basis? An empirical test of the factors governing moral sentiments regarding incest. *Proceedings of the Royal Society, London B, 270*, 819–826.

Lieberman, M. D., Eisenberger, N. I., Crockett, M. J., Tom, S. M., Pfeifer, J. H., & Way, W. M. (2007). Putting feelings into words: Affect labeling disrupts amygdala activity in response to affective stimuli. *Psychological Science, 18*(5), 421–428.

Liebowitz, M. R. (1983). *The chemistry of love*. Boston, MA: Little, Brown.

Lin, Z., & Murray, S. O. (2015). More power to the unconscious: Conscious, but not unconscious, exogenous attention requires location variation. *Psychological Science, 26*(2), 221–230.

Lindzey, G. (1967). Some remarks concerning incest, the incest taboo, and psychoanalytic theory. *American Psychology, 22*, 1051–1059.

Lipka, J., Miltner, W. H., & Straube, T. (2011). Vigilance for threat interacts with amygdala responses to subliminal threat cues in specific phobia. *Biological Psychiatry, 70*(5), 472–478.

Litowitz, B. E. (2007). Unconscious fantasy: A once and future concept. *Journal of the American Psychoanalytic Association, 55*, 199–228.

Loewald, H. (1960). On the therapeutic action of psychoanalysis. *Journal of the American Psychoanalytic Association, 41*, 16–33.

Loewald, H. (1962). Internalization, separation, mourning, and the superego. *Psychoanalytic Quarterly, 31*, 483–504.

Loewald, H. (1966). Review of *Psychoanalytic concepts and the structural theory*, by J. A. Arlow, & C. Brenner. *Psychoanalytic Quarterly, 35*, 430–436.

Loewald, H. (1979). The waning of the oedipal complex. *Journal of the American Psychoanalytic Association, 27*, 751–775.

Loewenstein, R. (1967). Defensive organization and autonomous ego functions. *Journal of the American Psychoanalytic Association, 15*, 795–809.

Lorenz, K. (1970). *Studies in animal and human behaviour* (Vol. 1). Cambridge, MA: Harvard University Press.

Low, B. (1920). *Psycho-analysis: A brief account of Freudian theory*. (Jones, E., introd.). London: Allen & Unwin.

Luborsky, L. (1973). Forgetting and remembering (momentary forgetting) during psychotherapy: A new sample. *Psychological Issues, 8*, 29–55.

Luborsky, L., & Barrett, M. S. (2006). The history and empirical status of key psychoanalytic concepts. *Annual Review of Clinical Psychology, 2*, 1–19.

Luborsky L., Blinder B., & Schimek J. (1965). Looking, recalling, and GSR as a function of defense. *Journal of Abnormal Psychology, 70*, 270–280.

Luborsky, L., & Crits-Christoph, P. (1998). *Understanding transference: The core conflictual relationship theme method* (2nd ed.). Washington, DC: American Psychological Association Books.

Luborsky, L., Crits-Christoph, P., & Alexander, K. J. (1990). Repressive style and relationship patterns: Three samples inspected. In J. L. Singer (Ed.), *Repression and dissociation* (pp. 275–298). Chicago, IL: University of Chicago Press.

Lyons-Ruth, K. (1999). The two-person subconscious. Intersubjective dialogue, implicit relational knowing, and the articulation of weaning. *Psychoanalytic Inquiry, 19*, 567–617.

Lyons-Ruth, K. & Jacobvitz, D. (2008). Attachment disorganization: Genetic factors, parenting context, and development transformation from infancy to adulthood. In J. Cassidy, & P. R. Shaver (Eds.). *Handbook of attachment: Theory, research, and clinical applications*, 2nd ed. (pp. 666–697). New York: Guilford Press.

Lyons-Ruth, K. and members of the Process of Change Study Group, Boston, MA (1998). Implicit relational knowing: Its role in development and psychoanalytic treatment. *Infant Mental Health Journal, 19*(3), 282–289.

McClure, S. M., Laibson, D. I., Loewenstein, G. & Cohen, J. D. (2004). Separate neural systems value immediate and delayed monetary rewards. *Science, 306*(5695), 503–507.

McGinnies, E. (1949). Emotionality and perceptual defense. *Psychological Review, 56*, 244–251.

Mack, A., & Rock, I. (1998). *Inattentional blindness*. Cambridge, MA: MIT Press.

McLoughlin, J. (2002). Unwittingly recapitulating Freud: Searle's concept of a vocabulary of the unconscious. *Ratio, 12*, 34–53.

Macmillan, M. (1991). *Freud evaluated: The completed arc*. New York: Elsevier Science.

McNally, R. J. (2006). Let Freud rest in peace. *Behavioral and Brain Sciences, 26*, 526–527.

Mahler, M. S. (1968). *On human symbiosis and the vicissitudes of individuation*. New York: International Universities Press.

Maier, M. A., Elliot, A. J., & Lichtenfeld, S. (2008). Mediation of the negative effect of red on intellectual performance. *Personality and Social Psychology Bulletin, 34*, 1530–1540.

Main, M., & Goldwyn, R. (1998). *Adult Attachment Interview scoring and classification manual: 6th version*. Unpublished manuscript, University of California, Berkeley.

Main, M., & Hesse, E. (1990). Parents' unresolved traumatic experiences are related to infant disorganized attachment status: Is frightened and frightening parental behavior the linking mechanism? In M. T. Greenberg, D. Ciccheti, & E. M. Cummings (Eds.) *Attachment in the pre-school years: Theory, research, and intervention* (pp. 161–182). Chicago, IL: University of Chicago Press.

Makari, G. (2008). *Revolution in mind: The creation of psychoanalysis*. New York: HarperCollins.

Malinowski, B. (1927). *Sex and repression in savage society*. London: Routledge & Kegan Paul.

Marcel, A. J. (1980). Conscious and preconscious recognition of polysemous words: Locating the selective effects of prior verbal context. In R. S. Nickerson (Ed.), *Attention and Performance VIII* (pp. 435–458). Hillsdale, NJ: Erlbaum.

Marcuse, H. (1966). *Eros and civilization: A philosophical inquiry into Freud*. Boston, MA: Beacon Press.

Marmor, J. (1962) Psychoanalytic therapy as an educational process. In J. Marmor (Ed.), *Science & psychoanalysis*. New York: Grune & Stratton.

Marquez, G. G. (1994/2014). *Love in the time of cholera* (Trans. E. Grossman). New York: Vintage.

Masling, J., & Cohen, I. S. (1987). Psychotherapy, clinical evidence, and the self-fulfilling prophecy. *Psychoanalytic Psychology, 4*, 65–80.

Maslow, A. (1954). *Motivation and personality*. New York: Harper & Row.

Masserman, J. H. (1944). *Behavior and neurosis*. Chicago, IL: University of Chicago Press.

Masserman, J. H. (1950). Experimental neurosis. *Scientific American, 182*, 38–43.

Masserman, J. H. (1953). Psychoanalysis and biodynamics: An integration. *International Journal of Psycho-Analysis, 34*, 13–42.

Masson, J. M. (1985) Ed. and Trans. *The complete letters of Sigmund Freud to Wilhelm Fliess: 1887–1904*. Cambridge, MA: Harvard University Press.

Mayes, L. C., & Cohen, D. J. (1996). Children's developing theory of mind. *Journal of the American Psychoanalytic Association, 44*, 117–142.

Meissner, W. (1981). *Internalization in psychoanalysis*. New York: International Universities Press.

Melden, A. I. (1961). *Free action*. London: Routledge & Kegan Paul.

Metcalfe, J., & Mischel, W. (1999). A hot/cool-system analysis of delay of gratification: Dynamics of willpower. *Psychological Review, 1*, 3–19.

Michael, R. T., Gagnon, J. H., Laumann, E. O., & Kolata, G. (1994). *Sex in America: A definitive survey*. New York: Warner Books.

Mikulincer, M. (1995). Attachment style and the mental representation of the self. *Journal of Personality and Social Psychology, 69*, 1203–1215.

Mikulincer, M. (1998). Attachment working models and the sense of trust: An exploration of interaction goals and affect regulation. *Journal of Personality and Social Psychology, 74*, 1209–1224.

Mikulincer, M., Dolev, T., & Shaver, P. R. (2004). Attachment-related strategies during thought suppression: Ironic rebounds and vulnerable self-representations. *Journal of Personality and Social Psychology, 87*(6), 940–956.

Mikulincer, M., & Horesch, N. (1999). Adult attachment style and the perception of others: The role of projective mechanisms. *Journal of Personality and Social Psychology, 76*, 1022–1034.

Mikulincer, M., Horesh, N., Eilati, I., & Kotler, M. (1999). The association between adult attachment style and mental health in extreme life-endangering conditions. *Personality and Individual Differences, 27*(5), 831–842.

Mikulincer, M., & Shaver, P. R. (2007). *Attachment in adulthood: Structure, dynamics, and change*. New York: Guilford Press.

Mikulincer, M., & Shaver, P. R. (2008). Adult attachment and affect regulation. In J. Cassidy & P. R. Shaver (Eds.), *Handbook of attachment: Theory, research and clinical applications* (pp. 503–531). New York: Guilford.

Miller, A. (1984). *Society's betrayal of the child*. New York: Farrar, Straus, Giroux.

Miller, M. L. (1948). Psychodynamic mechanisms in a case of psychodermatitis. *Psychosomatic Medicine, 10*, 309–316.

Miranda, J., & Persons, J. B. (1988). Dysfunctional attitudes are mood-state dependent. *Journal of Abnormal Psychology, 97*(1), 76–79.

Miranda, J., Persons, J. B., & Byers, C. N. (1990). Endorsement of dysfunctional beliefs depends on current mood state. *Journal of Abnormal Psychology, 99*, 237–241.

Mischel, W. (1961a). Father absence and delay of gratification: Cross-cultural comparison. *Journal of Abnormal and Social Psychology, 63*, 116–124.

Mischel, W. (1961b). Preference for delayed reinforcement and social responsibility, *Journal of Abnormal and Social Psychology, 62*, 1–7.

Mischel, W. (1961c). Delay of gratification, need for achievement, and acquiescence in another culture. *Journal of Abnormal and Social Psychology, 69*(4), 411–417.

Mischel, W. (1966). Theory and research on the antecedents of self-imposed delay of reward. In B. A. Maher (Ed.), *Progress in experimental personality research* (Vol. 3, pp. 85–131). New York: Academic Press.

Mischel, W. (1970). Sex typing and socialization. In P. H. Mussen (Ed.), *Carmichael's manual of child psychology* (Vol. 2, pp. 3–72). New York: John Wiley.

Mischel, W., & Ebbesen, E. (1970). Attention in delay of gratification. *Journal of Personality and Social Psychology, 16*, 329–337.

Mischel, W., Ebbesen, E. B., & Zeiss, A. R. (1972). Cognitive and attentional mechanisms in delay of gratification. *Journal of Personality and Social Psychology, 21*(2), 204–218.

Mischel, W., & Grusec, J. (1967). Effects of time and probability of occurrence on self-imposed delay for rewards and punishments. *Journal of Personality and Social Psychology, 5*, 24–31.

Mischel, W., & Metzer, R. (1962). Preferences for delayed rewards as a function of age, intelligence, and length of delay interval. *Journal of Abnormal and Social Psychology, 64*, 425–431.

Mischel, W., & Moore, B. (1973). Effects of attention to symbolically presented rewards on self-control. *Journal of Personality and Social Psychology, 28*, 172–179.

Mischel, W., Shoda, Y., & Peake, P. K. (1988). The nature of adolescent competencies predicted by preschool delay of gratification. *Journal of Personality and Social Psychology, 54*(4), 687–696.

Mischel, W., Shoda, Y., & Rodriguez, M. (1989). Delay of gratification in children. *Science, 244*, 933–938.
Mitchell, S. A. (1988). *Relational concepts in psychoanalysis: An integration*. Cambridge, MA: Harvard University Press.
Mitchell, S. A. (1998). The analyst's knowledge and authority. *Psychoanalytic Quarterly, 67*, 1–31.
Mitchell, S. A. (2002). *Can love last? The fate of romance over time*. New York: Norton.
Mittal, R., Russell, B. S., Britner, P. A., & Peake, P. A. (2013). Delay of gratification in two- and three-year-olds: Association with attachment, personality, and temperament. *Journal of Child & Family Studies, 22*(4), 479–489.
Modell, A. (1965). On having a right to life: An aspect of the superego's development. *International Journal of Psycho-Analysis, 46*, 323–331.
Modell, A. (1971). The origin of certain forms of pre-oedipal guilt and the implications for a psychoanalytic theory of affects. *International Journal of Psycho-Analysis, 52*, 337–346.
Modell, A. (1983). *Self preservation and the preservation of the self: An overview of the more recent knowledge of the narcissistic personality*. Paper given at a symposium on "Narcissism, masochism, and the sense of guilt in relation to the therapeutic process." Letterman General Hospital, San Francisco, California, May 14–15, 1983.
Money, J., & Erhardt, A. A. (1972). *Man and woman, boy and girl: The differentiation and dimorphism of gender identity from conception to maturity*. Baltimore, MD: Johns Hopkins University Press.
Moran, R. (2001). *Authority and estrangement: An essay on self knowledge*. Princeton, NJ: Princeton University Press.
Morehead, D. (1999). Oedipus, Darwin, and Freud: One big, happy family? *Psychoanalytic Quarterly, 68*(3), 347–375.
Morris, J. S., de Gelder, B., Weiskrantz, L., & Dolan, R. J. (2001). Differential extrageniculostriate and amygdala responses to presentation of emotional faces in a cortically blind field. *Brain, 124*, 1241–1252.
Morrison, A. P. (1989). *Shame: The underside of narcissism*. Hillsdale, NJ: Analytic Press.
Murray, E. J. (1956). A content-analysis method for studying psychotherapy. *Psychological Monographs, 70*, 1–31.
Nasrallah, M., Carmel, D., & Lavie, N. (2009) "Murder she wrote": Enhanced sensitivity to negative word valence. *Emotion*, 9(5), 609–618.
Newell, B. R. (2015). Decision making under risk: Beyond Kahneman and Tversky's Prospect Theory. In M. Eysenck & D. Groome (Eds.), *Cognitive Psychology: Revisiting the Classic Studies* (pp. 162–178). London: Sage Publications.
Newell, B. R., Wong, K. Y., Cheung, J. C. H., & Rakow, T. (2009). Think, blink, or sleep on it? The impact of modes of thought on complex decision making. *Quarterly Journal of Experimental Psychology, 62*, 707–732.
Nietzsche, F. (1974). *The gay science* (W. Kaufman, Trans.). New York: Vintage Books.
Nisbett, R. E., & Wilson, T. D. (1977). Telling more than we can know: Verbal reports on mental processes. *Psychological Review, 84*, 231–259.
Nordgren, L. F., & Dijksterhuis, A. (2009). The devil is in the deliberation: Thinking too much reduces judgmental consistency. *Journal of Consumer Research, 36*, 39–46.
O'Brien, G., & Jureidini, J. (2002). Dispensing with the dynamic unconscious. *Philosophy, Psychiatry and Psychology, 9*(2), 141–154.
Ogden, T. H. (1983). The concept of internal object relations. *International Journal of Psychoanalysis, 64*, 227–241.
Ohman, A., & Soares, J. J. (1994). "Unconscious anxiety": Phobic responses to masked stimuli. *Journal of Abnormal Psychology, 103*(2), 231–240.

Olafson, F. (1967). *Principles and persons: An ethical interpretation of existentialism*. Baltimore, MD: Johns Hopkins University Press.
Olson, S. L., Bates, J. E., & Bayles, K. (1990). Early antecedents of childhood impulsivity: The role of parent–child interaction, cognitive competence, and temperament. *Journal of Abnormal Child Psychology, 18*, 317–334.
Osgood, C. E., Suci, G. J., & Tannenbaum, P. H. (1957). *The measurement of meaning*. Urbana, IL: University of Illinois Press.
Panksepp, J. (2005). Affective consciousness: Core emotional feelings in animals and humans. *Consciousness and Cognition, 14*, 30–80.
Passman, R. H., & Erck, T. W. (1977, March). *Visual presentation of mothers facilitating play in childhood: The effects of silent films of mothers*. Paper given at the biennial meeting of the Society for Research in Child Development, New Orleans, LA.
Passman, R. H., & Longeway, K. P. (1982). The role of vision in maternal attachment: Giving 2-year-olds a photo of their mother during separation. *Developmental Psychology, 18*, 530–533.
Paul, I. H., & Fisher, C. (1959). Subliminal visual stimulation: A study of its influence on subsequent images and dreams. *Journal of Nervous and Mental Diseases, 129*, 315–340.
Pavlov, I. P. (1941). *Conditioned reflexes and psychiatry*. New York: International Publishers.
Payne, J. W., Samper, A., Bettman, J. R., & Luce, M. F. (2008). Boundary conditions on unconscious thought in complex decision making. *Psychological Science, 19*, 1118–1123.
Peake, P. K., Hebl, M., & Mischel, W. (2002). Strategic attention deployment for delay of gratification in working and waiting situations. *Developmental Psychology, 38*(2), 313–326.
Perry, J. C. (2001). A pilot study of defenses in psychotherapy of personality disorders entering psychotherapy. *Journal of Nervous and Mental Disease, 189*, 651–660.
Perry, J. C., & Bond, M. (2012). Change in defense mechanisms during long-term dynamic psychotherapy and five-year outcome. *American Journal of Psychiatry, 169*(9), 916–925.
Perry, J. C., Petraglia, J., Olson, T. R., Presniak, M. D., & Metzger, J. A. (2012). Accuracy of defense interpretation in three character types. In R. A. Levy, J. S. Ablon, & H. Kaechele (Eds.), *Psychodynamic psychotherapy research* (pp. 417–447). New York: Humana.
Persons, J. B., & Miranda, J. (1992). Cognitive theories of vulnerabilities to depression: Reconciling negative evidence. *Cognitive Therapy and Research, 16*, 185–502.
Pessoa, L., & Adolphs, R. (2010). Emotion processing and the amygdala: From a "low road" to "many roads" of evaluating biological significance. *Nature Review Neuroscience, 11*(11), 773–783.
Peterfreund, E. (1978). Some critical comments on psychoanalytic conceptions of infancy. *International Journal of Psychoanalysis, 59*, 427–437.
Peterfreund, E. (1983). *The process of psychoanalytic therapy: Models and strategy*. Hillsdale, NJ: Analytic Press (Erlbaum).
Piaget, J. (1971). Comments on developmental stages and developmental processes. In D. Green, M. Ford, & C. Flamer (Eds.), *Measurement and Piaget*. New York: McGraw Hill.
Pierce, J. D., O'Brien, K. K., & Dewsbury, D. A. (1992). No effect of familiarity on the Coolidge effect in prairie voles (*Microtusochrogaster*). *Bulletin of the Psychonomic Society, 30*, 325–328.
Pine, F. (1960). Incidental stimulation: A study of preconscious transformations. *Journal of Abnormal and Social Psychology, 60*(1), 68–75.
Pine, F. (1961). Incidental versus focal presentation of drive related stimuli. *Journal of Abnormal and Social Psychology, 62*, 482–490.
Pine, F. (1981). In the beginning: Contributions to a psychoanalytic developmental psychology. *International Review of Psycho-Analysis, 8*, 15–34.

Pinker, S. (2009). *How the mind works*. New York & London: W. W. Norton.

Pollet, T. V., van der Meij, L., Cobey, K. D., & Buunk, A. P. (2011). Testosterone levels and their associations with lifetime number of opposite sex partners and remarriage in a large sample of American elderly men and women. *Hormones and Behavior, 60*, 72–77.

Polanyi, M., & Prosch, H. (1975). *Meaning*. Chicago, IL: University of Chicago Press.

Portuges, S.H., & Hollander, N. C. (2011). The therapeutic action of resistance analysis: Interpersonalizing and socializing Paul Gray's close process attention. In M. J. Diamond, & C. Christian (Eds.), *The second century of psychoanalysis: Evolving perspectives on therapeutic action* (pp. 71–95). London: Karnac.

Potts, W. K., Manning, C. J., &Wakeland, E. K. (1991). MHC genotype influences mating patterns in semi-natural populations of Mus. *Nature, 352*, 619–621.

Potts, W. K., Manning, C. J., & Wakeland, E. K. (1992). MHC-based mating preferences in Mus operate through both settlement patterns and female controlled extra-territorial matings. *Chemical Signals in Vertebrates, 6*, 183–187.

Pötzl, O. (1917). The relationship between experimentally induced dream images and indirect vision. *Psychological Issues, 2*, 41–120.

Process of Change Boston Study Group. (1998). Report 1. Non-interpretive mechanisms in psychoanalytic therapy: The "something more" than interpretation. *International Journal of Psychoanalysis, 79*, 908–921.

Pryke, S. R., Andresson, S., & Lawes, M. J. (2001). Sexual selection of multiple handicaps in the red-collared widowbird: Female choice of tail length but not carotenoid display. *Evolution, 55*(7), 1452–1463.

Quine, W. V. O. (1969). *Ontological relativity and other essays*. New York and London: Columbia University Press.

Rajecki, D. W., Lamb, M. E., & Obmascher, P. (1978). Toward a general theory of infantile attachment: A comparative review of aspects of the social bond. *Behavior and Brain Sciences, 1*, 417–464.

Rand, N. (2004). The hidden soul: The growth of the unconscious in philosophy, psychology, medicine, and literature, 1750–1900. *American Imago, 61*, 257–289.

Rank, O. (1936). *Truth and reality* (J. J. Taft, Trans.). New York: Alfred A. Knopf.

Rapaport, D. (1967). *The collected papers of David Rapaport*. New York: Basic Books.

Reber, A. S. (1976). Implicit learning of synthetic languages: The role of instructional set. *Journal of Experimental Psychology: Human Learning and Memory, 2*, 88–94.

Reber, A. S. (1989). Implicit learning and tactic knowledge. *Journal of Experimental Psychology: General, 118*, 219–235.

Rey, A., Goldstein, R. M., & Perruchet, P. (2009). Does unconscious thought improve complex decision making? *Psychological Research*, 73, 372–379.

Ric, F., & Muller, D. (2012). Unconscious addition: When we unconsciously initiate and follow arithmetic rules. *Journal of Experimental Psychology: General, 141*(2), 222–226.

Ricoeur, P. (1970). *Freud and philosophy: An essay on interpretation*. New Haven, CT: Yale University Press.

Robles, R., Smith, R., Carver, C., & Wellens, A. R. (1987). Influence of subliminal visual images on the experience of anxiety. *Personality and Social Psychology Bulletin, 13*(3), 399–410.

Rock, I. (1970). Perception from the standpoint of psychology. *Research Publications, Association for Research in Nervous and Mental Disease, 48*, 1–11.

Rock, I. (1983). *The logic of perception*. Cambridge, MA: MIT Press.

Rofé, Y. (2008). Does repression exist? Memory, pathogenic, unconscious and clinical evidence. *Review of General Psychology, 12*(1), 63–85.

Rogers, C. R. (1951). *Client-centered therapy*. Boston, MA: Houghton Mifflin.

Rogers, C. R. (1959). A theory of therapy, personality and interpersonal relationships, as developed in the client-centered framework. In S. Koch (Ed.), *Psychology: A study of a science*, Vol. 3. *Formulations of the person and the social context* (pp.184–256). New York and Boston, MA: McGraw-Hill.

Rogers, C. R. (1960). Significant trends in the client-centered orientation. In L. E. Abt & B. F. Reiss (Eds.), *Progress in clinical psychology* (Vol. 4, pp. 85–99). New York: Grune & Stratton.

Roheim, G. (1950). The Oedipus complex, magic, and culture. In G. Roheim (Ed.), *Psychoanalysis and the social sciences*. New York: International Universities Press.

Rose, S., Brewin, C. R., Andrews, B., & Kirk, M. (1999). A randomized controlled trial of individual psychological debriefing for victims of violent crime. *Psychological Medicine, 25*(4), 793–799.

Rosenblatt, A. (2004). Insight, working-through, and practice: The role of procedural knowledge. *Journal of the American Psychoanalytic Association, 52*(1),189–207.

Rosenzweig, E. (2016). How and why awareness of the psychological immune system is compatible with its efficacy. *Perspectives on Psychological Science*, 11(2), 222–238.

Ross, J. M. (1982). Oedipus revisited: Laius and the "Laius complex." *The Psychoanalytic Study of the Child, 37*, 169–200.

Roy, C., Perry, J. C., Banon, E., & Luborsky, L. L. (2009). Changes in defensive functioning in completed psychoanalyses: The Penn Psychoanalytic Treatment Collection. *Journal of the American Psychoanalytic Association, 57*, 399–415.

Rubens, R. L. (1994). Fairbairn's structural theory. In J. S. Grotstein & D. B. Rinsley (Eds.), *Fairbairn and the origins of object relations* (pp. 151–173). New York: Guilford Press.

Rubinstein, B. B. (1976). On the possibility of a strictly clinical psychoanalytic theory: An essay in the philosophy of psychoanalysis. In M. M. Gill & P. S. Holzman (Eds.), *Psychology vs. metapsychology: Essays in memory of George S. Klein*. New York: International Universities Press.

Rubinstein, B. B. (1997). *Psychoanalysis and the philosophy of science: Collected papers of Benjamin B. Rubinstein* (R. R. Holt, ed.). Madison, CT: International Universities Press.

Runnion, B. R. (2009). Evidence for unconscious thought in complex decisions: The results of a methodological artifact or an active thought process? Montana State University, Bozeman, MT.

Russell, B. (1921). *Analysis of mind*. London: George Allen &Unwin.

Rutter, M. (1971). Parent–child separation: Psychological effects on the children. *Journal of Child Psychology and Psychiatry, 12*, 233–260.

Rutter, M., Quinton, D., & Hill, J. (1990). Adult outcomes of institution-reared children: Males and females compared. In L. N. Robins & M. Rutter (Eds.), *Straight and devious pathways from childhood to adulthood* (pp. 135–157). Cambridge: Cambridge University Press.

Sachs, H. (1944). *Freud: Master and friend*. Cambridge, MA: Harvard University Press.

Sand, R. S. (2014). *The unconscious without Freud*. Lanham, MD: Rowman & Littlefield.

Sandler, J. (1976). Countertransference and role-responsiveness. *International Review of Psychoanalysis, 3*, 43–47.

Sandler, J., & Freud, A. (1985). *The analysis of defense: The ego and the mechanisms of defense revisited*. New York: International Universities Press.

Sandler, J., & Joffe, W. G. (1967). Tendency to persistence in psychological function, development, with special reference to fixation and regression. *Bulletin of the Menninger Clinic, 31*, 257–271.

Sartre, J.-P. (1956). *Being and nothingness: A phenomenological essay on ontology*. Trans. H. E. Barnes. London: Methuen.

Scarfone, D. (2002). Sexual and actual. In D. Widlöcher (Ed.), S. Fairfield (Trans.), *Infantile sexuality and attachment* (pp. 97–111). London: Karnac.
Schachter, S., & Singer, J. (1962). Cognitive, social, and physiological determinants of emotional state. *Psychological Review, 69*, 379–399.
Schafer, R. (1968). *Aspects of internalization*. New York: International Universities Press.
Schafer R. (1976). *A new language for psychoanalysis*. New Haven, CT: Yale University Press.
Schafer, R. (1992). *Retelling a life: Narrative and dialogue in psychoanalysis*. New York: Basic Books.
Schimek, J. G. (1987). Fact and fantasy in the seduction theory: A historical review. *Journal of the American Psychoanalytic Association, 35*(4), 937–965.
Schlam, T. R., Wilson, N. L., Shoda, Y., Mischel, W., & Ayduk, O. (2013). Preschoolers' delay of gratification predicts their body mass 30 years later. *Journal of Pediatrics, 162*, 90–93.
Schmeidel, B. J., & Tang, D. (2015). Individual differences in executive functioning and their relationship to emotional processes and responses. *Current Directions in Psychological Sciences, 24*, 93–98.
Schmeing, J. B., Kehyayan, A., Kessler, H. Do Lam, A. T., Fell, J., Schmidt, A. C., & Axmacher, N. (2013). Can the neural basis of repression be studied in the MRI scanner? New insights from two free association paradigms. *PLoS One, 8*(4), e62358.
Schneider, M. A., & Hendrix, L. (2000). Olfactory sexual inhibition and the Westermarck effect. *Human Nature, 11*, 65–92.
Schore, A. N. (1994). *Affect regulation and the origin of the self: The neurobiology of emotional development*. Mahwah, NJ: Erlbaum.
Schwartz, G. E. (1990). Psychobiology of repression and health: A systems approach. In J. L. Singer (Ed.), *Repression and dissociation* (pp. 405–434). Chicago, IL: University of Chicago Press.
Searle, J. (1992). *The rediscovery of the mind*. Cambridge, MA: MIT Press.
Sears, R. R. (1943). Survey of objective studies of psychoanalytic concepts. *Social Science Research Council Bulletin* (No. 51). New York: Social Science Research Council.
Sears, R. R. (1944). Experimental analysis of psychoanalytic phenomena. In J. M. Hunt (Ed.), *Personality and other behavior disorders* (pp. 306–332). Oxford, UK: Ronald Press.
Sellars, W. (1963). Philosophy and the scientific image of man. In W. Sellars (Ed.), *Science, perception, and reality*. Atascadero, CA: Ridgeview Publishing.
Setchell, J. M., & Wickings, E. J. (2005). Dominance, status signals, and coloration in male mandrills (*Mandrillus sphinx*). *Ethology, 111*, 25–50.
Sethi, A., Mischel, W., Aber, J. L., Shoda, Y., & Rodriguez, M. L. (2000). The role of strategic attention deployment in development of self-regulation: Predicting preschoolers' delay of gratification from mother–toddler interactions. *Developmental Psychology, 36*(6), 767–777.
Shanks, D. R., & St. John, M. F. (1994). Characteristics of dissoluble human learning systems. *Behavioral and Brain Sciences, 17*(3), 367–447.
Shaw, R. E., Cohen, F., Doyle, B., & Palasky, J. (1985). The impact of denial and repressive style on information gain and rehabilitative outcomes in myocardial infarction patients. *Psychosomatic Medicine, 47*, 262–273.
Shaw, R. E., Cohen, F., Fishman-Rosen, J., Murphy, M. C., Stertzer, S., Clark, D. A., & Myler, R. K. (1986). Psychologic predictors of psychosocial and medical outcomes in patients undergoing coronary angioplasty. *Psychosomatic Medicine, 48*, 582–597.
Shedler, J., Mayman, M., & Manis, M. (1993).The illusion of mental health. *American Psychologist, 48*, 1117–1131.

Shepher, J. (1971). Mate selection among second generation kibbutz adolescents and adults: Incest avoidance and negative imprinting. *Archives of Sexual Behavior, 1*, 293–307.

Sheleff, L. (1981). *Generations apart: Adult hostility to youth*. New York: McGraw-Hill.

Sherwood, M. (1969). *The logic of explanation in psychoanalysis*. New York: Academic Press.

Shevrin, H., Williams. W. J., Marshall, R. E., Hertel, R. K., Bond, J. A., & Brakel, L. A. (1992). Event-related potential indicators of the dynamic unconscious. *Consciousness and Cognition, 1*(3), 340–366.

Shoda, Y., Mischel, W., & Peake, P. (1990). Predicting adolescent cognitive and self-regulatory competencies from preschool delay of gratification: Identifying diagnostic conditions. *Developmental Psychology, 26*, 978–986.

Shor, E., & Simchai, D. (2009). Incest avoidance, the incest taboo, and social cohesion: Revisiting Westermarck and the case of the Israeli kibbutzim. *American Journal of Sociology, 114*(6), 1803–1842.

Shybut, J. (1968). Delay of gratification and severity of psychological disturbances among hospitalized psychiatric patients. *Journal of Consulting and Clinical Psychology, 32*(4), 462–468.

Silberschatz, G. (2005). The Control–Mastery theory. In G. Silberschatz (Ed.), *Transformative relationships: The Control–Mastery theory of psychotherapy* (pp. 3–30). New York: Routledge.

Silberschatz, G., & Curtis, J. T. (1993). Measuring the therapist's impact on the patient's therapeutic progress. *Journal of Consulting and Clinical Psychology, 61*, 403–411.

Silberschatz, G., Fretter, P., & Curtis, J. (1986). How do interpretations influence the process of psychotherapy. *Journal of Consulting and Clinical Psychology, 54*, 646–652.

Silberschatz, G., Curtis, J. T., & Nathan, S. (1989). Using the patient's plan to assess progress in psychotherapy. *Psychotherapy, 26*, 40–46.

Silverman, I. W. (2003). Gender differences in delay of gratification: A meta-analysis. *Sex Roles, 49*(9–10), 451–463.

Silverman, L. H. (1979). The unconscious fantasy as therapeutic agent in psychoanalytic treatment. *Journal of the American Academy of Psychoanalysis*, 7, 189–218.

Silverman, L. H., & Weinberger, J. (1985). Mommy and I are one: Implications for psychotherapy. *American Psychologist, 40*(12), 1296–1308.

Simon, B. (1991). Is the Oedipus complex still the cornerstone of psychoanalysis? *Journal of the American Psychoanalytic Association, 39*, 641–668.

Singer, J. L., & Sincoff, J. X. (1990). Summary chapter: Beyond repression and the defenses. In J. L. Singer (Ed.) *Repression and dissociation* (pp. 471–496). Chicago, IL: University of Chicago Press.

Skolnick, N., & Scharff, D. (Eds.). (1998). *Fairbairn, then and now*. Hillsdale, NJ: Analytic Press.

Smith, D. L. (2007). *The most dangerous animal: Human nature and the origins of war*. New York: St. Martin's Press.

Smith, E. R., & Miller, F. D. (1978). Limits on perception of cognitive processes: A reply to Nisbett and Wilson. *Psychological Review, 85*, 355–362.

Smith, G. J. W., Spence, D. P., & Klein, G. S. (1959). Subliminal effects of verbal stimuli. *Journal of Abnormal and Social Psychology, 59*(2), 167–176.

Smith, H. F. (2003). Conceptions of conflict in psychoanalytic theory and practice. *Psychoanalytic Quarterly, 22*(1), 49–96.

Smith, J. L., Johnstone, S. J., & Barry, R. J. (2007). Response priming in the GO/NoGo task: The N2 reflects neither inhibition nor conflict. *Clinical Neurophysiology, 118*(2), 343–355.

Sorce, J. F., & Emde, R. N. (1981). Mother's presence is not enough: Effect of emotional availability on infant exploration. *Developmental Psychology, 17*, 737–745.

Spence, D. P. (1982). *Narrative truth and historical truth.* New York: Norton.

Spence, D. P., & Holland, B. (1962). The restricting effects of awareness: A paradox and an explanation. *Journal of Abnormal Social Psychology, 64,* 163–174.

Sperling, G. (1960). The information available in brief visual presentations. *Psychological Monographs: General and Applied, 74*(11, Whole no. 498), 1–29.

Spitz, R. A., & Wolf, K. M. (1946). Anaclitic depression: An inquiry into the genesis of psychiatric conditions in early childhood. *The Psychoanalytic Study of the Child, 2,* 313–342.

Sprecher, S., & Regan, P. C. (1998). Passionate and companionate love in courting and young married couples. *Sociological Inquiry, 68,* 163–185.

Sroufe, L.A., & Waters, E. (1977). Heart rate as a convergent measure in clinical and developmental research. *Merrill-Palmer Quarterly of Behavior & Development, 23*(1), 3–27.

Stern, D. B. (1983). Unformulated experience. *Contemporary Psychoanalysis, 19,* 71–99.

Stern, D. B. (2003). *Unformulated experience.* Hillsdale, NJ: Analytic Press.

Stern, D. N. (1985). *The interpersonal world of the infant.* New York: Basic Books.

Sternberg, G., Lindgren, M., Johansson, M., Olson, A., & Rosen, I. (2000). Semantic processing without conscious identification: Evidence from event-related potentials. *Journal of Experimental Psychology: Learning, Memory, and Cognition, 26*(4), 973–1004.

Stolorow, R. D., Atwood, G. E., & Orange, D. M. (2002). *Worlds of experience: Interweaving philosophical and clinical dimensions in psychoanalysis.* New York: Basic Books.

Stolorow, R. D., & Lachmann, F. M. (1980). *Psychoanalysis of developmental arrests: Theory and treatment.* New York: International Universities Press.

Stone, A. (2012). *Feminism, psychoanalysis, and maternal subjectivity.* New York: Routledge.

Stone, A. A. (1997). Where will psychoanalysis survive? *Harvard Magazine,* January/February, 35–39.

Stone, L. (1954). The widening scope of indications for psychoanalysis. *Journal of the American Psychoanalytic Association, 2,* 567–594.

Stone, M. H. (2012). Special section: Psychosis. *American Psychoanalyst, 46*(1), 18–20.

Strachey, J. (1934). The nature of the therapeutic action of psychoanalysis. *International Journal of Psycho-Analysis, 15,* 127–159.

Straube, T., Mothes-Lasch, M., & Miltner, W. R. (2011). Neural mechanisms of the automatic processing of emotional information from faces and voices. *British Journal of Psychology, 102*(4), 830–848.

Sugarman, A. (2006). Mentalization, insightfulness, and therapeutic action: The importance of mental organization. *International Journal of Psychoanalysis, 87,* 965–987.

Sullivan, H. S. (1953). *The interpersonal theory of psychiatry.* New York: Norton.

Sullivan, H. S. (1956). *Clinical studies in psychiatry.* New York: W. W. Norton.

Symons, D. (1979). *The evolution of human sexuality.* New York: Oxford University Press.

Szalai, J., & Eagle, M. N. (1992). The relationship between individual differences in defensive style and concept formation. *British Journal of Medical Psychology, 65,* 47–57.

Talmon, Y. (1964). Mate selection in collective settlements. *American Sociological Review, 29,* 491–508.

Tangney, J. P., Baumeister, R. F., & Boone, A. L. (2004). High self-control predicts good adjustment, less pathology, better grades, and interpersonal success. *Journal of Personality, 72*(2), 271–324.

Taylor, J. G. (1987). *Psychosomatic medicine and contemporary psychoanalysis.* Madison, CT: International Universities Press.

Taylor, S. E. (1989). *Positive illusions: Creative self-deception and the healthy mind.* New York: Basic Books.

Taylor, S. E., Kemeny, M. E., Reed, G. M., Bower, J. E., & Gruenewald, T. L. (2000). Psychological resources, positive illusions and health. *American Psychologist, 55*, 99–109.

Taylor, S. E., Klein, L. C., Gruenewald, T. L., Gurung, R. R., & Fernandes-Taylor, S. (2003a). Affiliation, social support and biobehavioral responses to stress. In J. Suls, K. A. Wallston, J. Suls, K. A. Wallston (Eds.), *Social psychological foundations of health and illness* (pp. 314–331). Malden, MA: Blackwell Publishing.

Taylor, S. E., Lerner, J. S., Sherman, D. K., Sage, R. M., & McDowell, N. K. (2003b). Are self-enhancing cognitions associated with healthy or unhealthy biological profiles? *Journal of Personality and Social Psychology, 85*, 605–615.

Thorsteinson, T. J., & Withrow, S. (2009). Does unconscious thought outperform conscious thought on complex decisions? A further examination. *Judgment and Decision Making, 4*, 235–247.

Tierney, J. (2003, Sept. 28). The struggle for Iraq: Traditions; Iraqi family ties complicate American efforts for change. *New York Times*. Retrieved from www.nytimes.com/2003/09/28/world/struggle-for-iraq-traditions-iraqi-family-ties-complicate-american-efforts-for.html?pagewanted=all

Titchener, E. B. (1898). Postulates of a structural psychology. *Philosophical Review, 7*, 449–465.

Titchener, E. B. (1909). *Lectures on the experimental psychology of the thought process*. New York: Macmillan.

Todes, D. P. (2014). *Ivan Pavlov: A Russian life in science*. New York: Oxford University Press.

Tomarken, A. J., & Davidson, R. J. (1994). Frontal brain activation in repressors and nonrepressors. *Journal of Abnormal Psychology, 103*, 339–349.

Treisman, A. (1969). Strategies and models of selective attention. *Psychological Review, 76*(3), 282–299.

Truax, C. B. (1966). Reinforcement and nonreinforcement in Rogerian psychotherapy. *Journal of Abnormal Psychology, 71*, 1–9.

Tsuchiya, N., & Koch, C. (2005). Continuous flash suppression reduces negative afterimages. *Nature Neuroscience, 8*, 1096–1101.

Tsuchiya, N., Koch, C., Gilroy, L. A., & Blake, R. (2006). Depth of interocular suppression associated with continuous flash suppression, flash suppression, and binocular rivalry. *Journal of Visualization, 6*, 1068–1078.

Tuch, R. (2016). Between knowing and believing: Salvaging illusion's rightful place in psychoanalysis. *Psychoanalytic Quarterly, 85*(1), 35–57.

Tulving, E. (1985). Memory and consciousness. *Canadian Psychology, 26*(1), 1–12.

Turvey, M. T. (1977). Preliminaries to a theory of action with reference to vision. In R. Shaw & J. Bransford (Eds.), *Perceiving, acting and knowing: Toward an ecological psychology*. Hillsdale, NJ: Erlbaum.

Turvey, M. T., & Fertig, J. (1970). Polarity on the semantic differential and release from proactive interference in short-term memory. *Journal of Verbal Learning and Verbal Behavior, 9*, 439–443.

Vaillant, G. (1976). Natural history of male psychological health. *Archives of General Psychiatry, 33*, 535–545.

Valenstein, A. (1962). Affects, emotional reliving, and insight in the psychoanalytic process. *International Journal of Psychoanalysis, 43*, 315–324.

Van den Berghe, P. (1990). *Human family systems: An evolutionary view*. Prospect Heights, IL: Waveland.

Vansteenkiste, M., Lens, W., Soenens, B., & Luyckx, K. (2006). Autonomy and relatedness among Chinese sojourners and applicants: Conflictual or independent predictors of well-being and adjustment? *Motivation and Emotion, 30*, 273–282.

Wachtel, P. L. (2003). The surface and the depths: The metaphor of depth in psychoanalysis and the ways in which it can mislead. *Contemporary Psychoanalysis*, *39*, 5–26.
Wachtel, P. L. (2009). Knowing oneself from the inside out and knowing oneself from the outside in. *Psychoanalytic Psychology*, *26*(2), 158–170.
Waelder, R. (1936). The principle of multiple function: Observations on over-determination. *Psychoanalytic Quarterly*, *5*, 45–62. (Original work published 1930.)
Wakefield, J. C. (1992). Freud and cognitive psychology: The conceptual interface. In J. W. Barrron, M. N. Eagle, & D. L. Wolitzky (Eds.), *Interface of psychoanalysis and psychology* (pp. 77–92). Washington, DC: American Psychological Association.
Wakefield, J. C. (2001). Do conscious mental states exist? Freud, Searle, and the conceptual foundations of cognitive science (Unpublished doctoral dissertaton). University of California, Berkley, Berkley, CA.
Wakefield, J. C. (2007a). Little Hans and attachment theory: Bowlby's hypothesis reconsidered in light of new evidence from the Freud archives. *The Psychoanalytic Study of the Child*, *62*, 61–91.
Wakefield, J. C. (2007b). Attachment and sibling rivalry in Little Hans: The fantasy of the two giraffes revisited. *Journal of the American Psychoanalytic Association*, *55*(3), 821–848.
Wakefield, J. C. (2007c). Max Graf's "Reminiscence of Professor Sigmund Freud revisited": New evidence from the Freud archives. *Psychoanalytic Quarterly*, *76*, 149–192.
Waller, G., & Barter, C. (2005). The impact of subliminal abandonment and unification cues on eating behavior. *International Journal of Eating Disorders*, *37*, 156–160.
Waring, E. M., Tillman, M. P., Frelick, L., Russell, L., & Weisz, G. (1980). Concepts of intimacy in the general population. *Journal of Nervous and Mental Disease*, *168*(8), 471–474.
Waroquier, L., Marchiori, D., Klein, O., & Cleeremans, A. (2009). Methodological pitfalls of the unconscious thought paradigm. *Judgment and Decision Making*, *4*, 601–610.
Waters, H. S., & Waters, E. (2006) The attachment working models concept: Among other things, we build a script-like representations of secure base experiences. *Attachment and Human Development*, *8*(3), 185–197.
Watson, M. W., & Getz, K. (1990). The relationship between oedipal behaviors and children's family role concepts. *Merrill-Palmer Quarterly*, *36*, 487–505.
Wegner, D. M. (1994). Ironic processes of mental control. *Psychological Review*, *101*, 34–52.
Weinberger, D. A. (1990). The construct validity of the repressive coping style. In J. L. Singer (Ed.), *Repression and dissociation* (pp. 337–386). Chicago, IL: University of Chicago Press.
Weinberger, D. A., Schwartz, G. E., & Davidson, R. J. (1979). Low-anxious, high-anxious, and repressive coping styles: Psychometric patterns and behavioral and physiological responses to stress. *Journal of Abnormal Psychology*, *88*, 369–380.
Weinberger, J. (2000), William James and the unconscious: Redressing a century-old misunderstanding. *Psychological Science*, *6*, 439–445.
Weiner, H., Thaler, M., Reiser, N. F., & Mirksy, I. A. (1957). Etiology of duodenal ulcer. *Psychosomatic Medicine*, *19*, 1–10.
Weisman, A. D. (1972). *On dying and denying: A psychiatric study of terminality*. New York: Behavioral Publications.
Weiss, J., & Sampson, H. (1985). Testing alternative psychoanalytic explanations of the therapeutic process. In J. M. Masling (Ed.), *Empirical studies of psychoanalytic theories* (Vol. 2). Hillsdale, NJ: Erlbaum.
Weiss, J., Sampson, H., & Mt. Zion colleagues (1986). *The psychoanalytic process: Theory, clinical observation, and empirical research*. New York, London: Guilford Press.
Westermarck, E. (1894). *The history of human marriage* (2nd ed.). London: Macmillan.
Whiting, J. W. M., & Child, I. L. (1953). *Child training and personality: A cross-cultural study*. New Haven, CT: Yale University Press.
Whyte, L. L. (1960). Developmental selection of mutations. *Science*, *132*, 954.

Whyte, L. L. (1967). *The unconscious before Freud.* London: Tavistock Publications.

Widlöcher, D. (2002). Primary love and infantile sexuality: An eternal debate. In D. Widlöcher (Ed.), *Infantile sexuality and attachment* (pp. 1–36). New York: Other Press.

Williams, L. E., & Bargh, J. A. (2008). Experiencing physical warmth promotes interpersonal warmth. *Science, 322*(5901), 606–607.

Williams, L. M., Liddell, B. J., Kemp, A. H., Bryant, R. A., Meares, R. A., Peduto, A. S., & Gordon, E. (2006). Amygdala-prefrontal dissociation of subliminal and supraliminal fear. *Human Brain Mapping, 27*(8), 652–661.

Wingfield, J. C. (1984). Androgens and mating systems: Testosterone-induced polygyny in normally monogamous birds. *The Auk, 101*, 665–671.

Winnicott, D. W. (1956). Primary maternal preoccupation. In *The maturational processes and the facilitating environment*, pp. 300–305. New York: International Universities Press.

Winnicott, D. W. (1965). Ego distortion in terms of true and false self. In *The maturational processes and the facilitating environment* (pp. 140–152). New York: International Universities Press.

Winnicott, D. W. (1969). The use of an object and relating through identifications. *International Journal of Psychoanalysis, 50*, 711–716.

Winston, B., Winston, A., Samstag, I. W., & Muran, J. C. (1994). Patient defense/therapist interventions. *Psychotherapy, 31*, 478–491.

Wittgenstein, L. (1938/1966). Lectures and conversations on aethetics. In C. Barrett (Ed.), *Psychology and religious belief.* Berkeley, CA: University of California Press.

Wolitzky, D. L., Klein, G. S., & Dworkin, S. F. (1975). An experimental approach to the study of repression. *Psychoanalysis and Contemporary Science, 4*, 211–233.

Wortman, C. B., & Silver, R. C. (1989). The myths of coping with loss. *Journal of Counseling and Clinical Psychology, 57*, 349–357.

Yamaguchi, M., Yamazaki, K., Beauchamp, G. K., Bard, J., Thomas, L., & Boyse, E. A. (1981). Distinctive urinary odors governed by major histocompatibility locus of the mouse. *Proceedings of the National Academy of Sciences USA, 78*, 5817–5820.

Yamazaki, K., Boyse, E. A., Mike, V., Thaler, H. T., Mathieson, B. J., Abbott, J., . . . Thomas, L. (1976). Control of mating preferences in mice by genes in the major histocompatibility complex. *Journal of Experimental Medicine, 144*, 1324–1355.

Yamazaki, K., Yamaguchi, M., Baranoski, L., Bard, J., Boyse, E. A., & Thomas, L. (1979). Recognition among mice: Evidence from the use of a Y maze differentially scented by congenic mice of different major histocompatibility types. *Journal of Experimental Medicine, 150*, 755–760.

Zajonc, R. B., Adelmann, P. K., Murphy, S. T., & Niedenthal, P. M. (1987). Convergence in the physical appearance of spouses. *Motivation and Emotion, 11*(4), 335–346.

Zeanah, C. H., Anders, T. F., Seifer, R., & Stern, D. N. (1989). Implications of research on infant development for psychodynamic theory and practice. *Journal of the American Academy of Child and Adolescent Psychiatry, 28*, 657–668.

# INDEX


Aarts, H. 65
Ablon, S. L. 250
Abraham, K. 11
Abramson, L. A. 247
abused women 166–168, 169
Ackerman, J. M. 65
Adam, K. S. 239
Adams, H. E. 80–81, 90
Adrian, Lord 3
Adult Attachment Interview (AAI) 31, 32, 81–82, 231, 267
affectionate and sensual currents 152
agoraphobia 11–12, 136
Akhtar, S. 208
Akkerman, K. 250
Albarracin, D. 61
Alexander, F. G. 194, 197, 198, 209, 260, 275
'aliment' 164
Alloy, L. B. 247
An, S. K. 59
anecdotal evidence, for Oedipus Complex 123–135
anti-libidinal ego 165
Antoni, M. 240
anxiety 178–180
Apfelbaum, B. 181
Aquinas 6
Arendt, H. 28–29
Armstrong-Perlman, E. 166
associative meaning 66, 88–89
attachment: compromise and 112–115; individual differences and 120–121; sexuality and 120–121, 141–142, 176–177
attachment patterns, defense and 241–243
attachment theory 2, 31–32, 44, 137–138, 185–186, 188, 199, 267–268, 269
attention, defense and 224–225
attentional distractions 202
attention cathexis 224
attention levels 74–78, 84, 89
attribute amnesia 64
attribution of unconscious mental states, validation of 12–17
Atwood, G. E. 48, 50, 192
auto-erotic fantasies 144, 175–176
autonomy 172, 203, 272–273, 277
Averbach, E. 63–64
avoidant attachment pattern/strategy 241–242, 268
avoidant/repressive defenses 80
awareness, influence of degree of 74–78
Ayduk, O. 202

baby-mother interaction 161
background smells 65
backward masking method 58, 59
Baeyens, F. 71
banality of evil 28
Banon, E. 251
Bargh, J. A. 65, 67–68, 82–83, 264, 265
Bateman, A. 52
Bateson, P. P. G. 112, 114
Baumeister, R. F. 149, 201, 218, 243–244
*Beast in the Jungle* (James) 208
behavior: not knowing reasons for 74; unconscious mental processes and 14–15
behaviorist school of psychology 11
"beneffectance" 227

Bentham, J. 105
Berman, M. G. 203
Bernat, E. 61
Betz, A. L. 59–60
Binet, A. 53
binocular suppression 58
Black, M. 20–21
Blake, R. 60
'blank screen' 68–69
Blatt, S. J. 185, 197, 250
Blinder, B. 80
bodily sensations 37
Bond, M. 250–251
Boone, A. L. 201
borderline personality disorder (BPD) 136
Bowers, K. S. 71–72
Bowlby, J. 2, 31, 44, 82, 137, 176, 188, 267, 268
Brandchaft, B. 173
Brenner, C. 18, 156–160, 182–183, 210, 273
Breuer, J. 40, 137, 148, 216–217
Briffault, R. 119
Burrows, L. 65
Busch, F. 257
Button-Molder 25
Buunk, A. P. 117
Byers, C. N. 247

Carlson, G. A. 250
Carmel, D. 61
Carr, V. 250
Carver, C. 59
Casey, B. 203
castration anxiety 96, 97, 121–123, 124, 153, 178
"cauldron, seething" 23, 25, 26, 30, 31, 34, 44, 49, 50, 182, 266
Charcot, J.-M. 40, 53, 232, 254
Chen, H. 64
Chen, M. 65
choice 18
Chomsky, N. 9
Christian, C. 208–209, 213
*Civilization and its discontents* (Freud) 234
Cleeremans, A. 70
closeness and engulfment 170–171
close process monitoring 49, 50–51, 91, 256, 257
Cobey, K. D. 117
cognitive behavior therapy 48
cognitive bias 227
cognitive conservatism 227
cognitive revolution 57
cognitive unconscious 7
Cohen, D. J. 126
Cohen, I. S. 68
Coifman, K. G. 240, 252, 255
color psychology 65–66
compromise formation 155–160
conditions of worth 48, 191–192, 229
conflict: between attachment and sexuality 176–177; between auto-erotic fantasies and object love 175–176; between autonomy and guilt 172; between closeness and engulfment 170–171; compromise formation and 155–156; conclusions regarding 206–208; core 204–205; "danger situations" and 150; between desire and self-image 149, 180–181; ego and 189–190; between ego structures 162–165; ego-superego 151–152; experimental neurosis in animals and 198–199; between fantasy and reality 169–170; between fantasy and relating 180; final thoughts on 208–213; id-ego 150–151, 181–183; id-superego 151; between immediate and delayed gratification 199–202; implications for treatment and 192–197; individuation and 183–184; between individuation and merger 171–172, 189; between individuation and parricide 171; between internal object relationships 165; between life and death instincts 160–161; between narcissism and object love 152–155, 186–189; nature of fundamental 176–177; in neo-Freudian theories 191–192; between pleasure and unpleasure 156–160; between pleasure principle and reality principle 149–150; between primary identification and separation 165–168; psychosomatic illness and 197–198; between pursuing nuclear program and ties to objects 173, 190–191; between relatedness and self-definition 184–186, 204; research on 197–205; between self-definition and relatedness 180
conflictual material 80
Confucius 54
connotative hierarchy 42
consciousness, expanding of 52–53
constancy principle 149, 150, 154–155, 179, 218
Control-Mastery theory 31, 44, 45, 48, 50, 52, 95, 172, 194, 205, 226, 228, 229, 260
convergent conflicts 173–175

Coolidge Effect 117–118
core 204–205
Core Conflict Relationship Themes (CCRTs) 203–204
corrective emotional experiences 260, 275
cortisol 117
Cosmides, L. 108
countertransference 91
Cousineau, T. M. 240, 252
Craig, T. K. 245
Cramer, P. 149, 221, 233–234, 250, 261
Crews, F. C. 2
Crowne-Marlowe Social Desirability Scale 238
Curtis, J. T. 205
Cushman, P. 269
Czyzewska, M. 71

Dale, K. 149
"danger situations" 46, 51, 97, 150, 179, 182, 195, 209, 218–219, 226, 228–230, 267–268; conflict and 150
David, A. S. 245
Davidson, R. J. 238
Davison, W. 50–51, 52
death, denial of 249
death instinct 153–155
DeBruine, L. M. 109
defense: adaptive nature of 233–234; analysis of 275–276; attachment patterns and 241–243; concluding comments on 260–262, 268–271; costs and benefits of 239–240; Freud on 234; interpersonal situation and 228–231; introduction to 216–217; maladaptive nature of 231–233; nature of 217–227; neural and physiological correlates of 244–245; psychotherapy and 250–252; research on 235–238, 252–260
defense analysis 49–50
defense hysteria 148, 217, 231, 275
defense mechanisms, research on 243–244
defensive exclusion 82, 268
degree of awareness 74–78, 84, 89
De Houwer, J. 71
denial 248–249
denial of death 249
Dent, L. 208–209, 213
depression 246–248, 255–256
depressive position 178
depressive realism 246
depth, unconscious as 24–30
depth psychology 24, 91
Descartes, R. 6, 13
descriptive unconscious 7, 57, 88, 92, 265
desire, self-image and 149, 180–181
Deutsch, F. 198
Deutsch, H. 11
Dewsbury, D. A. 118
Diamond, L. 118, 120, 176
Dijksterhuis, A. 65, 69–71
*ding-an-sich* 6
dissociation 164–165
divergent conflicts 173–175
Dolev, T. 242
Dollard, J. 11
domestic violence 166–168, 169
double-mindedness 54
Doyen, S. 66–68
dreaming/dream content 35, 58
drive derivatives 50
drive organization of cognition 42
drive theory 49, 90, 139, 150, 160
Dworkin, S. F. 81
dynamic unconscious 7, 30, 51, 57, 80–82, 84, 90, 264, 265–268

Eagle, M. N. 60, 75, 77, 80, 176–177
ecological validity 235–236
Eelen, P. 71
ego: conflict and 150–152, 153, 181–183, 189–190, 194–195; unity and 273–274
ego-alien experience 227, 272
egocentricity 227
ego functions 271–274
ego ideal 153
ego libido 153
ego psychology 210–213, 256
*Ego psychology and the psychoses* (Federn) 212
ego structures 162–165
Eichmann, A. 28–29
*Eichmann in Jerusalem* (Arendt) 28
Eigsti, I. M. 203
Eilati, I. 241–242
Elise, D. 128–130, 131–132
Elliot, A. J. 65–66
Emde, R. N. 203
emotional insight 54
endopsychic structure of personality 148, 162, 190
Enlightenment Vision 255–257, 274, 276
Erck, T. W. 203
Erdelyi, M. H. 220–221, 235–236
Erhardt, A. A. 33
Erikson, E. 181
Erikson, M. 100

erogenous zone, mother's gratification of 100–101
Eros 153–154, 155, 274
erotic desire and sense of transgression 103–104
Esterling, B. A. 240
Esteve, L. G. 248
event related potential (ERP) responses 60–61, 78
excitation 96, 104, 137, 149–150, 154–155, 218, 232–233
exotic states 14
Experience of Close Relationships (ECR) measure 242
experimental neurosis in animals 198–199
external stimuli, discrimination and encoding of 57–60, 265–266
extramarital sex 118, 169

Fairbairn, W. R. D.: conflict and 148, 162–170, 174, 180, 183–184, 188, 189–190, 269; defense and 219; Freud and 192–195; on Oedipus Complex 135, 136, 141; on therapist as "good" object 260; on unconscious 38–39, 41, 43; on unconscious mental processes 46–47
false consciousness 265
false memory debate 235
false self 219, 229
fantasy: auto-erotic 144, 175–176; and reality 169–170; and relating 180
Farooqui, A. A. 77
Farrugia, C. 119–120
Federn, P. 212–213
Fenichel, O. 181, 243
Feranil, A. B. 117
Fertig, J. 72–74, 265
fetal androgenization 33–34
Fingarette, H. 18, 32–33, 36, 49, 50, 221, 222–223, 224–225, 230, 237, 244
Fisher, C. 58, 75
fleeting consciousness experience 64, 91
Fliess, W. 8, 123
fMRI studies 244–245
Fodor, J. A. 6, 16, 57
Fonagy, P. 52, 117, 176, 209, 225, 231, 235
forgetting 80, 81, 90
Fosshage, J. 173
Fox, R. 99, 106, 115
Fraley, R. C. 107, 108–109, 110–111, 114, 241
Frelick, L. 120
French, T. M. 194, 198, 209, 260, 275
Freud, A. 49–50, 91, 150–151, 181, 220, 221, 233, 261
Freud, S.: anxiety and 178, 179; on conflict 149–156, 180–182, 184–185, 186–188, 192–195, 199–200, 211; on defense 224, 228, 234, 252–254, 261, 268, 275; on depression 246–247, 248; on descriptive versus dynamic unconscious 57; drive theory and 139; dynamic unconscious and 22–23, 84; on ego 33; on external stimuli 83; on hysterical symptoms 148; on id and ego 53; on incest taboo 127; James and 10–12; Lucy R. and 35; metapsychology of 20–21; on motivations 21, 22; narcissistic object choice and 110; on Oedipus Complex 94, 96, 97, 98, 99, 100–101, 102, 104, 105, 115, 130, 131, 177, 268–269; parental hostility and 123; on personal-level phenomena 85; on psychical impotence 120, 176; on repression 46, 48–49, 216–217, 218–221, 231–232, 233, 238, 239, 242; Rogers and 192; self-analysis of 101; on sexuality 140; on strangulated effect 164; subpersonal processes and 87; superego and 38–39; on treatment modality 3; on unconscious desires 86; on unconscious fantasy 23–24, 41, 42; on unconscious mental processes 6–8, 10–12, 13, 17, 19, 22–30, 40, 47–48; Wakefield and 9–10; Wittgenstein and 25; working through and 54–55
Friedman, L. 254
Friedman, R. C. 226
Fromm, E. 184, 191

Gagnon, J. H. 119
Gallese, V. 2–3
galvanic skin responses (GSR) 81, 241
Garcia Marquez, G. 170
Gedo, J. 101
generational envy 123
genetic kinship as mediator 108–112
genetic kinship estimator 108, 110
Gestalt therapy 48
Gettler, L. T. 117
Getz, K. 125, 126
Ghent, E. 273
Gibson, M. 35–36
Gill, M. M. 68
Gilroy, L. A. 60
Goldberg, B. 235–236
Gonzales-Vallejo, C. 70

Goodwin, F. K. 250
gratification: capacity to experience 208; conflict between immediate and delayed 199–202; death instinct and 154–155; delay of 207; personality functioning and 271–272; psychosomatic illness and 197; studies on delay of 203–204
Gray, P. 35, 49, 50, 52, 91, 230, 256, 275
Green, A. 140
Greenberg, J. 184
Greenson, R. R. 68
Greenwald, A. G. 149, 227
Groddeck, G. 82, 89
guilt 172, 177, 178–180, 196, 205
Guntrip 164, 170–171, 180

habituation as mediator 107–108
Hannula, D. E. 63
Havik, O. E. 248–249
Hazan, C. 119, 176
Helmholtz, H. 16
Hendrickx, H. 71
Hendriks, M. 65
Hendrix, L. 107
Hepler, J. 61
hidden meanings 19
Hill, A. B. 59
Hill, J. 27
Hill, T. 71
Hoffman, I. Z. 132, 249
Hoffman, L. 190
Hoffman, M. 190
Hogans, L. 119–120
holding environment 260
Holender, D. 64
Holland, R. W. 65, 76–77
Holmes, D. S. 235
Holmes, J. 117, 176
Holzman Rorschach Measure of Repression 237, 238
homogamy 114
homosexuality 153
homunculi 17–19, 33, 88, 221
Horesch, N. 241–242
horizons of awareness 48, 50, 228
Horney, K. 191
hostile wishes toward same sex parent 95–97
Huang, Y. 117
Hull, C. 198
Hullian learning theory 139
hypnosis 53–54, 81
hysterical symptoms 148

Ibsen, H. 25, 259
*Iceman Cometh, The* (O'Neill) 259
id: conflict and 150–151, 181–183, 195; unity and 273–274
implicit, unconscious as 37–39
implicit learning 72, 91
implicit procedural knowledge 37–38
implicit procedural unconscious 38
implicit relational knowing 26, 31, 91, 260
implicit relational procedures 38
"imprinting" mechanisms 113–114
"in and out program" 170–171
inattentional blindness 64
incest taboo 96, 97, 98–100, 101, 127
incestuous wishes: primacy of 96–97; universality of 95, 97–135
incidental stimulus 75–76
indeterminate unconscious mental contents 36–37
individual differences 78–80, 120
individuation 171–172, 183–184, 189
infantile form 45–46
infantile impulses, repressed 47–48
infantile sexuality 96, 100, 138–139, 144
*Infantile sexuality and attachment* (Widlöcher) 144
infant-mother attachment 96, 199
infant-mother interaction 161
inferential processing 16–17
inner conflict: concluding comments on 268–271; convergent and divergent 173–175; in Freudian theory 149–177; inevitability of 180–197; introduction to 148–149; in self psychology 172–173; unconscious processes and 39–41
instinctual derivatives 35
institution-reared children 27
integration 53–55
interactional structures 31, 85
internal mental contents, defense and 252–255
internal object relationships 165
internal objects 47–48, 163–165
internal obstacles 173
internal working models (IWMs) 31, 37–38, 81–82, 85, 89
interpersonalization 43–46, 91
interpersonal situation, defense and 228–231
intrapsychic conflict 18
Israëls, H. 101

James, H. 208
James, W. 5, 10–12, 17, 49, 64, 91

Janet, P. 40, 53, 164–165, 211, 216–217, 232, 254
Johansson, M. 78
Johnson, A. W. 102
Johnson, M. 6, 57, 198
Jones, E. 95, 101, 123, 162
Josephs, L. 127, 130–131, 132
Jung, C. 75
Jureidini, J. 85, 86
Jussim, L. J. 59–60

Kanaan, R. A. 245
Kandel, E. 3
Kang, J. I. 59
Kant, I. 6
Kemp-Wheeler, S. M. 59
Kernberg, O. F. 44, 103–104, 107, 209
Kierkegaard, S. 54
King, A. C. 187
Klein, G. S. 42, 58, 75, 81, 100, 141, 225, 226
Klein, M. 43, 123, 124, 160–161, 178, 190
Klein, O. 66–68, 70
Koch, C. 60
Kogan, I. 29–30
Kohut, H. 30, 122, 123, 133, 141, 172–173, 186–188, 190, 194, 206, 209, 211–212, 260
Kolata, G. 119
Kotler, Ml 241–242
Kris, A. 173–175, 197
Kris, E. 23, 148, 156, 208, 272–273
Krosnick, J. A. 59–60
Kubie, L. 198
Kumar, M. 240
Kuzawa, C. W. 117

labeling 62
Lacan, J. 118–119, 140, 184
Lachmann, F. M. 209
Laius Complex 102
Lakoff, G. 6, 57
Laumann, E. O. 119
Lavie, N. 61
Lazarus, R. S. 249, 255
Lear, J. 19, 24–25, 41, 42
LeDoux, J. E. 63
Lee, E. 59
Lee, S. Y. 59
legends 102–103
Levi, P. 29
Levine Denial of Illness Scale 248
Lévi-Strauss C. 99–100
Levithan, D. 170
Lewicki, P. 71, 85
Lewin, R. 250
libidinal cathexis of ego 152
libidinal ego 165
Lichtenfeld, S. 65–66
Liddell, B. J. 61, 84, 198
Lieberman, D. 108, 109–110
Lieberman, M. D. 62, 78
Liebowitz, M. R. 116
life and death instincts 160–161
Lin, Z. 78
Lindgren, M. 78
Lindzey, G. 98
Little Hans 98
Loewald, H. 134, 135, 171–172, 177, 178–179, 181, 183, 189, 206–207
logical behaviorism 14, 37
Lohr, B. A. 80–81
Longeway, K. P. 203
Lorenz, K. 112
love and desire, split between 115–121
*Love in the Time of Cholera* (Garcia Marquez) 170
Low, B. 154
Luborsky, L. 80, 90, 203–204, 236–237, 251
Lucy R. 35, 36, 49, 50, 81, 91, 180, 196, 222, 230–231, 261, 268
Lynn, A. R. 59–60
Lyons-Ruth, K. 26, 37–38, 39, 91, 260

Mack, A. 64
Maeland, J. G. 248–249
Mahler, M. S. 135
Maier, M. A. 65–66, 78
major histocompatibility complex (MHC) gene segment 107
Makari, G. 139, 140
maladaptive representations 275
Malinowski, B. 95
Manis, M. 245
Manly, T. 77
Marcel, A. J. 77, 265
Marchiori, D. 70
Marks, M. J. 107, 108–109, 110–111, 114
Marmor, J. 137
masking procedures 63
Masling, J. 68
Maslow, A. 187
Masserman, J. H. 198
masturbation 153
mate, choice of 96, 97, 104–115
Mayes, L. C. 126
Mayman, M. 245
McDade, T. W. 117
McLoughlin, J. 7

McNally, R. J. 236
Menninger, K. 198
mentalization 52–53, 209, 231, 257–260, 276
Mentalization Based Treatment (MBT) 258
merger, individuation and 171–172, 189
Metalsky, G. I. 247
metapsychology 20, 181
Meurs, T. 69
Michael, R. T. 119
Mikulincer, M. 241–243
Miller, A. 102
Miller, N. E. 11
Miltner, W. R. 63
Miranda, J. 247
Mirksy, I. A. 197
Mischel, W. 13, 14, 15, 200–201, 203, 207
Mitchell, S. A. 44, 118, 141, 228, 266
Modell, A. 122, 178, 179
modular theory of mind 16
momentary consciousness 10–11, 64, 91
momentary forgetting 80, 236–237
Money, J. 33
monogamy 116–117
mood-state hypothesis 247
Moran, R. 274
Morehead, D. 105, 106, 111, 113, 133
mother's gratification of erogenous zone 100–101
Mothes-Lasch, M. 63
motivated defensive forgetting 90
motivational explanation, skepticism toward 21–22
mourning 174–175
*Mourning & Melancholia* (Freud) 246, 255
Muller, D. 60
Muller, M. N. 117
Muller-Lyer illusion 16
multiple determination 22
multiple functioning, principle of 141
Murray, S. O. 78
myths 102–103

Namkoong, K. 59
narcissism, object love and 152–155, 186–189
narcissistic object choice 110
Nasrallah, M. 61
Nathan, S. 205
National Opinion Research Center 119
Newell, B. R. 70
*New Language of Psychoanalysis, A* (Schafer) 18
New York University Research Center for Mental Health 58, 75, 79–80
Nietzsche, F. 21
Nisbett, R. E. 74, 85, 264
Nivana principle 154, 155
Nocera, C. C. 65
Nordgren, L. F. 69, 70–71
nuclear program, pursuit of 173, 187–188, 190–191
Nuremberg trials 28–29

object libido 153
object love: auto-erotic fantasies and 175–176; narcissism and 152–155, 186–189
O'Brien, G. 85, 86
O'Brien, K. K. 118
Oedipal betrayal 128–133
Oedipus Complex: concluding comments on 145–146, 268–271; conflict and 177; implications of relinquishment of 135–145; inner conflict and 152; introduction to 94–95; Loewald on 171; nature of 95–97; reconceptualizations of 133–135; superego and 151; unconscious fantasy and 24
Ogden, T. H. 193
Ohman, A. 59
Olafson, F. 32
olfactory mediation 107
Olson, A. 78
Olson, S. L. 207
O'Neill, E. 259
*On Narcissism* (Freud) 153, 187
optimal similarity hypothesis 114
oral deprivation 34
Orange, D. M. 192
Ortof, E. 75, 77
Osgood Semantic Differential 72–73
otherness of oneself 236, 259
overall defensive functioning (ODF) 251
oxytocin 116

Panksepp, J. 64, 126
parricide, individuation and 171
partial denial 249
Passman, R. H. 203
Pavlov, I. P. 198
Peake, P. 203
perception 16–17
perceptual defense 244
Perry, J. C. 250–251
*Personality and Psychotherapy* (Dollard and Miller) 11, 198
personality development 271–274

personal processes 85–87
Persons, J. B. 247
Peterfreund, E. 159
Phillips, N. D. 70
physiological evidence 116–117
Piaget, J. 164
Pichon, C.-L. 66–68
Pierce, J. D. 118
Pine, F. 76, 88–89, 189, 265
Pinker, S. 99
Plato 35
pleasure and unpleasure 154, 156–160
pleasure principle 149–150, 154, 199–200
Plotinus 6
Pollet, T. V. 117
Polyani, M. 38
positive assortative mating 114
positive illusions 245–250, 255–256
Pötzl, O. 58, 75
Price-Williams, D. 102
primary identification and separation 165–168
principle of multiple functioning 22
procedural knowledge 26, 164
*Project for a scientific psychology* (Freud) 8, 10, 19
prolactin 117
*Protecting the self* (Cramer) 218
psychical impotence 120, 152, 176
psychoanalysis, influence of 1–3
*Psychoanalysis of developmental arrests* (Stolorow and Lachmann) 209
psychological evidence 117–120
psychopathology 39–46, 92
psychosexual development 96
psychosomatic illness 197–198
psychotic core 26–27, 34, 171, 189

Quine, W. V. O. 37
Quinton, D. 27
quota of affect 40, 155, 232, 252

Rank, O. 259
Rapaport, D. 42, 224, 272
reality principle 149–150, 199–200
rebound effect 238
*Recent developments in psychoanalysis* (Eagle) 209
red (color) 65–66
"reflected appraisals" 191
reflective capacity 258, 276
regions of experience 48, 50, 219, 228
Reiser, N. F. 197
relatedness, self-definition and 180, 184–186, 204
relational configurations 30–31
religious beliefs 246
representationality 9
Representations of Interactions Generalized (RIGs) 30–31, 37, 41, 72, 85, 89
repression: costs and benefits of 239–240; defense and 90–92; definition of 217; Freud on 40, 46, 47–49, 216–217, 218–221, 231–232, 233, 238, 239, 242; importance of lifting 195; studies on 235–238; *see also* defense
repressive style 236, 238, 240, 241
resolution of oedipal conflicts 96
Ric, R. 60
Ricoeur, P. 87, 265
Robles, R. 59
Rock, I. 16–17, 64
Rofé, Y. 235–236
Rogers, C. 48, 52, 68, 184, 187, 191–192, 229
Roheim, G. 2, 95
Roosevelt, T. 27–28
Rorschach assessment 213
Rorschach Index of Repressive Style (RIRS) 237
Rosen, I. 78
Ross, J. M. 102
Roy, C. 251
Rubens, R. L. 164, 168
Rubinstein, B. B. 8–9, 13, 15, 86, 87
rules, acquisition of without awareness 71–74, 84, 89
Russell, B. 25
Russell, L. 120
Rutter, M. 27, 158–159

Sachs, H. 101
Sampson, H. 31, 44, 45, 50, 172, 179, 184, 196, 205, 206–207, 229, 260
Sandler, J. 42, 43–45, 49–50, 91, 221, 261
Sartre, J. P. 18, 32–33, 54, 221, 222, 244
satisfaction, conflict and 153
Scarfone, D. 144
Schachter, S. 37
Schafer, R. 18
Scharff, D. 190
Schatzman, M. 101
Schimek, J. 80
Schlam, T. R. 203
Schmeidel, B. J. 203
Schmeing, J. B. 81, 244
Schneider, M. A. 107
Schneiderman, N. 240
Schore, A. N. 240

Searle, J. 7–8, 12
seduction, reports of 101
selective inattention 48, 224, 226
self actualization 187
self-deception 244, 265
self-definition, relatedness and 180, 184–186, 204
self-image 153, 180–181
self-knowledge 247, 256, 259, 274, 275–276
self-preservative instinct 153
self psychology 30, 172–173, 209, 211–212, 260, 269
self realism 247
self realization 187
self-regulating function 200, 202
sense of transgression 103–104
separation guilt 122, 178, 179
separation-individuation 135, 136
Sethi, A. 202
sexual instinct 96, 153
sexuality: attachment and 120–121, 141–142, 176–177; individual differences and 120–121
sexual reductionism 141
sexual system, compromise and 112–115
Shapiro, L. B. 198
Shaver, P. R. 241, 242
Shedler, J. 240, 245, 252
Sheldon-Keller, A. E. 239
Shepher, H. 106
Shevrin, H. 59, 60, 61, 78
Shoda, Y. 203
Shor, E. 106–107
"signal anxiety" 220, 221, 228
Silberschatz, G. 205
Simchai, D. 106–107
Sincoff, J. X. 237, 262
Singer, J. 37, 262
Singer, J. L. 237
skepticism 21–22, 66–68
skin conductance response (SCR) 59
Skolnick, N. 190
sleep 35
Smith, D. L. 28
Smith, G. J. W. 58
Smith, H. F. 159
Smith, R. 59
Snodgrass, M. 61
Soares, J.J. 59
Sommer, K. L. 149
Sorce, J. F. 203
Spence, D. P. 58, 76–77
Sperling, G. 63–64
Spiro 95
Spitz, R. A. 218
Sroufe, L. A. 241
state dependent cognition 247
Stenberg, G. 78
Stern, D. 229
Stern, D. B. 32, 36, 50, 219, 221, 222–223, 224–225
stimulus organization 74–78, 84
Stolorow, R. D. 48, 50, 192, 209, 219, 228
Stone, A. 20, 29–30, 209, 210
Stone, A. A. 236, 259
Stone, L. 210
Stone, M. 210
Strachey, J. 39, 178, 233
Strange Situation 199
strangulated affect 164, 252–253, 254, 273
Straube, T. 63
strength of instinct 232–233
structural conflicts 30
Structuralism 10, 11
*Studies on Hysteria* (Freud) 149
subliminal stimuli 60–62, 78, 88
subliminal studies 57–60, 62–80
subpersonal processes 85–87
success 153
Sugarman, A. 52, 257, 275
Sullivan, H. S. 48, 191, 224, 225, 226
superego 97, 151–152, 178
supraliminal stimuli 64–69, 78, 88–89
surface and depth 51
survivor guilt 122, 178, 179
Symons, D. 118
Szalai, J. 80

Talmon, Y. 106
Tang, D. 203
Tangney, J. P. 201
Taylor, J. G. 198
Taylor, S. E. 245, 246
template of parental figure 96
testosterone 116–117
Thaler, M. 197
Thanatos 153–154
Thematic Apperception Test (TAT) 201
Tierney, J. 115
ties to objects 173, 190–191
Tillman, M. P. 120
Titchener, E. B. 10, 11
Tomarken, A. J. 238
Tooby, J. 108
transference 68–69, 91, 228–229
transgression, erotic desire and sense of 103–104
trauma, defense and 235, 252–255

triadic relationships 133
true self 48, 229
Tsuchiya, N. 60
Turvey, M. T. 72–74, 265
"tyranny of the shoulds" 191

unarticulated, unconscious as 32–36
*Unconscious, The* (Freud) 57
unconscious computational process 86–87, 88
unconscious desires 86–87
unconscious fantasy 23–24, 41–46
unconscious inference 16
unconscious pathogenic beliefs 31, 85, 89, 172, 205
unconscious processes: concluding comments on 88–92, 265–268; contemporary psychoanalytic conceptions of 30–39; implications of research findings for 82–87; inner conflict and psychopathology and 39–41; integration and 53–55; introduction to 5–6; psychoanalytic conceptions of 22–30; psychopathology and 41–46; theoretical and conceptual issues regarding 6–22; treatment implications regarding 47–53
unconscious thought paradigm 69–71
unconscious wishes and desires 19–21
under determination of meaning by behavior 14
undeveloped implications 225
unformulated experiences 223–224
unity of personality 273–274

Vaillant, G. 250
validation of attribution 12–17
Van Avermaet, E. 71
van der Meij, L. 117
van Knippenberg, A. V. 65
van Olden, Z. 69
vasopressin 116

Wachtel, P. L. 24, 91
Waelder, R. 141
Wakefield, J. C. 9–10, 37, 92, 98
Waller, G. 28–29
warded off mental contents 48, 51–53
Waring, E. M. 120
Waroquier, L. 70
Waters, E. 32, 241
Waters, H. S. 32
Watson, M. W. 125, 126
Wegner, D. M. 238
Weinberger Questionnaire Measure of Repression 237
Weiner, H. 197
Weiss, J. 31, 44, 45, 50, 172, 179, 184, 196, 205, 206–207, 229, 260
Weisz, G. 120
Wellens, A. R. 59
Weltanschanung 255–256, 262, 276
Wessely, S. C. 245
West, M. 239
Westermarck, E. 105, 108
Westermarck hypothesis 105–107, 114, 133
whore-madonna complex 115
Widlöcher, D. 144, 175–176, 180, 193
*Wild Duck, The* (Ibsen) 259
Williams, L. E. 65
Williams, L. M. 78
Wilson, T. D. 74, 264
Wingfield, J. C. 116
Winnicott, D. W. 43, 48, 178, 184, 192, 219, 229, 260
Wittgenstein, L. 21, 25, 74
Wolf, K. M. 218
Wolitzky, D. L. 81, 90
working through, concept of 54–55
Wright, L. W. 80–81
Wylie, B. 64

Zeifman, D. 119, 176